Third World Lives of Struggle

HAZEL JOHNSON and HENRY BERNSTEIN
with RAÚL HERNÁN AMPUERO
and BEN CROW

for the Third World Studies *course*
at The Open University

HEINEMANN EDUCATIONAL BOOKS
in association with
THE OPEN UNIVERSITY

Heinemann Educational Books Ltd
22 Bedford Square, London WC1B 3HH
PMB 5205, Ibadan · PO Box 45314, Nairobi
IBADAN NAIROBI JOHANNESBURG
EDINBURGH MELBOURNE AUCKLAND
HONG KONG SINGAPORE KUALA LUMPUR
NEW DELHI KINGSTON PORT OF SPAIN
Heinemann Educational Books Inc.
4 Front Street, Exeter, New Hampshire 03833, USA

British Library Cataloguing in Publication Data

Third world lives of struggle. –(Open University
  Third World Readers; 1)
  1. Underdeveloped areas
  I. Johnson, Hazel II. Series
  909'.097240828 HC59.7

ISBN 0-435-96130-6

Cover photographs   top left: Unicef photo © Hewett, courtesy Alan Hutchison
Library; top right: © Romano Cagnoni; bottom left: © Margaret Murray;
bottom right: © Raissa Page.

Set in 9/10pt Baskerville by Northumberland Press Ltd, Gateshead
Printed in Great Britain by Richard Clay (The Chaucer Press) Ltd,
Bungay, Suffolk

Contents

Acknowledgements   ix
Introduction   xi

Part One *Struggles on the Land*

Introduction   2

1   The Horrors of the North-East Drought (Brazil)   6
    EXPEDITO SEBASTIÃO DA SILVA

2   Sentences by Mexican Peasant Indians   11
    K. J. JÄKLEIN

3   Fourteen Great Achievements of the Peasant Movement in Hunan
    (China)   13
    MAO TSE-TUNG

4   Forced Labour in Colonial Mozambique: Peasants Remember   31
    ALPHEUS MANGHEZI
    (i) The experience of chibalo   32
    (ii) Forced cultivation   34

5   Indra Lohar and the Due Process of Law (India)   35
    D. P. BANDYOPADHYAY

6   'The Agrarian Reform': Song Sung by Members of the Peasants'
    Federation in Ecuador   43
    Commentary by M. REDCLIFT

7   Childhood of a Mapuche Indian (Chile)   45
    ROSENDO HUENUMÁN

8   Mapuche Indians Organize (Chile)   50
    ROSENDO HUENUMÁN

9   *The Making of Rural Proletarians: Sugar Estate Workers in*
    El Valle (Colombia)   63
    ANDREW PEARSE

10   *The Senegal River Valley: What Kind of Change?*   67
    ADRIAN ADAMS

Part Two *Struggles in Town*

Introduction   92

11   *Migrant and Worker* (Chile)   96
    ROSENDO HUENUMÁN

12   *Work Songs of Mozambican Miners*   103
    ALPHEUS MANGHEZI
      (i) Leaving for the mines   104
      (ii) Working on the mines   104

13   *Looking for Work in Kingston* (Jamaica)   105
    MICHAEL THELWELL
      (i) The building site   106
      (ii) The suburbs   108
      (iii) 'The Harder They Come' – Jimmy Cliff   110

14   *Autobiography of an Urban 'Marginal': Miguel Duran*
    (Colombia)   111
    JUAN RUISQUE-ALCAINO and RAY BROMLEY

15   *Small Engineering Workshops in Howrah* (India)   125
    M. P. GHOSH

16   *Beedi-workers of Nizamabad* (India)   127

17   *The Sekondi–Takoradi General Strike, 1961* (Ghana)   131
    RICHARD D. JEFFRIES

18   *Interview with Luís Inácio da Silva ('Lula')* (Brazil)   142

19   *Hungerstrike of Moroccan Workers in Holland*   153
      (i) Statement of 'the 182'   154
      (ii) Individual statements by two hungerstrikers   155

Part Three *Women's Struggles*

Introduction   160

20   *Interviews with Mozambican Peasant Women*   164
      ALPHEUS MANGHEZI

      (i) Women are forced to grow rice   165
      (ii) Women plantation workers   166
      (iii) The life of a migrant's wife   168

21   *Poem by a Moroccan Woman*   173

22   *'Women Have to do Double Work'* (India)   174
      GAIL OMVEDT

23   *Conversation with Aída Hernández from a Peruvian Cooperative* 185
      AUDREY BRONSTEIN

24   *Production, Property, Prostitution: 'Sexual Politics' in Yumbe
      (Kenya)*   191
      JANET M. BUJRA

25   *'Poor Naïve Young Man'* (Morocco)   212

26   *Testimony of a Guatemalan Woman*   213
      LUZ ALICIA HERRERA

27   *Organizing the Annapurna* (India)   217
      MIRA SAVARA

28   *'The Union is Our Mother'* (India)   225
      GAIL OMVEDT

29   *At the International Women's Year Tribunal*   233
      DOMITILA BARRIOS DE CHUNGARA (Bolivia)

      (i) How a miner's wife spends her day   234
      (ii) At the International Women's Year Tribunal   236

Part Four *Understanding Struggles*

30   *Resistance and Hidden Forms of Consciousness among*
     African Workers   244
     ROBIN COHEN

Conclusion: Types of Struggle   259

Index   269

Acknowledgements

A number of people helped us with suggestions for material and with some of the details involved in editing this collection. We are grateful to all of them, and in particular to David Baytelman of the Institute of Social Studies in The Hague, Robin Cohen of the University of Warwick, Selina Cohen of the United Nations Research Institute for Social Development, Ruth First of the Centre of African Studies, Eduardo Mondlane University, Maputo, David Seddon of the University of East Anglia, and our friend and co-worker in Third World Studies at the Open University, David Wield.

Our largest debt is to two more of our friends and co-workers. Raúl Hernán Ampuero and Ben Crow played an important role in the general planning of this collection and in finding and discussing material from Latin America and India respectively, as well as writing the introductions to Readings 5 (Ben) and 7 (Raúl). Without their interest and specialized knowledge of these two major areas of the Third World, the work of the main editors would have been much more difficult and the collection itself poorer in content.

At the time of going to press we learned of the tragic murder by letter bomb of Ruth First, who fought against apartheid and for a more progressive future for Africa. We wish to convey our deep appreciation and respect for her work.

Hazel Johnson and Henry Bernstein

The editors and publishers would like to thank the following for permission to reproduce copyright material:

Readings 1, 2 and 6: *Journal of Peasant Studies* by kind permission of Frank Cass & Co Ltd, London

Reading 3: Foreign Languages Press, Peking

Readings 4, 12 and 20: Centre of African Studies, Eduardo Mondlane University, Maputo

Reading 5: Manohar Publications, New Delhi

Readings 7, 8 and 11 from the Spanish transcript by David Baytelman, translated by Susan Welsh, translation copyright © 1982 The Open University.

Reading 9: United Nations Research Institute for Social Development, Geneva

Readings 10 and 30: *Review of African Political Economy* 1978 and 1980

Readings 13(i) and 13(ii): © Michael Thelwell 1980 from *The Harder They Come*, published by Pluto Press Limited, London 1980 and Grove Press Inc., New York

Reading 13(iii): Words and Music by Jimmy Cliff, reproduced by kind permission of Island Music Limited; original soundtrack recording available on Island Records Limited (ILPS 9202)

Reading 14: John Wiley & Sons Limited, Chichester

Readings 15 and 16: *Economic and Political Weekly* 1980 and 1981

Reading 17: Longman Group Limited, London
Readings 18 and 26: *Latin American Perspectives* 1979 and 1980
Readings 19 and 21 from a special issue of the *Bulletin of the Committee of Moroccan Workers*, 1978, English translation ˙Gavin Hudson
Readings 22 and 28: Zed Press, London
Reading 23: War on Want Campaigns Limited in association with War on Want
Reading 24: *Cahiers d'études africaines* 1977
Reading 25: University of Texas Press, Austin
Reading 27: Institute of Development Studies, University of Sussex, Brighton
Reading 29: Stage 1, London
The publishers and editors have endeavoured to trace the copyright holders of all the readings. If any have inadvertently been overlooked, we will be pleased to make the appropriate arrangements at the first opportunity.

Introduction

This collection of readings has been prepared for the use of students taking an Open University course in *Third World Studies* together with a 'companion' volume *An Anthology of African and Caribbean Writing in English*.

Our first task was to try to find material that would prove informative and interesting to Open University students, and that they could use in engaging with some of the critical issues of the contemporary Third World. At the same time, we wanted to use this opportunity to provide an accessible source of information and ideas for a wider audience of people interested in such issues. They may be studying topics relevant to the Third World as part of their higher or further education; they may be participating in study and discussion groups organized by War on Want or the Workers' Educational Association, for example, or within the women's movement; they may simply be individuals interested in enhancing their knowledge of the Third World and of those who live in it.

These considerations have been the major factor in the selection and presentation of the readings contained in this volume which, in its comprehensiveness and variety, represents a substantial departure from what has been readily available up to now. First, and most important, we decided to concentrate on readings that portray the diverse conditions of everyday life of people in the Third World; that show how the majority of them have a continuous struggle to achieve any kind of decent existence; and that illustrate some of their responses and actions, both individual and collective.

Second, we have tried to do this as much as possible through the 'voices' of those who live these daily experiences, or as an alternative through the reporting of 'outsiders' who have lived with, or otherwise closely observed, the people whose lives they describe. Accordingly, much of the material in this collection takes the form of interviews, conversations, and autobiographical and biographical accounts, and there are also a number of poems and songs. We have mostly avoided the more conventional sources and types of academic literature, apart from a few readings that combine history and analysis with a strong sense of the circumstances, experiences and actions of those whose lives are being analysed (Readings 10, 17, 24, 27, 30).

Third, this volume is set out differently from the usual sequence of more or less uniform 'chunks' of reading matter. The juxtaposition of readings in terms of type of material and length is intended to make the use of the collection more attractive to those who are not necessarily practised in wading through academic journals and monographs. Just as important, we want the collection to be a 'resource' that readers can use in different ways according to their own interests and needs.

Certain common issues appear in different forms in all the three main sections; in several instances readings from the same source appear in more than one section because they illustrate various aspects of a particular area of struggle. The section introductions are intended to facilitate the use of the readings by providing 'pointers'; they lay no claim to being authoritative statements about the issues involved, nor are they exhaustive summaries of the material contained in the readings, which readers can use in their own way. Introductions to the readings, textual insertions and additional footnotes have been limited to conveying some essential aspects of context, translating foreign words, and explaining unfamiliar terms or events.

While we constructed this collection of readings as a 'resource', amenable to different uses by Open University students and others, we should say something more about our method of selection and organization, and how we hope it will be used. First, there was a deliberate decision to concentrate on the lives of those who are poor and who are subordinated socially, culturally and politically. In our view they are the majority of the people of the Third World, and it is their poverty and subordination that are the driving force of their struggles for a better life. Consequently, we have not given any space to other social groups such as political and military cliques, bureaucrats and judges, landowners and rich peasants, industrialists and merchants, who, in an important sense, are no less engaged in struggles to maintain or extend their relative wealth, power and prestige. Their presence is certainly manifested in most of the readings, but through the perceptions of those to whose 'voices' we have given priority.

Second, we have devoted a section to women's struggles because we believe that women peasants and workers confront specific forms of exploitation and oppression as a result of their gender, in addition to those experienced by all peasants and workers.

Third, we have included material from different regions and countries of the Third World with a rough 'parity' between the three continents of Africa, Asia and Latin America. Readers will notice, however, that with the exception of Reading 3 from China, Asia is 'represented' exclusively by India. Rather than give an illusory 'coverage' of Asia we thought it better to focus on the lives of people in one country that is 'sub-continental' in its social, economic and political diversity as well as in its geographical expanse and contrasts.

Fourth, the collection is somewhat unconventional in the range of sources it draws on, as already indicated. Some of the material is published in English for the first time, such as the life story of Rosendo Huenumán (Readings 7, 8, 11), extracts from the *Bulletin of the Committee of Moroccan Workers in Holland* (Readings 19, 21), and some of the Mozambican interviews and songs (Readings 4, 12, 20). With a few exceptions, most of the readings are recent in origin and documentary in nature. As well as the poems and songs referred to, there is the account of the peasant movement in Hunan in Reading 3, written by a world-famous political leader and dating from the 1920s, and Reading 13 which combines extracts from a novel, itself based on a film, with the words of a 'hit' reggae song by Jimmy Cliff. Our justification for the inclusion of all the readings is that, in their very different ways, they are vivid expressions and interpretations of important social realities as they are experienced in people's lives.

But how typical are the people whose lives are described here, and how accurate are the descriptions? We have not tried to achieve any notional 'typicality'. We have given considerable space to the 'voices' of those who became leaders in the struggles of the groups and communities they belong to, for example, Rosendo Huenumán (Reading 8), Lula (Reading 18), Aída Hernández (Reading 23), and Domitila Barrios de Chungara (Reading 29). Concerning 'typicality' more generally, we feel that this was addressed very well by Gail Omvedt in the introduction to her book on Indian women's struggles, from which two of our readings are taken. 'When I talk about my experiences of those days [when she was collecting the material for her book], I am invariably asked, with some amazement, "But was your experience typical? Were these women typical?" No, of course not. Why should they be? First, readers should remember that the events described here took place mainly in one part of India, the state of Maharashtra, which has a relatively high rate of women's [wage] work participation and a strong tradition of social–cultural revolt, both factors leading to a relatively vigorous expression of women's militancy. Second, the women I met for the most part (though not always) were in some way or another involved in organization and protest activity. They were not "typical" in the sense of being randomly chosen to represent a numerical average. But they are authentic. However much they are involved in fighting their society's traditional bondage, they are part and parcel of that society, their experiences and their concerns are those of all the women of the society.'[1]

The types of account presented in these readings, whether reported by those directly involved or by 'outsiders', cannot be 'neutral' or 'accurate' in any absolute sense. However, on one hand, the modes of reporting 'lives of struggle' drawn on here are intrinsically no more misleading than the supposed neutrality of statistical surveys and the 'averages' they produce, the biases and stereotypes of newspaper reports (see pp. 85–7 below), or the often spurious claims to represent the interests and needs of 'the people' or 'the nation' that are the stock in trade of politicians and official agencies. On the other hand, it is precisely because the 'voices' collected and reported here are not so accessible nor often heard that gives this volume its principal rationale.

The last sentence indicates another point we want to emphasize. While we have suggested that conditions of poverty and oppression define the struggle for existence of most people in the Third World, there is no necessary connection between being poor and oppressed and being engaged in struggles aimed at the radical transformation of those conditions. The collection includes examples of the latter that readers may find inspiring, as we have done, but they do not justify any 'revolutionary romanticism' detached from the recognition of social realities. Many of those who are poor and oppressed accommodate themselves to the circumstances of their daily lives, struggling to 'get by' or to improve their lot as individuals while remaining fatalistic about (or not envisaging) possibilities of social change. They too have a 'voice' in this collection.

The meaning of 'lives of struggle' in the title, therefore, is not limited to types of (collective) struggle with which the editors may sympathize. The contradictions of social reality, including the resignation and fatalism of many of those who are exploited and oppressed, have to be understood – especially by those committed to radical social change. In any case, struggles to achieve the latter are subject to many vicissitudes, and give rise to often complex questions of organization and leadership, ideology and strategy, tactics and political calculation, in particular sets of circumstances. They are never 'guaranteed' success; two of the outstanding local leaders whose 'voices appear here – Rosendo Huenumán from Chile and Domitila Barrios de Chungara from Bolivia – were forced into exile from their countries.

When students were testing a preliminary version of the Open University course in Third World Studies, one of them wrote that some of these readings 'said more than volumes of theory'. It is not difficult to agree with this assessment as far as some volumes of theory are concerned! However, we do not regard the 'voices' presented here as an *alternative* to the work of theory and analysis, but rather as expressions of experience that any effective theory and analysis must recognize and assimilate – *and* be able to 'speak' back to. To illustrate how this might be done we have included a brief final section on 'Understanding Struggles' which contains one reading of a more theoretical and generalizing character, together with our own Conclusion that picks out and analyses forms of struggle as they appear in the readings. We hope this is helpful as another guide to using the collection, by providing readers with concepts and ideas that they can test for themselves against the evidence contained in the readings.

Finally, we should make clear our view that 'lives of struggle' are not exclusive to the people of the Third World, but occur wherever exploitation and oppression occur and are experienced in more or less complex, more or less brutal, more or less subtle, ways. We believe that 'Third World lives of struggle', as portrayed here, have specific conditions and features of their own which at the same time are the product of common historical processes that have shaped the world we all inhabit.

NOTE

1. Gail Omvedt, *We Will Smash This Prison! Indian Women in Struggle,* Zed Press, London, 1980, p. 5.

Part One

Struggles on the Land

Introduction

The majority of the population of the Third World (albeit a declining proportion) derive their living from working on the land, at least half of them as tillers of the soil on small holdings. It is these people who have the major voice in this section, although there are other important social groups whose livelihood is derived from the land, such as pastoralists and agricultural wage workers. Reading 9 describes the lives of one group of wage workers on a sugar estate in Colombia, and Readings 20(ii), 22 and 26 also contain material on agricultural workers.

Our main focus here is on those who are conventionally termed 'peasants', suggesting agricultural producers who have the use of a plot of land which is cultivated with the labour of members of the family. The concept of peasants or peasantry is thus closely associated with that of the 'household' as a social unit of production, as well as of consumption.

As a descriptive term 'peasants' encompasses many groups of people who may be quite different from each other in terms of their relationship to their natural environment and to other social groups, their historical formation and experiences, and their cultures. It is difficult, therefore, to make significant generalizations about all those agricultural producers in the Third World who are termed 'peasants'. One important point, however, is that very few, if any, are today 'subsistence' farmers in the sense of satisfying their needs through producing everything they consume. All peasants are involved in the operations of the market and of monetary economy to a greater or lesser degree (and the general trend is towards more involvement). They need a cash income to pay taxes or rents, to purchase some of their consumption items and means of production too, such as tools and fertilizers, to pay for children's school fees and for medical treatment, and so on. Another important point is that farming is often combined, according to local circumstances, with livestock keeping, handicrafts or petty trading, and economic necessity often dictates working on the farms of others or longer distance labour migration. Reading 10 describes one rural area where the opportunity of earning a cash income from agriculture has been very limited, and men have migrated to the cities of Senegal and France to earn money (see also Readings 12, 20(iii)).

As we focus on the contemporary situation, not much space is devoted to the historical formation of different peasantries, although some readings indicate central themes in the history of peasants in the Third World (see the commentary in Reading 1, also Readings 4, 10 and 20). These include the experience of colonial rule, the effects of different systems of land tenure, and of incorporation into market relations (including those of the world market), with peasants growing crops for exchange or having to find some other way of acquiring money. The accounts from Mozambique (which achieved independence from Portuguese colonial rule as recently as 1975) in Readings 4 and 20 describe practices of forced agricultural labour in the colonial economy, and Reading 12 contains two songs composed by those who were recruited from the rural areas of southern Mozambique to work in the gold mines of South Africa.

With the exception of China, all the countries included in the readings of this section underwent a period of European colonial rule. China was a long-established empire that eventually collapsed under the combined pressure of peasant resistance to feudal exploitation, and of the spread of European imperialism and the concessions it demanded. Part of Mao Tse-tung's famous report of 1927 on the peasant movement in his native province of Hunan is reprinted here as Reading 3. It provides a vivid account of the lives of Chinese peasants at that time and an analysis of their struggles against poverty and oppression. These struggles both drew on a long history of peasant revolt against the feudal conditions of the old empire and fed into a new political movement for national liberation and socialism. Mao's report suggests useful points of reference and comparison for the other readings in this section.

While we have cautioned against generalizing about peasants in the contemporary Third World, certain themes recur which gain a particular content and 'feel' in the particular circumstances of different peasantries. One such theme is the struggle with nature expressed, for example, in trying to cultivate poor or deteriorating soils or surviving the often traumatic irregularities of rainfall, manifested in flood or drought. 'Just at the crucial time/the rains did not fall' records the poem in Reading 1, stating with laconic simplicity the precariousness of the relationship with nature that determines the existence of so many peasants, and which can be extended from north-east Brazil to many other parts of the Third World.

Another general theme is the distribution of land, and the conditions in which many peasants struggle to retain or acquire possession of land, their fundamental means of livelihood. This theme is a central one in the readings from China in the 1920s (3), from India (5), Ecuador (6) and Chile (8). In much of Latin America and Asia, peasants' use of land is dependent on renting from landlords, or some other form of tenancy such as sharecropping through which a substantial part of the product of the peasants' labour is appropriated by landowners as rent in kind. 'The landlord's wife gave me half a plot [of land]; I did the work and she took the product' (Reading 6). Moreover, the right to occupation and use of a piece of land is often very weak whether in legal terms or those of effective political power. The threat of dispossession and landlessness confronts the poor peasant with a prospect of even greater destitution (Reading 5).

The land farmed by peasants may be coveted by large-scale commercial farmers, themselves employing capital, modern machinery and wage workers, who want to expand their enterprises. This is shown in the attempted encroachment on the land of the Mapuche reservation (Reading 8), and in the loss of their land by the peasants who subsequently became sugar estate workers in Colombia (Reading 9). The calculation of profit also appears as a factor in the eviction of Indra Lohar by his landlord who wanted to bring in new sharecroppers to cultivate a special variety of rice, and to claim a larger share of their crop as rent (Reading 5).

It is the combination of the struggle with nature on one hand, with the exactions of economically, socially and politically more powerful groups on the other, that defines the struggle for existence of many peasants in the Third World. They typically cultivate with simple implements fuelled by human or animal energy, usually cannot afford to buy more advanced tools or means of irrigation, improved seeds and fertilizers, pesticides and insecticides, and are unlikely to accumulate reserves or savings to get them through hard times. In these conditions a crop failure or the illness of one of the family workers, a fall in the market price for the crops they sell or a rise in the price of the commodities they need to buy, can produce a crisis in the life of a peasant household. This may lead to indebtedness which easily becomes another vehicle of exploitation (Reading 3), perhaps culminating in the loss of land. This happened to one of the sugar estate workers in Reading 9, while three of his fellow workers were forced to evacuate their land due to the effects of chemical spraying on a neighbouring estate (as intended by its owners).

The pressures on peasants are not restricted to the effects of unequal land distribution, the extension of capitalist farming, and the workings of the commercial and monetary economy. As well as being economically 'squeezed', peasants are typically disadvantaged politically. The structure of legal and political power and the practices of the state are often experienced as contributing to the subordination of peasantries. Even when laws have been passed to reform the pattern of landownership and to redistribute land, their implementation is frequently obstructed by powerful social classes of landlords or agrarian capitalists and their allies (Readings 5, 6, 8). A Mexican Indian peasant makes the ironic observation that 'Everybody has rights, but there are many who don't have land' (Reading 2).

Another facet of the conditions of peasant existence is the view of their cultural inferiority, their 'backwardness' and 'conservatism' which those who are urban, richer and more powerful tend to subscribe to, and which is articulated in the ideologies of 'development' and 'modernization' promoted by most governments (see Reading 10). This is most marked when a peasantry is also an ethnic, linguistic or cultural minority, as with the Popoloca Indians of Mexico, the Mapuche people in Chile (Readings 2, 7, 8), and the Harijan ('untouchable') low caste and 'tribal' people of India (see the introduction to Reading 22). When Rosendo Huenumán led a Mapuche delegation to see a government official, he noted: 'I was well dressed, wearing shoes, a spotless suit, a tie, and speaking perfect Spanish . . . the secretary noticed the difference straight away, and he treats me very politely' (Reading 8).

Rosendo had spent eleven years or so in towns, where he had first gone so that he could pursue his education, and had also acquired political skills through his seven years as a coal miner and his knowledge of trade union activity (see Reading 11). His education and experience were a crucial catalyst in organizing his community on the reservation when he returned. Likewise, the person who initiated an association for collective agriculture in his native village of Jamaane in Senegal had returned after many years of working and living in a more metropolitan environment (Reading 10). Peasants can appreciate that education is a means to certain kinds of knowledge and perhaps power, but might feel ambivalent because such knowledge and power is part of the system by which they feel oppressed. A Popoloca Indian considers that what his children learn at school is 'all right for the city, but no good for the countryside' (Reading 2), a perception that converges with what Mao heard from peasants in Hunan in 1927 (Reading 3).

The difference between peasant life in the countryside and the life of the towns is another theme that recurs in the readings of this section, from China in the 1920s where 'the villagers were afraid of the townspeople' (Reading 3) to contemporary Brazil where the poem says 'living off the land/is just so different' (Reading 1). This difference is evidently firmly established in popular consciousness, and becomes an active division or opposition when the town is seen as the place where the wealthy, the powerful and the educated are concentrated. This often connects with another recurring theme, namely the combination of hard work and poverty that is definitive of their identity for many peasants. The Popoloca say of the local government officer, 'He never works. We don't know how he makes a living', and to the visiting anthropologist, 'Since you don't work, you don't know' (Reading 2); the song of the Ecuadorean peasants goes 'The poor work harder/even than oxen;/the rich do not work/and live like kings' (Reading 6).

Having pointed out some of the recurring themes of this section, it is still necessary to be cautious about easy generalizations. For example, some of the people whose lives are described here live in rural areas where there is a considerable differentiation or stratification of the peasantry. The introduction to Reading 3 provides a sketch of such differentiation, distinguishing poor, middle and rich peasants whose life experiences and ideologies are likely to reveal important divergences as well as certain similarities. Some peasants do succeed in improving their positions through successful development of cash crops or involvement in trade and transport, through advantageous connections with government officials or merchants, or some combination of these circumstances.

In this section we have selected readings that portray the lives of those peasants who are poorer and more subordinated, undoubtedly the majority of the rural population in most Third World countries. Here you will find these peasants' perceptions of those significant 'outsiders' they necessarily relate to in ways that enter the construction of the peasants' self-identity: the landowners, big farmers, merchants, priests, magistrates, government officials, policemen, development 'experts', and so on. Within the conditions faced by those who struggle to gain a living from the land, there are additional and particular problems experienced by women peasants and agricultural wage workers which are described in Readings 20, 22, 23 and 26.

EXPEDITO SEBASTIÃO DA SILVA

Commentary by Anthony Hall, Institute of Latin American Studies, University of Glasgow

Escutem bons brasileiros	Listen good Brazilians
con ordem de Pai Celeste	by order of Father Celeste
os horrores cruciantes	to the terrible horrors
que assolam o Nordeste	which lay waste to the North-East
onde o flagelo é sem nome	where the scourging has no name
proveniente da fome	but comes from hunger
e o ameaço da peste	and the threat of disease
O Nordeste onde outrora	The North-East which yesterday
parecia um paraíso	seemed like paradise
hoje quem vê-lo compara	who looks at it today
com um Dia de Juizo	compares it with the Day of Judgement
pois nos lares sertanejos	because in *sertanejo* homes
não existem mais gracejos	no longer does fun exist
e nem um tranquilo riso	nor even a tranquil smile
Porque no Norte e Nordeste	For in the North and North-East
quase nada se lucra	almost nothing is reaped
lá numa parte ou outra	there in one part or another
que a lavoura prosperou	where crops used to prosper
se torna em prejuizo	all is now destroyed
pois no momento preciso	for just at the crucial time
a chuva em geral faltou	the rains did not fall
É lamentável e tristonho	Lamentable and sad is
no Norte o desassossêgo	the suffering in the North
se vê homens pelas ruas	men in the streets
errantes como o morcêgo	wandering like bats
devido a necessidade	out of need
pedindo por caridade	begging work for the love of God
aos prefeitos emprêgo	from town councils
Muitos atrás de emprêgo	Many looking for work
nas prefeituras insistem	with town councils persist
porém não arranjam nada	although they can get none
pois trabalhos não existem	since there is no work
aqueles homens famintos	for these hungry men
apesar dos bons instintos	despite their good intentions
se não tomar, não resistem	if they don't grab they can't survive

Pois esses chegam em casa	For they arrive at home
sem nenhuma remissão	bringing no solace
encontram a mulher chorando	and find their women crying
e os filhos com precisão	and the children in need
por forte que o homen seja	however strong the man
a vida não mais deseja	he no longer cares to live
perde de todo a razão	he loses all his reason
Aí se vem forçados	Thus they are forced
embora contia a vontade	although against their will
ir atacar constrangidos	to go and attack
os mercados da cidade	the markets of the town
que triste situação . . .	what a sad situation
mas é ésta a soluçao	but this is the only solution
dos que tem necessidade	for those in desperate need
Muitos no Sul não conhecem	Many Southerners are ignorant
do nordestino o tormento	of the Northerner's agony
quando não existe inverno	when winter does not appear
e lhe falta o alimento	and he has no food
se de perto observassem	if they observed closely
talvez se penalizassem	perhaps they might share
com dó do seu sofrimento	the pain of his suffering
São homens que quando existe	These are men who
inverno pelo sertão	during winter in the _sertão_
quem a eles se chegar	whoever should be afflicted
com fome e sem remissão	by hunger with no remission
pode ficar conformado	may rest assured
que ficará arrumado	that he will be taken care of
e se acaba a precisão	and his need will be no more
Porém a fome cruel	Yet cruel hunger
faz aqueles nordestinos	drives these Northerners
abandonar suas roças	to abandon their plots
buscando novos destinos	looking for a new future
mas remissão não achando	but they find no consolation
terminam o pão implorando	and end up begging bread
como pobres peregrinos	like poor pilgrims
Quando em uma cidade	When in a town
chegam uns cem reunidos	some hundred souls arrive
o povo todo se alarma	the people become scared
trancando com alaridos	closing up with cries
as vendas e os mercados	their shops and markets
como sejam os flagelados	as if these _flagelados_
uma carga de bandidos	were a gang of bandits
Alí mais ninguém se lembra	Then no-one remembers
que foram aquelas figuras	that it was these people
as maiores produtoras	who were the biggest producers

das nossas grandes farturas
hoje como flagelados
se acham repudiadas
por diversas criaturas

É aquele mesmo povo
que no campo era dono
a qual por causa da sêca
deixou todo em abandono
onde antes descansando
não trocava seu roçado
pelo mais soberbo trono

Mas a crise insuportável
que a todo Nordeste assola
faz daqueles flagelados
uma miserável bola
os quais sem emprêgo achar
achando feio roubar
terminam pedindo esmola

Alguns que já atacaram
cidades e povoados
com certeza se achavam
com fome e necessitados
ou então sem sossêgo
sem encontrar um emprêgo
ficaram desesperados

Quase desequilibrado
se dispõe na mesma hora
bota na frente a família
dali triste vai embora
assim como retirante
sai pelo mundo errante
em busca duma melhora

Quando em uma cidade
chega toda aquela gente
vendo aquêles movimentos
logo muito mal se sente
aí a mulher 'engrossa'
porque o viver da roça
é daquele diferente

Aí ficam se batendo
sem ter onde se arranchar
o homen atrás de serviço
anda até se abusar
o que lhe dão é conversa
promessa e mais promessa
e êles fome a passar

of our abundance
who today as *flagelados*
find themselves rejected
by many people

It is that same people
who in the fields were kings
and who because of the drought
abandoned all their things
where once before
they would not exchange their plot
for the most splendid throne

But this unbearable crisis
that affects the whole North-East
turns these *flagelados*
into a miserable band
who without work
find it hard to steal
and end up by begging

Some who already attacked
towns and villages
surely found themselves
with hunger and in need
or without peace of mind
out of a job
and became desperate

Almost going mad
he decides at that very moment
to get his family prepared
and sadly leave his home
thus like an emigrant
he goes wandering in the world
searching for an improvement

When at a town
all these people arrive
seeing all that movement
they feel very ill
and the women get [. . . fed up]
since living off the land
is just so different

And here they stay
with no place to live
the man after a job
to the point of being insulted
for all he gets is talk
promises and more promises
that his hunger will pass

Se sabe que o governo	We know that the government
está dando alimento	is giving food away
pega um saco às carreiras	he grabs a sack in a hurry
a vai no mesmo momento	and goes straight away[1]
mais tarde volta sem nada	but later he returns home with nothing
pois não obteve entrada	for he could not take part
naquele fornecimento	in that share-out
Assim são todos aqueles	And such are they
que vem com a ilusão	who come with the illusion
de encontrar na cidade	of finding in the town
uma boa remissão	some reassuring consolation
mais aquela pobre gente	but these poor people
não encontra um só vivente	can't find a living soul
quem chegue e dê-lhe atenção	who will pay them attention
Vamos contritos a pedir	Let us go in penance to ask
ao nosso Pai Eterno	from our Eternal Father
pra que no ano vindouro	that in future years
nos conceda um bom inverno	he will give us a good winter
mas se for da mesma sorte	but if our luck is the same
por completo todo Norte	the entire North
se transforma num inferno	will become an inferno

The above lines were selected from one of the many popular poems which constitute perhaps the most important element in the written folk-lore of North-East Brazil. These poems are published in pamphlet form known as *folhetos*, usually with eight or sixteen pages, about six inches by four inches, and printed on cheap paper. Collectively they are known as *literatura de cordel* after the type of cord binding once used to hold the pages together. *Folhetos* are partly an extension of Portuguese literary tradition adapted from prose stories brought from the Iberian Peninsula during the colonial period. However, they are primarily the written development of an already existing tradition in North-East Brazil established by *cantadores* or oral poets. The cantador would travel to feasts, weddings and the like, and improvise verses on a whole range of subjects, usually at the invitation of the audience. Often, two poets would conduct a duel or *desafio* in improvized verse, always in the popular regional dialect.

Folhetos were at one time the only literature to which the rural population had access, being conceived, written and sold in the interior of the region. Even today, if a peasant cannot read he will listen to the salesman or *folheteiro* read out or sing the verses at the local market where the poems are usually sold. The poets themselves are invariably of peasant origins, although their skills have led many to earn most of their living outside of agriculture. With the gradual penetration of the mass media into North-eastern peasant culture, the popularity of this literature has diminished, and the popular poets who used to make their living by selling their poems to local publishers are fast disappearing.

These poems cover an infinite variety of subjects, including natural disasters which affect the North-east, such as floods and droughts, tales of brave bandits (*cangaceiros*) in their fight against the injustices of the police and landowners, moralistic stories and miracles. Subjects which are in the news also inspire the publication of *folhetos*. Their continued success is partly due to the speed with which a poem can be produced and distributed after a major event has taken place. Within two days of the death of Getulio Vargas,[2] for example, 70,000 poems commenting upon the events had been circulated. Other notable events to have been covered include the downfall of Hitler, the death of President Kennedy and the moon landings.

The extract quoted above is taken from one of many poems which describe the effects of the periodic droughts or *sêcas* which strike the semi-arid interior or *sertão* of the North-east. Droughts in the region have been recorded since the seventeenth century but they did not create enormous social and economic problems until the mid-nineteenth century. Until then, cattle-rearing on large estates was the only major rural activity, and cattle for slaughter provided an abundant supply of food. In the nineteenth century cotton cultivation was introduced, and flourished both as a source of income for landowners during the cotton shortage caused by the American Civil War, and as a source of cottonseed cake for cattle fodder. Peasants attracted from neighbouring regions into cotton cultivation became sharecroppers and were forced to grow their own food supply by means of subsistence farming. This was adequate in normal years, but drought caused crop failure and starvation, leading to large-scale emigration from the *sertão*. The 1877–79 drought caused half a million deaths in the state of Ceará alone.

During a *sêca* thousands of peasants are therefore forced to leave their small subsistence plots because they cannot produce their normal food supply. These emigrants have become known as *flagelados*, literally translatable as 'the flagellated ones'. The variety of tenancy arrangements with landowners invariably involves transactions in kind rather than cash; a typical arrangement would be for the peasant to pay the landowner half of his annual cotton crop in exchange for the right to plant a subsistence plot. The peasant is still overwhelmingly outside of the money economy, since not only is he paid in kind, i.e. the right to grow his own food, but he invariably sells his share of the crop to the landowner in exchange for goods. Left with no surplus during times of need, the peasant is totally dependent on his master or *patrão* for additional help at a time of crisis. However, many landowners feel it in their interest to force peasants off their land during a drought, rather than to give them alternative employment and a wage with which basic needs can be met. Some manage to find other jobs locally outside of agriculture, while others are employed on government 'work fronts' building roads. But many are forced to migrate, as the poem relates, to towns in the interior and on the coast, as well as to the major urban centres in the South such as Brasilia, Rio de Janeiro and São Paulo. The most hungry and desperate have been known to attack food stores and supply trains as a last resort. Newspaper reports corroborated the poet's description of the 1970 drought quoted above, and described the ransacking of food shops and vehicles by starving peasants. Despite government attempts to provide short-term relief, the usual problems of hunger and large-scale migration by the *flagelados* associated with each *sêca* were as serious as ever.

Reprinted from *Journal of Peasant Studies*, vol. 3, no. 3, 1976, pp. 355–9.

NOTES
   [1. i.e. to collect a food handout.]
   [2. Brazilian president 1930–45, 1951–54.]

2 Sentences by Mexican Peasant Indians

K. J. JÄKLEIN

The following sentences are taken from tape recordings and field notes gathered in the course of an anthropological study of the *Popoloca* Indians in Mexico. All the speakers are male – there is no particular reason for this – but are of different ages and social groups. They live in the village of San Felipe Otlaltepec, which has approximately 1,900 inhabitants (1974). The village is situated in the *municipio* of Tepexi de Rodríguez in the Southern part of the State of Puebla, Central Mexico. Most inhabitants are extremely poor, even in relation to Mexican rural conditions. The men work in agriculture, the women make mats.

They speak *Popoloca* among themselves. In conducting their affairs with the outside world they have to speak Spanish, and most of them manage to do so. Men tend to speak Spanish more frequently and more correctly than women, because they have more contact with Spanish-speaking outsiders.

The sentences presented here were selected from daily conversation. Only four sentences were originally spoken in *Popoloca*, the rest were in Spanish. None of them are proverbs. Individuals predominantly refer to themselves in the plural in speaking both *Popoloca* and Spanish.

Although a collection of sentences of this kind yields only an eclectic view of personal and social world views, convictions, justifications, ideologies and rationalizations, it is nevertheless important that field workers and researchers should be sensitive to daily speech and be able to select the representative statements. Further work on such material might provide the basis for understanding the syntax of ideology.

The sentences appear first in Spanish, then in English. Occasionally the context is briefly indicated in brackets at the end of the English version. (G. Rose, Oxford, helped with the translation from Spanish to English.) The English translation is only an approximation to the Spanish. The Spanish is more figurative than the English translation conveys. The sentences are not presented in any systematic sequence. The Spanish version is notated according to local pronunciation.

1. *Nosotro puro campesino. A vece trabajamo. A vece nomá estamo.*
We are only peasants. Sometimes we work. Sometimes we just exist.

2. *Lo jornalero no importa. Cuando no cae agua, pierde campesino.*
It doesn't matter to the daily labourer. When there is no rain, it is the peasant who loses.

3. *No hay tiempo para aprendemo escribemo. Trabajamo para comemo. Regresamo campo cansado. Comemo, dormimo, así andamo.*
There is no time for us to learn to write. We work in order to eat. When we come back from the field we are tired. We eat, we sleep, that's how we live.

4. *Aquí nacimo come chivo. Así estilo de nosotro.*
Here we breed like goats. That's our style.
(in reference to the absence of contraceptives)

5. *Si fuera animal ya me hubiera ido. Pero como son hijo, que hace uno? Necesita comida. Cuando crece, ya es otra cosa, ya ve.*
If I were an animal I would have left already. But since there are children, what can one do? They need food. When they grow, it will be different, you will see. (said in relation to the question of becoming a migrant worker)

6. *Estodo mujer de puro dinero.*
Those women never think of anything but money. (in reference to white women in towns)

7. *En esta vida hay pobre y hay rico como hay flor bonito y flor feo. Si miramo claro todo flor bonito.*
In this life there are poor and rich people just as there are beautiful and ugly flowers. If we try, we only see the beautiful ones.

8. *Donde hay peso hay justicia. Donde no hay, no hay justicia.*
Where there is money, there is justice. Where there is no money, there is no justice. (in reference to *la mordida* [= the bite], the bribe)

9. *Como to no trabaja, no sabe.*
Since you don't work, you don't know. (in reference to the visiting anthropologist)

10. *Cuando viene uno de lejo, corremo.*
If someone comes from far away, we run.

11. *Lo leye que rijen son leye de ella. Que hacemo nosotro?*
The laws which rule us are their laws. What can we do? (said by the local *presidente auxiliar* about the *municipio*)

12. *Cae mal al pueblo. Ese nunca trabaja. No sabemo como vive.*
The village does not like him. He never works. We don't know how he makes a living. (in reference to the *agente*, the local political representative of the government)

13. *El cura no sabe que pensamo.*
The priest does not know what we think. (said by a local *curandero* [= healer] who became a ministrant in order to study more closely his rival's practices of celebrating mass)

14. *Yo no me fio en los curas. Los curas y los ricos siempre andan juntos. La iglesia católica es iglesia de los ricos.*
I don't trust priests. The priests and the rich always stick together. The Catholic Church is the church of the rich. (said by an unusually self-educated, outstanding peasant)

15. *Nos tratan como animale.*
They treat us like animals. (given as a reason for preferring the local *curandero* to the doctor in the market town)

16. *Pa la ciudá, si sirve. Pa la vida del campo ni pensar. Pero que hacemo? Manda ela.*
That's all right for the city, but no good for the countryside. But what can we do? They give the orders. (in reference to what children learn at school)

17. *México es paí libre. Cada uno puede decir lo que quiere. Puede andar pa donde quiera. Hay educasión y justicia.*
Mexico is a free country. Everybody can say what he wants to say. Everybody can go where he wants to go. There is education and justice. (said by the *agente* to the visiting anthropologist)

18. *Cosa nueve no tiene palabra. Buscamo palabra.*
New things don't have names. We look for names. (in reference to satellites)

19. *Ya no hablamo legítimo Popoloca. Todo sale revuealta. Así estilo nosotro. Todo revuelto.*
We don't speak correct Popoloca any more. Everything is upside down. That's our style. Everything upside down. (in reference to medicinal plants)

20. *Habla Popoloca lo pobre y lo tonto, que no saben nada, ni castilla.*
The poor and the stupid speak Popoloca – people who don't know anything, not even Spanish. (said by an eleven year old son to his father)

21. *Habla Popoloca perjudica a castilla.*
Speaking Popoloca spoils our Spanish. (said by an eleven year old son to his father)

22. *La tierra da. Es buena. A vece se enoja. Tiembla.*
The land gives. It is good. At times it is enraged. Then it shakes.

23. *El día que sale uno, otro lo trabaja. Falta terreno.*
When somebody leaves, somebody else will work the land. Land is lacking. (in reference to migrant labour)

24. *Todo tiene derecho, pero hay bastantes que no tiene terreno.*
Everybody has rights, but there are many who don't have land.

25. *Lo que nos dirige es el hambre.*
Hunger is our master.

26. *No esperamo ayuda.*
We have no hope of help.

27. *Somo sufridore en grande.*
Our suffering is infinite.

Reprinted from *Journal of Peasant Studies*, vol. 2, no. 2, 1975, pp. 226–8.

3 Fourteen Great Achievements of the Peasant Movement in Hunan

MAO TSE-TUNG

Editors' introduction

This is the concluding section of Mao Tse-tung's famous 'Report on an Investigation of the Peasant Movement in Hunan'. Early in 1927 Mao visited five counties of the province of Hunan, at that time the centre of the peasant movement in China. 'In the thirty-two days from January 4 to February 5, I called together fact-finding conferences in villages and county towns, which were

attended by experienced peasants and by comrades working in the peasant movement, and I listened attentively to their reports and collected a great deal of
material.'

A brief outline of the political situation in China in 1927 is necessary to understand the context of Mao's report, and a number of the references it makes. In
1911 the Chinese Republic was established after a long period of social upheaval,
and the disintegration of the last imperial dynasty of the Manchus. This process
combined massive rebellions based in the peasantry, such as the T'ai'ping
rebellion of the mid-nineteenth century and the 'Boxer' rebellion at its end, with
the disruptive role of foreign economic, political and military penetration of
China. The establishment of the Republic is associated with the nationalist and
modernizing goals of Dr Sun Yat-sen and the Kuomintang party he founded, but
real power rested with the generals. The years from 1916 to 1928 are known as the
'warlords period' because a number of regionally based military governors
dominated (and exploited) large areas of the country in the absence of any effective
central political authority. In 1923 the Kuomintang and the Chinese Communist
Party (founded in 1921) formed an alliance to establish the integrity of the
republican state, and received substantial Russian aid. Chiang Kai-shek, who
succeeded Sun Yat-sen as leader of the Kuomintang on the latter's death in 1925,
led the Northern Expedition in 1926 to overthrow the predatory warlords.

There were differences within the nationalist and communist parties, as well as
an uneasy alliance between them. For example, the Kuomintang headquarters
referred to below as represented in local councils in Hunan were the headquarters
at county level which often contained left-wing nationalists who were sympathetic
to the politics of the peasantry, unlike the national leadership of Chiang Kai-shek
and his associates. On the other hand, Mao undertook his investigation of the
peasant movement in Hunan to provide material against influential leaders of the
Communist Party who denigrated the revolutionary role of the peasantry because
they conceived the revolution as the exclusive task of the urban working class, and
because they were afraid of compromising the alliance with Chiang Kai-shek. As it
happened, the latter's successful Northern Expedition culminated in the wholesale
massacre of communists and workers in Shanghai in April 1927, and the attempt
to eliminate the communists and their supporters throughout China. This ushered
in a new period of civil war, combined with war against Japanese invasion and
conquest in the 1930s, that finally saw the communists under Mao's leadership
succeed in establishing their rule in 1949.

Mao distinguished three stages in the development of the peasant movement in
Hunan. January to June 1926 was a period of 'underground activity'; from July to
September, as the Northern Expeditionary Army defeated the forces of the
warlords in Hunan, the peasant associations emerged into open political activity.
From October 1926 to the time of Mao's visit the peasant movement generated a
mass following and engaged in 'revolutionary action' of the kind presented in the
'fourteen great achievements'.

Finally, the following is an extract from earlier on in Mao's report in which he
describes the class composition of rural Hunan (based on a survey of one of the
counties he visited) which is extremely important for understanding the social
content of the struggles he analysed: 'The poor peasants comprise 70 per cent, the
middle peasants 20 per cent, and the landlords and the rich peasants 10 per cent of
the population in the rural areas. The 70 per cent, the poor peasants, may be subdivided into two categories, the utterly destitute and the less destitute. The utterly
destitute, comprising 20 per cent, are the completely dispossessed, that is, people

who have neither land nor money, are without any means of livelihood, and are forced to leave home and become mercenaries or hired labourers or wandering beggars. The less destitute, the other 50 per cent, are the partially dispossessed, that is, people with just a little land or a little money who eat up more than they earn and live in toil and distress the year round, such as the handicraftsmen, the tenant-peasants (not including the rich tenant-peasants) and the semi-owner peasants. This great mass of poor peasants, or altogether 70 per cent of the rural population, are the backbone of the peasant associations. . . .'

*   *   *

Most critics of the peasant associations allege that they have done a great many bad things. I have already pointed out that the peasants' attack on the local tyrants and evil gentry is entirely revolutionary behaviour and in no way blameworthy. The peasants have done a great many things, and in order to answer people's criticism we must closely examine all their activities, one by one, to see what they have actually done. I have classified and summed up their activities of the last few months; in all, the peasants under the leadership of the peasant associations have the following fourteen great achievements to their credit.

Organizing the peasants into peasant associations

This is the first great achievement of the peasants. In counties like Hsiangtan, Hsianghsiang and Hengshan, nearly all the peasants are organized and there is hardly a remote corner where they are not on the move; these are the best places. In some counties, like Yiyang and Huajung, the bulk of the peasants are organized, with only a small section remaining unorganized; these places are in the second grade. In other counties, like Chengpu and Liling, while a small section is organized, the bulk of the peasants remain unorganized; these places are in the third grade. Western Hunan, which is under the control of Yuan Tsu-ming [. . ., a warlord], has not yet been reached by the associations' propaganda, and in many of its counties the peasants are completely unorganized; these form a fourth grade. Roughly speaking, the counties in central Hunan, with Changsha as the centre, are the most advanced, those in southern Hunan come second, and western Hunan is only just beginning to organize. According to the figures compiled by the provincial peasant association last November, organizations with a total membership of 1,367,727 have been set up in thirty-seven of the province's seventy-five counties. Of these members about one million were organized during October and November when the power of the associations rose high, while up to September the membership had only been 300,000–400,000. Then came the two months of December and January, and the peasant movement continued its brisk growth. By the end of January the membership must have reached at least two million. As a family generally enters only one name when joining and has an average of five members, the mass following must be about ten million. This astonishing and accelerating rate of expansion explains why the local tyrants, evil gentry and corrupt officials have been isolated, why the public has been amazed at how completely the world has changed since the peasant movement, and why a great revolution has been wrought in the countryside. This is the first great achievement of the peasants under the leadership of their associations.

Hitting the landlords politically

Once the peasants have their organization, the first thing they do is to smash the political prestige and power of the landlord class, and especially of the local tyrants and evil gentry, that is, to pull down landlord authority and build up peasant authority in rural society. This is a most serious and vital struggle. It is the pivotal struggle in the second period, the period of revolutionary action. Without victory in this struggle, no victory is possible in the economic struggle to reduce rent and interest, to secure land and other means of production, and so on. In many places in Hunan like Hsianghsiang, Hengshan and Hsiangtan Counties, this is of course no problem since the authority of the landlords has been overturned and the peasants constitute the sole authority. But in counties like Liling there are still some places (such as Liling's western and southern districts) where the authority of the landlords seems weaker than that of the peasants but, because the political struggle has not been sharp, is in fact surreptitiously competing with it. In such places it is still too early to say that the peasants have gained political victory; they must wage the political struggle more vigorously until the landlords' authority is completely smashed. All in all, the methods used by the peasants to hit the landlords politically are as follows:

Checking the accounts. More often than not the local tyrants and evil gentry have helped themselves to public money passing through their hands, and their books are not in order. Now the peasants are using the checking of accounts as an occasion to bring down a great many of the local tyrants and evil gentry. In many places committees for checking accounts have been established for the express purpose of settling financial scores with them, and the first sign of such a committee makes them shudder. Campaigns of this kind have been carried out in all the counties where the peasant movement is active; they are important not so much for recovering money as for publicizing the crimes of the local tyrants and evil gentry and for knocking them down from their political and social positions.

Imposing fines. The peasants work out fines for such offences as irregularities revealed by the checking of accounts, past outrages against the peasants, current activities which undermine the peasant associations, violations of the ban on gambling and refusal to surrender opium pipes. This local tyrant must pay so much, that member of the evil gentry so much, the sums ranging from tens to thousands of yuan. Naturally, a man who has been fined by the peasants completely loses face.

Levying contributions. The unscrupulous rich landlords are made to contribute for poor relief, for the organization of co-operatives or peasant credit societies, or for other purposes. Though milder than fines, these contributions are also a form of punishment. To avoid trouble, quite a number of landlords make voluntary contributions to the peasant associations.

Minor protests. When someone harms a peasant association by word or deed and the offence is a minor one, the peasants collect in a crowd and swarm into the offender's house to remonstrate with him. He is usually let off after writing a pledge to 'cease and desist', in which he explicitly undertakes to stop defaming the peasant association in the future.

Major demonstrations. A big crowd is rallied to demonstrate against a local tyrant or one of the evil gentry who is an enemy of the association. The demonstrators eat at the offender's house, slaughtering his pigs and consuming his grain as a matter of course. Quite a few such cases have occurred. There was a case recently at Machiaho, Hsiangtan County, where a crowd of fifteen thousand peasants went to the houses of six of the evil gentry and demonstrated; the whole affair lasted four days during which more than 130 pigs were killed and eaten. After such demonstrations, the peasants usually impose fines.

'Crowning' the landlords and parading them through the villages. This sort of thing is very common. A tall paper-hat is stuck on the head of one of the local tyrants or evil gentry, bearing the words 'Lord tyrant so-and-so' or 'So-and-so of the evil gentry'. He is led by a rope and escorted with big crowds in front and behind. Sometimes brass gongs are beaten and flags waved to attract people's attention. This form of punishment more than any other makes the local tyrants and evil gentry tremble. Anyone who has once been crowned with a tall paper-hat loses face altogether and can never again hold up his head. Hence many of the rich prefer being fined to wearing the tall hat. But wear it they must, if the peasants insist. One ingenious township peasant association arrested an obnoxious member of the gentry and announced that he was to be crowned that very day. The man turned blue with fear. Then the association decided not to crown him that day. They argued that if he were crowned right away, he would become case-hardened and no longer afraid, and that it would be better to let him go home and crown him some other day. Not knowing when he would be crowned, the man was in daily suspense, unable to sit down or sleep at ease.

Locking up the landlords in the county jail. This is a heavier punishment than wearing the tall paper-hat. A local tyrant or one of the evil gentry is arrested and sent to the county jail; he is locked up and the county magistrate has to try him and punish him. Today the people who are locked up are no longer the same. Formerly it was the gentry who sent peasants to be locked up, now it is the other way round.

'Banishment'. The peasants have no desire to banish the most notorious criminals among the local tyrants and evil gentry, but would rather arrest or execute them. Afraid of being arrested or executed, they run away. In counties where the peasant movement is well developed, almost all the important local tyrants and evil gentry have fled, and this amounts to banishment. Among them, the top ones have fled to Shanghai, those of the second rank to Hankow, those of the third to Changsha, and of the fourth to the county towns. Of all the fugitive local tyrants and evil gentry, those who have fled to Shanghai are the safest. Some of those who fled to Hangkow, like the three from Huajung, were eventually captured and brought back. Those who fled to Changsha are in still greater danger of being seized at any moment by students in the provincial capital who hail from their counties; I myself saw two captured in Changsha. Those who have taken refuge in the county towns are only of the fourth rank, and the peasantry, having many eyes and ears, can easily track them down. The financial authorities once explained the difficulties encountered by the Hunan Provincial Government in raising money by the fact that the peasants were banishing the well-to-do, which gives some idea of the extent to which the local tyrants and evil gentry are not tolerated in their home villages.

Execution. This is confined to the worst local tyrants and evil gentry and is carried out by the peasants jointly with other sections of the people. For instance, Yang Chih-tse of Ninghsiang, Chou Chia-kan of Yuehyang and Fu Tao-nan and Sun Po-chu of Huajung were shot by the government authorities at the insistence

of the peasants and other sections of the people. In the case of Yen Jung-chiu of
Hsiangtan, the peasants and other sections of the people compelled the magistrate
to agree to hand him over, and the peasants themselves executed him. Liu Chao of
Ninghsiang was killed by the peasants. The execution of Peng Chih-fan of Liling
and Chou Tien-chueh and Tsao Yun of Yiyang is pending, subject to the decision
of the 'special tribunal for trying local tyrants and evil gentry'. The execution of
one such big landlord reverberates through a whole county and is very effective in
eradicating the remaining evils of feudalism. Every county has these major
tyrants, some as many as several dozen and others at least a few, and the only
effective way of suppressing the reactionaries is to execute at least a few in each
county who are guilty of the most heinous crimes. When the local tyrants and evil
gentry were at the height of their power, they literally slaughtered peasants
without batting an eyelid. Ho Mai-chuan, for ten years head of the defence corps
in the town of Hsinkang, Changsha County, was personally responsible for killing
almost a thousand poverty-stricken peasants, which he euphemistically described
as 'executing bandits'. In my native county of Hsiangtan, Tang Chun-yen and Lo
Shu-lin who headed the defence corps in the town of Yintien have killed more than
fifty people and buried four alive in the fourteen years since 1913. Of the more
than fifty they murdered, the first two were perfectly innocent beggars. Tang
Chun-yen said, 'Let me make a start by killing a couple of beggars!' and so these
two lives were snuffed out. Such was the cruelty of the local tyrants and evil gentry
in former days, such was the White terror[1] they created in the countryside, and
now that the peasants have risen and shot a few and created just a little terror in
suppressing the counter-revolutionaries, is there any reason for saying they should
not do so?

Hitting the landlords economically

*Prohibition on sending grain out of the area, forcing up grain prices, and hoarding and
cornering.* This is one of the great events of recent months in the economic struggle
of the Hunan peasants. Since last October the poor peasants have prevented the
outflow of the grain of the landlords and rich peasants and have banned the forcing
up of grain prices and hoarding and cornering. As a result, the poor peasants have
fully achieved their objective; the ban on the outflow of grain is watertight, grain
prices have fallen considerably, and hoarding and cornering have disappeared.

   Prohibition on increasing rents and deposits;[2] *agitation for reduced rents and deposits.* Last
July and August, when the peasant associations were still weak, the landlords,
following their long-established practice of maximum exploitation, served notice
one after another on their tenants that rents and deposits would be increased. But
by October, when the peasant associations had grown considerably in strength and
had all come out against the raising of rents and deposits, the landlords dared not
breathe another word on the subject. From November onwards, as the peasants
have gained ascendancy over the landlords they have taken the further step of
agitating for reduced rents and deposits. What a pity, they say, that the peasant
associations were not strong enough when rents were being paid last autumn, or
we could have reduced them then. The peasants are doing extensive propaganda
for rent reduction in the coming autumn, and the landlords are asking how the
reductions are to be carried out. As for the reduction of deposits, this is already
under way in Hengshan and other counties.

Prohibition on cancelling tenancies. In July and August of last year there were still many instances of landlords cancelling tenancies and re-letting the land. But after October nobody dared cancel a tenancy. Today, the cancelling of tenancies and the re-letting of land are quite out of the question; all that remains as something of a problem is whether a tenancy can be cancelled if the landlord wants to cultivate the land himself. In some places even this is not allowed by the peasants. In others the cancelling of a tenancy may be permitted if the landlord wants to cultivate the land himself, but then the problem of unemployment among the tenant-peasants arises. There is as yet no uniform way of solving this problem.

Reduction of interest. Interest has been generally reduced in Anhua, and there have been reductions in other counties, too. But wherever the peasant associations are powerful, rural money-lending has virtually disappeared, the landlords having completely 'stopped lending' for fear that the money will be 'communized'. What is currently called reduction of interest is confined to old loans. Not only is the interest on such old loans reduced, but the creditor is actually forbidden to press for the repayment of the principal. The poor peasant replies, 'Don't blame me. The year is nearly over. I'll pay you back next year.'

Overthrowing the feudal rule of the local tyrants and evil gentry — smashing the *tu* and *tuan*

The old organs of political power in the *tu* and *tuan* (i.e., the district and the township), and especially at the *tu* level, just below the county level, used to be almost exclusively in the hands of the local tyrants and evil gentry. The *tu* had jurisdiction over a population of from ten to fifty or sixty thousand people, and had its own armed forces such as the township defence corps, its own fiscal powers such as the power to levy taxes per *mou*[3] of land, and its own judicial powers such as the power to arrest, imprison, try and punish the peasants at will. The evil gentry who ran these organs were virtual monarchs of the countryside. Comparatively speaking, the peasants were not so much concerned with the president of the Republic, the provincial military governor or the county magistrate; their real 'bosses' were these rural monarchs. A mere snort from these people, and the peasants knew they had to watch their step. As a consequence of the present revolt in the countryside the authority of the landlord class has generally been struck down, and the organs of rural administration dominated by the local tyrants and evil gentry have naturally collapsed in its wake. The heads of the *tu* and the *tuan* all steer clear of the people, dare not show their faces and push all local matters on to the peasant associations. They put people off with the remark, 'It is none of my business!'

Whenever their conversation turns to the heads of the *tu* and the *tuan*, the peasants say angrily, 'That bunch! They are finished!'

Yes, the term 'finished' truly describes the state of the old organs of rural administration wherever the storm of revolution has raged.

Overthrowing the armed forces of the landlords and establishing those of the peasants

The armed forces of the landlord class were smaller in central Hunan than in the western and southern parts of the province. An average of 600 rifles for each county would make a total of 45,000 rifles for all the seventy-five counties; there may, in fact, be more. In the southern and central parts where the peasant movement is well developed, the landlord class cannot hold its own because of the tremendous momentum with which the peasants have risen, and its armed forces have largely capitulated to the peasant associations and taken the side of the peasants; examples of this are to be found in such counties as Ninghsiang, Pingkiang, Liuyang, Changsha, Liling, Hsiangtan, Hsianghsiang, Anhua, Hengshan and Hengyang. In some counties such as Paoching, a small number of the landlords' armed forces are taking a neutral stand, though with a tendency to capitulate. Another small section are opposing the peasant associations, but the peasants are attacking them and may wipe them out before long, as, for example, in such counties as Yichang, Linwu and Chiaho. The armed forces thus taken over from the reactionary landlords are all being organized into a 'standing household militia'[4] and placed under the new organs of rural self-government, which are organs of the political power of the peasantry. Taking over these old armed forces is one way in which the peasants are building up their own armed forces. A new way is through the setting up of spear corps under the peasant associations. The spears have pointed, double-edged blades mounted on long shafts, and there are now 100,000 of these weapons in the county of Hsianghsiang alone. Other counties like Hsiangtan, Hengshan, Liling and Changsha have 70,000–80,000, or 50,000–60,000, or 30,000–40,000 each. Every county where there is a peasant movement has a rapidly growing spear corps. These peasants thus armed form an 'irregular household militia'. This multitude equipped with spears, which is larger than the old armed forces mentioned above, is a new-born armed power the mere sight of which makes the local tyrants and evil gentry tremble. The revolutionary authorities in Hunan should see to it that it is built up on a really extensive scale among the more than twenty million peasants in the seventy-five counties of the province, that every peasant, whether young or in his prime, possesses a spear, and that no restrictions are imposed as though a spear were something dreadful. Anyone who is scared at the sight of the spear corps is indeed a weakling! Only the local tyrants and evil gentry are frightened of them, but no revolutionaries should take fright.

Overthrowing the political power of the county magistrate and his bailiffs

That county government cannot be clean until the peasants rise up was proved some time ago in Haifeng, Kwangtung Province. Now we have added proof, particularly in Hunan. In a county where power is in the hands of the local tyrants and evil gentry, the magistrate, whoever he may be, is almost invariably a corrupt official. In a county where the peasants have risen there is clean government, whoever the magistrate is. In the counties I visited, the magistrates had to consult the peasant associations on everything in advance. In counties where the peasant power was very strong, the word of the peasant association worked miracles. If it demanded the arrest of a local tyrant in the morning, the magistrate dared not delay till noon; if it demanded arrest by noon, he dared not delay till the afternoon. When the power of the peasants was just beginning to make itself felt in the countryside, the magistrate worked in league with the local tyrants and evil gentry against the peasants. When the peasants' power grew till it matched that of the landlords, the magistrate took the position of trying to accommodate both the landlords and the peasants, accepting some of the peasant association's suggestions while rejecting others. The remark that the word of the peasant association 'works miracles' applies only when the power of the landlords has been completely beaten down by that of the peasants. At present the political situation in such counties as Hsianghsiang, Hsiangtan, Liling and Hengshan is as follows:

(1) *All decisions are made by a joint council consisting of the magistrate and the representatives of the revolutionary mass organizations.* The council is convened by the magistrate and meets in his office. In some counties it is called the 'joint council of public bodies and the local government', and in others the 'council of county affairs'. Besides the magistrate himself, the people attending are the representatives of the county peasant association, trade union council, merchant association, women's association, school staff association, student association and Kuomintang headquarters. At such council meetings the magistrate is influenced by the views of the public organizations and invariably does their bidding. The adoption of a democratic system of county government should not, therefore, present much of a problem in Hunan. The present county governments are already quite democratic both in form and substance. This situation has been brought about only in the last two or three months, that is, since the peasants have risen all over the countryside and overthrown the power of the local tyrants and evil gentry. It has now come about that the magistrates, seeing their old props collapse and needing other props to retain their posts, have begun to curry favour with the public organizations.

(2) *The judicial assistant has scarcely any cases to handle.* The judicial system in Hunan remains one in which the county magistrate is concurrently in charge of judicial affairs, with an assistant to help him in handling cases. To get rich, the magistrate and his underlings used to rely entirely on collecting taxes and levies, procuring men and provisions for the armed forces, and extorting money in civil and criminal lawsuits by confounding right and wrong, the last being the most regular and reliable source of income. In the last few months, with the downfall of the local tyrants and evil gentry, all the legal pettifoggers have disappeared. What is more, the peasants' problems, big and small, are now all settled in the peasant associations at the various levels. Thus the county judicial assistant simply has nothing to do. The one in Hsianghsiang told me, 'When there were no peasant associations, an average of sixty civil or criminal suits were brought to the county government each day; now it receives an average of only four or five a day.' So it is that the purses of the magistrates and their underlings perforce remain empty.

(3) *The armed guards, the police and the bailiffs all keep out of the way and dare not go near the villages to practise their extortions.* In the past the villagers were afraid of the townspeople, but now the townspeople are afraid of the villagers. In particular the vicious curs kept by the county government – the police, the armed guards and the bailiffs – are afraid of going to the villages, or if they do so, they no longer dare to practise their extortions. They tremble at the sight of the peasants' spears.

Overthrowing the clan authority of the ancestral temples and clan elders, the religious authority of town and village gods, and the masculine authority of husbands

A man in China is usually subjected to the domination of three systems of authority: (1) the state system (political authority), ranging from the national, provincial and county government down to that of the township; (2) the clan system (clan authority), ranging from the central ancestral temple and its branch temples down to the head of the household; and (3) the supernatural system (religious authority), ranging from the King of Hell down to the town and village gods belonging to the nether world, and from the Emperor of Heaven down to all the various gods and spirits belonging to the celestial world. As for women, in addition to being dominated by these three systems of authority, they are also dominated by the men (the authority of the husband). These four authorities – political, clan, religious and masculine – are the embodiment of the whole feudal–patriarchal system and ideology, and are the four thick ropes binding the Chinese people, particularly the peasants. How the peasants have overthrown the political authority of the landlords in the countryside has been described above. The political authority of the landlords is the backbone of all the other systems of authority. With that overturned, the clan authority, the religious authority and the authority of the husband all begin to totter. Where the peasant association is powerful, the clan elders and administrators of temple funds no longer dare oppress those lower in the clan hierarchy or embezzle clan funds. The worst clan elders and administrators, being local tyrants, have been thrown out. No one any longer dares to practise the cruel corporal and capital punishments that used to be inflicted in the ancestral temples, such as flogging, drowning and burying alive. The old rule barring women and poor people from the banquets in the ancestral temples has also been broken. The women of Paikuo in Hengshan County gathered in force and swarmed into their ancestral temple, firmly planted their backsides in the seats and joined in the eating and drinking, while the venerable clan bigwigs had willy-nilly to let them do as they pleased. At another place, where poor peasants had been excluded from temple banquets, a group of them flocked in and ate and drank their fill, while the local tyrants and evil gentry and other long-gowned gentlemen all took to their heels in fright. Everywhere religious authority totters as the peasant movement develops. In many places the peasant associations have taken over the temples of the gods as their offices. Everywhere they advocate the appropriation of temple property in order to start peasant schools and to defray the expenses of the associations, calling it 'public revenue from superstition'. In Liling County, prohibiting superstitious practices and smashing idols have become quite the vogue. In its northern districts the peasants have prohibited the incense-burning processions to propitiate the god of pestilence. There were many idols in the Taoist temple at Fupoling in Lukou, but when extra room was needed for the district headquarters of the Kuomintang, they were all piled up in a corner, big and small together, and no peasant raised any objection. Since then, sacrifices to the gods, the performance of religious rites and the offering of sacred lamps have rarely been practised when a death occurs in a family. Because the initiative in this matter was taken by the chairman of the peasant association, Sun Hsiao-shan, he is hated by the local Taoist priests. In the Lungfeng Nunnery in the North Third District, the peasants and primary school teachers chopped up the wooden idols and actually used the wood to cook meat. More than thirty idols in the Tungfu Monastery in the Southern District were burned by the students and peasants together, and only two small images of Lord Pao[5] were snatched up by an old peasant who said, 'Don't commit a sin!' In places where the power of the peasants is predominant, only the older peasants and the women still believe in the gods, the younger peasants no longer doing so. Since the latter control the associations, the overthrow of religious authority and the eradication of superstition are going on everywhere. As to the authority of the husband, this has always been weaker among the poor peasants because, out of economic necessity, their womenfolk have to do more manual labour than the women of the richer classes and therefore have more say and greater power of decision in family matters. With the increasing bankruptcy of the rural economy in recent years, the basis for men's domination over women has already been weakened. With the rise of the peasant movement, the women in many places have now begun to organize rural women's associations; the opportunity has come for them to lift up their heads, and the authority of the husband is getting shakier every day. In a word, the whole feudal–patriarchal system and ideology is tottering with the growth of the peasants' power. At the present time, however, the peasants are concentrating on destroying the landlords' political authority. Wherever it has been wholly destroyed, they are beginning to press their attack in the three other spheres of the clan, the gods and male domination. But such attacks have only just begun, and there can be no thorough overthrow of all three until the peasants have won complete victory in the economic struggle. Therefore, our present task is to lead the peasants to put their greatest efforts into the political struggle, so that the landlords' authority is entirely overthrown. The economic struggle should follow immediately, so that the land problem and the other economic problems of the poor peasants may be fundamentally solved. As for the clan system, superstition and inequality between men and women, their abolition will follow as a natural consequence of victory in the political and economic struggles. If too much of an effort is made, arbitrarily and prematurely, to abolish these things, the local tyrants and evil gentry will seize the pretext to put about such counter-revolutionary propaganda as 'the peasant association has no piety towards ancestors', 'the peasant association is blasphemous and is destroying religion' and 'the peasant association stands for the communization of wives', all for the purpose of undermining the peasant movement. A case in point is the recent events at Hsianghsiang in Hunan and Yanghsin in Hupeh, where the landlords exploited the opposition of some peasants to smashing idols. It is the peasants who made the idols, and when the time comes they will cast the idols aside with their own hands; there is no need for anyone else to do it for them prematurely. The Communist Party's propaganda policy in such matters should be, 'Draw the bow without shooting, just indicate the motions.'⁶ It is for the peasants themselves to cast aside the idols, pull down the temples to the martyred virgins and the arches to the chaste and faithful widows; it is wrong for anybody else to do it for them.

While I was in the countryside, I did some propaganda against superstition among the peasants, I said:

'If you believe in the Eight Characters,⁷ you hope for good luck; if you believe in geomancy,⁸ you hope to benefit from the location of your ancestral graves. This year within the space of a few months the local tyrants, evil gentry and corrupt officials have all toppled from their pedestals. Is it possible that until a few months ago they all had good luck and enjoyed the benefit of well-sited ancestral graves, while suddenly in the last few months their luck has turned and their ancestral graves have ceased to exert a beneficial influence? The local tyrants and evil gentry jeer at your peasant association and say, "How odd! Today, the world is a world of committeemen. Look, you can't even go to pass water without bumping into a committeeman!" Quite true, the towns and the villages, the trade unions and the peasant associations, the Kuomintang and the Communist Party, all without exception have their executive committee members – it is indeed a world of committeemen. But is this due to the Eight Characters and the location of the ancestral graves? How strange! The Eight Characters of all the poor wretches in the

countryside have suddenly turned auspicious! And their ancestral graves have
suddenly started exerting beneficial influences! The gods? Worship them by all
means. But if you had only Lord Kuan[9] and the Goddess of Mercy and no peasant
association, could you have overthrown the local tyrants and evil gentry? The gods
and goddesses are indeed miserable objects. You have worshipped them for
centuries, and they have not overthrown a single one of the local tyrants or evil
gentry for you! Now you want to have your rent reduced. Let me ask, how will
you go about it? Will you believe in the gods or in the peasant association?'
My words made the peasants roar with laughter.

Spreading political propaganda

Even if ten thousand schools of law and political science had been opened, could
they have brought as much political education to the people, men and women,
young and old, all the way into the remotest corners of the countryside, as the
peasant associations have done in so short a time? I don't think they could. 'Down
with imperialism!' 'Down with the warlords!' 'Down with the corrupt officials!'
'Down with the local tyrants and evil gentry!' – these political slogans have grown
wings, they have found their way to the young, the middle-aged and the old, to the
women and children in countless villages, they have penetrated into their minds
and are on their lips. For instance, watch a group of children at play. If one gets
angry with another, if he glares, stamps his foot and shakes his fist, you will then
immediately hear from the other the shrill cry of 'Down with imperialism!'
In the Hsiangtan area, when the children who pasture the cattle get into a fight,
one will act as Tang Sheng-chih, and the other as Yeh Kai-hsin;[10] when one is
defeated and runs away, with the other chasing him, it is the pursuer who is Tang
Sheng-chih and the pursued Yeh Kai-hsin. As to the song 'Down with the
Imperialist Powers!' of course almost every child in the towns can sing it, and now
many village children can sing it too.
Some of the peasants can also recite Dr Sun Yat-sen's Testament. They pick out
the terms 'freedom', 'equality', 'the Three People's Principles'[11] and 'unequal
treaties' and apply them, if rather crudely, in their daily life. When somebody who
looks like one of the gentry encounters a peasant and stands on his dignity, refusing
to make way along a pathway, the peasant will say angrily, 'Hey, you local tyrant,
don't you know the Three People's Principles?' Formerly when the peasants from
the vegetable farms on the outskirts of Changsha entered the city to sell their
produce, they used to be pushed around by the police. Now they have found a
weapon, which is none other than the Three People's Principles. When a policeman strikes or swears at a peasant selling vegetables, the peasant immediately
answers back by invoking the Three People's Principles and that shuts the policeman up. Once in Hsiangtan when a district peasant association and a township
peasant association could not see eye to eye, the chairman of the township
association declared, 'Down with the district peasant association's unequal
treaties!'
The spread of political propaganda throughout the rural areas is entirely an
achievement of the Communist Party and the peasant associations. Simple
slogans, cartoons and speeches have produced such a widespread and speedy effect
among the peasants that every one of them seems to have been through a political
school. According to the reports of comrades engaged in rural work, political

propaganda was very extensive at the time of the three great mass rallies, the anti-British demonstration, the celebration of the October Revolution and the victory celebration for the Northern Expedition. On these occasions, political propaganda was conducted extensively wherever there were peasant associations, arousing the whole countryside with tremendous effect. From now on care should be taken to use every opportunity gradually to enrich the content and clarify the meaning of those simple slogans.

Peasant bans and prohibitions

When the peasant associations, under Communist Party leadership, establish their authority in the countryside, the peasants begin to prohibit or restrict the things they dislike. Gaming, gambling and opium-smoking are the three things that are most strictly forbidden.

Gaming. Where the peasant association is powerful, mahjong, dominoes and card games are completely banned.

The peasant association in the 14th District of Hsianghsiang burned two basketfuls of mahjong sets.

If you go to the countryside, you will find none of these games played; anyone who violates the ban is promptly and strictly punished.

Gambling. Former hardened gamblers are now themselves suppressing gambling; this abuse, too, has been swept away in places where the peasant association is powerful.

Opium-smoking. The prohibition is extremely strict. When the peasant association orders the surrender of opium pipes, no one dares to raise the least objection. In Liling County one of the evil gentry who did not surrender his pipes was arrested and paraded through the villages.

The peasants' campaign to 'disarm the opium-smokers' is no less impressive than the disarming of the troops of Wu Pei-fu and Sun Chuan-fang [warlords] by the Northern Expeditionary Army. Quite a number of venerable fathers of officers in the revolutionary army, old men who were opium-addicts and inseparable from their pipes, have been disarmed by the 'emperors' (as the peasants are called derisively by the evil gentry). The 'emperors' have banned not only the growing and smoking of opium, but also trafficking in it. A great deal of the opium transported from Kweichow to Kiangsi via the counties of Paoching, Hsianghsiang, Yuhsien and Liling has been intercepted on the way and burned. This has affected government revenues. As a result, out of consideration for the army's need for funds in the Northern Expedition, the provincial peasant association ordered the associations at the lower levels 'temporarily to postpone the ban on opium traffic'. This, however, has upset and displeased the peasants.

There are many other things besides these three which the peasants have prohibited or restricted, the following being some examples:

The flower drum. Vulgar performances are forbidden in many places.

Sedan-chairs. In many counties, especially Hsianghsiang, there have been cases of smashing sedan-chairs. The peasants, detesting the people who use this conveyance, are always ready to smash the chairs, but the peasant associations forbid them to do so. Association officials tell the peasants, 'If you smash the chairs, you only save the rich money and lose the carriers their jobs. Will that not hurt our own people?' Seeing the point, the peasants have worked out a new tactic

– considerably to increase the fares charged by the chair-carriers so as to penalize the rich.

Distilling and sugar-making. The use of grain for distilling spirits and making sugar is everywhere prohibited, and the distillers and sugar-refiners are constantly complaining. Distilling is not banned in Futienpu, Hengshan County, but prices are fixed very low, and the wine and spirits dealers, seeing no prospect of profit, have had to stop it.

Pigs. The number of pigs a family can keep is limited, for pigs consume grain.

Chickens and ducks. In Hsianghsiang County the raising of chickens and ducks is prohibited, but the women object. In Hengshan County, each family in Yangtang is allowed to keep only three, and in Futienpu five. In many places the raising of ducks is completely banned, for ducks not only consume grain but also ruin the rice plants and so are worse than chickens.

Feasts. Sumptuous feasts are generally forbidden. In Shaoshan, Hsiangtan County, it has been decided that guests are to be served with only three kinds of animal food, namely, chicken, fish and pork. It is also forbidden to serve bamboo shoots, kelp and lentil noodles. In Hengshan County it has been resolved that eight dishes and no more may be served at a banquet. Only five dishes are allowed in the East Third District in Liling County, and only three meat and three vegetable dishes in the North Second District, while in the West Third District New Year feasts are forbidden entirely. In Hsianghsiang County, there is a ban on all 'egg-cake feasts', which are by no means sumptuous. When a family in the Second District of Hsianghsiang gave an 'egg-cake feast' at a son's wedding, the peasants, seeing the ban violated, swarmed into the house and broke up the celebration. In the town of Chiamo, Hsianghsiang County, the people have refrained from eating expensive foods and use only fruit when offering ancestral sacrifices.

Oxen. Oxen are a treasured possession of the peasants. 'Slaughter an ox in this life and you will be an ox in the next' has become almost a religious tenet; oxen must never be killed. Before the peasants had power, they could only appeal to religious taboo in opposing the slaughter of cattle and had no means of banning it. Since the rise of the peasant associations their jurisdiction has extended even to the cattle, and they have prohibited the slaughter of cattle in the towns. Of the six butcheries in the county town of Hsiangtan, five are now closed and the remaining one slaughters only enfeebled or disabled animals. The slaughter of cattle is totally prohibited throughout the county of Hengshan. A peasant whose ox broke a leg consulted the peasant association before he dared kill it. When the Chamber of Commerce of Chuchow rashly slaughtered a cow, the peasants came into town and demanded an explanation, and the chamber, besides paying a fine, had to let off firecrackers by way of apology.

Tramps and vagabonds. A resolution passed in Liling County prohibited the drumming of New Year greetings or the chanting of praises to the local deities or the singing of lotus rhymes. Various other counties have similar prohibitions, or these practices have disappeared of themselves, as no one observes them any more. The 'beggar-bullies' or 'vagabonds' who used to be extremely aggressive now have no alternative but to submit to the peasant associations. In Shaoshan, Hsiangtan County, the vagabonds used to make the temple of the Rain God their regular haunt and feared nobody, but since the rise of the associations they have stolen away. The peasant association in Huti Township in the same county caught three such tramps and made them carry clay for the brick kilns.

Resolutions have been passed prohibiting the wasteful customs associated with New Year calls and gifts.

Besides these, many other minor prohibitions have been introduced in various places, such as the Liling prohibitions on incense-burning processions to propitiate the god of pestilence, on buying preserves and fruit for ritual presents, burning ritual paper garments during the Festival of Spirits and pasting up good-luck posters at the New Year. At Kushui in Hsianghsiang County, there is a prohibition even on smoking water-pipes. In the Second District, letting off firecrackers and ceremonial guns is forbidden, with a fine of 1.20 yuan for the former and 2.40 yuan for the latter. Religious rites for the dead are prohibited in the 7th and 20th Districts. In the 18th District, it is forbidden to make funeral gifts of money. Things like these, which defy enumeration, may be generally called peasant bans and prohibitions.

They are of great significance in two respects. First, they represent a revolt against bad social customs, such as gaming, gambling and opium-smoking. These customs arose out of the rotten political environment of the landlord class and are swept away once its authority is overthrown. Second, the prohibitions are a form of self-defence against exploitation by city merchants; such are the prohibitions on feasts and on buying preserves and fruit for ritual presents. Manufactured goods are extremely dear and agricultural products are extremely cheap, the peasants are impoverished and ruthlessly exploited by the merchants, and they must therefore encourage frugality to protect themselves. As for the ban on sending grain out of the area, it is imposed to prevent the price from rising because the poor peasants have not enough to feed themselves and have to buy grain on the market. The reason for all this is the peasants' poverty and the contradictions between town and country; it is not a matter of their rejecting manufactured goods or trade between town and country in order to uphold the so-called Doctrine of Oriental Culture.[12] To protect themselves economically, the peasants must organize consumers' co-operatives for the collective buying of goods. It is also necessary for the government to help the peasant associations establish credit (loan) co-operatives. If these things were done, the peasants would naturally find it unnecessary to ban the outflow of grain as a method of keeping down the price, nor would they have to prohibit the inflow of certain manufactured goods in economic self-defence.

Eliminating banditry

In my opinion, no ruler in any dynasty from Yu, Tang, Wen and Wu down to the Ching emperors and the presidents of the Republic has ever shown as much prowess in eliminating banditry as have the peasant associations today. Wherever the peasant associations are powerful, there is not a trace of banditry. Surprisingly enough, in many places even the pilfering of vegetables has disappeared. In other places there are still some pilferers. But in the counties I visited, even including those that were formerly bandit-ridden, there was no trace of bandits. The reasons are: First, the members of the peasant associations are everywhere spread out over the hills and dales, spear or cudgel in hand, ready to go into action in their hundreds, so that the bandits have nowhere to hide. Second, since the rise of the peasant movement the price of grain has dropped – it was six yuan a picul[13] last spring but only two yuan last winter – and the problem of food has become less serious for the people. Third, members of the secret societies have joined the peasant associations, in which they can openly and legally play the hero and vent their grievances, so that there is no further need for the secret 'mountain', 'lodge', 'shrine' and 'river' forms of organization.[14] In killing the pigs and sheep of the local tyrants and evil gentry and imposing heavy levies and fines, they have adequate outlets for their feelings against those who oppressed them. Fourth, the armies are recruiting large numbers of soldiers and many of the 'unruly' have joined up. Thus the evil of banditry has ended with the rise of the peasant movement. On this point, even the well-to-do approve of the peasant associations. Their comment is, 'The peasant associations? Well, to be fair, there is also something to be said for them.'

In prohibiting gaming, gambling and opium-smoking, and in eliminating banditry, the peasant associations have won general approval.

Abolishing exorbitant levies

As the country is not yet unified and the authority of the imperialists and the warlords has not been overthrown, there is as yet no way of removing the heavy burden of government taxes and levies on the peasants or, more explicitly, of removing the burden of expenditure for the revolutionary army. However, the exorbitant levies imposed on the peasants when the local tyrants and evil gentry dominated rural administration, e.g., the surcharge on each *mou* of land, have been abolished or at least reduced with the rise of the peasant movement and the downfall of the local tyrants and evil gentry. This too should be counted among the achievements of the peasant associations.

The movement for education

In China education has always been the exclusive preserve of the landlords, and the peasants have had no access to it. But the landlords' culture is created by the peasants, for its sole source is the peasants' sweat and blood. In China 90 per cent of the people have had no education, and of these the overwhelming majority are peasants. The moment the power of the landlords was overthrown in the rural areas, the peasants' movement for education began. See how the peasants who hitherto detested the schools are today zealously setting up evening classes! They always disliked the 'foreign-style school'. In my student days, when I went back to the village and saw that the peasants were against the 'foreign-style school', I, too, used to identify myself with the general run of 'foreign-style students and teachers' and stand up for it, feeling that the peasants were somehow wrong. It was not until 1925, when I lived in the countryside for six months and was already a Communist and had acquired the Marxist viewpoint, that I realized I had been wrong and the peasants right. The texts used in the rural primary schools were entirely about urban things and unsuited to rural needs. Besides, the attitude of the primary school teachers towards the peasants was very bad and, far from being helpful to the peasants, they became objects of dislike. Hence the peasants preferred the old-style schools ('Chinese classes', as they called them) to the modern schools (which they called 'foreign classes') and the old-style teachers to the ones in the primary schools. Now the peasants are enthusiastically establishing evening classes, which they call peasant schools. Some have already been opened, others are being organized, and on the average there is one school per township. The peasants are very enthusiastic about these schools, and regard them, and only them, as their own. The funds for the evening schools come from the 'public revenue from superstition', from ancestral temple funds, and from other idle public funds or property. The county education boards wanted to use this money to establish primary schools, that is, 'foreign-style schools' not suited to the needs of the peasants, while the latter wanted to use it for peasant schools, and the outcome of the dispute was that both got some of the money, though there are places where the peasants got it all. The development of the peasant movement has resulted in a rapid rise in their cultural level. Before long tens of thousands of schools will have sprung up in the villages throughout the province; this is quite different from the empty talk about 'universal education', which the intelligentsia and the so-called 'educationalists' have been bandying back and forth and which after all this time remains an empty phrase.

The co-operative movement

The peasants really need co-operatives, and especially consumers', marketing and credit co-operatives. When they buy goods, the merchants exploit them; when they sell their farm produce, the merchants cheat them; when they borrow money or rice, they are fleeced by the usurers; and they are eager to find a solution to these three problems. During the fighting in the Yangtse valley last winter, when trade routes were cut and the price of salt went up in Hunan, many peasants organized co-operatives to purchase salt. When the landlords deliberately stopped lending, there were many attempts by the peasants to organize credit agencies, because they needed to borrow money. A major problem is the absence of detailed, standard rules of organization. As these spontaneously organized peasant co-operatives often fail to conform to co-operative principles, the comrades working among the peasants are always eagerly enquiring about 'rules and regulations'. Given proper guidance, the co-operative movement can spread everywhere along with the growth of the peasant associations.

Building roads and repairing embankments

This, too, is one of the achievements of the peasant associations. Before there were peasant associations the roads in the countryside were terrible. Roads cannot be repaired without money, and as the wealthy were unwilling to dip into their purses, the roads were left in a bad state. If there was any road work done at all, it was done as an act of charity; a little money was collected from families 'wishing to gain merit in the next world', and a few narrow, skimpily paved roads were built. With the rise of the peasant associations orders have been given specifying the required width – three, five, seven or ten feet, according to the requirements of the different routes – and each landlord along a road has been ordered to build a section. Once the order is given, who dares to disobey? In a short time many good roads have appeared. This is no work of charity but the result of compulsion, and a little compulsion of this kind is not at all a bad thing. The same is true of the embankments. The ruthless landlords were always out to take what they could from the tenant-peasants and would never spend even a few coppers on embankment repairs; they would leave the ponds to dry up and the tenant-peasants to starve, caring about nothing but the rent. Now that there are peasant associations, the landlords can be bluntly ordered to repair the embankments. When a landlord refuses, the association will tell him politely, 'Very well! If you won't do the repairs, you will contribute grain, a *tou* for each work-day.' As this is a bad bargain for the landlord, he hastens to do the repairs. Consequently many defective embankments have been turned into good ones.

All the fourteen deeds enumerated above have been accomplished by the peasants under the leadership of the peasant associations. Would the reader please think it over and say whether any of them is bad in its fundamental spirit and revolutionary significance? Only the local tyrants and evil gentry, I think, will call them bad. Curiously enough, it is reported [. . .] that Chiang Kai-shek, Chang Ching-chiang [another Kuomintang leader] and other such gentlemen do not altogether approve of the activities of the Hunan peasants. This opinion is shared by [. . .] other right-wing leaders in Hunan, all of whom say, 'They have simply gone Red.' But where would the national revolution be without this bit of Red? To talk about 'arousing the masses of the people' day in and day out and then to be scared to death when the masses do rise – what difference is there between this and Lord Sheh's love of dragons?[15]

Extracted from Mao Tse-tung, *Selected Works,* vol. 1, Foreign Languages Press, Peking, 1967, pp. 34–59.

NOTES

[1. 'White terror' is counter-revolutionary terror exercised by the ruling class of the old regime; it is 'white' in opposition to the 'Red terror' of the revolution. These terms were adopted in China from their usage in the Russian (Bolshevik) revolution.]

2. A tenant generally gave his landlord, as a condition of tenancy, a deposit in cash or kind, often amounting to a considerable part of the value of the land. Though this was supposed to be a guarantee for payment of rent, it actually represented a form of extra exploitation.

3. The tax per *mou* was a surcharge on top of the regular land tax, ruthlessly imposed on the peasants by the landlord regime.

4. The 'standing household militia' was one of the various kinds of armed forces in the countryside. The term 'household' is used because some member of almost every household had to join it. After the defeat of the revolution in 1927, the landlords in many places seized control of the militia and turned them into armed counter-revolutionary bands.

5. Lord Pao (Pao Cheng) was prefect of Kaifeng, capital of the Northern Sung Dynasty (A.D. 960–1127). He was famous in popular legend as an upright official and a fearless, impartial judge with a knack of passing true verdicts in all the cases he tried.

6. This reference to archery is taken from *Mencius.* It describes how the expert teacher of archery draws his bow with a histrionic gesture but does not release the arrow. The point is that while Communists should guide the peasants in attaining a full measure of political consciousness, they should leave it to the peasants' own initiative to abolish superstitious and other bad practices, and should not give them orders or do it for them.

7. The Eight Characters were a method of fortune-telling in China based on the examination of the two cyclic characters each for the year, month, day and hour of a person's birth respectively.

8. Geomancy refers to the superstition that the location of one's ancestors' graves

influences one's fortune. The geomancers claim to be able to tell whether a particular site and its surroundings are auspicious.

9. Lord Kuan (Kuan Yu, A.D. 160–219), a warrior in the epoch of the Three Kingdoms, was widely worshipped by the Chinese as the God of Loyalty and War.

10. Tang Sheng-chih was a general who sided with the revolution in the Northern Expedition. Yeh Kai-hsin was a general on the side of the Northern warlords who fought against the revolution.

[11. The Three People's Principles were Sun Yat-sen's principles and programme for the bourgeois–democratic revolution in China on the questions of nationalism, democracy and people's livelihood. In 1924, in the Manifesto of the First National Congress of the Kuomintang, Sun Yat-sen restated the Three People's Principles, interpreting nationalism as opposition to imperialism and expressing active support for the movements of the workers and peasants. The old Three People's Principles thus developed into the new, consisting of the Three Great Policies, that is, alliance with Russia, co-operation with the Communist Party, and assistance to the peasants and workers. The new Three People's Principles provided the political basis for co-operation between the Communist Party of China and the Kuomintang during the First Revolutionary Civil War period.]

12. 'Oriental Culture' was a reactionary doctrine which rejected modern scientific civilization and favoured the preservation of the backward mode of agricultural production and the feudal culture of the Orient.

[13. 1 picul = 60 kilos.]

14. 'Mountain', 'lodge', 'shrine' and 'river' were names used by primitive secret societies to denote some of their sects. The members were mainly bankrupt peasants, unemployed handicraftsmen and other *lumpen*-proletarians. In feudal China these elements were often drawn together by some religion or superstition to form organizations of a patriarchal pattern and bearing different names, and some possessed arms. Through these organizations the *lumpen*-proletarians sought to help each other socially and economically, and sometimes fought the bureaucrats and landlords who oppressed them. Of course, such backward organizations could not provide a way out for the peasants and handicraftsmen. Furthermore, they could easily be controlled and utilized by the landlords and local tyrants and, because of this and of their blind destructiveness, some turned into reactionary forces.

15. As told by Liu Hsiang (77–6 B.C.) in his *Hsin Hsu*, Lord Sheh was so fond of dragons that he adorned his whole palace with drawings and carvings of them. But when a real dragon heard of his infatuation and paid him a visit, he was frightened out of his wits. Here Comrade Mao Tse-tung uses this metaphor to show that though Chiang Kai-shek and his like talked about revolution, they were afraid of revolution and against it.

4 Forced Labour in Colonial Mozambique: Peasants Remember

ALPHEUS MANGHEZI

Editors' introduction

European colonialism in Africa, as elsewhere, was a central feature of the development and expansion of capitalism. The participation of the indigenous peoples in commodity production and monetary economy was brought about in various ways, including measures of legal and political coercion (see Reading 30). These measures were used to enforce, on one hand, the commercialization of small-scale agricultural production to supply commodities to the colonial and metropolitan markets (Readings 4(i), 20(i)), and, on the other hand, the provision of labour for large-scale capitalist enterprises in mining (Readings 12, 20(iii)) and plantation agriculture (Readings 4(i), 20(ii)).

The term *chibalo*, or variations of it, was widespread in Central and Southern Africa from the late nineteenth century to describe different types of labour introduced by the combination of colonial rule and the impact of capitalism. These included forced labour (whether paid or not), low-paid wage labour, and long-term contract labour (for example, in the mines). In Readings 4(i) and 20 *chibalo* is used in the sense of compulsory labour service on large colonial plantations, although it was also applied in Mozambique to forced cultivation of particular crops by peasants on their own land (Readings 4(i) and 20(i)).

Forced labour was generally more extensive and lasted longer in Portugal's African colonies than those ruled by Britain and France. It was still widespread in the early 1960s, which is why the people interviewed by Alpheus Manghezi retained vivid memories of their *chibalo* experiences. The Portuguese colonial state stipulated that all adult males had to perform *chibalo* labour for six months each year. The conditions of work and the pay on plantations in Mozambique were so poor that many men migrated to South Africa to work as contract labourers in the gold mines there, this being the lesser of two evils (see Readings 12 and 20(iii)). The person speaking in the first extract below was in his home village between labour contracts in South Africa when he was 'caught' by the authorities and sent to perform *chibalo* on a banana plantation. These extracts (and also Reading 20(i)) give a picture too of the role of 'chiefs' and 'sub-chiefs', appointed by the colonial state as part of its system of local government (and termed 'Native Authorities' in British colonies), in enforcing *chibalo* and other oppressive measures.

(i) The experience of *chibalo*

Can you tell us, very briefly, about your experience of chibalo?

Yes, I will give you a garbled version of this experience, I won't be able to tell everything.

Okay, go ahead!

Before I went to the mines, some people in our community had been complaining, privately, about our family. They wanted to know why none of us had been arrested and sent for *chibalo* until then. The fact was that my father was one of the *indunas* [assistants] of the chief [. . .] and was therefore 'exempt' from *chibalo* (his family and other relatives, could, at least temporarily get away without being taken for forced labour). [. . . Then] during one of my holidays from the mines I was arrested and taken away for *chibalo* with lots of other people from Khambane. They said we were going to do some road work. When we reached the Administration at Homoine, we were locked up in jail until next morning when we were issued with *'guias de macha'* [travel passes] and then driven off to Manhiça. In Manhiça we were delivered to Kolichi's place where the *induna* was a man called Duvulane ('to shoot at'). The white proprietor was known by the nickname of Mukhulwane ('the big one'). We were paid 10$00 per month (with deferred pay to be collected at the administrator's office at the end of the contract – 600$00 for a contract of 6 months).[1]

We worked in the fields, with the adults going in first to clear the bush and the small boys following from behind and doing the planting – it was a banana plantation.

Do you mean there were also small boys doing chibalo *with you?*

Yes, there were small boys doing *chibalo*. This was the reason why I decided against desertion from *chibalo*: I said to myself, well, if even the small boys are made to work with exactly the same tools as I am using, it cannot mean that I actually suffer more than they do. I had thought of the (miserable) 600$00 I would have in my pocket (at the end of the contract), and had planned to desert if the work was too hard. But if I did that now, and abandoned these children here, that would mean I was a damned coward. I decided to persevere, saying to myself, let me serve this punishment and then see if they (the colonial authorities) can find some other accusation to lay against me! When we worked the fields, there were songs which we sang – with 12 men or even 20 men standing in a line with their hoes. One song we sang against Duvulane, the *induna*, was:

Leader: Duvulane, my mother
Chorus: Oh! he makes me suffer
Ah! poor me, he makes me suffer
Leader: Duvulane, my mother, I have old reserves (of energy)
Chorus: Oh! he makes me suffer
Leader: The whiteman's tractor, what can I do?
Chorus: Oh! he makes me suffer
Leader: Let us go on mother, yes!
Chorus: Oh! he makes me suffer
Leader: I have wandered in whiteman's lands (colonies)
To whom shall I talk about this (my problems/sufferings)?
Chorus: Oh! he makes me suffer.

Meanwhile, the whiteman (landowner) would be swearing: 'hei! you *capataz*, shit!'[2] You lag behind and sing for nothing; you talk about nothing!'

This is how we worked. We would sing and cut the long creeping plants, and if you did not watch out you could have the whole creeper wound around you (so that you fell down in a heap). It was after these big creepers had been removed by the men that the small boys came along to plant bananas. The small boys had also to cut the bananas when they were ready and they also had to dig the potatoes – this was the job of the small boys and not for the adults. Water for drinking had to be fetched from a long distance and this was done by the small boys. Shortage of water caused some people to drink water from the furrows cut between rows of bananas and this water was contaminated because some of it came from the latrines. When people were desperately thirsty, they were forced to drink some of this water and some of them got dysentery. The fresh water which was brought from a distance of some 10 km by small boys in drums was not sufficient for all the workers. Food was brought to the work place in boxes. This was porridge.[3] You had to eat exactly where the lunch hour found you, whether there was shade or in the open blazing sun. We all wore old sacks as our work clothes. I shall stop here and I hope you have got some idea of how we did *chibalo*.

(ii) Forced cultivation

Alfredo Sithole, what do you know about forced cotton growing?
Cotton? I have seen the introduction of forced cotton growing.

Can you tell us something about when and how cotton was introduced in this area?
[. . .] It was in 1938 that cotton was introduced [. . .] we were all summoned to the *regulo*'s [chief's] place where we were told that we had to open cotton fields. They (the authorities) then started distributing land – measuring out tracts of land with a string, and after that we started cultivating cotton. In some places cotton grew very well, but it did not come out in other places. If you refused to cultivate cotton or failed to finish the cotton plot allocated to you, they would beat you up. We had to plant the cotton in straight lines, using a string as a guide. After the introduction of cotton then came forced rice cultivation, and it was the same story all over again. They supplied us with rice seed and we planted it in our fields. After harvest, all the rice had to be delivered to the government and we had to buy it back (if we wished to consume some of it). If you were found absent from your cotton plot, because you wanted to attend to your maize field, they would whip you.

Have all these things you are telling us happened to you personally – did you have a personal experience of all this?
I was beaten up!

You were beaten up? Tell us what happened on that day when you got beaten up?
I went to my aunt for a visit. My aunt had invited me to visit her, and I spent the whole day there, returning to the fields the next day. I was told upon my return that 'the police man came looking for you, old chap!' As I started hoeing, I saw the car driving towards my field, and when they came to where I was working they asked, 'who is the owner of this field?' When I said I was the owner, they then asked, 'where were you yesterday?' I was not even given the chance to explain because they started beating me up.

Who was driving in the car?
It was 'Galachani', the fat Portuguese who came here to introduce forced rice cultivation. (Galachani means a robber – a term applied to all recruiters to the mines and *chibalo* who made false propaganda about the conditions of work.)

Do you know the name of the policeman who actually gave you the hiding?
They are all dead now – it was Xikwanda and Whate and their chief, Valente.

For how long did you cultivate cotton?
For one year. We abandoned cotton cultivation because the soil was not suitable for it.
[. . .]

We have heard that people tried to resist forced cotton growing in different ways, for example, some roasted the seed before planting it, and as the seed could not germinate, then they were able to 'prove' to the colonial authorities that the soil was not suitable for cotton. What do you know about this?
[In Gijana] they boiled cotton seed before they planted it. They boiled the seeds thoroughly and when it failed to germinate, the Portuguese decided to abandon forced cultivation in Xihakelani and then concentrated on [...] Bileni-Masiya where the soil is very good for cotton.

Extracted from material collected at the Centre of African Studies, Eduardo Mondlane University, Maputo, in southern Mozambique during 1979. Alpheus Manghezi conducted the interviews and recorded the songs (see Readings 12 and 20), translated them from Shangaan to English, and provided the explanations in brackets in the text.

NOTES
   [1. 1$00 = £0.01 or 1p.]
   [2. *Capataz* means foreman; presumably used here as the landowner is referring to the man leading the singing.]
   [3. Made of maize meal and water.]

5   Indra Lohar and the Due Process of Law

D. P. BANDYOPADHYAY

Editors' introduction

Indra Lohar lived in a village about one hundred miles north-west of Calcutta. He was a *bargadar*, or sharecropper, which means that he paid a share, a fixed proportion, of his harvest to the landowner as rent for the use of the land. Sharecropping was a common form of tenancy, particularly in north-east India, at the time of India's independence in 1947. It allows most of the costs and risks of an agriculture subject to considerable weather variations to be borne by the tenant. He generally provides the seeds, animal power, plough, and, of course, all the labour required for cultivation. The landowner supplies the land and receives at least half of the crop.
   Two processes led to a decline of sharecropping after India's independence. First, landowners evicted many tenants in anticipation of the implementation of land reform laws designed to provide security of tenure to tenants and to limit the amount of land held by any one individual. Second, the coming of 'Green Revolution' agriculture – with irrigation, new high-yielding seeds, fertilizer, pesticides, and tractors – reduced the risks of agricultural production and

increased its returns. Many landowners therefore evicted their sharecroppers and others with weak tenancy rights in order to reap a bigger proportion of the harvest for themselves.

This account of Indra Lohar's unusually brave and persistent fight against eviction was written by the former Land Reforms Commissioner for West Bengal as a case study for the Task Force on Agrarian Relations of the Indian government's Planning Commission. D. Bandyopadhyay also wrote an obituary of Indra Lohar (who died in 1979), an extract from which follows the main account as a postscript. In 1981 Shyam Benegal, one of India's best-known film directors, made a film based on the story of Indra Lohar.

Radical changes were made in the West Bengal Land Reforms Act, 1955, in 1970 through a President's Act. *Bargadars* (sharecroppers) were given substantial rights under this amendment. Their right to cultivation was made heritable. Where they supplied the inputs of agriculture their share of crop was raised from 60 per cent to 75 per cent. Eviction through the process of law from the land held by *bargadars* was made practically impossible (see Appendix A). This amendment was held by many as a progressive piece of legislation and it was hoped in the official circles that it would usher in a new era of agrarian relationships in rural West Bengal.

No systematic attempt was made to find out whether sharecroppers did in fact reap the benefit of this law. A concurrent assessment made in late 1970 ('Bargadars of Salihan') indicated that things were happening in a manner quite different from the wishful thinking in the top administrative echelons. Anyway, 1970 was too early to make an assessment of the performance of a law passed in that very year. Untoward happenings in a particular village, where a group of organized *bargadars* were badly trounced by the *jotedars* [landlords] taking undue advantage of the due process of law, could not be the basis of any generalization. Moreover, signs of unrest in the rural areas in 1970 and 1971[1] were effectively and sternly dealt with by the administration and order and peace were restored all over the countryside. With the law already amended in a progressive manner and with the restoration of order in the rural areas there were good reasons to encourage complacency about agrarian relations in the State, and to create an expectation that everything should be all right everywhere in rural Bengal.

This is a story of a simple, hard-working and loyal *bargadar* of village Vora, Police Station Vishnupur, District Bankura in West Bengal. Indra Lohar would never dream of embarrassing his *Raja* [master, lord], late Bibhuti Bhusan Mondal, in any way. Though he had been cultivating Plot No. 9 of Mauza Tala, measuring approximately five acres, for more than a couple of decades, he did not get his name recorded during the last revisional settlement operation (1955–62) as that might have been interpreted as an act of disloyalty by his master. The late Bibhuti acquired this plot of land through a mortgage deed and recorded it in the name of his daughter, Annapurna Devi. It was a piece of *benami* land.[2] Indra took orders from Bibhuti and delivered the share of crop to his (Bibhuti's) *khamar* (barn). He kept this secret to himself and did not betray it to anyone, even during those tumultuous years of the hunt for *benami* land in the late sixties, when this information and evidence before a revenue official might have led to the vesting of the plot of land in him with prospect of two acres being settled permanently on him free of cost.

In Indra's system of values, laws of the land and the current social trends did not play any part. He continued to pay 55 per cent of the share of the crop to his landowner even though under the law he was required to pay only 40 per cent of the gross produce. His loyalty was reciprocated by his master's trust in him, as he was engaged by Bibhuti generally to look after his vast landed properties most of which were kept *benami* to evade and avoid the ceiling provisions of the West Bengal Estates Acquisition Act, 1953.

After the death of Bibhuti a year and a half ago his son Sachinandan appointed a village quack, Badal Karmakar, known for his shrewdness and ruthlessness, as his estate agent. After the completion of the winter harvest of 1971–72, Indra was summoned by this agent and was told that the new owner would not recognize him as a *bargadar*, he was advised that he should immediately give up possession of the plot of land as well as the produce therefrom to the agent if he valued his life. In a moment the make-believe world of Indra was shattered. He did not have a scrap of paper to support his claim as a *bargadar*. Hardly anyone would come forward against this formidable person to tender oral evidence in his favour. He asked for the reason for this severe punishment. He was curtly told to clear out from the land and not to argue. Perhaps, Indra thought, he knew too much about late Bibhuti's clandestine holdings which made the new master nervous. He tried to propitiate his new master by making a further concession in the sharing of crops. He was told that new *bargadars* who would cultivate this plot of land had already agreed to give a higher share than what he offered and they would cultivate IR-8 paddy [a 'Green Revolution' rice] for which the vacant possession of the land would be required at once. Dejected and helpless, Indra started looking around for a friend. Strangely enough, he found some sympathetic response from two persons who belonged to a political party and who had tried to harm his dead master and whose company he used to avoid scrupulously lest they got out of him any secrets about his late master's landed properties. They suggested that Indra should move a petition before the [. . . Magistrate], Vishnupur, through a lawyer who was known to them.

On 29 January 1972 Indra Lohar filed a petition under Section 144 Cr.P.C. in the court of [. . . the] Magistrate, Vishnupur. He alleged that though he was in possession of Plot No. 9 of Mauza Tola as a *bargadar*, one Sachinandan Mondal, brother of Annapurna, the recorded owner of the plot, and Badal Karmakar were trying to evict him forcibly from that land. He further alleged that though the crop of the land was already harvested and stacked in his own *khamar* [barn] he was prevented from threshing the paddy for fear of assault by the said Sachinandan and Badal Karmakar. The [. . .] Magistrate admitted the petition (Case No. 16 Miscellaneous Petition, 1972) and directed the Junior Land Reforms Officer, Vishnupur, to enquire into the matter. He also directed the Officer-in-Charge, Vishnupur Police Station, to maintain peace and *status quo* in the area. The Junior Land Reforms Officer (JLRO) while submitting the enquiry report enclosed a compromise petition purported to have been signed by Indra Lohar in which he had disclaimed his entitlement as *bargadar* of the said land. Indra's version was that on the date on which an Officer from the JLRO's office went to the field he was surrounded by a large number of supporters of the landowner who forcibly took his thumb impression on a piece of white paper which was later produced as a letter of compromise. He immediately filed another petition challenging the enquiry report of the JLRO and further alleged that the so-called compromise petition was obtained from him under duress.

The [. . .] Magistrate, thereafter, ordered a further enquiry by the Agricultural

Extension Officer of Vishnupur Block. The report of the Agricultural Extension Officer (AEO), Vishnupur, revealed that though Indra's name did not feature in the record of rights there was overwhelming local evidence to substantiate his claim as a *bargadar*. Meanwhile, before the Agricultural Extension Officer's report was submitted Badal Karmakar filed a counter-petition before the [...] Magistrate, Vishnupur, on 12 February 1972 praying for action under Sections 107/117 (3) of the Cr.P.C. (security for keeping peace and good behaviour) against Indra Lohar and his brother Gour Lohar. This was sent to the Officer-in-Charge of the Vishnupur Police Station for enquiry who promptly, on 14 February 1972, recommended action under section 144 Cr.P.C. against both parties and action under Sections 107/117 (3) Cr.P.C. against Indra Lohar. His report, however, did not contain any material for taking action under the said sections against Indra excepting a very cryptic remark that there was an apprehension of breach of peace. As a follow up of this report Sachinandan filed another petition under Section 144 Cr.P.C. (Case No. 25 M.P. of 1972) on 17 February 1972 praying *inter alia* that Indra should be restrained from threshing his paddy stacked on Plot No. 2493, Mauza Vora (*khamar* of Indra Lohar). The [...] Magistrate ordered on 19 February 1972 that since both the cases (16 M.P. and 25 M.P. of 1972) were interrelated and since the enquiry report of AEO was still awaited both the cases would be taken up on 22 February 1972.

In the meantime the administrative machinery, particularly the Executive Magistracy of Vishnupur, got involved in the preparation and conduct of the General Elections of 1972. As a result hearing of the pending cases had to be postponed till after the election. While the Executive Magistracy got involved in the emergent problems relating to conduct of General Elections, the landowners took advantage of this temporary diversion of the attention of the Magistracy to carry through their desire of ousting Indra Lohar through other means.

On 18 April 1972 police raided the house of Indra Lohar and seized twenty-two bags of paddy, three *kahans* of straw and some quantities of unthreshed paddy. All these seized materials were given to one Netai Karmakar, a close relation of Badal, for safe custody. A subsequent enquiry revealed that these properties were seized by the police neither in connection with any specific case nor under order of any Court. It was also found that there were no entries in any of the registers in the Police Station regarding this seizure, nor were any other papers available. Obviously, the police took this inappropriate action at the behest of the landowners who made no secret of their intention of ousting Indra from the land by harassing him till he complied with their desire. The fact of seizure was reported to the Sub-divisional Executive Magistrate, who called for an explanation from the police about this unauthorized seizure and started a separate case (No. 62 M.P. of 1972) on it. This case, together with two other previous cases connected with the same issue, was finally transferred on 22 May 1972 to [another] Magistrate [...], Vishnupur, for final disposal, who fixed the next date for hearing on 25 May 1972.

Having found that the matter was not progressing in the desired manner in the court of the Executive Magistrate, Sachinandan and Badal thought out another line of action to achieve their objective. On 23 May 1972 Sachinandan filed a title suit (No. 86 of 1972) in the Court of *Munsif* [a subordinate local judge], Vishnupur, in the name of Annapurna Devi [the nominal owner of the land] who appeared as a plaintiff and prayed for issue of an injunction order restraining Indra Lohar from proceeding with the Case No. 16 M.P. of the [...] Magistrate's Court, Vishnupur. The Munsif ordered: 'In view of urgency, plaintiff's prayer for *ad interim* injunction is allowed. Defendant No. 1 Shri Indra Lohar is temporarily restrained from proceeding with the Case No. 16 M.P. of 1972 of the Court of S.D.O., Vishnupur, till the disposal of this injunction petition.' Events moved rather fast thereafter. In the early hours of 27 May 1972 there was an attack on the house of Indra Lohar by a gang of armed men at the instigation of Badal Karmakar. He was seriously wounded. The remaining stock of paddy, which had not been seized by the police earlier, was looted. His brother and the womenfolk of his family were also severely beaten up. The police later recovered a substantial amount of the looted paddy from Badal's house, who was also arrested. Indra was admitted as an indoor patient to the Subdivisional Hospital, Vishnupur, with serious wounds. The Medical Officer reported:

> Examined one Indra Lohar, 65, male, Hindu, son of late Suchand Lohar of Vill. Vora, P.O. Bishnupur, on 27.5.72 at 11 a.m. and the history of assault:
> (1) 1½ " long ¼ " wide and 2" deep incised wound over the out aspect of middle ... of (RT) thigh;
> (2) ½ " long incised wound over the upper part of (RT) leg antiriosly.
> All the injuries are of recent origin and might have been caused by a sharp cutting weapon.
> Prog. uncertain at present.

The focus, thereafter, shifted to another arena. On 27 May 1972, while Indra was lying in the hospital, his case came up for hearing before the [. . .] Magistrate as scheduled. Sachinandan, the landowner, was present and he produced the certified copy of the order of the Munsif on the title suit No. 86 of 1972 in which Indra Lohar was injuncted from pursuing Case No. 16 M.P. of 1972 in the court of [. . . the] Magistrate. The Magistrate in his order, *inter alia* noted: 'The order (of Munsif) seems to be anomalous. I think there has been interference with the powers and jurisdiction of the Court.' From the hospital Indra Lohar sent another petition to the Magistrate on 31 May 1972 in which he alleged among other things that it was quite improper on the part of the learned Munsif to have issued an *ex parte* injunction order against him restraining him from pursuing his case before the Magistrate and suggested that but for the injunction order his opponent would not have dared assault him and loot his paddy. Thereafter, both the [. . .] Magistrate [. . .] and the Munsif moved the High Court at Calcutta separately for initiating action under contempt of court against each other. The Munsif also prayed that contempt of court proceedings should also be started against Indra Lohar and his lawyer Bimal Sarkar who moved the petition on 31 May 1972 before the [. . .] Magistrate for 'willingly and without any reason creating an atmosphere regarding the dignity and prestige of this court which is clearly contemptuous'. The High Court of Calcutta took cognizance of the complaint of the Munsif and initiated Criminal Miscellaneous, Case No. 1307 of 1972, on 4 August 1972 against Shri S. Saha, Executive Magistrate and Shri Indra Lohar. Regarding Indra it was ordered:

> Rule also do issue to Indra Lohar to show cause why he should not be proceeded against for contempt of the court of Munsif Bishnupur, for wilfully criticizing and making derogatory and contemptuous allegations in his petition dated 31.5.72 filed in the court of S. Saha against the order of *ad interim* injunction passed by the Munsif Bishnupur in T.S. No. 86/72 and thereby creating atmosphere affecting the dignity and prestige of the court.

Incidentally, the [. . .] Magistrate's complaint on the similar issue was rejected by the High Court. On a subsequent date Indra came to Calcutta to put in a personal appearance before the High Court. Ashen-faced and trembling, he entered the red gothic structure of the High Court which stands out, aloof in its medieval grandeur, on the city's skyline. Inside, his lawyer tendered an unqualified apology on his behalf and secured discharge of the Rule against him (Appendix B).

We may summarize in chronological order the ordeal that Indra Lohar had to undergo in his attempt to enforce the rights bestowed on him under the West Bengal Land Reforms Act, 1955, as amended up to date. Being faced with forcible eviction from his land he filed one case under Section 144 Cr.P.C. against Badal Karmakar and Sachinandan Mondal on 29 January 1972 – Case No. 16 M.P. of 1972, Vishnupur. It was followed by two other cases involving him in the court of the Sub-divisional Executive Magistrate (Case Nos. 25 M.P. and 62 M.P. 1972). In the meantime, on 18 April 1972, the police in an unauthorized manner, acting presumably under section 154 I.P.C., seized and took away a large portion of the paddy that he had harvested as a *bargadar* in the year 1971–72. On 23 May 1972, a title suit was filed against him in the court of the Munsif, Vishnupur, and he was despoiled and the rest of the paddy was looted. He was admitted to the hospital on the same day as an indoor patient. On 31 May 1972 he filed a petition protesting against the Munsif's order before the Executive Magistrate for which he was hauled up by the High Court on 4 August 1972 in Criminal Miscellaneous Case No. 1307 of 1972. From Vora he travelled to Calcutta, appeared before the High Court, tendered an apology and was acquitted. Thus, he became directly involved in five judicial proceedings including a contempt of court proceeding in the High Court in the course of eight months – from January 1972 to August 1972. He was assaulted and his house was ransacked twice – once by the strong arm of law and then by the ruffians engaged by his landowner.

When he was admitted to the hospital after being wounded, Indra's prognosis was uncertain. It is not so now. Persecuted by his *jotedar* [landlord], assaulted and plundered by hired hoodlums, harassed and intimidated by the police, restrained by the Civil Court from preferring his legal claim before the appropriate legal forum, hauled up by the 'High Court of Judicature at Fort William in Bengal' for lowering the 'dignity and prestige' of the Court, Indra Lohar lost his will to fight for his right. He paid rather dearly for his temerity to assert his notional rights embodied in law. Maimed and feeble, defeated and dejected, Indra has now bowed down before the majesty of the established order and stands dispossessed of his land.

A couple of issues stem from this tragic episode. The attitude of the bureaucracy (inclusive of all the organs of State machinery) cannot be taken for granted for the proper implementation of land reform laws. Experience shows that it is generally indifferent and apathetic and sometimes it may even be positively hostile. Often we have found how the Executive Magistracy and the local police smartly short-circuit the entire gamut of land reform laws and the Government instruction thereon. Though the Executive Magistracy here was taking an objective view of the problem and initiating certain action as warranted by facts and the laws, other organs of the State machinery promptly intervened and completely checkmated the initiative of the Magistracy. The facile explanation of the link with the landed interests is not quite applicable to the Calcutta-based middle class bureaucracy of West Bengal. The reason lies elsewhere. The attitude of the bureaucracy is moulded and conditioned by the prevailing administrative and judicial tradition and usage. Where the entire burden of the civil and criminal laws, judicial pronouncements and precedents, administrative tradition and practice, are heavily weighted in favour of the existing social order based on the inviolability of private property and the existing property relationships it is very natural for the bureaucracy to develop a bias against any isolated law aimed at even a slight alteration of the existing social arrangements. Further, any benefit even given to the weak by a corresponding abridgement and diminution of rights and interests of the strong is bound to be ephemeral in the absence of a strong mass organization of the beneficiaries. The stronger group would hit back with such ferocity that the beneficiaries might not be able to withstand the onslaught. This may result in a situation where the post-reform condition of the weak might even be worse than it was in the pre-reform stage. It is an essential prerequisite of the success of any reformist measure that the beneficiaries should have a strong and militant mass organization to secure and consolidate the gains as well as resist, with some degree of militancy, if necessary, the sanctions that would be applied against them by the entrenched interests. Indra Lohar fought alone and lost, and in the process the fate of his fellow *bargadars* of the entire region was sealed. If this lone battle of Indra had developed into a collective action of the *bargadars* of the area, the result might have been otherwise.

Appendix A

The rights of *bargadars* in West Bengal are contained in the West Bengal Land Reforms Act, 1955. The Act was amended in 1970 and 1971 further safeguarding the interests of *bargadars*. The Act as amended provides for:

1. Regulation of crop-share payable to the landowner. It has been provided that the produce of the land cultivated by the *bargadars* shall be divided as between the *bargadars* and the owner

(a) in the proportion of 50:50 in case where plough, cattle manure and seeds necessary for cultivation are supplied by the person owning the land; and
(b) in the proportion of 75:25 in all other cases.

2. Security of tenure. The *bargadar* has been conferred fixity of tenure. The landowner is permitted to terminate cultivation of land for bona fide personal cultivation provided, however that

(a) the extent of land so resumed by the owner along with any other land under his personal cultivation does not exceed seven and a half acres; and
(b) the *bargadar* is left with at least two acres for his cultivation.

3. By the recent amendment, the *bargadar* has been conferred heritable right in respect of land he cultivates.
4. In case the landowner should refuse to accept his share of the produce or refuse to tender a receipt for the same, the *bargadar* can deposit the same with the prescribed officer or authority.
5. The *bargadar* is not liable to eviction on ground of non-payment of rent and the orders for eviction on this ground are not to become effective if the *bargadar* delivers to the person whose land he cultivates the dues within such time and within such instalments as the officer or authority making the order, having regard to the circumstances of the case, may specify in this behalf.
6. The prescribed officer or authority has exclusive jurisdiction in respect of disputes between the *bargadar* and the owner, subject to an appeal to the Subdivisional Officer.

Appendix B

Shri S. Saha, Executive Magistrate First Class, Vishnupur, tendered an un-qualified apology before the High Court. An excerpt from the judgement of the High Court of Calcutta in the Criminal Miscellaneous Case No. 1307 of 1972 dated 4 October 1972 is given below:

The learned advocate for the State Mr. Sudhindra Kumar Palit has also sub-mitted that the words used tend to come very much within the mischief of what constitutes contempt as now defined in the Contempts of Court Act, 1971. But Mr. Palit also submitted that . . . the Executive Magistrate was misled to use the language which he borrowed from the paragraphs in the petition of the Party made before him. Mr. Palit, however, has not opposed the prayer of Mr. Sanyal made on behalf of the contemner present in the Court that the unqualified and bona fide apology now tendered should be accepted. We do so and let off contemner with a warning which we deliver to him directly in the Court.

In exercise of the powers under section 161 A of the Cr.P.C. we direct that the two sentences in the order dated 27.5.72 in case No. 16 M.P. of 1972 reading: 'The order seems to be anomalous. I think there has been interference with the powers and jurisdiction of the Court,' be expunged from the records. . . . The rule is disposed of accordingly.

Reprinted from A. N. Das, V. Nilakant (eds), *Agrarian Relations in India*, Manohar Publications, Delhi, 1979.

Postscript   (Reprinted from *Mainstream*, New Delhi, 30 June 1979.)

Lame and disillusioned, Indra Lohar kept largely to himself. But the poor men of the village looked upon him with awe and respect. It was only Indra among them who could question the authority of the landowner.

Landowners always pointed to the case of Indra as an example of what would happen to a recalcitrant sharecropper who tried to assert his right in the belief that the law was on his side. Others did not have the courage to protest against the insult and injustice that they suffered at the hands of the landowners.

But in their mind the lame and old Indra Lohar was a hero. He was the fulfil-ment of their innermost desire to rise against and challenge the unjust system. Indra was a lone rebel who fought his battle alone [. . .] Through his defeat he charted the path of victory; the only way to secure and establish rights was to suffer and fight collectively.

NOTES

[1. During the late 1960s a number of peasant and labour movements rose to prominence in the countryside of West Bengal and several other states of India. Of these the best known was the 'Naxalite' movement which saw its tasks as very similar to those of the Chinese peasant movement described by Mao Tse-tung (see Reading 3), and whose actions included the seizure of land and the assassination of particularly hated landlords.]

[2. Land registered in the name of a relative or employee of the true beneficiary in order to circumvent 'land ceiling' laws intended to outlaw holdings above a certain size.]

6 'The Agrarian Reform'

Song sung by members of the Peasants' Federation in Ecuador

Commentary by M. REDCLIFT

La Reforma Agraria

Quieren Reforma Agraria
todos los campesinos:
que ordeñen a las vacas
y no a los inquilinos.

Cuando pare la chancha
me duele el corazón,
se come mis chanchitos
el hijo del patrón.

No seremos más siervos,   (chorus)
no [. . . seremos] mas parias
cuando los campesinos
hagan [la] 'Reforma Agraria'.

El toro bien cebao
y el potro regalón;
pero a los campesinos
les niegan la ración

Me dio una chacra a medias
la mujer del patrón
yo me llevé el trabajo
[y] ella la producción

No seremos más . . .

El fuerte en automóvil,
nosotros en carreta;
estas son las delicias
del régimen paleta.

El fuerte bien calzado,
nosotros con [. . . ojotas;]
el fuerte bien vestido
y nosotros en pelotas.

The Agrarian Reform

All the peasants
want an Agrarian Reform:
so that it is the cows that
are milked . . . not the tenants.

When the sow gives birth
my heart aches;
the son of the landlord
eats my piglets.

We will no longer be serfs,
there will be no pariahs,
when the peasantry
makes an 'Agrarian Reform'.

The bull is fattened up
and the foal is provided for,
but rations are denied
to the peasants

The landlord's wife
gave me half a plot (of land);
I did the work
and she took the product.

The boss goes by car
we travel by cart;
these are the delights
of our landlord's rule.

The boss is well-heeled
we walk about in sandals.
The boss is well dressed;
we are without a stitch . . .

Los pobres trabajamos más	The poor work harder
que los mismos bueyes,	even than oxen;
los ricos no trabajan	the rich do not work
y viven como reyes.	and live like kings.
No seremos . . . etc.	
El cura de mi pueblo	The priest from my village
me dijo que esperara,	told me to wait . . .
pero yo no aguanto:	But I cannot endure any more
quiero 'Reforma Agraria'.	I want an 'Agrarian Reform'.

This is the text of a song [. . . sung] by members of the Ecuadorian Peasant Federation, FENOC *(Federación Nacional de Organizaciones Campesinos)* during an 'induction' course, held at Balzár on the Ecuadorian Coast in June 1975.[1] This course was organized for *campesinos* from the Sierra, who were prospective peasant leaders and most of whom were either small-holders *(minifundistas)* or ex-*huasipungeros,* that is, former labour tenants on estates who have either bought their land or have been adjudicated land under the 1964 Agrarian Reform Law.

The distribution of agricultural land in Ecuador was even more unequal than that of the other six countries studied by the Interamerican Committee for Agricultural Development (CIDA) in the early 1960s. Ecuador had the highest percentage (89·9 per cent) of farm units classified as 'sub-family' units (CIDA, 1965). At the other end of the scale barely 1 per cent of the total number of farms occupied almost 57 per cent of the agricultural land (CENSO, 1954). As elsewhere in Andean Latin America. the economic and social relations between the *latifundia* and the *campesino* population are symbiotic and exploitative. The institution of the *'huasipungo'* exemplifies this relationship. In return for the usufruct of a piece of land on the estate (the *huasipungo*), the *huasipungero* was expected to undertake so many days labour service on the *hacienda.* The severity with which this labour obligation was enforced varied widely, but the peasant was dependent on the landlord not only for the land he cultivated, but also for access to urban centres and markets. The conditions under which *huasipungeros* worked were probably no worse than those of *minifundistas*; their subjugation to the landlord was merely more direct.

The 1964 Agrarian Reform Law, under which the *huasipungo* system was formally abolished, did not bring about the expected redistribution of land in Ecuador. Five years after the 1964 Law was introduced it was calculated that, at the rate at which land was being handed over to former *huasipungeros*, it would be one hundred and seventy years before all the 'feudal' tenants in Ecuador received land (Ortiz, 1970, 128). Of the estimated 176,000 such tenants only about 21,000 *huasipungeros* benefited from the 1964 Reform (CESA, 1974: 19). Plots of land were subdivided, and sold to middlemen instead of *campesinos.* Those *huasipungeros* who could count on the support of landlords often received the best land. In other cases 'beneficiaries' had to work for wages in an attempt to pay for the land they received; because not every *huasipungero* received the land as of right (Galarza, 1973: 216). Well before the 1973 Agrarian Reform Law was passed – with significantly little improvement – it had been agreed by most commentators that the 'agrarian reform' of 1964 had not worked. Most *campesinos*, and their leaders, knew that it had never been tried.

Reprinted from *Journal of Peasant Studies,* vol. 4, no. 2, 1977.

REFERENCES

CENSO, 1954, *Primer Censo Agropecuario Nacional,* Quito.

CESA, 1974 *(Central Ecuatoriana de Servicios Agricolas),* Una Experiencia en desarrollo rural, Quito.

CIDA, 1965, *Ecuador: Tenecia de la Tierra y Desarrollo Socio-Economica del Sector Agrícola,* Washington DC.

Ortiz, M., 1970, *El Cooperativismo, un Mito de la Democracia Representativa,* Universidad Central, Quito.

Galarza, Jaime, 1973, *Los Campesinos de Loja y Zamora,* Universidad Central, Quito.

NOTE

[1. Raúl Hernán Ampuero tells us that this song was widely sung in Chile in the 1950s and 1960s and is also known by peasants in other Latin American countries.]

7   Childhood of a Mapuche Indian

ROSENDO HUENUMÁN

Editors' introduction

In 1980 David Baytelman met Rosendo Huenumán who had been forced into exile from Chile following the overthrow of the Allende government in 1973. Rosendo is a Mapuche Indian, a member of an ethnic minority in Chile, and a person whose experiences of life, of work and politics, express the struggles that he and his people fought – and still fight – in their native land. David Baytelman recorded Rosendo Huenumán's account of his life, having asked him to concentrate on what he believed to be his most important experiences. This was not an interview, in the sense that no questions were asked to direct Rosendo to specific points. The result is a verbatim 'autobiography' with the rhythm and directness of speech, and which is presented here with its original idiosyncrasies and minor inconsistencies concerning, for example, dates and times.

The whole of Rosendo's autobiography is reproduced here, divided into three parts. The first part which follows covers his childhood on the Mapuche reservation. The second part recounts Rosendo's experiences in towns where he first migrated to gain an education, and worked as a domestic servant in Temuco and subsequently as a coal miner in Lota (Reading 11, 'Migrant and Worker'). On returning to his reservation after some years away Rosendo played a leading role in the struggles over land between the Mapuches and neighbouring landowners, and in setting up communal activities in education and agriculture (Reading 8, 'Mapuche Indians Organize').

The Mapuches seem to have been the most numerous of the different indigenous peoples whom the Spanish encountered in Chile in the sixteenth century.

By contrast with the comparative ease with which the Spanish *conquistadores* defeated the Inca empire in Peru, they had to wage a protracted war to establish their domination over the Mapuches. This struggle continued well into the nineteenth century when the ethnic status of the Mapuches was established in law as a means for their subjugation. For centuries they had been pushed further and further back, first by the Spaniards and then by the governments of independent Chile which were anxious to open up the fertile lands of the south to colonization. In this process landowners and foreign immigrants settled and exploited the lands which had once belonged to the Mapuches, who were continually displaced into less fertile areas, their rights eroded and abused. Today interspersed over a wide area of southern Chile – there are about 300,000 Mapuche or roughly 10 per cent of the rural population – their 'reservations' exist as a reminder of an ethnic identity and rich culture that has been largely forgotten and is only exceptionally acknowledged beyond myth, folklore and rhetoric.

The lack of land has driven increasing numbers of Mapuches to leave their shrinking reservations for the cities where they are usually employed in casual, low-paid jobs in domestic service, bakeries, and in the building industry. In this process of partial 'integration' with the wider society of Chile, the Mapuches still strive to preserve their identity at the same time as they become involved in the common struggles of workers and peasants.

Rosendo's life story encapsulates in an extraordinary and vivid way the past and the present of the Mapuche people, and, more broadly, the experiences of a wide range of Chileans. After all, there seems to be little difference in the way peasants are robbed of their land, miners risk their lives, or domestic servants are exploited. Nevertheless, Rosendo's self-identity as a Mapuche asserts itself vigorously in his account. He speaks about *'huincas'* (generally non-Mapuche people), *'gringos'* and 'Chileans' as 'the others'. It is only after his first engagement in trade unionism and politics (see Reading 11) that significantly the first and last terms disappear; he continues to use the term *'gringos'*, however, for those landowners of foreign ancestry who occupied Mapuche land a century ago.

Equally illustrative is the Mapuches' battle through the maze of bureaucratic and legal procedure to ascertain and defend their rights to land (Reading 8). Their pilgrimage to the *Gobernación* and *Intendencia* (*Gobernadores* and *Intendentes* were regional administrative and political representatives of the executive, in charge of 'law and order'), and their fruitless calls to the *Juzgado de Indios* (courts dealing with Indian affairs) have their counterparts in other readings in this collection.

The struggle of the Mapuche people in Chile is by no means over, and Rosendo points to this forcefully (Reading 8). It will not be, he says, just a Mapuche struggle. The general reassertion of peasants, he believes, is of increasing relevance as the gains achieved by Chilean peasants, including the Mapuches, during the short-lived socialist government of Allende have been drastically overturned since the military seized power in 1973. The land that was expropriated from large landowners and redistributed to peasants under the Agrarian Reforms of the Christian Democratic government (1964–70) and, on a more significant scale, of the Allende administration (1970–73) has now been handed back to its previous owners.

Well, I am going to tell you the story of my childhood. Like all sons of Mapuche peasants, I too went out into the world at an early age. They leave home, their parents and so did I . . .

I was born in a 'ruca' [Indian hut]. My mother's name is Margarita García Huenumán. She is illiterate. She works on the land and on the loom. That is my mother's profession. She is an unmarried mother. I was brought up in my grandparents' house. My grandfather was about 1.5m tall, kind, likeable, who had many children . . . about seventeen children. I knew fifteen of them . . . many aunts . . . seven women and eight men, of whom there are only three living today, two men and one woman, my mother.

Well, my life has been pretty hard, particularly my childhood. I started work at an early age. I remember that I first earned money by cutting oats . . . Cutting oats for some peasants, one of them called Guillermo Estoy, of German origin, who are neighbours of our reservation. And my reservation is called Hueñaluhuén; it is in the district of Puerto Saavedra in the Province of Cautín. I cannot remember the year I started work but I was very young.

A task, 'tarea', as the agreed piece of work was called . . . was fifty metres wide by seventy metres long approximately. I cut a 'tarea' of oats in three days, with a sickle. I remember that I completed three 'tareas' of oats and one of linseed, this had to be pulled.

They paid me, for this 'tarea' . . . three pesos in those days. Well there were three 'tareas' so they paid me nine pesos.[1] But they paid me a little more for the linseed, three pesos fifty cents. So I earned about twelve pesos in the summer season, in the harvest . . . mm? . . . The rich, the 'Parceleros' (smallholders) when they are shorthanded contract other farmworkers and give them casual work as a 'trato', as the Chileans say. That was my first experience of work and of earning money through my own work and, without a doubt, I felt that I was no longer a child but a young man able to earn a living.

This money enabled me to buy some clothes, trousers, . . . a shirt and I remember that I also bought a pair of football boots. And of course it was a great day when I bought the pair of football boots and started playing with a ball of seaweed with shoes . . .

The next year I travelled further away from my reservation to do the same work, cutting wheat. Three of us went, a cousin and another youth who is a brother on my father's side, his name is Félix Huenumán and my cousin's name is José Bernardo Carrasco Huenumán. We were a group of three and we went out together to cut wheat in the summer. We were working near Carahue for a whole month and a half. There we took on whole fields of wheat, they were seven and three-quarters cuadras, . . . mm? . . . . A 'cuadra' is larger than a hectare. They are one hundred and twenty-five metres long by one hundred and twenty-five metres wide. So seven and three-quarters cuadras . . . we were still children . . . we cut that field in a fortnight and there was still more wheat to be cut. There were other peasants, smallholders who were not landowners, . . . mm? . . . they were medium-sized farmers who had between three and four hundred hectares; well we used to cut the wheat for them.

And in that same year, in April, we also went to pick potatoes on the estate of Messrs King. [. . .] The potatoes were harvested with a large hoe and payment was by the sack, . . . mm? . . . and they paid with ten kilos of potatoes for every sack we picked. We used to do this to take home potatoes for the winter . . . instead of paying us with money, as they did other people, they paid us with potatoes. Of course we used to take them home. And so I started learning how to earn a living and how to help at my grannie's home because my grandad dies. I hardly knew

him. My grannie is left alone . . . my uncles got married and left home and some of
the aunts and uncles who remain at home, at my grannie's house, do not behave
very well . . . and so the time and the year had arrived for my mother to take on the
responsibility of managing the house . . . the work at home and in the field.
My grandfather's land was not very big. They, as Indians established on this
reservation and according to the 'título de merced' [order by which land was
apportioned] had nine hectares allocated to each one. So between the two – my
grandad and grannie – they had eighteen hectares . . . and all that was cultivable
land only . . . eighteen hectares of not very good soil, bad, therefore it didn't
produce enough for us to exist on, and so we had to go away to other places to
work, to other regions, to bring in money or at least food with which to face the
rough winter in that area.

And there was another way of earning a living. For example, we, the Mapuches
of that area live near the sea, so the shellfish is also a product which helped us
survive. From a very early age I practised catching sea-urchins . . . diving, diving
into the water very early in the morning and fetching out sea-urchins, and the
water there is freezing. Well you had to face up to it. I used to bring out many sea-
urchins . . . great quantities . . . 'locos' [a sort of shellfish] . . . and I was also the
youngster who was expert at cutting and collecting seaweed[2] . . . mm? . . .
Because the people who live in that area, not only the Mapuches, but other people
who are not Mapuches, do that work. They gather the seaweed, cultivate it and
take it to other areas, such as Imperial, Temuco, Lautaro, Pitrufquén . . . as far as
Cunco . . . Curacautín, Galvarino, well . . . as far as Los Angeles . . . Los Sauces
. . . by waggon, to sell seaweed. The sale is always made by bartering . . . they
exchange the seaweed for wheat, for beans . . . well . . . for any cereal that will last.
No doubt it was also exchanged for money, but usually it was by bartering . . . and
that is how those people live, those people who live by the sea. Well, every year the
Mapuches go in great caravans of waggons full of seaweed, shellfish, 'luche'
[another seaweed] . . . dried fish, and so on. Those trips last twenty days, sometimes twenty-five days, depending on the distance. A journey from Puerto
Saavedra to Curacautín takes thirty days, that is, one month.

Later on, I also did this work, but, from a very early age my mother took me
with her, I used to go with her . . . she did this work, with two waggons of seaweed
and she used to sell a lot. Of course we didn't go very far afield, we always went to
a place called Huapi Budi, to the Nor . . . to the South of Puerto Saavedra. Well,
there [. . .] we used to sell a waggonload of seaweed. We would sometimes
collect four sacks of wheat, two sacks of oats, half a sack of beans, maize, peas . . .
sometimes we would come back with seven, eight sacks of cereals for the house.
On occasions we made two trips a year. We went towards Carahue, Taise, to
Quechucahuiri, Capecuye . . . all that area we covered. One might say that it took
longer because it was further away, but we were home within a fortnight. We did
this every year, I used to go with my mother, she used to take me, so from a very
early age I knew all those places, all those areas. There is no doubt that these trips
were very gruelling, arduous. It's hard. One does not sleep under cover. You have
to sleep in the open and you have to look after the oxen or else they might be
stolen. . . . The oxen are tied to the waggon, and you have to sleep right by
them. . . . So all these are enormous sacrifices.

On one of those trips, whilst accompanying an aunt and uncle who went out in
two waggons full of seaweed to the North of Imperial, at a place called Río Molco
(roundabout Labranza), well around there . . . ah? . . . I was with my aunt, my
aunt was called Luisa, María Luisa. She was single. I remember that I was barely

six years old and still not very strong. I could not, for example, harness up the oxen. . . . I could not manage the harness. Of course I was good enough for leading the oxen, keeping an eye on them, looking after them whilst they were grazing. . . . I was good enough for that. So my aunt took me with her on those trips. . . . And it was there that misfortune struck, a misfortune which hit me badly and when one is still a child, when something happens that has serious consequences . . . mm . . . it remains stuck in your mind, and this, I cannot forget. . . . And sometimes, when I think, I reconstruct all those journeys . . . it seems as though it only happened a short time ago.

The fact is that my aunt had a baby. Or rather, on one of those trips when we are far from home, my aunt gives birth to a baby, delivers a baby without any medical help . . . at the home of a Mapuche woman who lived alone . . . very poor, very humble . . . we were staying at that house and my uncle was elsewhere, far away (they had parted because two waggons could not travel together, it took longer to sell our goods . . . so they had agreed to separate for a while, for a few days). My uncle went to another place and we went around that area of the Manío . . . Molte, with my aunt. I remember that one night she became ill in childbirth. As day broke she gave birth to a son. But as she was not assisted by a doctor nor any specialist person in midwifery, but coped as best she could she became very ill . . . some complications and she was gravely ill. She couldn't get up. . . . On the third day my aunt dies, at about three in the afternoon. I was only a child, all on my own, without knowing the place. . . . It was very serious . . . all I could do was cry. I cried and cried. . . . I would go and see my aunt lying on a mattress on the floor, because the house was very poor . . . she was dead and the baby, the new born baby was crying, crying from hunger the baby was. Well I didn't, did not, did not know what to give him. And then the poor woman would feed him, I don't know what with, the fact is that he survives and . . .

The woman with whom we were staying had some sons . . . so when I gave them an idea of the place where my uncle might be they went out to look for him, and they find my uncle . . . luckily, and he arrives at the house where I was with my dead aunt.

Of course, we had to start the return journey immediately. There were goods still left to sell but we had to return immediately with my dead aunt . . . by waggon and . . . the child, we gave him to a family who was sort of related to my grandfather. That woman was called Rosalía Huenumán. I think she was a first cousin of my grandfather. She lived in a place called Peleco. . . . We left the child in this woman's care and we returned . . . and about . . . about a week later we were back in our own home. There is no doubt that this journey was very sad, very hard. Well I have lived all this drama, I have suffered it . . .

Well, so my childhood has some dramatic passages . . . and so did my youth, my adolescence. . . . To learn to read and write I had to leave my reservation. Where I lived, a family, not a Mapuche family, opened a school, a fee paying school because there were a large number of young illiterate men and women. There was no school nearby, all the schools were about forty kilometres away. . . . She was called Luzmira Jiménez . . . she thought of teaching all those young people who had grown up illiterate.

That is how my cousins learnt to read. . . . They were older than I. Well, they went to the school, my uncles paid the fees, they were paid monthly. . . . I cannot remember how much you paid a month, the fact is you paid every month. Well then, when one of my cousins learnt to read I always went up to him, to look at his books . . . he used to talk to the books, and I used to look at him respectfully . . .

curiously.... I used to ask him why he talked to the book. And he explained that the letters are spoken, that you have to know the letters and then say them, and that is how books are read, newspapers are read, well, everything that is written and you also write them. And so my cousin started teaching me the letters and I, with that, with that interest in learning, learnt to read without going to school, my cousin taught me ...

Specially translated for this volume by Susan Welsh from the Spanish transcript provided by David Baytelman of the Institute of Social Studies, The Hague.

NOTES

    [1. About 1.2 pesos = £1 (1945).]
    [2. This seaweed is eaten.]

8 Mapuche Indians Organize

ROSENDO HUENUMÁN

[*See introduction to Reading 7*]

So all this experience accumulated, and later, when I return to my community ... there is a latent and serious problem, nothing less than the fourth time that some ambitious men had put up fences ... as all rich, ambitious landowners do. These gentlemen, one of them was Don Alfonso Estoy de la Nuez and the other Leopoldo Astorga, had an agreement to exploit one hundred and sixty hectares, more or less, of untouched mountain that had very good quality wood. But all this land, this mountain, belonged to the reservation of Hueñaluhuén.

I remember that when I was a child, a very young child ... when I just about knew my grandad, he had this lawsuit with other citizens, with a certain Francisco Ulloa ... over this land. And so my grandfather dies and the land passed over to the possession of my uncles, and with the land also ... the defence of the conflict which had been going on for no one knows how long ... so my uncles headed the lawsuit, the case. But never ever was a solution found, only promises and more promises.... Well, the bourgeois authorities of that time were very corrupt, and still are, so, well ... the rights of the poor (and more so if they are Mapuche), the racial discrimination and all that ... were ignored.

Those who were not Mapuches simply put up fences wherever they felt like it, and were even accompanied by the police, the 'Carabineros'.

This not only happened on my reservation. Well, the fact is that when I return in the year 1959, I return in January to my reservation and the first news I receive at my mother's house.... I arrive at night and I start to ask after my family, after my uncles, the neighbours and so on.... And they tell me 'Look, there is a very alarming situation. The "carabineros" have already been here to summon eight people to appear before the Gobernador [head of regional authority]*1 in February and they want to evict them. The eviction is being requested by Señor Estoy and Señor Astorga.'

Well, the following day I go to see my uncle, the nearest one, he lived about two kilometres away from my mother.... He was my eldest uncle, he was called José Agustín García, he was illiterate. Well, all the peasants were illiterate in that area. When I went to see him the first thing he said to me was, 'Look nephew, we have a lawsuit here. We have been moved back three times, and this is the fourth. And even our cemetery... mm? ... they want to take it away as well. The "carabineros" have been and so have some surveyors to measure, and the line goes along there, over by that hill.' – he points.

So this meant that my uncles and other neighbours had to leave and go nearer to the seaside so as to leave all that area free, especially that huge mountain. And for the fourth time these men would move their fence.

So I say to him, 'This cannot be. This is an injustice. This reservation must have a "Título de Merced" [an order allocating the land] and this "título de merced" must state its dimensions, how many hectares it has, and how many people were settled there at the time. Who has that document?' I ask him.

He says, 'The Chief of the reservation has it.' The Chief was an old man, also illiterate. He had the paper but he didn't know what it said. And it included a sketch and a small plan of the reservation. And so I go to speak to the Chief (my uncle and I went), he shows me the document, the famous 'título de merced', the sketch and the small plan. When I read the 'título de merced' I see that it clearly says: 'The Community of Hueñaluhuén headed by Chief José Painecura . . . mmm . . . at the time that it was established . . . has four hundred . . . ahem . . . seven hundred and forty-eight hectares . . . no?' And it gave its boundaries, from North to South so many metres and from East to West so many metres, and I start to observe, to walk round the hill, to see how many metres there are from here to there, just a mental calculation . . . like that . . . a visual calculation, and I say, 'That cemetery must be within the boundaries given on the plan and the "título de merced". It cannot be acceptable that this land be taken from us again. Something must be done.' And so I say to my uncle, 'Well, and what have you done about it? Have you spoken to the people? To your friends? To the authorities?'

'No, to nobody. We are waiting for the day to go and give evidence . . . well, there we will say that we are not usurping the land from the "gringos",* but that they are the usurpers.... That is what we are going to say, we are agreed.'

But that is what my grandad did, before, when he headed the lawsuit, he used to speak like that . . . and so did other neighbours and the truth is that nobody listened to them, and so the same thing was going to happen when those eight people who were to be evicted appeared before the court.

And so I say, 'Well, the land cannot be handed over, it must be defended, come what may. The eviction must be opposed. Enough is enough!' When I left, I said, 'I remember that my grandfather had that lawsuit. And I return now, a fully grown young man, a young man with experience, I know how to fight, I know how the union works, I can judge the bourgeois and the capitalist.... I also understand all about injustice. . . .'

And so I start talking to my uncle about all this, and I propose that we arrange a meeting with everybody on the reservation, men and women . . . even the children, the elderly, that is, with everybody. My uncle agrees. He speaks to the other eight neighbouring peasants, who are also Mapuches, they agree and go off out to let the others on the reservation know. The meeting took place one Sunday.

It is here that I speak for the first time, speak about organization, on my reservation. I talk to them about the union. Undoubtedly they did not understand what a union was. The little bit of dialect I had learned as a child was almost forgotten. It is very difficult for me to speak in Mapuche so that they can understand what I have been trying to explain in Spanish. But I did all I could so they would understand, by speaking very simple words ... mm? ... by giving them examples.... The fact is that this meeting lasts about four hours. They convince themselves, at least the first eight do because they have a bigger interest, for they are the victims ... and they begin saying, 'Very well, we agree with what this lad says ... we think that this is the way we can defend our land.'

It is then that I insist that if we are all in agreement we must constitute ourselves. 'A committee must be organized.' My uncle asks me what a committee is. And so I say, 'Well, a committee is an organization that groups together a great number of people, men and women, they unite, a chairman is nominated, a directive is given ... and so on.... It's the same as on this reservation, for example, the Chief Don Juan Llancapán (who was present) is the Chief of this reservation. He has a certain authority, for example to perform [...] religious feasts. When he orders you obey, all of you support him. The committee is the same thing. It has that similarity. The difference is that this committee is now going to fight to defend and recover all this land that has been usurped over the years and also the mountain which they now want to take. And so now, all the reservation, all the people, men and women, the old people, we have to unite to recover this territory. Not just accept the eviction ... mm?.... So we must name leaders to do just that. Two or three men, the best and the bravest, the most self-sacrificing, and they must also be knowledgeable, understand what is happening.'

And they say, 'That is all very well, but we don't know how to read, we don't even speak Spanish properly ...' mm.... I had some cousins who, ... those cousins who had learnt to read at the small school before me.... But years have gone by and they haven't practised reading, they don't read, so they forget how to read ... the youth ... my cousin? ... he has forgotten how to read. It is difficult for him to read. Well, the fact is we proposed that he too should be part of the leadership. And of course they ask me ... unanimously. They all started talking about me helping and that I should accept the leadership ... ahem?.... And I had only gone to my reservation for a few days, to see my mother, because when I arrived in Temuco I made plans, I said to myself, 'I am not staying in Chile, I am going to Argentina to work ... to look for better horizons.' But I have to give up that plan because I saw the enormous need here ... seeing that everyone, including my family, my relatives are not able to defend themselves. The need was great and I agreed to stay.

I say to them, 'All right, look, I'll stay here for three months. I will help you in the beginning so that you understand how a committee works, what has to be done, and how the land has to be defended.' Well, once this proposal had been accepted everyone was happy and we provisionally constitute ourselves because there were immediate jobs to be done to prevent this new eviction. I propose that we travel to the 'gobernación' [regional authority]* immediately, this was in Nueva Imperial, with the eight peasants who are on the eviction list; amongst them was my uncle.

One day we went to the 'gobernación'. We were a group of eight and we left on foot. We walked for twelve hours to reach Carahue.... We left the reservation before daybreak (about one in the morning) and we arrived about five in the afternoon. We stayed at a small boarding house there before taking the bus and arriving the next day at the 'gobernación' of Nueva Imperial. And so I arrive there with my Mapuche companions. ... Some of them tired by the walk, not being youngsters . . . mmmm . . . and not having eaten, without breakfasting . . . and so on . . . but . . . first we wanted to meet the 'gobernador' and then find somewhere to eat. And of course I hardly knew the city, I didn't know where the offices of the Authorities were, but by asking and asking we arrive. There I speak to the Secretary, I say, 'I need an audience with the "gobernador" . . .'. The secretary looks at me. Well, of course, he thought, perhaps, that I had the appearance of a lawyer . . . as I was the only one accompanying a group of Mapuches, who was well dressed, wearing shoes, a spotless suit, a tie, and speaking perfect Spanish. The secretary noticed the difference straight away and he treats me very politely. He says, 'Just a moment, sir, I will inform the "gobernador" immediately and see if he can receive you now.'

And so he did. Only a few minutes went by before I was called. I went into the office. There was the 'gobernador', sitting in an armchair, next to him was his secretary with a typewriter, he was smoking a cigar . . . mm?. . . . I introduce myself by saying 'Mr "Gobernador" I am so and so.'

'Pleased to meet you. What problem do you bring?' Well, I sit in front of him, at his desk, and I explain: 'This is the problem, it's happening in this reservation and I need to know on what grounds the eviction was authorized on that date without any previous investigation. I think this is unjust, even an error . . . ahmm? . . . according to our legislation,' I say, 'neither this Office nor any Public Office can intervene, only the Tribunal known as the "Juzgado de Indios" [Court for Indian Affairs]* which operates in Temuco can do so. This Court is authorized to solve any conflict or problem which may arise on the Indian reservations.'

So the 'gobernador' calls the secretary and asks him to bring all the previous records, and so on. He saw the copy of the order that was already in the hands of the Criminal Court for fulfilment and there were only eight days left before this order was to be carried out. We discussed it for a little while. I showed him the 'título de merced' and the plan which the Chief had given me. I say, 'Our reservation is here, and the "título de merced" states so many metres from North to South and so many from East to West' and so forth. And then I say to him: 'There is a line, a boundary, that has been put up three times. Of course Señor Estoy didn't put it up, this fence was put up by a certain Francisco Ulloa . . . whom I don't know. But now Señor Estoy and Señor Astorga want to run the fence along here. See here, all this, it is a huge mountain of about one hundred and sixty hectares and here is a cemetery, and they want to take this cemetery as well. . . . How then are we going to allow them to take this land, for a fourth time? We have all agreed that we'll not accept any more evictions, we'll oppose and resist them. . . . If you don't get the right information and you don't rescind the order that exists now in the Law court, there will be consequences and these consequences will be your responsibility, Mr "Gobernador". We have all agreed that we'll not accept any more evictions. On the other hand, had this order come from the "Juzgado de Indios" in Temuco we might have been able to accept it, but this order comes from here, from this office, and the law says that only the Juzgado de Indios can intervene in any conflicts where Indian territories are in dispute. Therefore as soon as this interview has ended we are going to Temuco and there we are going to lodge our complaint because we cannot allow . . . if it is possible we are going to speak to the "Intendente" [government representative in the province]* and we are going to ask him as well to send some officials to investigate on the actual site, so that it can be ascertained who is right.'

All these discussions, well . . . when the 'gobernador' saw the file . . . then . . . well . . . he says, 'Oh well, you are right. How would you feel if I wrote an official letter immediately and you could take it by hand and give it to the Judge in the Court?'

'Agreed,' I say.

He immediately gives his secretary the order, the letter is written and given to me and I take it by hand to Temuco. The next day we were in Temuco. There we requested an audience with the Judge and we explained the problem. The Judge issues a summons immediately, a summons, for a meeting between Señor Estoy, Señor Astorga and ourselves. This was to take place within twenty days. We had stopped the eviction.

When the hearing took place Señor Estoy arrived with his solicitor and Señor Astorga to tell lies. Firstly they accuse us, they say we are usurping their land, accustomed, as always, to lie to the Authorities. The Judge produces the map of the province and the reservation is marked on it. ... I say, 'Here. This is the reservation of Hueñaluhuén whose Chief was José Painecura but he died many years ago. The present Chief is Juan Llancapán and he is also very old. ... We didn't want to bring him because it is too big a sacrifice. That is why we came. I'm also a member of the reservation. I was born there so of course I know all about the problem.'

So the Judge says, 'Very well then, we shall send another order for the "carabineros" to collect evidence and information, and according to their report, which I will study, we'll resolve the case. But in the meantime all conflict is suspended and no one provokes or attacks any one. You must show mutual respect for each other. Neither you, Señor Estoy, nor you, Señor Astorga, can carry on bothering the Indians, neither can you, sirs, carry on bothering Señor Estoy and Señor Astorga. Agreed?'

We said, 'Agreed, even though we had never bothered them. They are the ones who have always created the conflicts, not us. But so that the matter can be clarified and a report from the "carabineros" returned here we accept.' And we signed an agreement, there, before the Tribunal in Temuco.

Of course, we returned very happy. It gave us some security, the eviction order would not be carried out. Well, the 'carabineros' came and twenty days later the new report went to the 'Juzgado de Indios' in Temuco. We are summoned again. ... And the report shows in our favour. The 'carabineros' report that in fact it is not the Indians who are the usurpers but that the private individuals are, Señor Estoy and Señor Astorga, and another man who has taken some land belonging to the reservation of Hueñaluhuén a little further to the North. So the Judge says, 'Very well then, we shall send some surveyors to go and measure, to mark out the boundaries of the reservation and then you must enclose it, put up a fence so that there are no more conflicts.'

'Agreed.'

'Well, listen to me, within twenty-five days we shall send the officials there. There will be a surveyor and a secretary, two people to work on this.'

'Agreed.'

The twenty-five days go by. A month, two months, a year, and nothing. The officials never arrive. ... The second year comes. We carry on persisting, trip after trip. But no, only promises and the Judge says, 'Wait. Have patience. I have no more staff.'

Lies. All that waiting, and a year and a half go by. In the year 1962 the situation changes. The people understand what organization is, they know how to intervene ... then the youth has another restlessness. But I had been taking advantage of all this problem and that disquiet from the moment when the committee was

organized. . . . We constituted it officially, I remember it was one 21st May. This
is a holiday in Chile. So the Committee was officially constituted. We ordered a
seal to be made. . . . The foundation of the Committee was explained. . . . It was a
Mapuche Committee of Hueñaluhuén founded the 21st May, 1960.

And . . . I see a need . . . all the youth that lives there, men and women, are all
illiterate . . . and I start teaching reading. And so the idea emerges of building
some small premises for a school, because the enthusiasm for learning how to read
was growing.

And so we built a small hut, a 'ruquita', . . . well it took two days and we had a
good little house, it only had one room but there was space for thirty people. We
held our classes there. That was a literacy class. I taught a great number of young
peasants, men and women, and some children and old people. And, as soon as a
few had learned to read, my cousin for example, they understood better my talks
on organization. I used to talk about political orientation as well, the class struggle
. . . all this I explained as I taught them to read, what they read in books and in
magazines, well I was giving them all these ideas as well . . . how we would need to
fight later on, who were our real enemies. Why land was not only being usurped in
that region but at a national level. . . .

Well, after that it was easier for me. During that year the idea emerged that the
committee should not only devote itself to defending the territory but that we
should organize collective employment. . . . It was in a way, going back to the old
ideas, because I can remember and so can my Mapuche friends who are older than
I, that was what used to happen in old days. There was always a fraternity and a
solidarity and that is very important. They helped each other with their work in
those days . . . they helped each other, that is what one says . . . for example the
'huincas'* called it 'el mingaco' [voluntary communal labour]. 'El mingaco' is
a form of collective work, all together, of helping each other. And that idea
emerged we made it materialize, there was agreement, and we set to work collectively. We made a plan for sowing wheat, oats, potatoes, linseed . . . all the crops
of that area. And so we helped each other. We counted how many people had oxen
and harnesses . . . on our reservation there were twelve peasants who had oxen,
twelve yokes of oxen and harnesses. . . . All peasants drive their own plough, well
the tools of their trade, and we started to work to break up the stones for the newly
planned crops. Everyone came to look . . . Goodness . . . the twelve yokes of oxen
ploughed the ground and we cleaned it, well we did other things . . .

That year our reservation produced a harvest as never before. So that was a
very exciting year. Everybody sowed everything, harvested everything, stored food for
the winter and the people like this form of work. And new ideas surged forward
from the warmth of this united work. For example, it was there we agreed, seeing
the importance of the school, because the children were growing up, and so we
said, 'Why don't we build a real school, a building that looks like a school?' . . .
Well, we have no money, wood is so expensive . . . and so on . . . and so forth . . . it
would be difficult to buy it immediately. But my uncle, the one who had some
experience as a labourer on those ranches on those huge estates . . . says, 'I once
worked splitting wood with a hand-saw and we cut up sixty planks a day . . . and
my neighbour, Don Juan Fonseca, who is a friend of mine says he has a hand-saw
and we can cut the wood with that saw. I can borrow it, because he is a good bloke
that Juan Fonseca, a very good friend . . .'.

Once my uncle's proposal is accepted he promises to go and borrow the saw. . . .
Juan Fonseca gives it to him, I think, and my uncle arrives the next day with his
hand-saw on his shoulder. And on the third day we started installing a bench on

the mountain-side. ... I call it a bench because there was no carpenter's bench there ... they called it a 'burriquete', a saw-horse. We put down a great base, some posts about one and a half metres high, other planks across, and so on, so the wood had something firm to sit on. ... Well, and then ... the hand-saw. One pulling upwards and the other down. The one pulling down had to do so with more force so that it would cut.

And so we started work, splitting wood with a hand-saw. That's the way we got the planks to build premises with. A school eight metres long by five metres wide. We built them with wood cut with that hand-saw and we made tiles. Tiles cut with a 'machete'. We made tiles by hand ... for the roof. So the school was made with wooden walls and a wooden roof. We built the school. ... We opened it with a huge party. And so, well, we had no teacher. ... The youth I was preparing could teach literacy, could teach reading, they were able to, but they were only able to teach reading, that is make people literate. ... So I was the only one who had more education ... although I had not finished my sixth grade I knew more than they did and so they make me a proposal, that I should dedicate myself to teaching reading and they would pay me a salary between them so that I could live, but I must give up farming and dedicate myself exclusively to teaching. I accepted ... I started a register ... ehm? ... the first year. ... That same year, 1962, I start work. I have an attendance of about sixty-five children, aged from seven to sixteen years ... the school is almost full ... the enthusiasm is great ... but we had no resources, no exercise books ... we looked for any pieces of paper, cardboard, cement sacks, all those things we used. We had no chalk so we used charcoal. We wrote with charcoal. And then we discovered coloured soil on our reservation. That served as paint ... it replaced the chalk ... those were our resources which we used.

Working there every day, from Monday to Friday, I taught children aged seven to sixteen years old and on Saturdays and Sundays the adults, men and women. Well, that was a very important experience for me ... no? ... And the fight goes on. We never abandon the fight to recover our territory ... until ... the authorities will have to solve our problem, one day ... the recovery of our land.

The year 1962 saw the occupation of land in the Province of Malleco. In Lolocos, Loncomahuida, there was a confrontation with the police, seven 'carabineros' were injured and about fifteen Mapuches were seriously injured and thirty were arrested. ... This was published by the daily newspaper *Diario Austral* of the Province of Cautín. I had made many journeys activating our problem, trying to get a solution to our conflict in Temuco. ... I always bought the paper on these journeys, and there it is in the *Diario Austral*, this event.

And so I go back with the paper. I call a meeting and at the meeting I read the article about the incident, about what the Mapuches of Malleco had done ... and I say to them, 'Well, there is an identical problem to ours there. The bureaucratic proceedings are the same. That is why our Mapuche companions quite rightly took that decision and I think this will be the solution here. Why can't we get ready and learn from that experience, adopt the same attitude and take back our land? Well, we can see that justice is done by ourselves. We can move the fence, and need respect no longer the boundary that is there, made by these "huincas". We know up to where our territory went before. That great field over there, that one, was my grandfather's and that one another neighbour's. But now they are exploiting it, all those "huincas" are working that land and making themselves rich, fattening their animals, and so on. One will never know how much money they have made all these years. ...'

And then I make a fiery speech and they understand me, and also by that time I was speaking Mapuche fluently. ... I speak in Mapuche and in Spanish and in Mapuche ... and there is no doubt that they understand me. They understand what I had explained and an agreement was reached. Then they all say, 'We are in agreement. We will also take our territory, we will throw all the animals of these "gringos" out towards the sea. Let them go to the Devil! The fact is that we won't let them tread on our land again.'

And so we put this agreement into practice on New Year's Eve of 1962. We chased the animals out, we moved the fence to where we thought it should be, we did this between everybody and people from other reservations helped ... we made a boundary ... a strong boundary, we built a huge fence, with almost whole trees, so that neither the animals nor the 'gringos' could get in. Of course this was an act that provoked ... provoked anger in the first place on the 'gringos' side ... Señor Astorga and also on the side of the Authority.

As soon as we did this we were accused of being Communists. And, there is no doubt that the responsibility for it was laid on me, I was the promoter. I was the dangerous Communist and there I was urging the peasants to war.

Well, the New Year ... we celebrated the New Year of 1962 building houses, because we had the hand-saw we had planks of wood.

We built eight houses on New Year's Day. The next day about another eight ... we used up all the ground, two kilometres from North to South ... ehmm? ... as we had worked it out, and that land, those open fields, which had been like that for years and years, were the work of our grandparents, of our parents ... and so ... oh well ... that is where the houses were built.

And so, after a fortnight the 'carabineros' came to find out what was going on. But they did not arrive in an aggressive mood, but ... there ... they looked at the houses, 'Sure enough the land is now populated' ... and, well. ... 'there is a huge fence as a dividing line.'

They go away and afterwards we were summoned. They summoned us to the 'Juzgado de Indios'. There we made a statement ... but the Judge says we have violated the agreement and that is bad, breaking an agreement is breaking the law and breaking the law is a crime. And I say to him, 'We are totally in agreement with you, Señor Usía. But not fulfilling an agreement is also a crime isn't it? We have waited so many years and you have promised us so many times and we are fed up with so many lies. We can no longer believe the authorities. ... That is why we are forced to take this measure and because we believe we are right and justified to do so. The Officials you have promised us have never arrived.'

'But I only have one surveyor for the whole province and I've hurried him and I have to send surveyors to other provinces also, Valdivia, Osorno ... there are conflicts there as well. ... I have no more staff' as an excuse.

In the end the Tribunal says we must leave the land until the surveyor arrives. I say, 'Well, we'll let our people know. At this moment I am only the leader. I don't make the decisions. The people decide. Whatever happens I promise you that I'll take the information that you give me back, but there is no agreement here ... I, at least, won't take any action against the will of the majority.'

Well, we returned home. That same year, the 13th April ... but first, before the 13th April, 'carabineros' had come on two occasions to evict us ... in March, we are harvesting. As all the work is collective we were all in the fields harvesting the crops and the houses were alone most of the day. We returned at night and on two occasions the 'carabineros' had taken advantage of the houses being empty and had started destroying them. When we returned at night we found the houses destroyed and it was the 'carabineros' who had done it ...

But by April we had all the crops harvested. We have more time. Again someone informs us that a new eviction is being prepared and that this time it is to be an
eviction, and it is almost April 13th. By now we had contacts in Carahue,
Imperial, Temuco . . . ehm? . . . We have contact with the Trade Unions* in
Temuco . . . mm . . . we have dealings with the Party. . . . By now I'm a member of
the Party.

Talking about membership, I joined the Party in 1959, the very same year that I
arrived back at my reservation. I remember that I went around asking in Carahue
who was a Communist and no one wanted to tell me, but later on I asked who sold
the daily *El Siglo* there. A lad who was selling the *Diario Austral* says, 'Over there is
a gentleman who sells *El Siglo.*' This same lad takes me to him.

I find him and say, 'Look sir, is *El Siglo* sold here?'

'Yes.'

'Look, I need to talk to a comrade from the Communist Party.'

And he says, 'I am a Communist.'

'Very good.'

The man had, . . . I mean, this comrade had a greengrocer's shop, a shoe shop
and a barber's shop as well. I asked him, 'Well, what do I have to do to become a
Communist?'

'Look,' he says, 'we Communists have a card and every month we pay a subscription according to our means. Where do you work?'

'No, . . . I . . . I'm a peasant, I'm on the Hueñaluhuén reservation, but I was a
miner before and I met many Party leaders,' I said, 'but I was a sympathizer of
the CP's youth organization. I have not been a Party member, that's why I'm
asking what I have to do to join the Party.'

'Very well,' he says, 'you fill up this paper,' he took out a paper, 'you write
your address, your name, your occupation and you sign here and the Card costs so
much.'

I immediately fill in the form, give it to him, produce my money and say, 'I
want the card.'

And that is how they gave me the Card and I return to my reservation and there
I show my Party Card. 'Now I'm a Communist.' That's how I joined the Party.

Well, let's continue with the issue of the struggle for our territory. As I was
saying, the contact I had with the Party and with the Trade Unions gave us
encouragement, . . . and success, the success of the struggle . . .

Sure enough, a contingent of policemen arrived on April 13th, 1962 . . . armed
to the teeth. It was then that we saw submachine guns. . . . Seventy-five 'carabineros' plus the Civil Police . . . mmmm . . . 'los tiras' as they are called, . . . and
the 'gringos', also armed.

This event was quite novel, a bit alarming. Everybody saw the caravan of police
pass along the road, the jeeps full of police armed to the teeth . . . as they advanced
towards our reservation, the people running behind to see what was going to
happen. They all said, 'There is going to be a confrontation and goodness knows
how many will die.' And many people who were following in the police wake,
along the road, were taking up positions, joining our side.

They arrive at about one-thirty in the afternoon. We are awaiting them. A
Captain arrives. A huge blond man, his surname was Quintana. . . . He was the
Captain of the 'carabineros' of Nueva Imperial, very overbearing. . . . 'I want to
meet the Chief.' And I say, 'There is no Chief here, I am Mr So-and-So but I am
the Leader of the Committee and the Chief of this reservation is at home because
he is very old.'

'Ah, you are Mr So-and-So?'

'Yes.'

'Well then, it's with you I have come to speak. I don't want to speak to the Chief, I want to speak to you.'

'Agreed.'

'Look here,' he says, 'I have brought an eviction order and you must leave this land this very instant. This is why we are here, to carry it out.'

And I say, 'I'm surprised, Captain. We are here on our own reservation. This community is called Hueñaluhuén, there is a "título de merced", there is a map, a ground plan. If you will allow me I'll show you it and you will locate us. You are mistaken. We're not conflicting with anyone here.'

He asked me to show him the 'título de merced' and the map. He looked at it and realized that we were within our rights, within our own reservation. So he calls the 'gringos' who were with them and says, 'Where is it? Where is the conflict?'

Then the 'gringo' shouts, 'It's here, this land is mine, the Indians have taken this land away from me.' He was shouting hysterically.

'Well,' he says (the Captain), 'I'm not mistaken then.'

'Well, if you look at it that way . . . but we are not going to accept the order. You must read the order first. We can't accept you just saying it.'

There were about fifteen of us there at the time. Where were the others? They were placed at strategic points on the mountain. At that moment we must appear to be very well organized. There was an important plan of attack.

Well, he didn't want to hand over the order. After the fifteen of us insisting he read, in a loud voice: 'The eviction, it says, in the high place called Alto Llupehue . . .'

First mistake. He finishes reading the order and I say, 'Captain, you are indeed mistaken. That order is for Alto Llupehue, as you have said. You said it and Alto Llupehue is more than fifteen kilometres from here . . . behind that hill that we can just see. . . . There is Alto Llupehue. And sure enough Señor Estoy has some land there and the conflict must be there and not here . . . so you have come here mistakenly.'

'No, it's here.'

'No,' . . . and I ask . . . 'May I see the order? I also know how to read.'

He handed me the order and the order didn't say 'eviction', it said 'destruction of houses' . . . and it was indeed for Alto Llupehue and not Hueñaluhuén. . . . This order was mistaken and it also said 'destruction of houses', and so, once I had read the order I had another argument: 'Captain, this order . . . for one thing it is wrong and also it's not an eviction order. It says here "destruction of houses" and it is for Alto Llupehue, not here, and so we don't have to accept this order, do we?'

But he persists. He says, 'No, it's for here. There aren't any conflicts anywhere else. It's here, and so you must leave this place.'

I say, 'No' . . .

After ten minutes or so of discussion the Captain changes his mind, he calls me aside, he takes me about fifty metres away from the others and says, 'Look here, may I give you some advice? Go away, hide in the mountains, remain hidden, because if you don't we'll destroy everything. The "carabineros" will act, they will respect nothing. You have things here, furniture, belongings, . . . that have cost you money. Take them away with great care and hide in the mountains. Afterwards, after we've gone you can come back, because we'll not return.'

And I say to him, 'Look, . . . in the first instance I am in agreement with you, but I'm not the one who makes decisions. I will tell everybody. If they accept we will go. But if they don't we shan't agree to do so.'

That is what we did. I said to the others, 'Look, the Captain says this . . . that we should go, take our belongings and hide in the mountains, and afterwards, when they have gone, we should return to live here. What do you think?' They all shouted in unison, 'We don't agree. Neither can we leave this territory nor are we taking territory from anyone . . . we will not be removed from here. They can only put us out if we're dead.'

So I say, 'This is their answer, Captain. Therefore I must agree with them and do as they say. I don't agree . . .'

On hearing our reply he says, 'Well, I haven't come here to argue. I have come to carry out orders.' And he orders the 'carabineros' to proceed. The 'carabineros' get going immediately, ten of them go to a small house they knock it down, the women run out and surround the next house, holding knives, sticks, sickles . . . well . . . anything that will cause injury.

So after knocking down the first house the 'carabineros' go on to the next and the women don't let them in and the alarm is given. A comrade starts blowing the Horn, 'el cacho' as it is called, in the mountain, to signal the attack.

That was the warning that the attack should begin. People came out, in groups, from all over the place in groups of twenty, fifteen, thirty people . . . mm? . . . Within ten minutes we have them surrounded. When the 'carabineros' see so many people coming down from the mountain they begin to look alarmed and they move around and the people get nearer . . . mm? . . . and the 'carabineros' are panicking, looking to all sides, running from side to side, changing their positions. And there are still 'carabineros' demolishing houses, they still hadn't got through to the second house, they couldn't get through the cordon of women. They daren't . . . mm? . . . and all along the Captain was holding a gun at my chest. Then he decides to break up the barrier of women.

They tied my hands behind my back with a rope, they tied up my hands and . . . they put a corporal at my right and another on my left pointing a gun at my ribs . . . to frighten me. . . . The Captain wants to break through the barrier of women. So he goes over, takes hold of a Mapuche and says, 'Move away, Mapuche, move aside or we will kill you here and now.' . . . He hadn't finished speaking when he was hit an enormous blow with a stick, I don't know how they hit him . . . but there he was, down, the Captain, he tried to push himself up with his hands but the women carried on hitting him . . . eventually he manages to move away on all fours. . . . As soon as he found himself somewhat more free, some forty metres away, with the women still chasing him, he straightened up and ran. And then he was free, and gaining ground, fifty metres away, and he orders, 'Withdraw.' The 'carabineros' withdraw, each one choosing a better route. . . . They ran with the peasants in pursuit, each trying to catch a 'carabinero' . . .

The fact is we chased them away. . . . It had all taken about two hours. . . . We chased them from the place . . . and . . . only anger remained.

The others return, they untie me . . . and . . . I am free. And I say to them, 'But what happened? Why didn't you disarm a "carabinero"?' Because that had been the arrangement, to catch a 'carabinero', not hit him, but take his gun away. Well that didn't happen. They got away. Well, the fact is, as I say, there was anger because the older ones blamed each other. 'It was your fault, why didn't you catch him?' or 'Why didn't you hit him?' 'Oh well, I don't know . . .' 'You're a coward' . . . and so they wanted to fight amongst themselves. And all the time I was appeasing them, pacifying them. 'No, we can't do that because we are not our own enemies . . . the important thing is that there wasn't a catastrophe, no crime was committed, no one was killed. The "carabineros" have gone and I don't think they will return. In any case we will have to be ready in case they return tonight. Nobody will sleep here tonight. We must be vigilant.'

Taking advantage of the people all being gathered together, some from other communities, some five hundred people had arrived from different places, we organized a meeting ... it was agreed immediately that a messenger should be sent to either Temuco or Carahue to notify the authorities of the occurrence ... to denounce the incident. It was proposed that I should go, that I should leave for Carahue immediately. I left at night, about nine o'clock from home. ... Dawn saw me riding my horse towards Carahue. In Carahue ... I arrived about seven o'clock in the morning, I had to take the bus to Temuco. I arrive in Temuco. Our comrades there already know about it, so some of the leaders of the CUT [Chilean Trade Union Congress] of Temuco, who had supported me in other negotiations were waiting for me.

We talked to the officer in charge of the 'carabineros' to the Intendente, and from there I went to the 'Radio de la Frontera' [a radio station]. There I was interviewed and the news broadcast. The *Diario Austral* had to publish the facts. ... Well ... we were famous ... mmm?

Meanwhile the 'carabineros' were given a huge banquet at the house of the 'gringo' Alfonso Estoy de la Nuez. They got drunk, they ate a whole calf, they were there for three days. And on the second day the rain came. It made the road impassable, it was an earth road. They faced enormous difficulties getting back. Also great solidarity was shown, repudiation of them. Other peasants who were far away from us, who were on the way back to us, destroyed some bridges, they demolished two bridges. They blocked the road with huge trees, to impede the return of the 'carabineros'. That was the work of other peasants, as a sign of repudiation, of protest. ... It was, without a doubt, out of solidarity with us. ... So their return was very difficult. ... They ruined three vehicles whilst trying to repair the bridge, they fell off the bridge. Seven 'carabineros' were injured, their ribs were broken, oh, I don't know ...

All this gives rise to an investigation. A telegram was sent to the Chamber of Deputies in Santiago where our Parliamentary Representatives laid the problem. A Committee was appointed to investigate the case, and Juan Acevedo, who was a Deputy in those days, came out to the province.

It was at that time that I met Juan Acevedo. He went to the Tribunal and investigated the case and as a result the officials ... who had been promised for so long ... came along. It was only then that the judge in Temuco was able to send the surveyor and an assistant to measure, draw and re-establish the boundaries of our reservation. And we have recovered the land. In that way. Under those conditions. With a fight. And the territory we have recovered we have turned into cooperative farming. Of course we were already operating as a cooperative, but now we have more land ... enthusiasm has grown. The Committee is stronger ... it is a cooperative. ... And it is agreed: 'We will no longer exploit the mountain as in olden days. We are not going to burn it as our parents, our grandparents did. No, we are really going to exploit the mountain now. We will buy a power saw to saw the wood and transform the "rucas" [huts] ... so that we may have a proper house, a better shelter before we die.'

And that is how it was done. We all contributed. Whatever we could, some had an animal, a pig. ... Oh, I don't know ... some lambs. ... We sold all we had, we managed to gather five million pesos more or less and we bought a power saw that had been discarded, thrown out by a capitalist. So, bit by bit we bought this machine and my cousin who had worked for the 'gringo' Estoy at the timber yard cutting up wood, and also helping to maintain the equipment ... and ... because

at one time he helped install a saw, whilst working there he learnt all that.
He was the craftsman, who installed all the machinery, worked on it until it functioned. The bench arrived. We started sawing the timber. [. . .] The straw 'rucas' are transformed by lining them with wood, tiled roofs . . . even glass windows.

During the Popular Government of 1970 our Committee was officially recognized as a cooperative. In the year 1972 we received our first loan from a bank, our organization had received a loan for the first time.

That loan helped us enormously. We bought new belts for the saw with it, some pipes for the engine which worked on steam and some other parts which were old and needed renewing. And we started selling the wood to ECA[2] and we bought roofing materials with the proceeds.

The Committee still functions. The Committee manages the cooperative. The cell of the Party grew. The older people worked in a planned way, we made roads with the money that we gathered, we had enough to build fifteen kilometres of roadway . . . mm? . . . And we did that with our own resources, with the willpower of the peasants. We begin to see great progress.

And, in 1969, I start the proceedings towards making our school legal. In the last year of Frei's Government there was an Official in the Department of Education of Nueva Imperial, a Department Inspector. He was a Socialist, Heriberto Pavéz, and his superior – the Secretary – was a Christian Democrat (I can't remember his name) . . . but this, this Christian Democrat helped us most of all, he was more . . . more . . . he took a greater interest, he helped us solve the problems in the . . . the creation, in giving the school a number. Of course it was not a state school, it was still a private school, but a teacher arrived to work there. It was only then that I was able to free myself from the job of teaching and I was able to dedicate myself to running the Committee . . . the Cooperative.

I gained a very important experience there, the value of the work of the cooperatives to the peasants. That convinced me that following the election of the Popular Government . . . the cooperatives must be promoted . . . and as a result of this experience I was able to convince the Indian peasants of my province and we were able to form thirty-seven cooperatives of this kind. [. . .] And there is no doubt that they all achieved good results.

Now, had I been on a course for cooperative workers at that time, I would have been of more help, I could have guided the people better . . .

We made mistakes, of course. For example, we never worked out our plans properly . . . mm? through lack of scientific knowledge, through lack of methods because we hadn't studied them at school.

But all things considered, once we had put our ideas into practice we solved many problems . . . we were able to move forward, we made progress . . . the needs were many, the poverty my family had lived in and so had all the peasants on the reservation of Hueñaluhuén. And so, as I was saying, everything that I went to learn in the coal-mine, all that knowledge that I acquired in the Lota Mineworkers' Union[3] I was able to put into practice on my own reservation, and later on in my province. I'm convinced that the direct solution and the most appropriate for small farmers, and for the medium-sized ones and especially for the Indian communes is the cooperative life. There is no better way in this kind of situation.

That is why when the day comes that we can free ourselves from fascism, from that hated, despotic regime, that regime introduced by Capitalism, by Imperialism . . . when the day comes that our people are free, this work on the land will return.

And not only will there be small cooperatives but large ones as well, great cooperative complexes. The farming industry will take off.

There will be a big awakening of the peasants, they will surge like great torrents
of strength, and that will be the future of the peasants and of the Chileans.

And like that, in that way we'll secure the liberation of our Fatherland and we
shall, with pride, offer our solidarity to other peoples.

NOTES

[1. Terms marked with an asterisk are explained in the introduction to Reading 7.]
[2. A state purchasing and marketing commission; in practice it served mainly the large
landowners.]
[3. i.e. of the Lota Mining Company.]

9   The Making of Rural Proletarians:
Sugar Estate Workers in El Valle

ANDREW PEARSE

Editors' introduction

The following account uses material collected by Salomon Rivera, a Colombian
sociologist. Published here for the first time, it was prepared for the United
Nations Research Institute for Social Development by the late Andrew Pearse as
one of a series of 'vignettes' illustrating the effects of new agricultural technologies.

The reading describes aspects of the lives and work of five sugar plantation workers
and their families, who were formerly peasant smallholders. Pradera is in El Valle, a
flat and fertile valley to the west of the Andes and near the city of Cali (see Reading 14).
El Valle exemplifies the transition to capitalist agriculture by landowners or
commercial companies which rent large tracts of land for this purpose (see the account
of the first worker). In the first place, this process involves competition between
capitalist enterprises and peasants for land. The hold of many peasants over land was
weakened as a result of the Colombian civil war of 1948–58 (commonly known as *La
Violencia*); other measures such as land sales by peasants to pay off debts, litigation over
land ownership, and evacuation of land because of aerial spraying by large estates
(intended to have this effect) have all contributed to the expansion of large-scale
commercial enterprises on to land formerly worked by peasants.

Secondly, capitalist agriculture requires wage workers, and dispossessed and
displaced peasants form a 'reserve' of labour for such employment. Apart from a
permanent wage-labour force, sugar estates recruit a lot of casual labour on a temporary basis, with fewer rights and lower rates of pay. Because casual labourers
are less protected and can be dismissed more easily, the numbers of those
employed can be adjusted by the estates according to seasonal requirements and
the 'logic' of the market (i.e. calculations of profitability). Insecurity of employ-

ment and low rates of pay mean that additional income has to be found to maintain any 'household' members beyond the individual worker, and here we see how the women who live with the estate workers have to engage in petty production and services to earn money, and even food, for themselves and their children.

As well as those former peasants who are entirely landless, there are others who have insufficient land to maintain themselves and their families and also have to work for the sugar plantations. Their situation is summed up by an anthropologist who lived for many years in an area near El Valle. 'Peasants are well aware that wage labour on the plantations is an enormous energy drain in comparison with peasant labour. ... They fetishize the cane as a plant which "dries one up. ..."￼ "I would rather be fat without money than old and skinny with money" is how young peasant labourers and peasant landowners put the issue. But when they have less than three *plazas* (one *plaza* = 0.64 hectare) and have to provide for children, then they are forced to increase their income and intensify their labour through wage work on the plantations or large farms.'[1]

The first of the workers said that his father had occupied his farm for forty years, having paid the former occupier a sum of money for the value of the 'improvements'. In the 1960s, the farm suffered periodic flooding from the waters of the large neighbouring estate. As a result of aerial fumigation contracted for by the larger neighbour, his animals died and his children suffered from sores and vomiting. The owner of the large estate to whom complaints about the flooding and the fumigations were made, denied responsibility since the farm was rented out to a commercial company: the company's representatives claimed that they paid rent in order to exploit the land, and that this included draining it and having it properly fumigated. Complaints to the municipal authorities were unavailing. In 1965, the neighbouring estate owner was able to obtain an order from a judge for the return of the property on the grounds that the peasant holding stood on land which was a part of the estate. The father agreed to make over half of the farm (the part which suffered from flooding) to the estate owner in return for payment of the improvements, and two years later, after the fumigation became more intense, made over to him the other half.

The second worker explained that his father, like the other small proprietors in his area, was obliged to leave his farm because of the fumigation which killed off fowl, pigs, cats and dogs. There was also the 'black pest'[2] which attacked and destroyed the cacao plants when the fumigation began. His father could not find a serious purchaser for the farm because of the fumigation, and a sale was arranged with the legal representatives of a neighbouring estate, who imposed the price. He reported that he only knew the proprietor's surname but had never met him. It was 'like that with most of the large proprietors thereabouts'.

Of the remaining three workers interviewed, one blamed the fumigation and the black pest, and another left because a part of the farm had to be sold to pay off debts. The last said that after living on their farm for 25 years, his parents were ordered by a judge to hand it over to the neighbouring estate owner since a study of titles showed that it formed a part of the estate lands. 'Formerly nobody made demands like this. My father had a document showing that he had bought the improvements. The man who sold them had been there for fifty years.'

Between the time they left their peasant homes and the time when they achieved the relative stability of their jobs in modern commercial agriculture,[3] all had undergone a longer or shorter peregrination in search of work, which had led all of them to Bogotá (national capital), Cali (capital of the Department of El Valle) and Cartago (rapidly growing city and communications centre in the same Department) and to various market towns, while four of them had found work for a time in Buenaventura, the Pacific Coast port.

In their previous search for work the most common occupations, reported by four, were market porter, unskilled construction worker and lorry-loader. Jobs mentioned twice were newspaper seller, coffee picker and cleaner. Waiter, brothel assistant, market hawker, warehouse porter and stevedore were mentioned. The variety of skills needed for running a mixed family farm, and the country school, do not qualify a young man for anything more than unskilled work in the city.

The organization of a sugar estate consists of three main levels: on top are directors, who may or may not be the owners, and who are in any case empowered to take entrepreneurial decisions. Below them are the permanent staff, looking after administrative, clerical and supervisory work; minding machines and means of transport, and in constant touch with the direction. Below them, making a voluminous bottom to the pyramid, are the workers; like the bees in the hive they are constantly in motion to supply the machines with the primary product from the cane fields scattered widely through the countryside, but unlike the bees they are subject to constant turnover.[4]

The directors have no contact with the workers, whose management in a number of enterprises has been given a pseudo-military character by the employment of retired Army NCOs as personnel managers. They have been able to build a system of subordination around military discipline and the inculcation of an *esprit de corps* which however is sufficiently discriminatory as to allow dismissal on one week's notice of any worker without question for offences against the system. Nevertheless, the five workers had held their present jobs for 7, 6, 11, 2 and 24 months respectively.

Although dismissal was easily earned, the sugar estates were exigent in recruitment, and required the job-seeker to present his National Identity Card, his Military Service Book and the 'Certificate of Juridical Antecedents'. He was also expected to have written recommendations from local establishment figures such as the priest and the political boss. The requirements for keeping the job, in the eyes of the five workers, are given as follows:

(a) This depends on your yield *(rendimiento)* and on your friends and so how far you can make friends with the Field Sergeant or the Corporal of the Sugar-Cane. In the sugar estates they are looking for high-yielders.

(b) They are always having new ideas for getting the highest yield out of the work for the least pay.

(c) It depends on your yield. The strongest and toughest *(aguantadòr)* earns most.

(d) The labour contractors *(enganchadores)* use every sort of trick to make a man work harder and harder. (In some cases the labour contractors are employees of the enterprise.) Those who yield most and keep quietest are the ones with most opportunities.

(e) The worker must be obedient, he must not make any sort of change in the work. He must not say anything or he will be suspended. . . . The contractors keep a common list and you cannot get work again; you must leave the area or die of hunger. Control is firmest in the Sugar Estates.

The five workers, like most of their class of in-migrant peasants. were unable to establish a family like that from which they came. They set up house with women of similar background who had also been obliged to leave home to go into domestic service, usually in the larger cities, and who sooner or later had become mothers but without stable domestic life, and had become accustomed to fending for themselves as best they could, working in cafés or brothels if alone, and doing needlework, laundry, etc. if they managed to set up house with a wage-earner. All five homes as a result had two earners since the women could not rely on their men's permanent presence or their continued employment, and anyhow in four cases the women had children of their own from earlier liaisons whom they wished to educate. The ways in which the women made their contribution to the aggregate livelihood are given below:

(a) She made pies and distributed them to neighbouring shops each afternoon, collecting 70 per cent of the selling price from the shopkeeper next morning, and taking back those unsold, which could be fed to her children. This lady bought household and 'trade' inputs together, and was unable to calculate her profits, but she felt that if there really were no profit, her family would be eating much worse than they were.

(b) She washed and ironed clothes for a number of town families, at whose homes she received her midday meal as part payment. The money she received was used for costs connected with her son's schooling.

(c) She worked as a cleaner in cafés and bars, where she spent most of the day, leaving her children with a neighbour. She received food in part payment and was able to supplement her children's meals.

(d) She washed and ironed clothes, and received some items of food and soft drinks in part payment.

(e) She washed and ironed clothes for single wage-earners living in rooming-houses. The washing was done in a public wash house on the margin of the town. She spent her earnings on food.

Within domestic groups, while the women's earnings were mainly a contribution to the cost of food, and also attempted to cover the children's schooling expenses, the men devoted about one-quarter of their salaries to rent and rather more than a quarter to food. The rest was spent on clothes, medicines and week-end drinking and cinema. The most common foods were *arepas* (maize cakes) and bread, fried plantains, sugar-water *(agua de panela)*, some chocolate or cocoa, rice or macaroni soup, eggs and, with good fortune, some meat.

Meat, sugar, chocolate and cooking oil had all become very expensive at the time when the study was made, due to a policy of exporting these articles. Although the standard of living was poor, especially in comparison with 15–20 years before, it was found that the contemporary peasant diets compared even worse with the earlier period, because of the very low level of income from sales [of their crops] and the high cost of supplementary foodstuffs, clothing, etc.

The workers expressed apprehension that sooner or later their jobs would be dispensed with.

'The companies daily seek ways of eliminating man-power.'
'Any day now the machines will arrive to take over our jobs.'
'They are going to finish with cane-cutting with *machetes*.'
'They continue to put machines in the place of men – what are we to do next? – we have no land of our own to return to.'

The workers and their families, like most others in similar conditions, live in houses rented out by the room or part thereof, one family to a room of approxi-mately 3 by 4 metres, divided by a curtain between a dormitory area and a living–cooking area, where some sort of oil stove is used.
Lavatories are shared between the several families occupying the house,

amounting to between 16–30 persons, without clear responsibilities for cleaning areas of communal use. Permanent competition and tension reign in connection with the shared space of the house.

Extracted from an unpublished report prepared for the United Nations Research Institute for Social Development.

NOTES

1. M. Taussig, 'Peasant economics and the development of capitalist agriculture in the Cauca valley, Colombia', *Latin American Perspectives*, vol. 5, no. 3, 1979, p. 85.
2. One explanation of the 'black pest' is that the *overkill* by fumigation released a contagion hitherto controlled by insects.
3. Four of the five worked in large sugar-cane enterprises, considered in local labouring circles to be the most desirable form of manual employment at that level. The fifth had also been so employed until he was dismissed for non-fulfilment of the quasi-military regulations imposed in one of the sugar-cane enterprises. He had since been excluded from all of them through the working of a black-list.
4. The bee-hive image is Salomon Rivera's.

10   The Senegal River Valley: What Kind of Change?

ADRIAN ADAMS

Late in April 1975, in a village on the left bank of the Senegal River, a meeting took place. It was held in the courtyard of a private dwelling-house, not in the village forum; for it involved, not the village as a whole, but the members of the village association for collective agriculture, which had been in existence for just over a year. They numbered about 270 at the time: 200 men and 70 women, almost half the active population then present in the village, evenly distributed throughout its 70-odd households. Many of them were at the meeting. Their designated spokesmen were seated on mats at the front of the gathering: six *chefs d'équipe*, heads of work groups, and the association's chairman, vice-chairman and treasurer. Near them sat observers from neighbouring villages where similar associations had been formed. Seated at a table, facing the assembled people, were the visitors who had caused the meeting to be held. One was a familiar figure, a French agricultural technician who had been in the area for a year. The others were not. One was the organizer of an agricultural improvement scheme about 200 miles downstream, the other was a representative of the Société d'Aménagement et d'Exploitation des Terres du Delta du Fleuve Sénégal (SAED), which had shortly before been placed in charge of agricultural development on the river. These two men were Senegalese, but from nearer the coast; they spoke in French, which was then translated into Soninke, the language locally spoken. The three men, accompanied by assistants who took no active part in the meeting, had arrived in the village together.

The man from downstream spoke first. He understood the people's worries, he said, because he had experienced the same problems himself. When the youth centre he ran started a farming scheme, they were anxious to preserve their freedom of action, because they had seen for themselves, in their own village, how peasant farmers working for SAED could be drawn into a cycle of debt. But they had solved the problem now. By coming to terms with SAED, they had gained access to international aid: the Senegalese authorities had sent observers, and the scheme was now receiving substantial support, especially from USAID [United States Agency for International Development]. 'You must cooperate with SAED,' he urged. 'You need modern technology; if you say No to SAED, you are saying No to modern technology. You should say Yes to all organizations which can help you. It is to be hoped that God will help us to be like Europe or America. SAED is the government's agent; it is your agent. It belongs to all of us.'

The SAED representative spoke next. He announced that SAED had been placed in charge of development along the river, and that the area within which the village was located was one of the few which was suitable for extensive rice cultivation. His task, he said, was to explain how SAED was going to organize work in the area, so as to dispel any misunderstandings. As the son of a peasant, he understood their problems well. 'A technician, in Senegal, is a peasant. The son of a peasant is no other than a peasant.' Once they had talked things over, everything would be clear.

The chairman of the village association then spoke briefly. People in the village, he said, had heard about SAED, but they had heard nothing from SAED, until now. They had started working on their own, with the help of the French technician; then they had suddenly heard, through this technician, that they should work with SAED. 'One day we were told that SAED would send us a master.' If they were all fellow-countrymen, why could SAED not address them directly, instead of treating them like things? In reply, the SAED representative said that now that the Government had given the Senegal River Valley to SAED, the technician referred to was the direct agent of SAED, in which capacity he would continue to do all he could to help the peasants. There was no need to worry about debts; debts were caused by foolish rivalry between neighbouring villages. The man from downstream added that they were lucky to have a technician to advise them; they would achieve take-off all the sooner, and then rich people would help them.

These initial exchanges set the pattern for the entire meeting, which lasted several hours. The line put forward by the SAED representative, and supported, with variations, by the man from downstream, denied that there could be any real difference of interests between the peasants and the authorities; the peasants' reasons for thinking otherwise were presented as trivial, arising from parochialism and fear of change. 'We are all peasants,' they said, 'my father was a peasant.' Although the village's technician now worked for SAED, they should continue to trust him; there was only one way to modernize. The peasants could rest assured that SAED would not favour the nearby town at the village's expense. 'You must work hard; then you will see what has been done for you.' The spokesmen of the village association, on the other hand, stressed their sense of separateness, their fear that cooperating with SAED might weaken their control over the future of the work they had begun on their own. Their technician had come to help them develop, they said, now they heard he had become a SAED agent. If SAED's interests were the same as their own, why not explain clearly what SAED wanted? The association's chairman recalled how he had been left waiting outside, while the French technician conferred with SAED officials in Saint-Louis. Was that right?

Towards the end of the meeting, patience wore thin, and a revealing exchange took place. One of the *chefs d'équipe*, a middle-aged man locally renowned as a Koranic scholar, asked whether they would be compelled to work with SAED. 'We live in a democratic country,' he was told. 'In that case,' he said, 'ever since the village was founded, we have been able to live by farming. God will give us a living. Let SAED make the sky fall; then we'll join SAED.' The SAED representative protested that he was 100 per cent Muslim. The man from downstream went further. Peasants [he said] were stubbornly opposed to the diffusion of new ideas and techniques. His activities [. . .] were based upon the Koran. God helped those who helped themselves. 'It is God who created SAED. We must collaborate with SAED. I advise you to do so.' The French technician remained silent throughout, except to say that he had no official connection with SAED, a statement directly contradicted by the SAED representative.

This meeting was inconclusive; it was not the first of its kind in the village, nor would it be the last. For one observer at least, it seemed a particularly clear sign of a general predicament, with far-reaching implications: for the people of the area, for Senegal and her neighbours on the river, and for the prospects of agricultural change in Africa. To understand why, one has to understand what the meeting was really about.

The record to date

Until the war

Seen on the flight from Paris, as the plane, leaving Mauritania's air space, begins the descent towards Dakar, the Senegal River looks surreal: a band of blue-green water meandering through desert. Close at hand, it retains that quality. After months without rain, when the countryside is bleached and tinder-dry, and the river itself choked with sand, the green grass at its edge still draws the eye. Like the Gambia River, the Senegal flows down from the heights of Futa Jalon; but the Gambia flows west to the sea, while the Senegal flows north. Fed by the rains of Futa Jalon, it crosses regions of steadily-decreasing rainfall; when it finally curves westward towards the Atlantic, true desert lies not far north. For much of its course, the Senegal River Valley is like an oasis, set apart from the tropical world. From its earliest recorded history, the area has indeed been known as an oasis, a granary, a magnet for peoples of the surrounding semi-arid lands. Arab chroniclers spoke of the settlements on the 'Nile': of Tekrur, whence derives 'Tukulor', the name now used to designate the dominant sedentary population of the Middle Valley, the historical region of Futa Toro; of Yaressi and Silla, on the upper rivers, near goldfields, which may refer to the earlier settlements upon which waves of Soninke migration built the state of Gajaaga after the 12th-century decline of the central Soninke kingdom of Wagadu. Moors, Fulani and Bambara encroached upon, but did not disrupt, this pattern of population. From the 17th century, French travellers explored the length of the river. Some, like Mollien, remarked upon its farmlands: 'The land on the banks of the river may be compared, for fertility, with the best French soil. The inhabitants till it with great care.' (1818, in Deschamps, 1967: 160)

The relative agricultural wealth of the Senegal River Valley, was of secondary interest to such travellers. Their chief concern was with trade: gold, gum from the Moors on the right bank of the Middle Valley, slaves from the Soninke merchant-clerics who brought them from the east to trading stations on the upper Senegal. Agriculture in the Valley concerned them only as it affected the availability of supplies for trading posts, and for the French establishment in Saint-Louis; thus Futa Toro, where a system of twice-yearly harvests drew upon the potential of the Middle Valley's alluvial floodlands, was noted less for its millet surplus than for its rulers' obstruction of trading vessels bound upstream. It was not until the early 19th century, when the export slave trade was officially prohibited, that some notion emerged of using the river's agricultural resources. It was decided, in 1818, to establish colonial plantations on the banks of the Senegal, in order to provide France with a new source of tropical agricultural produce, especially cotton and sugar, which would compensate for the decline in productivity of her West Indian plantations. Futa Toro seemed the most promising location; but its hostility to the French shifted the first plantations to the Wolof kingdom of Waalo, on the lower river. From the beginning, the scheme was beset with countless difficulties. The local population took a dim view of French attempts to establish ownership of the land required; the *habitants* [inhabitants] of Saint-Louis, set in the ways of trade, were averse to investing in agriculture; and there were great difficulties in obtaining labour. As Baron Roger, the governor most actively involved in the plan, remarked: 'The habit the Negroes have of working for themselves, makes it very difficult to employ them in our plantations. These men have very independent ways; they rightly say, "We are as free as you are", and their chiefs have very little authority.' (Barry, 1972: 253.) These difficulties could not possibly be overcome, given the nature of the French presence in Senegal at the time; the technical difficulties alone were enough to discourage the venture, in spite of the efforts of Richard, a gardener brought from France for the purpose, whose efforts are remembered in the place-name Richard-Toll, 'Richard's garden'. In 1831, the plan for an agricultural colony was a failure.

The vagaries of French interest in the agricultural promise of the Senegal River Valley during the 18th and early 19th century, in fact established a pattern of response which was to endure throughout the colonial period, and beyond: persistent lack of interest in existing subsistence agriculture in the Valley, unless it could be seen as servicing other, profitable enterprises; with fitful surges of speculation about the potential of the River for producing some export crop, usually coinciding with periods when the other enterprises seemed less profitable. The main difference, from the mid-19th century, was that the focus of French economic interest was no longer trade on the river, but trade in the groundnuts being cultivated for export in Western Senegal. The Senegal River remained of some interest until the end of the century, as the axis of French military penetration of the Western Sudan; while that lasted, the 'granary' was needed to provide supplies. After 'pacification', the servicing role of subsistence agriculture in the Valley became indirect; under pressure of taxation, it began to supply labour to the groundnut-growing areas of Senegal. The Senegal River basin was divided into three, its geographic unity unheeded since unneeded. The area became marginal, in both a real and a figurative sense, to the central preoccupations of the French colonial administration in each territory.

Perusal of 20th-century colonial archives is instructive in this respect, the scarcity of information on the Senegal River Valley, an area notionally covered by three sets of territorial records, being significant in itself. The normal focus of the archives' coverage of economic activity, is groundnut production: directly for Senegal, and indirectly for Soudan, where the main concerns are the supply of seasonal agricultural labour to Senegal, then the extension of groundnut production by the construction of the Dakar–Niger railway line, and later still the supply of labour to the Office du Niger. (The Mauritania archives neglect the sedentary populations almost entirely; their prime concern is the turbulent affairs of the Moors.) There was little groundnut cultivation in the Senegal River area. Outside periods of crisis in the groundnut trade, the records note this fact with melancholy, if at all, and tend to ascribe it to natural factors; in fact, the main reason appears to have been the lack of viable marketing circuits, due to high transport costs, which made commercial groundnut cultivation unprofitable even in areas where groundnuts were grown for local consumption. Millet cultivation is mentioned only as an early source of income for tax payment. The 1922 *rapport économique* [official economic report] for Senegal, for instance, notes that 'it seems likely that the inhabitants of regions adjacent to the River will find it difficult, if not to supply their own wants, at least to derive from their harvests the wherewithal to pay taxes'. However, the compensating dry-season floodland crop provides a solution, for the administrator at any rate: 'They have grown beans, manioc and sweet potatoes, which will enable them to sell their millet and maize in order to procure the cash needed to pay their debts and taxes.' Crop failures along the Senegal River are also noted because, as well as directly affecting the inhabitants' ability to pay taxes, they lead to increased seasonal labour migration to the groundnut-growing areas of Senegal; while acceptable in itself, this causes administrative anxiety because the migrants may elude taxation.

In periods of crisis in the groundnut trade, however, as during World War I and again in the early 1930s, the records display a sudden awareness of the fact that 'groundnut cultivation has done harm to subsistence farming; millet is having to be supplied (from outside the groundnut areas)'. The endurance of subsistence farming in the Senegal River Valley, is consequently seen to have advantages: 'This year [1917], the River will be able to supply the requirements of *cercles* [districts] less rich in sorghum.' (Sorghum is a floodland crop along the River.)[2] During the 1930 crisis, the *rapport économique* for Senegal stresses the dangers of a one-crop economy and the need to encourage *cultures vivrières* [food crops], then notes with relief: 'At any rate, no such measures will be necessary in the River *cercles* . . . In this region, the difficulty of evacuating groundnuts has kept subsistence crops in constant favour. Furthermore, a fortunate peculiarity of the region is that its inhabitants can grow an additional yearly crop on land flooded when the river overflows its banks.' In 1932, an abundant grain crop 'will help compensate for the collapse of the groundnut market'.

This intermittent rediscovery by the French colonial administration, in periods of crisis, of the Senegal River's potential for agriculture, never led to any suggestion that its people might be systematically encouraged to produce a constant surplus of grain to supply the groundnut-growing areas. There is no mention, for instance, of the possibility of organizing a marketing system for millet, sorghum or maize, as an alternative to importing rice from Indochina. There is, indeed, a marked inability to connect awareness of the groundnut areas' growing food deficit, with awareness of the plight of the 'marginal' grain-producing areas, where lack of a local cash-earning outlet for surplus production forced farmers to seek work elsewhere, so that food production steadily regressed there too, year by year. In the same year (1936) one administrative report deplores that Senegal should be 'dangerously dependent upon outside sources for its natives' food', while another deplores that Soudan should still be predominantly a subsistence economy, with trade confined to the colony itself and neighbouring territories, for 'Soudan, like the other colonies, has a duty to develop trade with the outside, and in particular to supply the Métropole with raw materials'. Subsistence agriculture was a convenient safety-net; but to invest in local food production was quite simply unthinkable. Whenever the notion of increased grain production is evoked, the end in view is always its potential use in France. Thus in 1916, there is a note to the effect that a good harvest had made it possible for Senegal to export 5,000 tons of sorghum for use as fodder by the French cavalry. In 1920, it was suggested that increased millet production could be exported to feed cattle in France, thus enabling French farmers to devote more of their energies to producing wheat. A canny early explorer of the economic potential of the Western Sudan, had already suggested that the Senegal River Valley could best be used for growing millet and maize ... to transform into alcohol. (Bailland, 1902: 23.)

With that order of priorities, there was no particular need to restrict the search for likely export crops to those already grown as food crops; there was no necessary connection between the *ad hoc* short-term usefulness of the Valley as supplier of surplus grain or surplus labour, and the possible long-term role of the Senegal River as an asset of French colonial strategy. The potential of the Senegal River for hydro-agricultural development on a large scale, is a recurrent theme of administrative reports. Several missions were sent to explore the possibility of reviving Baron Roger's old dream; they all confirmed that, in the words of a 1910 report, 'the Senegal River is an immense reservoir, well able to supply the quantities of water needed to irrigate large surfaces'. The World War I crisis, and the attendant fears that groundnuts might not be a viable export crop, caused schemes for the *mise en valeur* [exploitation] of the Senegal River to be given serious consideration. But the groundnut economy recovered during the 1920s, and the Dakar–Niger rail link was completed. In 1929, Governor-General Roume announced that the Niger was more suitable for large-scale irrigation than the Senegal; in 1932, the Office du Niger was instituted to conduct a massive cotton-growing scheme. In the 1930s, economic crisis revived interest in the Senegal River, in a minor key; the Mission d'Aménagement du Sénégal, set up in 1938, was not to become active until after the war.

An article by A. Minot (1934; 387–388) gives a particularly clear account of colonial attitudes towards the Senegal River Valley between the wars, and is worth quoting at some length:

It may be stated that at the time of the war, the river was no longer an immediate preoccupation of the colonial administration.

For a long time, only its role as a navigable waterway had been considered. Mazeran, in his report, had made a few suggestions about irrigation, and Hardel had said a few words on the same topic. The idea did not catch on, because it bore no relation to current interests: the country's activities were centred upon groundnut cultivation, which spread to new areas as the railway line was extended.

At the beginning of the war, however, interest shifted slightly, and Younès and Yves Henry were sent to look at the area of the Lac de Guiers. Later, especially after the end of the war, this move was intensified. The métropole's needs were growing, and its energies were being channelled first into war industries, then into the reconstruction of devastated regions; its sinking currency caused growing fears of foreign economic domination. All this led governments to try and use the colonies to bolster national production; and the agricultural potential of the Senegal Valley began to arouse active interest.

However, the administration's initial efforts were directed towards the Niger Valley, more densely populated, with a better labour supply. Senegal's activities were centred upon groundnuts. This crop, which could be sold for sterling whereas the necessities of life were paid for in francs, was indirectly favoured by the exchange-rate battle, and trade in groundnuts grew considerably. This meant that its collapse was all the more brutal, and the world crisis had an even more disruptive effect on the life of the country. This has caused acute awareness of the need to develop Senegal's resources in various ways, and has made the problem of the *mise en valeur* of the River Valley more topical than ever.

After outlining the technical specifications of engineering work suggested by previous studies of the river, he concludes:

> It must be pointed out that the problem of *mise en valeur* of the lower Senegal Valley, needs to be seen in agricultural and demographic terms. In the river's natural state, water supplies are available and can be put to use by technicians and engineers. The first question to ask, is what crops are possible and desirable. Is there a suitable plant which could be sold in Europe, while leaving the farmer in Senegal a reasonable profit? Is there an equivalent for the clay soils of the River Valley, which can be irrigated with a bit of effort, of what the groundnut has been for the sandy soils of Cayor, of Baol, of Sine?

This statement is interesting, not only for what it clearly states, but for what it implicitly assumes: that the Niger Valley was more suitable than the Senegal from the point of view of labour available, and that *mise en valeur* of the Senegal Valley would naturally focus on the lower reaches of the river. In fact, it was not true that the Niger offered better supplies of labour; the history of the Office du Niger is one of systematic recruitment of forced labour from outside the area of the scheme. The Senegal River Valley is densely populated on its upper and middle reaches, but the Lower Valley is thinly populated. The choice of the Niger by the colonial administration may have been prompted by considerations transcending demography, rather like the considerations which caused Baron Roger's short-lived plantation scheme to be located in the lower Senegal: the presence, in the Middle Valley, of an active, well-entrenched population with a highly developed land tenure system. In 1919, the archives note that 'the regions where irrigation would be feasible, are precisely those where the land belongs to the natives, who will never consent to give it up'. In 1923, a mission was sent to ascertain what land in the Middle Valley was free of customary tenure, and whether any other land might by some device be made over to European agricultural enterprises. And in 1935, when the River Valley was again of interest, three detailed studies of land tenure in Futa Toro were published (Gaden; Vidal; Kane; 1935). Thus the enduring relative prosperity of African agriculture in the Senegal Valley may have deflected colonial interest towards the Niger, where such impediments did not exist; and may have directed colonial interest in the Senegal itself, towards the sparsely populated Lower Valley. Outlining the background to the post-war activities of the Mission d'Aménagement du Sénégal, Lucien Papy (1954) writes, 'The presence of populations attached to their techniques, their customs, their property rights, was a barrier to undertaking large-scale agricultural projects; all hopes were therefore placed upon the Niger Valley, a new, thinly-populated zone . . .' He also writes that whereas in Futa Toro, the land has been used for centuries by a peasant population, in the Lower Valley and especially the Delta 'there is ample scope for experimenting with modern European techniques'.

Since the war

After the war, which had starkly revealed the extent of Senegal's dependence on imported rice, the colonial administration focused renewed attention upon the Senegal River, more specifically, upon the Delta. At Richard-Toll, where the first attempt at a colonial plantation had been made 125 years before, the Mission d'Aménagement du Sénégal (MAS) determined to establish rice cultivation on a large scale. An experimental 120-hectare plot was established in 1946; by 1949, work had begun on a 6,000-hectare scheme. This project did not involve the population of the Valley. It was located in a thinly populated area: 1 to 5 inhabitants per square kilometre, as against an average density of 32 for the Valley as a whole, according to 1951 estimates. Cultivation was highly mechanized, on the American model, and required very little manpower: 18 workers per 100 hectares at peak periods. A small area (330 hectares) of the project's land was made available, under pressure, to Senegalese settlers, who were to hire farm machinery and services from MAS; but this came to nothing. As an experiment in new methods of rice cultivation, the scheme was a mitigated success: the area under cultivation expanded fourfold, from 1,335 to 5,400 hectares, between 1953 and 1960, although average yields receded; average yearly production was 15,000 tons, one-tenth of Senegal's consumption. Financially, it was an unmitigated failure: the scheme cost a total of 2,700 million CFA Francs,[3] and a State subsidy was needed every year to cover deficits ranging from 8 to 50 million CFA.

After Independence, Richard-Toll was entrusted between 1961 and 1965 to the Government-run Société de Développement Rizicole du Sénégal, while the Organisation Autonome du Delta (OAD) was entrusted with the remainder of the Delta. In 1965, it was decided to renew the attempt at rice-growing on a large scale: 30,000 hectares of the Delta were to be brought under cultivation within a period of ten years, through a combination of mechanization and planned settlement. A new organization was created, replacing both SDRS and OAD, to handle the manifold tasks involved: the Société d'Aménagement et d'Exploitation des Terres du Delta du Fleuve Sénégal (SAED), described as a *Société d'Etat à caractère industriel et commercial* [Industrial and Commercial State Enterprise]. Peasant farmers were to grow the rice, on land made over to SAED by the State and distributed through cooperatives, but SAED would exercise close supervision, providing seed and fertilizer, hiring out machinery and marketing the crop; SAED itself would be accountable to the Ministry of Rural Economy.

As the area of the project was peopled largely by nomadic Fulani herdsmen, with only one sedentary village, population was to be shifted to the area from outside. The plan was to have 9,000 families settled in the area by the time the entire 30,000 hectares had been brought under cultivation. Six new villages were built between 1964 and 1967, and peopled by retired soldiers, immigrants from the Middle Valley, and a high proportion of people from villages on the bank of the lower Senegal. Plans proceeded at the intended pace until 1967; about 20,000 people moved to the project, and there were 29 cooperatives, with 4,436 members. Difficulties had arisen, however, even before the disastrous season of 1968, when

8,000 hectares yielded only 500 tons of rice. The terrain itself presented certain difficulties. 19,000 of the planned 30,000 hectares were found to be too salty to be used. A substantial part of the remaining land had been brought under cultivation, but crop losses were heavy, averaging 30 per cent, because of the technique of flooding unlevelled ground, which gave only limited control over the supply of water. After the 1968 crop failure, due to lack of water, SAED began to install pumping stations and improve the irrigation network; but it also called a halt to further settlement of the Delta. The settlement scheme had also presented certain difficulties.

The decision to aim for rapid extension of large-scale rice cultivation, meant intensive mechanization and heavy investment in the hydro-agricultural infrastructure; in other words, SAED intervention on a massive scale. The work which could be done by untrained peasants amounted to very little: sowing and threshing, only 40 days or so a year. SAED did the rest. SAED built and maintained houses, roads and irrigation works; this was not charged to the peasants. Fertilizer, seed and hired machinery were provided on credit to the individual peasant farmer, whose work was closely supervised by SAED personnel: an engineer for every 1,500 hectares, a technician for every 400 hectares, and for every 100 hectares, an *encadreur de base* [sort of extension worker] to supervise the day-to-day organization of work. Obtaining credit, purchasing supplies, marketing produce, reimbursing debts – all these activities were channelled through SAED.

The high cost of SAED services, the peasant farmers' low productivity, and their tendency, in the absence of subsistence crops, to consume much of their harvest themselves, combined with technical difficulties to draw the peasants ever deeper into debt. The year's debts often exceeded the cash value of the year's produce, and debts accumulated from one year to the next; at the end of the 1969–70 season, unpaid debts averaged 20,000 CFA Francs[4] per hectare. A French company specialized in advising on the diffusion of agricultural techniques, the Société d'Aide Technique et de Coopération (SATEC) was called in as early as 1967; in the circumstances, it proved difficult to improve peasant productivity.

The role imparted [to] the cooperatives was negligible. Like their counterparts in the groundnut-growing areas of Senegal, they were essentially administrative devices for marketing and credit allocation; unlike the groundnut cooperatives, which might be based in established peasant communities, the Delta cooperatives were based in new or displaced villages, with no communal landholdings, and had no contractual rights on the land parcelled out among their members. Accounts were kept by SAED. The members of the cooperatives had little in common. A SATEC report remarks that 'positive factors exist only where village organization provides some basis for solidarity: when the shift to the Delta involved an entire village, or when a new village is populated by retired soldiers'. After 1968, peasants left the Delta in increasing numbers, either returning to their former homes, or seeking work in towns. SAED suspended plans for bringing further surfaces under cultivation.

A report on SAED (Rodts, 1971) comes to this conclusion:

SAED's main object in the Delta was to reduce Senegal's food deficit. The aim, therefore, was increased production. But this aim was to be achieved under satisfactory economic and social conditions, among which one may cite the following:

- financial equilibrium at SAED level;
- financial equilibrium at cooperative level;
- self-management of SAED and cooperatives;
- regionalization of the developmental process.

At the present time, it may be said that none of these goals have been achieved. As long as all efforts are concentrated upon rice cultivation, which affords peasants only two or three months' employment a year, rather than agricultural activity as a whole, it will be impossible to integrate peasants into a progressive monetary economy. They will remain SAED sharecroppers; but temporary sharecroppers.

From 1972, while attempting to consolidate activities in the Delta by improving irrigation systems and dividing large cooperatives into small *groupements producteurs* [producer groups] of 15 to 20 members, SAED has sought to extend its operation to the more densely populated areas upstream, where heavy mechanization and settlement schemes would not be appropriate. Here, a larger proportion of the work would be done by the peasants already living in the area, trained through small-scale experimental plots, *petits périmètres*, which would rapidly be expanded into *grands périmètres*. SAED control would cover the same range as in the Delta: allocating credit; providing seed, fertilizer, fuel and machinery, technical supervision; crop marketing. There would be some diversification of crops.

At Dagana and Nianga, in the Lower Valley, work began in 1973–74. At Dagana, 200 hectares were being farmed in 1975: 160 hectares of tomatoes, 30 of wheat. The Nianga project was expected to have 810 hectares under cultivation by October 1975, involving five villages, over 4,000 people; this was later to be extended to a *grand périmètre* involving 32 villages and over 8,000 people. In 1975, SAED activities moved even further upstream: to Matam, in the Middle Valley, where there had been no previous attempt to introduce new crops or techniques. Since Independence, the valley upstream from the Delta had been under the nominal control of the Organisation Autonome de la Vallée, which had undertaken a few small pilot-projects, notably at Guédé; at Matam, there was only the recently-established FAO research station.

Rice-growing at Matam began on a very small scale. An expatriate SATEC agent, whose original brief had been to improve sorghum production, set up three *petits périmètres*, 25 hectares in all. People were recruited locally, in Matam and neighbouring villages – Diamel, Tigueré, Nabadji – where farmers were in distress because of drought: about 150 in all. They were given food, and lent picks and spades; they cleared land for the project, built irrigation canals, then were each allocated a small individual plot of land within the *périmètre*. After the rice, peasants were encouraged to grow wheat; as they could not process this for consumption themselves, they would have to sell it, thus obtaining cash which could be used to cover the costs of irrigating the rice-fields. It was planned to extend operations in the Matam area; both by multiplying *petits périmètres*, and by undertaking larger schemes, 200 hectares or so. This would presumably mean a reinforcement of SAED organizational control, hitherto more notional than real; all the more so, as SAED was since December 1974 officially in charge of all agricultural development projects along Senegal's stretch of the left bank of the river, from Saint-Louis, where SAED headquarters are, to the Mali border. By then, SAED was already moving further upstream: to the Bakel area, where they met with some unexpected difficulties.

Peasant initiative in the Bakel area

The shift of interest towards the groundnut trade, affected the Senegal River Valley as a whole. It might be said, however, that Soninke country, the historic state of Gajaaga, which had been at the centre of the river-borne trade in the 18th and early 19th century, has become the most marginal area of all. The Tukulor of Futa Toro remain a presence on the Senegalese scene, whether as local notables, religious leaders, or, increasingly, city-dwellers; Futa Toro stagnates, land remains untilled, but there is a road from Matam to Dakar, and by now roughly 100,000 Tukulor, one in three, live in Dakar or other urban centres of Senegal. The Soninke refer to Senegal as to a foreign country. Divided between three colonial territories – now 30,000 or so in Senegal, the same in Mauritania, 300,000 in Mali – and peripheral to the main interests of all three administrations, left stranded by the ebb of the European trade to which they had so thoroughly and successfully adapted, they too took to temporary migration in search of cash earnings. Typical Soninke labour migration has been long-distance, international migration. Soninke have worked as stokers and stewards in the French navy and merchant marine, as petty traders in all the countries of West Africa; but the recourse to temporary migration has always been superimposed upon a relatively stable system of subsistence agriculture. Migrants supported their families at home; and they always returned home in the end. Since the early 1960s, the loss of earlier employment opportunities, as shipping declined and newly independent nation-States sought to reserve the petty trading sector for their own nationals, combined with French demand for a new source of cheap labour to replace Algeria, redirected Soninke labour migration towards France. More and more men travelled to France, living in communal hostels, working as sweepers, as dustmen or in factories, sending money home and returning home every three years or so, often to leave once more. In most of the riverside villages near Bakel, almost half the men of working age, and almost all the young men, are away. These massive departures, combined with the severe drought of recent years, have weakened the fabric of subsistence farming. In recent years, money sent home has been used to buy millet; and even, now that the rains have returned, to hire agricultural labourers from outside the area. Older men had derived pride from the feeling that whatever happened, they could feed their families as they had always done: tilling their fields with the *daba* or short-handled hoe, sowing millet, waiting for rain; and growing sorghum, maize, sweet potatoes and beans as a second crop, as the river receded from flooded ground. They express some confidence that things could return to normal; but sometimes recognize the possibility that labour migration, which in the past acted to compensate imbalance and preserve a kind of equilibrium at home, has now become increasingly difficult, and is doing harm to the society it was intended to preserve. One old man said:

> The young people should stay here to work, but there's no way of paying the tax; we have to let them go, so that they can send money for taxes and food. Now they're having trouble ... We old men are here in the village, powerless; we let the young men go, to get something to live on, but they can't manage now. We have nothing. The village will die. The country will die.

In recent years, some people in the Bakel area began to think of a possible way out of this cycle: not permanent emigration, which for most Soninke is unthink-

able, but returning to the land, making it more productive, growing new things.
It all started in the early 60s, when a man from Jamaane, a large village on the
river-bank upstream from Bakel, returned there after 25 years as a cook in the
French navy and merchant marine, to find that things had not changed; there was
still no way of obtaining locally the cash needed to supplement subsistence farming. Yet the soil was good; would it not be possible to develop its resources, to
grow new crops as well as the old, to use oxen for ploughing? He had seen what
was done in other countries. The thought remained with him, until finally, in the
late 60s, he went to Paris to find work, as many others were doing, but with a
central aim in view: to acquire some means of improving farming at home. When
he returned home, in early 1973, he brought with him a cultivator and a small
pump; but he also brought the promise of an agricultural technician for the area.
He had discussed his ideas with people he had met in Paris, in particular with an
engineer who had worked in Africa and elsewhere, and who knew of an organization called the Compagnie Internationale de Développement Rural (CIDR), which
trained personnel for work on small-scale agricultural projects in Third World
countries, funded by international relief agencies. CIDR was contacted, and set
things in motion by writing to the député of Bakel. Back in Jamaane, people were
non-committal. 'They said, Would we be working for ourselves, or for
Europeans? And I said, For ourselves; it's called development. Then they said,
We'll see when he gets here.'
     In March 1974, the technician arrived; a Frenchman, who had worked in South
America before. His salary was to be paid by two British charities; he was to help
the villages along the river, in the vicinity of Bakel, to improve the productivity of
traditional crops and try out market gardening. He stressed that this was to be a
collective undertaking, for the people themselves; that he had come to the area as a
result of their fellow-villager's initiative, to help people work for themselves, not
for him. At the first village meeting, only 40 came forward. A plot of land near the
river was chosen for the *champ collectif* [collective field]. The group fenced the
one-hectare plot and dug a well; this was done by May 1974. Another meeting was
held, to urge village people to give more support to the undertaking. 'Old people,'
I said, 'you have travelled a great deal, you have lived a long time. Travel makes
people clever. I wish you would help with this development, since you know what
it is. If you don't help, that means you want the country to remain undeveloped
forever.' The old people said, 'Yes, you're right, we'll help you; in three years,
we'll think again.'
     By the time the well had been dug, the rains were near; so the first crops grown
on the Jamaane *champ collectif* were millet and maize. These were sold locally, to
provide the group's first working funds; and tomatoes, lettuce and onions were
grown, for the first time in the village, with some measure of success.
     It seems that the hardest task, in that first year, was to convince the people of the
river-bank villages that it was both possible and desirable for them to undertake
agricultural improvements on a collective basis. More people in Jamaane joined
the initial group; by early 1975, it had 270 members, 200 men and 70 women, and
had organized as an association, designating as chairman the man who had started
the group. Soon after the French technician's arrival, he and the Jamaane chairman had visited neighbouring villages to explain what was planned and encourage
them to take part. The villages of Gabou, Gougnian and Aroundou grew vegetables the first year, as did people in Bakel, the nearby administrative centre.
Other villages came to agree in principle, although they did not become active
until 1975, when most of them grew collective fields of millet. By mid-1975,

groups had been formed in all the villages along the river, from Balou, near the Mali border, to Moudéri. The villagers had been somewhat wary of the plan at the outset; but it was presented to them by someone they knew and trusted, and came to seem something they themselves could control. Wariness turned to hope, in some cases to enthusiasm.

Was it local civil servants, the *fonctionnaires* of Bakel, who first drew official attention to these new developments? Was it the French technician, eager to acquire new means for 'his' development project, who sought to consolidate his position in order to be able to obtain aid more readily? Did the authorities then bring pressure to bear upon him, to integrate his project with their plans? Probably a combination of all three. At all events the technician went to Saint-Louis to consult SAED. Shortly thereafter, on 13 December 1974, the Minister of Rural Development visited the Bakel area, accompanied by the Director of SAED. The French technician made a speech on that occasion in which he stated that the purpose of his work in the region was 'the technical and moral preparation of the population for the great task of *aménagement* [making the land fit for irrigation] of the Senegal Valley'; that 'CIDR was working in close collaboration with national agencies like SAED'; and that in the near future, the area's basic crop would be rice. He soon left Jamaane and went to live in Bakel. In January 1975, a team from USAID came to visit the area and inspect work already done by the villagers; as a result, USAID made a grant of 14 million CFA Francs (US$60,000)[5] for the purchase of equipment requested by the technician: essentially motor-pumps and other material for motorized irrigation. The question then arose, How was this aid to be channelled? The technician and the chairman of the Jamaane association travelled together to Saint-Louis; the peasant leader was left waiting outside, while the technician met with SAED officials and *fonctionnaires* from Bakel.

In mid-March 1975, the technician came to Jamaane, to explain that it would be necessary to place the village associations under the aegis of SAED, in order to take delivery of the machines promised by USAID. There would be no harm in doing so, he said. He did not bring up the points he had made in his speech to the Minister of Rural Development. When he left, the *responsables* [leaders] of the Jamaane association – the chairman and other officers, the heads of the six men's work teams – discussed what he had said. It was clear that they regarded this new step as contrary to the basis upon which collective agriculture had been set up in the villages; the peasant associations were to be free and independent, geared to the needs of local communities. They said that if outside aid were conditional upon subordination to outside control of any kind, they would do without outside aid, and continue with collective fields of millet and maize, until they had saved enough to acquire by themselves whatever equipment they might need. A few days later, the technician returned for another meeting, to explain that the peasants could make use of SAED, without risk to their autonomy. The connection with SAED, the nature of which he did not specify, would be a mere formality, to comply with Senegalese legislation prohibiting a non-citizen like himself from receiving foreign aid funds. The *responsables* once more stated their unwillingness to accept the idea of administrative subordination to SAED; they refused to be co-opted on the pretext of aid transfers. They had been working hard for a year now, on their own. SAED had never been heard of before in the region. Let SAED make contact with them directly; weren't they Senegalese citizens?

The result was a series of meetings involving peasant associations and personnel from SAED, which took place in Jamaane and in other villages; the Jamaane meetings can stand for all. The first was the meeting which has already been described; it took place at the end of April. That meeting's failure to achieve any agreement, was attributed by the authorities to a 'misunderstanding'. On 2 May, the Préfet of the *département de Bakel* visited Jamaane to express strong displeasure at the peasants' mistrust of the authorities' plans. He was listened to politely; then the same arguments as before were stated.

On 15 May 1975, another SAED delegation, higher-ranking than the previous one, arrived in Jamaane to hold another meeting. The tone was less urbane, more explicit than at the previous meeting. In Senegal, the visitors announced, all official decisions were to be shared by *la base* [i.e. the producers]. The programme for Bakel had been decided by the government; however, *le Sénégal, c'est le dialogue* [i.e. 'in Senegal, we believe in dialogue']. Just as no Muslim could be a good Muslim without knowing God's law, no peasant could be expected to accept SAED without first knowing about it. At the base, knowledge must start with elementary things. We will tell you about cooperatives and how they function; solidarity, of course, is an African tradition. Their cooperatives would be provided with *personnel d'encadrement* [extension workers]. In the Delta, the population had made an effort to learn; with the help of their SAED supervisors; they had one for every 30 or 40 peasants. People were even learning to read in their own language. Peasants in the Bakel area could learn to read in Soninke; the textbooks were ready. 'We are all one family. Our development is one and the same. I have spoken to you as a Muslim. May God help you to understand what I have said.'

The peasants answered this, in terms they had already used at previous meetings. A speaker told once again how their *développement* had started, stressing the part played by their chairman. They had begun work before ever hearing of SAED interest in the area, and from what they had heard of SAED's activities in the Delta, it seemed that SAED-run cooperatives were not free to choose what crops they wanted to grow, and had to organize their work according to SAED specifications, which meant contracting debts for equipment, and having to grow more and more cash-crops; this was also the plight of peasants in the cooperatives of the groundnut areas. The chairman of the village association repeated that they did not reject mechanization and technical advice as such; they merely wanted to control its use themselves, not commit themselves to wholesale acceptance of plans dictated from outside. A local government official suggested that this amounted to being against the Government; the village chairman became angry at this, and spoke in anger, denying the accusation. He was rebuked by another member of the official delegation, a man half his age, who stated that without Government control, there could be no development. If the chairman of the village association had been to France, it was because the Government had enabled him to do so. 'I advise you to work hand in hand with the administration.' Once more, the French technician remained silent.

A few days later, the CIDR team (the initial technician having been joined by two assistants) were informed that they were henceforth to consider themselves SAED agents, and implement SAED directives; the village agricultural associations were to become cooperatives on the SAED model, so that their activities could be more closely supervised by SAED. The peasants, they were told, were not *mûrs pour le dialogue* ['mature enough for dialogue']. It was suggested that they had fomented opposition to government plans among the peasants. Surfaces had been mapped out, and norms established, for expanded rice production in the vicinity of Bakel; the technicians accepted this as a *fait accompli*.

The Jamaane association received yet another visit from SAED: the Director himself came, to assure them that they would not be forced to do anything against their will. The matter rested there as far as the peasants were concerned; the rains were near, and in addition to their own millet-fields, they were preparing to grow rice for the first time, on a 4-hectare field where they had dug irrigation canals. They would be using a motor-pump they had received as part of USAID's initial grant. Balou, and of course Bakel, would also be growing rice.

The confrontation between the peasants and SAED was revived a few months later in muted form, as a confrontation between village associations and Bakel. The Bakel association had always differed from the others, in that while members of the village associations were peasants who did the work that needed to be done with their own hands, many of the members of the Bakel association, 25 out of 70 at one stage, were local civil servants who hired others to do the work for them. Village members felt that this was not right, and suspected that the Bakel civil servants might have been partly responsible for SAED's attempts to impose its own methods on the area; would it not have meant new jobs, and a chance to exercise new influence, in an area where Government presence had previously been tenuous and restricted to Bakel? This latent opposition flared into open conflict, as a result of events associated with the visit to Bakel of civic representatives of the town of Apt, in the South of France. This visit took place towards the end of July, and was intended to explore the possibility of twinning the two towns. Some local civil servants, members of the Bakel agricultural association, made contact with the Apt delegation on their own account; and two of them accepted the offer of a round-trip ticket to France. They also composed a circular letter dated 28 July 1975, addressed to migrant workers from the *département* of Bakel residing in France. This letter, written in a somewhat high-flown style, praised the migrant workers for their efforts to keep their village alive, but suggested these efforts were misdirected. Rather than continue to remit money to their villages, where it would at best keep things as they were, and at worst, who knows, be embezzled, they should invest their earnings in a series of projects hazily outlined in the letter – hotels to develop tourism in the Bakel area, local industries ... The present development which made such hopes possible was, of course, the emergence of agricultural development plans in the area, this was ascribed to government interest. The three motor-pumps newly installed in the area, were cited as 'a gracious gift from the Senegalese Government, whose constant solicitude towards our peasants no longer needs proof'. To this document were appended the names of the heads of the village associations. When they became aware of the contents of the letter, the village associations took exception to what they regarded as a breach of trust, compounding their grievances against Bakel. The villages upstream from Bakel threatened to cut themselves off from Bakel; whereupon peasant women in the Bakel association announced that in that case, they would no longer work in the Bakel field, but would walk to Jamaane and work with the association there. The matter was smoothed over somehow; but there remained a feeling that the position of the Bakel group, at least that of some of its members, was not straight-forward.

In September 1975, representatives of one of the funding agencies which had from the beginning provided financial support for the French technician's acti-vities visited the Bakel area. They had become increasingly uneasy about the prospect of SAED assuming control of the village agricultural associations, and more specifically about the role imparted [to] the CIDR team in this move. They learned that USAID was to grant the Senegalese Government US$3.1 million to be used to finance the extension of rice cultivation in the Bakel area. In the first instance, 15 *petits périmètres*, totalling 1,320 hectares, were to be brought under cultivation in the river-bank villages, by cooperatives working under SAED supervision and control. USAID would provide, through this grant, the equipment needed to install and maintain surface irrigation systems: pumps, bulldozers, tractors, trucks. This project was seen as the nucleus for later larger-scale *périmètres*, totalling 2,000 hectares, to be implemented as soon as possible. The CIDR team would be useful, in this perspective, in grafting the SAED type of structure onto existing collective work groups. (The CIDR team had known about the USAID plan for some time; bemused by its scale, they tended to regard it as probably destructive, but inevitable. Peasant association leaders knew scarcely anything about it.)

These matters were discussed at length with the technicians and with representatives of the village associations, in particular the chairman of the Jamaane association. The funding agency representatives expressed their disquiet, and suggested that the CIDR team revert to the objectives of the original project. Peasant leaders hoped that this would be possible, as the technicians, however discredited, still constituted their only source of information and advice; shortly thereafter, however, it appeared to the funding agency that the CIDR team would not be able to do this, and they terminated their financial support for the technicians, considering it inappropriate to finance SAED's agents. Subsequently, USAID agreed to make funds available for the salary of the first-arrived French technician, now officially designated as head of the 'Bakel project', and his assistants.

On 15 January 1976, representatives of all the village associations met in Bakel. Several matters were discussed, including the letter circulated in France by the Bakel civil servants, and the recent distribution of relief grain supplies, which the peasants felt had been inequitably handled by the CIDR technicians. The main subject, however, was the need to create a formally instituted federation of village associations, to ensure solidarity between villages and the coordination of work. The matter had arisen the previous summer, when the matter of the circular letter had caused dissent between groups; the January meeting decided that statutes of the Fédération des Paysans Organisés en Zone Soninké de Bakel should be drawn up on the basis of drafts submitted by the Jamaane and Bakel associations. This document was later drawn up; it laid down detailed regulations governing the operations of the Fédération, designed to ensure regular consultation and exchange of information, joint planning of work, and open discussion of any conflicts which might arise, while maintaining the discipline needed for the association to present a common front. The document sought to define clearly the form of future relations between the Fédération and SAED; crucial sections in this respect are III, IV and V. Chapter III states that the Fédération and its constituent associations intend to manage their own administrative and financial affairs, 'in accordance with the spirit of the reform of local government in Senegal'; while accepting the principle of technical assistance from SAED when needed, they reserve the right to obtain supplies from another source if it proved advantageous to do so, and to market their produce likewise. SAED cannot require the associations to contract debts. Chapter IV asserts the Fédération's right to accept help from development agencies other than SAED. Chapter V declares the non-political nature of the Fédération. It was intended to submit the statutes of the Fédération's existence. The peasants continued work. Jamaane, and the other villages which had grown rice, harvested their first crop. The French technician came to collect the money owed SAED for fuel and fertilizer. These villages, and several others, planned to grow more rice in the coming season; but they worried about costs. It seemed unlikely that they would receive any outside technical assistance or material aid; USAID's equipment was for SAED, not for them. The Fédération was determined to continue as before; but the future seemed uncertain. In April 1976, the chairman of the Jamaane association summed up the position:

We, the peasants of the Senegal River, have formed an association to try and develop our country, which has never been developed. We all agreed to begin working together, with our *daba* and our hands. The first year, our technician came to live in my house, and we all agreed on the work to be done. Our brothers, our children, have all vanished to work elsewhere. If the country were developed, we could work for ourselves.

Our technician came from Paris to live here. Nine months later, SAED came to him and said, 'Now we're going to organize you.' I said, 'What do you mean, organize *(encadrer)*? Four hundred people in one town all working together, that's organization for you. That's what I call development: free, independent, peasants working together. Since SAED is available, if we want something on credit, we'll ask you for it; if we want to buy something, we'll ask you for it. Apart from that, just let us work independently.' We discussed that a great deal, last year. This year, too, the SAED technicians are in Bakel, saying they'll help us; but the peasants still have the same way of thinking.

Last year, two towns grew rice; one grew four hectares, the other ten. This year, several of them are growing five, six, seven hectares. The season before, after the rice we in Jamaane grew maize, and it did well; we grew tomatoes, and they did well too. Up to now, all of us, men and women, are determined to work independently. I think we have the heart for it. If this peasant development continues, it will be good for the people of the River. If there's too much SAED development, it will be bad for us; we'll have to give up. But if the peasants themselves benefit from their own work, we'll continue. That's certain. That's what we want.

We're not against SAED. But we've seen how SAED tells peasants nothing, and gets them into debt. Early in the season, they tell you 'Look, you need so much fertilizer, so much this, so much that'. At the end of the season, they say, 'Now you owe me 400,000, 500,000 francs.'[6] Even if the peasant sells all his crop, he can't earn that amount; he's left with debts. The following year, a determined man thinks, 'I'll pay off those debts.' He takes the same fertilizer, hires machinery, and so on: that year too, he has 400,000 worth of debts. So the peasant is always in debt. A man like that is not free. In the end, all he wants is to be released from debt and forget about development. That's what we're against.

SAED doesn't make anyone any presents. SAED makes profit out of peasants, and makes them incur debts. So if people farm 20 or 30 hectares, they'll be 500,000 francs in debt. On 20 hectares there'll be 400 people working. SAED gets 500,000 francs; and what of the man who does the work, and all the people in his household, 10 or 20 people? Will he be able to make ends meet? No. He can't possibly manage. So people give up. If SAED takes over development on the Senegal River, people who understand things will stop taking part. Then development will have failed. This first year, we grew four hectares, and we owed 174,000 francs for fertilizer and fuel; at that rate, if we have 20 hectares, we'll owe 500,000 francs. That's what we have against SAED. We don't reject SAED; we want to be free to say what we want to buy, and to keep our own accounts. We don't need much fertilizer, because the soil is good. It's not old soil. SAED would say, take 20 sacks, 30 sacks – then we're in debt. We don't want that.

SAED works for SAED, not for the peasants. All the Senegal River peasants know that. We've seen what goes on in Matam. So we want to work as free independent peasants; even if we earn only a little, it will be our own. If peasants can't profit by their own work, then they can just continue with their own farming, as before. Our grandfathers made a living out of farming; so long as we have our *daba*, no one need be in want. Now we hoped to have something more; by working together, for ourselves. What little we get is for ourselves. This year we had 10 tons of rice; we sold it in the town, at 50 francs a kilo, and everyone was pleased. If we had sent it off to SAED, we would have had nothing.

So, we know about SAED, SAED is the government; and we are the peasants. We are here. SAED exists; but the peasants have to exist as well. We have to live, like the rest of the world. Our development is based on that idea. If that is set aside, development will be worthless.

Future prospects

'*Développement de fonctionnaires*' or '*développement paysan*'

At the meeting with which this paper opens, peasants and SAED officials were unable to come to terms, because each group held different and incompatible views about what constituted 'development'. For the SAED delegation, there was only one kind of development, defined in terms of technological innovation. Modernization therefore imposed its own objective constraints; once the peasants had chosen progress, there could be no sound reason for them to reject the production techniques and styles of organization which progress required. For the leaders of the peasant association, on the other hand, there were two kinds of development, two ways of bringing agricultural change to the area; the choice was not between innovation and stagnation, but between change evolved from within, and change imposed from without. They had organized on their own, and had shown themselves capable of adapting to new crops and new techniques: that was *développement paysan*. The SAED takeover, they felt, could not be justified in objective terms; its purpose was to deprive them of the freedom to control their own productive activity and its fruits, and make them work for outside interests rather than for the good of their own community. That was *développement de fonctionnaires*. The SAED officials often spoke in terms of national interest, one and undivided; but the peasants saw no necessary fit between their interests and those of officialdom. The evidence available suggests that the peasants' view of the situation is nearer the truth.

The type of development which SAED has sought to promote in the Senegal River Valley, is directly related to the earlier initiatives described above. It shares their reliance on capital-intensive techniques and large-scale irrigation schemes for cash-crop production; it also shares their indifference to the people of the area, their wishes and needs. The only difference is one of scope, not of perspective. Whereas previous ventures confined plans for systematic direct exploitation to the Delta, leaving the Middle and Upper Valley to be exploited directly as an intermittent source of surplus millet and constant source of labour, SAED's most recent ventures are designed to extend direct exploitation of labour to the more populous areas of the Valley. Baron Roger was in no position to compel the people of the Valley to work on his plantations. Direct colonial exploitation, after a period of vacillation, bypassed the Senegal River in favour of the Niger, where a vast irrigated cotton scheme was worked by Mossi forced labour. In the colonial powers' post-World War II rush to be seen to develop their territories, such techniques were out of the question; MAS's efforts to turn the Delta into a major rice-producing area treated it as virgin land, using intensive mechanization. When SAED inherited the Delta, it had recourse to the formula of *colonat paysan* [war veterans who colonized the Delta through a government scheme], in the hope that it would prove more economical as well as politically more acceptable. This was not the case; given the initial decision to grow rice on a large scale, bringing 3,000 additional hectares under cultivation every year, very little of the work could be done by inexperienced peasant farmers, who therefore incurred large debts for services rendered by SAED, and could not hope to pay off these debts because there was insufficient work available to them. They fell back upon subsistence farming in their home areas, or wage-earning in towns. In the words of the report quoted above, they became part-time sharecroppers for SAED.

It is sometimes suggested that SAED has altered its priorities as a result of this experience, and that its current activities are based on new principles. It seems more accurate to say that SAED's priorities and aims remain unchanged, but that its short-term tactics have changed, to suit conditions up-river. Reliance on immediate introduction of large-scale rice cultivation, has given way to the *petit périmètre* strategy, where peasants are gradually drawn into cash-crop production, initially presented as a way of earning locally the indispensable cash supplement to subsistence farming. In areas where subsistence farming is still a major component of the peasant economy, part-time share-cropping becomes a viable transitional stage; local food production, and income from labour migration, can act as safety nets, enabling peasants better to bear the costs and risks of the new scheme. The essential aim, however, remains large-scale production of rice, to be marketed through SAED; ultimately, therefore, full-time share-cropping, with some diversification of crops in order to employ peasants over a longer period of the year. Claims that SAED's new strategy is intended to improve local food production and provide an alternative to labour migration, seem in fact more suitable for export, than for local consumption; they improve the tone of foreign aid negotiations, but the facts of the matter rather contradict them.

A three-part article which appeared in Senegal's daily newspaper, *Le Soleil*, for 4, 5 and 6 February 1975, may serve to illustrate the version of SAED's priorities approved for presentation. Part 1 is headlined: 'Avec la SAED, c'est maintenant LE DELTA DE L'ESPOIR' ['with the intervention of SAED, the Delta now became the land of HOPE'], and announces, 'All the tomatoes we need, from 77'. The article reports the forecast by SAED's Director that SAED will be able to supply all of Senegal's rice by the year 2000, and that if the dam at Diama is built, it will also be supplying the country's wheat requirements by 1985. It then suggests that this forecast is excessively cautious; with research, unheard-of new agronomic wonders may become possible. Part 2 discusses the different types of project implemented by SAED: their technical specifications, the hydro-agricultural works required, their production, the number of people employed. It is sometimes difficult to tell whether the article is referring to present achievements or plans for the future. Part 3, title 'Développement du milieu humain' ['Development of human resources'], in fact describes the machinery hired out by SAED, and the processing and marketing of rice and tomatoes. This article addresses the urban consumer, who is quizzed for his addiction to the national dish of rice-and-fish, and told that 'we' must make sacrifices to help achieve SAED's goals; 'we' must force ourselves to eat Senegalese rice, instead of the Indochina rice for which we have acquired a taste. 'Let us become conscious of what is required of us, that these hopes may be fulfilled.'

If you and I are the consumers, who are the producers? The answer: SAED, its machines, its technicians, the dams which will be built.

There is an Eisenstein film called *Spring*, which presents the collectivization of Russian agriculture as a lyrical crescendo of plenty: beaming peasants are surrounded by heaving seas of corn, floods of pigs, and their rural bliss is contrasted with the sterility of the town's bureaucracy, which the heroine successfully beards in its den. The *Soleil* article enthusiastically portrays the reverse process: the bureaucracy miraculously conjures up bulldozers, irrigation canals, tons of tomatoes. The sky's the limit; SAED will have its own 'planes. And those who are remote and passive, are the peasants.

The peasants, we are told, are grateful. 'Many times we observed their commitment, which borders upon fervour. (A peasant woman) told us how SAED's action among the peasants was appreciated. A young schoolboy also expressed his gratitude.' But peasants as producers are invisible; they don't exist. Machinery is progress; peasants can only become worthy of machinery, hence progressive, by long training. It is the 400 permanent SAED technicians, not the 30,000 peasants involved in SAED schemes, who do the work: 'Not only have they spared neither time nor trouble, nor yet their knowledge; they have also carried out admirable training efforts in the vicinity of their *périmètres*. The idea that agricultural development is something which is imposed from without upon a passive peasantry, is linked in the article with the assumption that the only suitable crops for development are those for which urban consumers in Senegal acquired a taste during the colonial era – rice, tomatoes, wheat; not the crops grown by Senegalese peasants for their own use. The only such crop mentioned is sorghum; and it is mentioned only because a new experimental variety is being tested in SAED's laboratories. The negation of peasants as consumers matches their negation as producers.

Part 3 of the article is headed by two photographs. One, captioned 'The peasant can already do this', shows ten men riding in an ox-cart laden with agricultural machinery. The second shows a single man driving a tractor; it is captioned, 'The peasant must achieve this'. Where will the others go to find work? Is that new?

When SAED representatives met peasants in Jamaane, they did not claim that SAED intended to bolster local food production and provide an alternative to labour migration. These were the aims of the peasant association which SAED wished to supplant; yet when the peasants stated these aims, the SAED delegation did not assent, but attempted to demonstrate the convergence of SAED interests and peasant interests in abstract terms – shifting uneasily from modernity to Islam, from Islam to Government authority. It would have been useful to be able to claim that SAED's concrete aims were identical with the peasants', but that was not possible; for the peasants knew that SAED had never acted in support of local agriculture, and that the authorities' main concern about labour migration from the area, was to find some way of channelling the money remitted home into more productive forms of investment. The SAED representatives had no choice but to be evasive; not because they were dishonest men, but because claims that SAED was promoting a new, peasant-based form of development, which can be heard in Dakar and read in reports, could not survive confrontation with a genuine attempt at peasant-based development. SAED's strategy would have been shown up for what it was: *développement de fonctionnaires*, not the objective embodiment of modernity, but the expression of the interests of a particular sector of Senegalese society.

There are grounds for considering that peasants and bureaucrats are the key groups in Senegalese society today. The question is too complex to discuss here (see O'Brien, 1971; Dumont, 1972), and there would be no reason for confining it to the present context, which is not unique. That peasant resistance to innovation is not to be ascribed to a supposed 'peasant conservatism', but to a perception that such innovation is often not in the interests of peasants, has been demonstrated in other settings (e.g. Raynaut, 1975). The peasants of the Bakel area would generally be considered more 'conservative' than others in Senegal, not less; 'Saracolés bavards, criards, nonchalants, les plus conservateurs aussi' ['the Sarakholé,[7] who are great talkers, braggards, listless workers and the most conservative too'], as Sembene Ousmane, cumulating the more common stereotypes, described them in an early (1956) novel. What makes their case particularly clear, is that resistance to alienating innovation is expressed in terms of a positive alternative, resulting from peasant initiative. That may be due in part to that very 'conservatism': the sense of self-reliance induced by a century of marginality, during which the continuity of life at home was sustained by resourceful temporary migration. If peasant initiative in the Bakel area were to be defeated, they would probably become bitter opponents of 'development'. It must be acknowledged that their present position is vulnerable.

This vulnerability is due to outside factors, not internal dissent. The present associations are not seen as a direct challenge to village order, although they cut across the hierarchy of 'royal' families, clerical families, artisans and 'slaves', and their internal organization by no means invariably reflects that hierarchy. Opposition to the associations cannot be ascribed to any particular stratum within village society. Latent opposition seems rather confined to those persons in village society who might be seen as new notables, signs of a tentative reproduction, within the villages, of the class structure of Senegalese society as a whole: persons who have accumulated wealth, often parlayed out of migrant workers' earnings, and have sought to establish links with officialdom on their own account. In time, these latent conflicts of interest would no doubt give rise to internal divisions. At present, however, the main threat to the peasant associations lies outside the villages: in Bakel, for a start, where signs of SAED presence multiply daily, where teams of experts come and go; where there is equipment and technical knowledge to which the peasants cannot have access on their own terms; where plans for the future of the area are laid down, in meetings and reports which the peasants do not know about. It is this growing isolation, this encirclement, which makes the future uncertain.

Lack of equipment is not at the moment felt as keenly as might have been expected, because of peasant leaders' awareness that technology is not neutral, and 'presents' always have to be paid for in the end. As the associations seek to develop their activities further, the lack of mechanical aids, and the lack of transport, is bound to prove crippling, and will severely strain their members' resolve. The lack of impartial technical advice inhibits planning; commonsense and extrapolation from previous experience cannot compensate in the long run. But these are secondary issues at present; that which makes the associations most vulnerable, is their lack of information about what is planned for the area. Most peasants in the area are unable to read or write French, although some are literate in Arabic. This means that while their mastery of the spoken word, through memory and oratorical skill, is often considerable, they are vulnerable to mystification through written words. A man's 'papers' – household tax rolls, identity cards, birth certificates, seaman's papers, social security forms, addresses of former employers – are both instruments of survival and signs of bondage, as ambivalent as labour migration itself. That which circulates in writing, is quite beyond the peasants' control.

The meetings at which they have spoken have left no trace; the opposition they voiced there cannot compete with the reports being circulated which make no mention of the existence of autonomous peasant associations, and subsume all past and present organized agricultural developments in the Bakel area, under the heading 'SAED projects'. The drafting of the statutes of the Fédération des Paysans Organisés en Zone Soninké de Bakel is an attempt to break through this barrier, by requesting official recognition of the Fédération's existence. Under present circumstances, it is difficult to see how it can succeed.

The very existence of the draft statutes points to the fact that the peasant associations do have some contacts with the literate; but these relations are themselves ambiguous. This is not the place to discuss the role of the petty-bourgeois intelligentsia, if indeed that is the correct term, in Senegalese society. (But see Cabral's 1967 analysis of Guinéa-Bissau.) The account given of recent events in the Bakel area, indicates the diverse and fluctuating positions adopted by representatives of that group: the Bakel *fonctionnaires*, the 'man from downstream', even SAED technicians. The local *fonctionnaires* first courted SAED, then sought to establish a dominant position within the Bakel association; the ensuing conflict with peasant members has subsided, but has not been forgotten. The 'man from downstream' who spoke at the April 1975 meeting, is the organizer of an agricultural development project which resisted SAED attempts to take it over, and managed to retain some degree of autonomy. He suggested that this created a hopeful precedent for the peasant associations in the Bakel area, but it might equally well stand for the exception which proves the rule: his relative success might be attributed to the fact that his project was based on a nucleus of literate young people, he himself being an ex-schoolmaster, and managed to bypass SAED control by becoming directly dependent on outside aid. As for the SAED representatives, their repeated appeals to the bonds of filial respect and shared belief which linked them with the peasantry, would seem to indicate some uncertainty about the part they were playing. It seems possible that these various positions might shift and become clearer with the passage of time; but there may not be time. SAED's haste to be seen to operate effectively along the full length of Senegal's territory on the left bank, is certainly not unconnected with the recent rush of plans for the development of the Senegal River Valley as a whole: plans which now seem likely, having received international financial backing, to be implemented within the next few decades. A full discussion of their implications is beyond the scope of this paper. It is clear, however, that their aims and methods resemble those of SAED. [...]

Postscript (January 1978)

The village associations and the Fédération remain in existence. The Jamaane association in particular has extended its activities, heightened active solidarity between its members and achieved a clear sense that what distinguishes their approach to 'development' from SAED's is their determination to use diversified, collective irrigated farming as a complement to rainy-season family-based subsistence farming: as a safeguard in years of poor rainfall, with increased production of irrigated maize and group purchases of grain, and as a source of revenue in good years, for reinvestment in production and also, it is hoped, in community

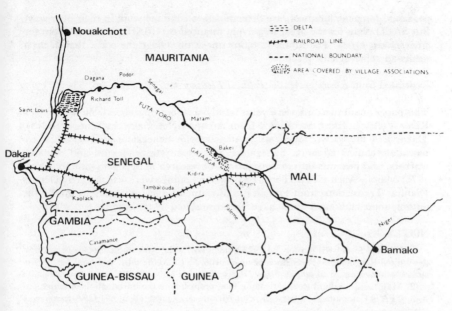

projects. The difference between *développements de fonctionnaires* and *développement paysan*, first perceived in terms of long-term priorities and organized control, is seen to extend to concrete choices to be made here and now.

Until late 1977, Jamaane saw relatively little of SAED. Technical assistance was nominal: 'we have become our own technicians'. The French SAED agents (who have now left the area) suggested repeatedly that collectively farmed land be divided into individual family plots; this was rejected. During this period of surface tranquillity, there was a build-up of SAED presence in Bakel; and since December 1977, there has been renewed SAED activity. The Director of SAED toured the area to announce the start of the new USAID-financed project; this meant, he said in Jamaane, that villagers must grow much more rice and sign a contract with SAED. He also announced that SAED policy required, in the interest of the peasants themselves, that irrigated land be divided among individual families. This was followed by a visit from local government representatives, urging the same message. Village spokesmen forthrightly stated their own priorities, as outlined above. 'What will you pay us for rice? Forty francs a kilo? That's four thousand francs for a hundred-kilo sack. The cheapest millet costs six thousand francs a hundred-kilo sack. And we live on millet here; not rice.' They once more rejected the idea of a shift to irrigated farming on an individual family basis, and suggested that the proposed contract was not relevant to their needs.

SAED remains free to pay lip-service to the Fédération in speeches, while denying its existence in reports and projects; the Fédération has still not applied for official recognition. This is now due to the delaying tactics of 'educated' members of the Bakel group, who have also been playing on peasants' fear of the authorities with suggestions that the Fédération leadership is anti-government, and that it would be wise to accept SAED's conditions.

The situation has not yet changed fundamentally; it has developed further, as latent tendencies have become more explicit. The village associations represent the only visible form of agricultural development in the area so far; and a solid core of peasants, Jamaane foremost, are determined to continue work in their own way. But SAED plans for the area, massively financed by USAID, leave no room for *développement paysan*. The future remains uncertain. Given the odds, that in itself seems an achievement. [. . .]

Reprinted from *Review of African Political Economy,* no. 10, 1978, pp. 33–59.

This paper has drawn on several years' study of labour migration from the Senegal River Valley utilizing documents from Archives Nationales du Sénégal (ANS), Dakar and interviews, taped and untaped, with Senegalese civil servants, expatriate technical advisers, Senegalese and expatriate academics and research workers, and peasants during two periods of research in Senegal (January–June 1975, March–April 1976).[1] Tapes recorded in Soninke were translated by Demba Diabira. Translations from French [. . . documents and conversations are by the author; some additional terms have been translated by the editors].

NOTES

1. This article was written for the 1976 conference of the African Studies Association of the United Kingdom, and has since been incorporated into the third and final part of the author's *Le long voyage des gens du Fleuve* (Paris: François Maspero, 1977).

[2. Millet and sorghum were the staple food crops before the introduction of maize.]

[3. CFA is Communauté Financière de l'Afrique de l'Ouest; about 691 CFA francs = £1 (1955).]

[4. About 624 CFA francs = £1 (1969).]

[5. About 475 CFA francs = £1 (1975).]

[6. About 434 CFA francs = £1 (1976).]

[7. Sarakholé was the name given by the French to the Soninke people.]

REFERENCES

Bailland, Emile, 1902, *Sur les outes du Soudan,* Toulouse.
Barry, Boubacar, 1972, *Le royaume du Waalo: le Sénégal avant la conquête,* Paris.
Cabral, A., 1969, 'Brief analysis of the social structure of Guinée-Bissau', in *Revolution in Guinea.*
Deschamps, Hubert, ed., 1967, *L'Afrique Occidentale en 1818 vue par un explorateur français,* Gaspard Theodore Mollien, Paris.
Dumont, René, 1972, *Paysanneries aux abois:* Ceylan, Tunisie, Sénégal.
Gaden, 1935, 'Du régime des terres de la vallée du Sénégal au Fouta antérieurement a l'occupation française', *Bulletin du Comité d'Etudes Historiques et Scientifiques de l'A.O.F.*
Kane, A. S., 1935, 'Du régime des terres chez les populations du Fouta Sénégalais', *B.C.E.H.S. de l'A.O.F.,* 1935.
Minot, A., 1934, 'Contribution à l'étude du fleuve Sénégal', *B.C.E.H.S. de l'A.O.F., XVII.*
Ousmane, S., 1956, *Le docker noir,* Paris, 1973.
Papy, Lucien, 1954, *La vallée du Sénégal: agriculture traditionelle et riziculture mécanisée,* Les Cahiers d'Outremer, October/December.
Raynaut, C., 1975, 'Le cas de la région du Maradi (Niger)', *Sécherres et famines du Sahel, II,* Paris.
Rodts, R., 1971, *Etude économique de la SAED,* June 1971.
Vidal, M., 1935, 'Etude sur la tenure des terres indigènes au Fouta', *B.C.E.H.S. de l'A.O.F.*

Part Two

Struggles in the Town

Introduction

A growing proportion of people in the Third World live in towns and cities. The distribution of population between countryside and town varies greatly from country to country; in some countries the urban population exceeds that of the rural areas. The movement of people between countryside and town, and between towns, is referred to in nearly all the readings in this section, and is typically connected with the search for a living (see also Readings 9, 24, 26). As in the previous section, our focus here is on the great majority of urban inhabitants who have to engage in a daily struggle to secure even a modest existence.

While one of the main issues for peasants in gaining their living is the struggle to secure means of production, first of all land, the basic 'fact of life' in the urban context is the need to find wage employment or some form of self-employment in order to survive. This theme is vividly illustrated in Readings 13 and 14, and the latter shows that it applies as much to those who are born in the city as to those who arrive as migrants from the countryside like Rosendo Huenumán (Reading 11) and Ivan Martin (Reading 13).

Definitions of urban employment, unemployment and underemployment in the Third World are contentious, as are attempts to measure and interpret data on various forms of employment (or lack of it). Generally speaking, however, it is clear that 'modern' sector industry and services (including the distribution of goods, and office work) employ a lower proportion of the urban population than in Western countries. The term 'modern' or 'formal' sector refers to large-scale enterprises and employers, private and public (for example, government services). It conveys the idea that in the 'modern' sector employment is more stable, wages are higher, regulations concerning conditions of work, pay and social insurance are observed more closely, and workers have more opportunity to organize themselves in trade unions.

All this is by way of contrast with conditions prevailing in the so-called 'informal sector' encompassing self-employment, casual and irregular wage work, employment in personal services or in small-scale enterprises in manufacturing and services. In Latin America the term 'marginalization' was coined to refer to the effects of 'modern' capitalist industrialization (and agricultural development) which, it is argued, provides fewer and fewer jobs relative to the numbers of those seeking them. Those unable to find (or retain) regular wage employment – the 'marginals' – consequently swell the ranks of the 'informal sector', forming an increasing proportion of the urban population.

The readings in this section illustrate some of the ways of pursuing and making a living in the 'informal' and 'formal' sectors, including the search for wage employment (Readings 11, 13), and for viable means of self-employment (Reading 14). In the 'informal' sector we encounter employment in domestic service (Reading 11; see also Reading 26), and a series of attempts to 'make it on one's own' in various small-scale undertakings, both legal and illegal (Reading 14). Readings in other sections give a picture of other types of self-employment, whether as a primary means of livelihood (Readings 24, 26, 27), or to supplement inadequate household incomes from wage work (Readings 9, 29(i)). Conditions in different types of 'informal' sector manufacturing are described in the two pieces from India. Reading 15 is about small engineering workshops, and Reading 16 is about 'factories' making *beedies* (hand-rolled cigarettes), although the use of the term 'factory' here is rather special as the introduction to the reading explains. In the case of Moroccan migrant workers in Holland, the introduction to Reading 19 suggests that many of them are employed in the 'informal' sector of a Western economy, that is, in smaller-scale, less capitalized and non-unionized businesses ('sweat shops', cleaning, catering), which find immigrant workers 'cheap to hire and easy to fire'. However, some big companies in Western Europe and the United States employ large numbers of immigrant workers in the same way and for the same reason, notably in agriculture, construction, and in services such as laundries, restaurants and hotels.

In contrast to the struggles of those who are unemployed, or employed in the often precarious activities of the 'informal' sector, Readings 17 and 18 portray the struggles of two groups of 'modern' sector workers in a Ghanaian port and railhead town and in the major industrial city of Brazil. Together with Rosendo Huenumán's account of his experience as a coal miner in Chile, and the conclusions he draws from it (Reading 11), these readings reveal issues of trade unionism and rank-and-file politics which are common to the industrial working classes in all capitalist countries, despite significant differences in their historical formation and the conditions in which their struggles are conducted. Here politics takes on a sharper definition, and is articulated with greater sophistication, than was generally the case in the previous section. All seats of government and important state agencies are situated in major cities, as are most large-scale industries, and the nature and conduct of workers' struggles are as much a concern of Third World governments as of those in the West – perhaps more so given that trade unions can serve as the vehicle for more general political discontent and opposition when other means of expression are not available (Reading 17).

While the distinction between the 'formal' and 'informal' sectors is often useful for descriptive purposes (like the term 'peasants'), it can easily be misleading if used to suggest two self-contained and separate 'compartments' of social reality. First, the 'informal' sector is a residual category, that is, one that contains everything excluded by definition from the 'formal' (or 'modern' or 'developed') sector. Accordingly, it encapsulates a heterogeneous mixture of activities and people, whether children hawking matches and newspapers and generally 'hustling' on the streets (Reading 14), prostitutes (Readings 14, 24), petty criminals (Reading 14), women cooking and selling food in their homes (Reading 27), or skilled machine operators and craftsmen in small workshops (Reading 15). Second, certain forms of organization and activity combine characteristics ascribed to both sectors, for example, the *beedi* 'factories' which bring together large numbers of workers (the criterion of scale), but in a 'labour process' which is completely individualized and uses only human energy and dexterity rather than any machinery (Reading 16). Third, 'informal' and 'formal' sector activities are linked in all sorts of ways through the social division of labour and market exchanges. For example, 'informal' sector engineering is typically linked directly or indirectly to larger scale industry, as Reading 15 suggests; the production of cheap cigarettes (Reading 16) and of services like meals (Reading 27) and prostitution (Reading 24) contribute to the consumption of the urban poor, who usually include a sizeable proportion of 'single' male migrants from the countryside. Finally, while 'formal' sector industry may make collective organization, including trade unionism, easier, it contains no guarantee of job security. Large numbers of Brazilian car workers have been laid off and made redundant in the face of worldwide recession (60,000 in the first eight months of 1981), in the same way as workers in the capitalist countries of the West.

Some of the readings in this section indicate that the boundaries between countryside and town are not as definite in practice as they appeared in the perceptions of the peasants in the previous section. This is partly because people move between them frequently, and many urban inhabitants retain connections with their (or their families') areas of origin in the countryside. The pattern of movement between countryside and town is exemplified in the life of Rosendo Huenumán (Reading 11; also Readings 7 and 8), in the patterns of 'rotational' migration of men from the Senegal River Valley (Reading 10) and southern Mozambique (Reading 12), and in the testimony of the Guatemalan woman in Reading 26.

Another reason for the blurring of boundaries is that certain groups of workers, notably those in extractive industries like mining, live in communities that are 'industrial villages' relatively isolated from larger towns and cities (see Reading 29(i)). The Mozambican miners (Reading 12) are a 'special case' in that the mining companies of southern Africa have always used large numbers of fixed-contract migrant workers from rural areas (for both economic and political reasons). These workers are housed in segregated compounds and 'barracks' at the mines, rather than being urban residents in any fuller social or cultural sense. Again, the nature of the technical conditions of *beedi* manufacture (Reading 16) shows that it is not necessarily an 'urban–industrial' occupation, as it can be carried out at home and sometimes is, unlike the kinds of production in the great industrial zones of São Paulo, for example (Reading 18).

On the other hand, the peasants' stereotype and distrust of urban life and people is reciprocated by the view of Miguel Duran, a thoroughgoing big city 'type', that country people are 'incredibly dumb and humble', providing easy prey when they come to town (Reading 14). More important, the railway workers of Sekondi–Takoradi (Reading 17) and the metalworkers of São Paulo (Reading 18) provide examples of working classes fully committed to industrial work and urban existence, that are of increasing social and political importance in many countries of the Third World.

These introductory comments have focused on the 'basic fact' of securing and protecting a living, but a number of other facets of urban existence and experience are revealed in the readings in this section. In both Cali, Colombia (Reading 14) and in Kingston, Jamaica, as portrayed in the film and book of *The Harder They Come* (from which Reading 13 is taken), the lives of the poorest and most desperate urban dwellers are marked by everyday physical violence, whether inflicted by police and prison officers or on each other. This has its counterpart in the social violence with which Ivan Martin's pleas for work are met by the 'party henchman' at the building site and the affluent woman in the suburban villa (Reading 13).

The need for identity papers and permits of various kinds enables officials and employers to harass the poor and keep them insecure, to extract bribes from them, and to maintain their subordination (Readings 9, 14, 17, 19). Larger-scale bribery and other forms of corruption among politicians, government officials and trade union leaders figure large in the urban consciousness (Readings 16, 17).

Finally, we can see from the readings in this section that the struggle for daily existence in the towns and cities of the Third World takes very different forms. These include highly individualized responses (Readings 13(iii), 14); cooperation and mutual support, whether of an informal or more organized kind, between those pursuing 'individual' occupations (Readings 24 and 27 respectively, in the next section); and the impulse to collective organization and action among those whose work in larger enterprises, often combined with other common social conditions, gives them a strong shared identity (Readings 11, 16, 17, 18, 19, and see also Readings 28, 29).

ROSENDO HUENUMÁN

See introduction to Reading 7

That made me think. Later on, I would be about seven years old, perhaps eight
... a brother, called José Luis Huenumán (half-) brother on my father's side, was
studying in Temuco. ... He was studying to be an accountant and worked in a
company of a large concern which at that time belonged to Messrs Rivera & Co.
The company, a brewery, was 'The José Rivera & Co. United Brewery'. During
one of his holidays my brother came out to the country and met me. I had learned
to read and write without having been to school, my mother had encouraged me to
study. ... Well, that was all my ... the period of my childhood. And now, here
was my brother, José Luis, trying to persuade me to go to Temuco, he would find
me work and he would pay me ... if I did not find work, he would pay for my
food. I became excited at the prospect.

I liked that offer very much. So I went home and told my mother, I said, 'Look,
I have been talking to my brother and he proposes taking me to Temuco so that I
may study.'

My mother did not agree at first. She spoke to my grannie who agreed even less,
in fact strongly opposed the idea. I couldn't sleep for thinking about it, firstly I
would learn to read properly and another thing getting to know the town.

My brother did not have many more days left with us. The last day came and I
still did not have a reply. Always a negative answer. Then I decided to run away. I
left about eleven at night. Everybody was asleep. I went to bed early and I got up a
little later because I could not sleep ... well I took my few rags and left. My
brother was staying some distance away, about twelve kilometres. I arrived with
my small bundle of clothes and said 'I am going with you.' 'But have you their
permission?' 'No, they have not given me permission but I am going with you
regardless.'

Well, he made up his mind and took me to Temuco, making himself responsible
for me. Upon our arrival in Temuco he looked for what was obviously a good job
for a child, as a houseboy. I went to work at the house of Mr Carlos Gregos, who
was an official at CORFO (National Development Corporation) in Temuco. This
happened about 1948, one thing I do remember is the date.

I worked at that house for three months. They paid me one peso twenty a
month.[1] Mr Gregos was later transferred to Osorno. He wanted to take me with
him. When I told my brother he said, 'No, you must stay here because you must
not miss out on your studies.'

I worked during the day and studied at night. So my brother took me to work at
the house of Messrs Rivera. There I was taken on as a houseboy by Mrs Engracia
de Rivera. She was my boss. And I had a rise. They paid me three pesos a month
... but three pesos a month even then was paltry, because a pair of shoes cost
between seven and twelve, eighteen ... twenty-five pesos ... depending on the
quality of them. But for a child ... seven pesos. The ... but that bought only shoes

and what about shirts and underwear? I remember that a shirt used to cost between seventy-five cents and one peso twenty cents. ... Well, I worked for that wage. I was there for almost three years.

It was very hard work. At Mrs Engracia de Rivera's house there were two married couples ... some of her children who were married. The eldest, Don Juan de Rivera, who had five children, and a daughter who used to live next door ... not in the same house, but next door. Her name was Erica Rivera, married to a Captain ... Aguilera ... I believe he was called Luis Aguilera and he was a Captain of the Tucapel Regiment at that time.

I had to look after and serve Captain Aguilera's house and the two families at my employer's house. I did the shopping every day, I had to go to the market, thank goodness the market was nearby, to buy things for lunch ... every day ... I did the cleaning and the housework, fed the chickens, did the gardening, cleaned the garden up ... well, all the jobs in both houses. The workload was enormous.

I went to school in Temuco from half past seven every evening until midnight. During the years that I was in Temuco I passed my fifth grade of primary schooling. In the last year, that was about 1952, when I was in the sixth grade a problem arose ... I was fed up with the excessive amount of work and the exploitation. Because during the second year I was in the Rivera household, whenever workmen were absent from the factory – the brewery – they used to send me to replace that workman and of course I then worked there for eight hours, but I was paid the same wage of three pesos a month.

And so that made me think and take action. I thought it was unjust, a great injustice. ... I started to claim that the days when I went to work in the factory I should be paid as a labourer because I went to take the place of a labourer who was absent and was going to do the same work. So I thought, that wage, that salary, belonged to me. ... But that was not happening, instead at the end of the month they handed me three pesos. So I became discontented ... and there was still the excessive workload. Sometimes I went to bed at two in the morning because I had to leave the house clean and tidy and also had to sleep.

I got home from my classes at midnight, had something to eat and immediately started the housework ... and I did not have enough time to do the work the teachers gave me. So I used to go to school twenty, fifteen or ten minutes early and quickly do my homework. That's how I managed to get by. Nevertheless I managed to make progress because several times after the six monthly tests I was put up a grade. This happened from the fourth to the fifth grade. In the fifth grade, however, the work must have been harder, more difficult ... but my brother helped me, you understand. He had been to university so he had enough knowledge to be able to help me, and he helped me a lot. And so that was the way I got good marks at school.

But by 1952 I had had enough and so I asked for a rise. I went to the Inspección del Trabajo [office for the arbitration of labour problems] and said 'Look, I have been working in the Rivera household for so long. My employer is Mrs Engracia de Rivera and I get three pesos a month, they have no insurance card for me, and they make me work in the factory when any labourers take a Monday off. ...'

The inspector found in my favour. A summons arrives for my employer to present herself at the Inspección, but she did not go, instead she sent her solicitor and there he discovers that I had made a claim.

Well to keep me happy an insurance card was taken out for me, contributions were paid for me from the date that I started work. And that card was not stamped for three pesos – they had to put it right. This was done with the help of the solicitor. 'Well this child earns so much ...' – it ends up the minimum rate for insurance ... mmm ... labourer. And the wages stay put. They gave me my card up to date but I carry on claiming for a better wage.

My demand was quite high as I had asked for a rise from three pesos to fifteen pesos[2] a month. They did not want to pay fifteen pesos but my pay did go up to twelve pesos. I accepted twelve pesos for two months. At that time there was a coalminers' strike. One morning – I used to collect the paper from the terrace where the newsboy left it – I glanced at the paper, well I used to do so every morning, glimpsed at the news ... and on the first page I saw that the conflict at the Lota coalmine had been resolved. A victory, another victory for the miners. It said, 'The conflict with the miners had been resolved by giving them a wage for an eight hour shift. Forty-three pesos a month ...' ... a month it was. Forty-three pesos a month. Then I worked it out. I am earning twelve pesos a month and a labourer there for eight hours' work ... is earning forty-three pesos a month and they have other privileges, family allowance, public holidays and here I have no public holidays and am earning a pittance.

I decided to push for a new claim for twenty-four or twenty-five pesos a month. They do not accept this but do give me fifteen pesos ... what I had asked for in my first claim, fifteen. And so they paid me fifteen pesos and not twenty-five. But the work in the factory also went up. Now I was not only working when the labourers failed to turn up but when they felt like making me do so, they 'phoned for me to go and work in the factory for half a day or just two hours ... three hours. ... This I used to do two and sometimes three times a week ... and earning fifteen pesos a month ... and I get tough, firm and keep on insisting: 'Well, if you make me work in the factory you must pay me what you pay a labourer in the factory.' Then my claim ... I insist ... and to top it all I have a disagreement with the cook.

The cook was a single lady, Spanish, called Hipólita Delgado, about fifty years old, blonde, with blue eyes ... she was an hysterical woman, very hysterical, neurotic. As you know I used to go shopping to the market every morning, one morning she gave me back the vegetables. She said, 'These vegetables are bad, they are no good.' It was some chicory ... well, I had selected the best in the market, I had looked for the best ... and she made me take them back. I speak to the man there, the owner of the vegetable warehouse ... he chose some more himself, and ... I went to speak to other colleagues. ... Well, there were none better. I returned home, she won't accept this lot and makes me return those vegetables and get better ones. And I am telling her the whole time that there are no better ones: that these are the best in the market. ... She doesn't believe me, makes me go back again. Well I am beginning to feel that I've had enough. I could not find any better ones. When I returned the third time and she turned them down again I objected 'I am not going back a third time to return the vegetables. If that's what you wish you can go and choose them yourself.'

She insulted me and said 'What do you think you are saying, you insolent boy.' ... Well, she upset and insulted me ending up by saying '... you indian so-and-so.' That I could not tolerate and I lost my temper. I insulted her and tried to hit her ... I actually hit her ... I hit her, I felt like killing her. The maids intervened ... because I had her by the neck, squeezing it, her tongue was sticking out ... I was like a wildcat ...

All this caused a nervous crisis in me. I hated this woman, I could stand her no longer. This made me decide, very quickly, very quickly, not to continue working in that house. I had made up my mind, 'I'll leave on such and such a day.' I go the Inspección to give notice, 'I am leaving the Rivera household on such and such a day.' I gave fifteen days' notice in accordance with the law at that time. The fifteen days were up and I went to collect the salary due to me, two months' pay, and asked for my insurance card to be up to date. I was very firm. Then, when my employer realized that my mind was made up she offered me the twenty-five pesos; if I would stay she would pay me twenty-five pesos. I refused. I refused because I could not stand the cook . . . I could not abide her any more. I hated her. I had made up my mind to go to Concepción.

I arrived in Concepción, in that mining town without knowing anyone. On the last night that I was at school in Temuco I put my problem to my teacher. I said 'I'm going to Concepción to work. I need a transfer certificate because if I get to Concepción I want to start school straight away.' There was no problem. They granted me the certificate and a recommendation for being an excellent pupil at the school.

I arrived in Concepción. There I start looking for work. I used to buy the daily paper *El Sur*. I used to tour the city every day. . . . I found work but was not employed on account of my young age. According to my documents I was perhaps seventeen years old but to be able to work in a factory I had to be turned eighteen. And I didn't want to work as a houseboy again, I loathed the job. At the time I wanted to be a labourer.

So there I was for three months paying a very cheap rent for a humble room. The day arrived when my money ran out and I could not pay my digs . . . so then I go to the railway station at Concepción and carry luggage . . . 'to earn a crust' as we say in Chile. But that is also quite complicated because there were days which went well for me and I did it to carry on with my studies, my sixth year . . . primary. Unfortunately I was unable to finish it because things went badly in the station and I was forced into going to the Lota coalmine because I had a cousin there.

When I arrived in Lota my cousin made this offer 'Look, you have no problems here, I'll pay your digs and you can carry on at school here. There are also night schools.' This I did but my cousin didn't keep his word so . . . I couldn't carry on living there asking for charity. So off I go to the offices on my own, to the company's offices to ask for a job.

Of course they asked me my age. I was eight . . . seventeen years old and only three months and twenty days to go, or something like that, to my eighteenth birthday. One of the officials was looking at me and he said to the other one 'Well, why don't we put his name down, perhaps a surface job will come up?' 'All right', the other one agrees, and they take my name down.

Fifteen days later I was summoned to the office where I am told that I have been successful, there is a vacancy, but in the mine. So I had no alternative but to accept the job.

I worked in the mine, I started work but it was the end of my studies. There were only twenty days to go to the end of term, I went to ask for my certificate and they wouldn't give it to me because I had not finished the term . . . so I lost a whole year of studies and I start work in the mine . . . in October in 1952 . . . yes, I cannot remember whether it was the eighth or the fourth of October, but it was in the month of October. There I worked until 1959 . . . the twenty-four . . . the twenty-third of December . . . because they dismissed me the day before Christmas . . .

There is no doubt that working in the mine was a valuable experience for me. Maybe this experience of my youth is very important in my life, up to the present day. Because there I came into contact with the union, there is where I saw what the organization of the workmen meant and there I understood what the class struggle was all about, there I came to understand better the exploitation that the miner is victim of in the huge mining industry.

At that time . . . the owners of the mine were Messrs Cousiño. The Cousiño Company . . . mmm.

Of course the work in the mine is very risky, a permanent danger . . . The work in the mine is permanently dangerous.

Well, now this story will take a little time to tell, the story of those six years in the mine. The work in the mine was an impressive experience for me, unforgettable. Those first days, when I saw the mine under the sea, when I had to go down three hundred and seventy metres in a cage and then walk towards the workings under the sea . . . with a lamp . . . a battery powered lamp which gives as much light as a torch. . . . When I got to the bottom of the mine I thought I was in another world, a different world. It was under the sea, kilometres and kilometres away.

I began to observe the vast machinery, great air compressors, water pumps taking the water out: water which accumulates in the mine shaft. . . . I observed enormous cables which carry the electricity to the bottom of the mine, the trucks that take out the coal and the clay, the stones . . . mm . . . trucks that weigh a ton. And by then I had begun to notice the coal, areas propped with heavy timbers, which are called 'los laboreos' – 'los tráficos' as they are called in the mine are bigger, wider parts where one can move about more safely. They are two metres thirty high by four metres wide, where one can walk perfectly easily – but on the other hand working on the face, where the so called 'el laboreo' is, here is where the coal is extracted, work is difficult here because the coal seams are only three-quarters of a metre high. There are medium seams . . . a metre twenty high; a tall seam is nearly two metres high, one metre sixty, one metre eighty in some places, where it's possible to work more comfortably. But the small three-quarter metre seams, it's terrible to work there and many miners work there, many face workers. I knew veterans, men who had worked thirty years in the mine, some forty years . . . their legs, for example . . . one side of their legs and their ribs, the elbow and the arm tough, tough like the sole of a shoe from working on their side, lying down, on their side to extract the coal. . . . And to be working in that uncomfortable position for eight hours is dreadful.

And the dangers the miners are in . . . the face workers take the biggest risks, those who are extracting the coal . . . there are also the prop erectors, 'los enmaderadores', those are men who put up boards at certain intervals to support the hill and so the stones don't become loose and fall on a face worker . . . so the prop erectors must take great care – and so does the face worker because he has to watch the hill . . . to see if it is firm or if it is weakening. Because there are places where the hill is wet, the water gets through and it rains salt water, sea water . . . when the hill is wet it is very dangerous because that is when the falls happen and the falls are very dangerous. The worst accidents happen through rock falls . . . and . . . how is the hillside, which is being emptied of coal, being supported? Well, it's filled with the clay which is left on the floor, which has to be dug out and lowered to make enough height so the truck and the man, who is working there, can go in . . . pushing the truck in, pulling it out, full, pushing it in empty and pulling it out full. So the floor has to be lowered and all that rubble fills in the empty pits.

All that is hard work, furthermore the air which is breathed in the pit is asphyxiating.

A man can be very healthy physically but the eight hours' shift exhausts him. That is the state of the miners when they come out, after eight hours, they come to the surface with quite a changed character . . . mm . . . all the exhaustion . . . and they are unrecognizable through the coal dust and the exhaustion.

So it is very hard work, inhuman. But that's what the work is like for the miners in my time. When I worked in the mine ... I was working as a face worker for eight months, then they moved me off that job, face work ... and then I came to know about mining construction.

Well I started off as a labourer, what they call 'el apir' ... mmm ... that's what he's called in the mine, el apir [mineworker], but he's really just a labourer, an operative. ... And I also worked as a builder, 'contratista', making those big openings two metres by four metres wide, putting up huge wooden beams, mainly eucalyptus. After this I became 'el empaquetador'. 'El empaquetador' fills in the old pits with rocks and clay.

I also operated a cutting machine ... electric machines, which cut the coal in the ground ... then ... and then well, you drilled some blast holes for dynamite, six feet, seven feet deep ... you also place four or five sticks of dynamite ... mm ... and then you ignite it to loosen the coal. That is also very dangerous because if the prop is not secure, the force of the blast as the dynamite explodes shakes up the whole hillside, it moves, and there are huge rock falls, and if one is not protected by secure beams the rocks fall on you and squash you like a rat. Well, all those are the dangers of working in a mine ... as I said especially at the coalface ...

I had been in ... I had worked in almost every part of the mine. And the mine ... all that, that experience, the exploitation of the miner with a miserable wage and the way of life including the notorious 'pabellones' (sleeping quarters). ... Because there are people who take in these miners, especially single blokes, as lodgers. In some houses there are up to twelve lodgers ... mm? and they all work on different shifts ... first, second and third ... mm? and from there comes the saying 'the hot beds'. Of course the bed is always warm. The man on the first shift goes out in the morning, in comes the man from the third shift ... mm? and sleeps in the same bed ... when the man on the third shift goes to work at night along comes the one from the second shift, who finishes at about eleven at night and gets into the same bed ... still warm. And so on ... the way of life in the notorious 'pabellones de Lota'.

Well, all this work in my youth was having its effect on me and I used to think about the mine   and used to say 'I must not grow old and give all my youth to working here in this mine. One day I must leave and find other work that I can do when I'm older and a job that is not as dangerous, where you don't think of accidents and death.'

In 1959 the Lota Company said it had been over-producing. There was too much coal mined, stockpiled, and there was no market. They ordered a cut-back in the working hours ... this meant that we started working a three-day week ... and ... it also threw up another choice. They said: 'Every miner has the opportunity to leave voluntarily and will receive redundancy pay.' Well, when this happens ... to be working three days a week and with a miserable wage ... then the majority of the miners were unable to pay their rent, that is those who paid rent. Well, the married ones ... those who had lodgers got by a little better because, well, the wife took in lodgers and that gave them an income. But those of us who paid rent did not have enough to even pay the rent. That was a serious problem and many miners took voluntary redundancy and I was thinking of doing so when ... by coincidence ... whilst at work one night, a Sunday, I had a disagreement with the 'disparador' [shot-firer], as he is called, the man who ... is a company employee ... whose job it is to fire the sticks of dynamite, that is why he is called a shot-firer. But this man also has a status. He plays the role of foreman: gives directions and instructions, and gives orders. With this shot-firer I had a disagreement, as I say, that night when I was working, to top it all ... it was an urgent job.

And so to earn myself a bonus – because he who worked on Sundays was paid double – I agreed to work that Sunday and by coincidence my group were working under this shot-firer. About halfway through the shift, as was usual, we took out our roll which we took to eat and a small bottle of coffee, 'la charra' as it is called, and an aluminium water bottle, litre size, the coffee was for dunking our bread and the water to quench our thirst ... mm? At that time I worked with three operatives because I was a builder, a 'contratista', but at that moment I was working as a face worker ... and my operatives ... I say to them, 'We've filled enough trucks, now we can have a short rest and eat our roll.' No more than ten minutes had gone by, when we were finishing our bread the shot-firer came and grumbled 'that we are lazy, that we are taking advantage, and that we are paid to work and not to sit down'. So very respectfully, I say 'Sir, we've hardly had ten minutes. We sat down to eat our bread and we have already filled enough trucks and after we've eaten our bread we will fill that extra truck.' Then the firer said 'Well, I am the one who gives orders here and not you and if you don't return to work immediately I won't pay the shift.'

I said 'Please, let us finish eating our roll and we will return to work immediately.' He insists and he insults me, he provokes me. So I stand up and say 'I cannot put up with such insults.' He tries to hit me, but I saw it coming and was ready for him, I had to defend myself. I picked up the shovel and aimed it at his head. It was fortunate that he ducked or maybe there would have been a firer buried in the mine. He ran away from me.

But on the way out, in the morning, as we were leaving the mine, in the office where we clocked out there was a note summoning me to the administration office. They had a suspension order ready for me there, for assaulting the firer.

Well, I defended myself. I explained to the bosses that I was not the aggressor but that I was attacked by him first. Also I have witnesses, what he has reported is quite false. ... Nevertheless I ended up without a job and the company did not want to pay me any redundancy money, they wanted to refuse me my redundancy pay. So the union intervened ... hmm. They investigate the case, the witnesses testify, and the case is found in my favour. But in spite of this I was suspended, however the most important outcome was that they gave me my redundancy pay. And so I finished work in December, 1959.

And so off I went to my homeland. That land which had seen my birth. That land where I had taken my first steps, on the shores of the great Pacific Ocean ... that huge expanse of salt water which had tanned my skin ... where I had spent my early childhood. I returned to my reservation ... and when I return to my reservation I encounter another problem ... Hmm ...? A problem which was as unjust as the way the miners were treated in the mines. Because the fact is, the treatment of the miners, when I worked in a mine, was so unjust, so inhuman ...

But first, I am going to tell you what I learnt in the mine. I did not sacrifice my youth in vain during those six years in the mine. Because not only did I learn but I experienced capitalist exploitation. I went there to learn and to understand better, as they say, the class struggle and I went there to understand class unity and I also went there to understand the importance which the union organization has. That union organization was for me, without doubt, as good an education as six years at university would have given me. I was able to listen to and get to know many union leaders who were labourers, miners. The majority were of peasant origin. I went there to find out the strength, the wisdom and the intelligence of the proletariat. I was very impressed ... by the leaders ... when they spoke at union assemblies. But the leader who probably stirred me most, who touched upon my pride, was comrade Jorge Montes, on his first visit to the province of Concepción. I was very fortunate to be able to listen to his ardent and frank speech. He spoke of the exploitation of capitalism. He talked about economic power, about abuse, and he also talked about landowners. When talking about landowners he also referred to the seizure of the lands of the peasants, of the settlers and of the Mapuches. This speech made me think a lot. Another piece of luck, perhaps, through working in the mine I was able to participate and help with the propaganda work the young Communists were doing in Comrade Montes' campaign. So I learnt how to move around at night, painting slogans, drawing and putting up wall posters, all that.

NOTES

[1. About 2.4 pesos = £1 (1948).]
[2. About 5.3 pesos = £1 (1952).]

12   Work Songs of Mozambican Miners

ALPHEUS MANGHEZI

Editors' introduction

Ninety per cent of African men in the southern third of Mozambique today have worked in South Africa, as did their fathers, grandfathers, and probably their great-grandfathers. Portugal, the poorest and most backward of the European colonial powers in Africa, was unable to stimulate much capitalist development in its colonies. Colonial Mozambique was effectively an appendage of the South African economy. In 1897 the Portuguese and South African governments signed an agreement to provide Mozambican migrant workers for South Africa, and above all for the gold fields of the Transvaal. Between 1904 and 1976 Mozambique contributed an annual average of 90,000 workers, the principal component of the labour force on which the South African gold-mining industry was built.

Recruitment was highly organized through the Witwatersrand Native Labour Agency (Wenela), set up by the mining companies and with offices and transit stations throughout southern Mozambique. Maghalangu, whose name provides the title of the first song, was a particularly vicious and notorious agent of Wenela in the area of Homoine. This song and the interjections that accompany its performance refer to the effects of labour migration to 'Joni' or Johannesburg (strictly speaking, the mining compounds rather than the city) on those left behind as well as those migrating (see also Reading 20(iii)). The second song conveys something of the conditions of work in the mines where Mozambican miners performed some of the most arduous and dangerous tasks such as 'lashing', that is,

shovelling the debris on to trolleys after dynamite blasting had broken up the hard
quartz into rocks, rubble and dust.

(i) Leaving for the mines

Maghalangu

Leader: Maghalangu Maghalangu Maghalangu
Chorus: Heeyoo! Maghalangu
Leader: Maghalangu has taken his son
Chorus: Heeyoo! Maghalangu
Leader: Maghalangu has killed his son
Chorus: Heeyoo! Maghalangu
Leader: Maghalangu has taken his wife
Chorus: Heeyoo! Maghalangu
Leader: Maghalangu Maghalangu Maghalangu
Chorus: Heeyoo! Maghalangu

In between the leader and the chorus the following comments or phrases are
thrown in by members of the chorus:

- drive carefully, we are going to Joni (Johannesburg or the mines)
- drive carefully otherwise our provisions will spill off!
- father, please buy your son a pair of trousers (woman)
- you must take good care of my field – cultivate it properly and plant every
  crop . . .! (man)
- you must write letters, father!
- I will send the money for hut tax, I shall send the money!
- please, don't forget us here at home! (woman)

Do you sing this song when you are saying gooodbye?
Yes, when we left Maghalangu's recruiting station.

And you say Maghalangu is taking my son away? etc.
The women are saying that Maghalangu, the recruiter, is (stealing) their sons to
Joni. Maghalangu was the recruiter for Wenela.

Maghalangu is taking away my son who might get killed in Joni and never return.
Maghalangu is taking the man away who, upon his return from Joni, may find
that his wife has gone with another man!

(ii) Working on the mines

Xikwembu xa Muhliwa

Leader: The god that is being exploited/cheated, (back to) my mother

Chorus: Lasher, mechanical loader/shovel!
Leader: I work without pay, myself.
Chorus: Lasher, mechanical shovel!
Leader: The whitemen of Joni have got me/are oppressing me
Chorus: Lasher, mechanical shovel!
Leader: I work without pay, my father
Chorus: Lasher, mechanical shovel!
Leader: Because it is the black skin working, my father
Chorus: Lasher, mechanical shovel!
Leader: They point with fingers; I am tired/exhausted father
Chorus: Lasher, mechanical shovel!
Leader: I am suffering, I am exhausted indeed!
Chorus: Lasher, mechanical shovel!
Leader: I came to Joni because of poverty, indeed!
Chorus: Lasher, mechanical shovel!
Leader: I earn half escudo per day
Chorus: Lasher, mechanical shovel!
Leader: Because I am the god that is being exploited/cheated
Chorus: Lasher, mechanical shovel!
Leader: The Boers make us work; I am exhausted, father.
Chorus: Lasher, mechanical shovel!

What does this song say?

The song means that it is by fate (the will of god) that we have landed here in Joni. The miner becomes, inevitably, an exploited person because he has been forced to come here by poverty. He is an exploited worker because *they* make him work hard but he does not earn as much as *they* earn. He earns very little compared to what *they* earn – those who loaf about or do nothing while he does all the work.

Who are 'they'?

The white man of Joni. He sits down and points with the finger ('Do this! do that!'). He does that because I have a black skin.

SOURCE
See Reading 4.

---

13 Looking for Work in Kingston

MICHAEL THELWELL

Editors' introduction

The Harder They Come is the title of a remarkable film made in the slums of West Kingston, Jamaica, the title of a record of its soundtrack performed by reggae singers and musicians, including Jimmy Cliff who stars as the central character, and the title of a novel by Michael Thelwell which was inspired by the film. The book tells us that the story 'is based on the life and exploits of Rhygin, the legendary gunman and songwriter who lived in and around Kingston in the late 1950s'.

Growing up in the countryside and drawn by 'visions of wealth and fame, Rhygin goes to Kingston – the vibrant, squalid, rip-off city – where his innocence is rudely lost. There, hounded by the hard-driving rhythm of reggae, the ritualized violence of the streets, the hypocrisy of religion and the utopian dreamings of the Ras Tafarians, Rhygin re-forms into the mythical urban hero: reggae star, stud, ganja (marijuana) trader and a gunman. In one stunning image, we find Rhygin dodging his police pursuers as his number one hit song "The Harder They Come" plays on radios across the country.' The adjective 'rhygin' in Jamaican speech means 'spirited, vigorous, lively, passionate with great vitality and force; also sexually provocative and aggressive. Probably a form of English *raging*.'

The film starts with the arrival in Kingston of Ivan, who is to become Rhygin, but the novel gives an extraordinary evocation of Ivan's rural upbringing and the people who inhabited it, prior to his experiences in the city. Of these his attempts to find a job make up an early stage of his loss of innocence. The desperation and frustration of Ivan's search for work are conveyed in the two extracts that we reprint from the novel, glimpses of situations that are confronted daily by masses of people in the cities of the Third World. The transition from Ivan to Rhygin is expressed in the words of Jimmy Cliff's song 'The Harder They Come', which completes the items in this reading.

(i) The building site

[...] The construction site was hidden behind a tall plywood fence. The metal gate at the entrance was chained and locked. A couple of security men wearing hard hats and pistols at their waists patrolled the gate. Ivan's heart sank when he arrived at six o'clock. Already the line of men stretched from the gate and out of sight around the corner.

'Line up,' one of the security men bawled unnecessarily. 'One line dere.'

Men continued to arrive, look at the line, shake their heads, and take their place anyway. Like Ivan, most were dressed in the eclectic style dictated by poverty and chance. None could have been said to look particularly hopeful – not even the elite minority who wore efficient-looking work clothes of blue denim, and who appeared, with their hard hats and lunch boxes, very experienced and professional. At eight-thirty a jeep with four policemen arrived. They carried pistols on their hips and in a rack behind the driver the shiny squat butts of riot guns were clearly visible. They sat in the jeep smoking and drinking coffee, occasionally directing a cold stare at the line of men through the lenses of their aviator-type glasses.

At eight forty-five, three men came out through the gate and set up a table, at which one of them sat with paper in front of him. The foreman, a beefy fellow in a steel hat and heavy boots, stood next to the clerk's table. The third man, casually dressed in loafers and sports clothes, seemed different to Ivan, not like a worker.

'Who dat?' Ivan asked the man in front of him as they approached the gate.
'Shh,' the man said, then whispered, 'Das de party henchman.'[1]
'Oh?' said Ivan.
'You no understan'?'
'Not really.'
'Is government work, dis – only dem party member dem get work here.'
As they crept toward the table Ivan could feel the tension mount among the men around him. His own belly tightened. The man in front of Ivan, one of those in work clothes who had been talking confidently of the various buildings he had worked on, began to mop his face. His metal lunch box trembled where he had it cradled against his side. Ivan's stomach started to hurt. He had eaten the last of the bread and sardines he had bought with Sufferah's dollar that morning. Now it felt like a lump of sour lead in his belly. The man in front didn't look at the foreman. For some reason he seemed to be standing at attention.
'Whe' you used to work?' the foreman asked sharply.
'Mullers, sah.'
'What kinda work?'
'Carpenter work, Maastah carpenter, sah.'
'Why you leave?'
'Job finish, sah.'
The man gave his answers in a low voice and stood gazing at the middle distance. Ivan could see a muscle in his temple twitching. A sheen of sweat coated his face. He stood rigid as the foreman paused and then said:
'All right, give you name to Mr Jackson.'
'Yes, sah!' the man shouted and started to the table, a huge smile cracking his face.
'One minute, dere!' The party representative's voice was commanding.
The carpenter stopped in midstride in an attitude of comic surprise. '*Me*, sah?'
'Yes you, sah.' The party henchman's expression was hard and suspicious. 'Yes you, sah – don't I see you somewhere before? What party you defen', eh?'
'Me no support none, sah.'
'You damn lie! You's a big unionite – don't I see you over Mr Maxwell headquarters de other day?'
'Me, sah? Me, sah? No, sah, don't run dem kinda joke deh, sah . . .' The man was out of control, his voice shrill with outrage. 'Is t'ree month me no work, me have to get de little work yah today. What my baby fe eat eh, sah? 'Im deh a yard now sick wid hungry knot up 'im tripe. No, sah, no run dem joke deh at all, *at all*.'
If the man was acting, he was a hell of an actor because the desperation in his voice sounded very real.
Two of the policemen approached. The foreman looked uncomfortable. 'You sure?' he asked the party man. 'We need carpenters, you know.'
'All right. 'Im can go through – but jus' fe today.' He pointed at the carpenter. 'An' you don't t'ink you get away wid nutten, y'know. Ah going check you out.'
There was a movement in the back of the line. Some of the men were leaving. They went and stood some distance away and were talking excitedly among themselves. The party man looked at the police.
'Move dem! Don't make no crowd congregate here!'
'Either get on line or leave!' the cop shouted.
Ivan stepped up to the foreman.
'What party you follow?' the henchman asked.
'None, sah,' Ivan answered truthfully.

'Well, choose one,' the man said. 'You mus' follow one.'

'What kind of work you do?' the foreman asked.

'I can do anyt'ing, y'know, sah,' Ivan answered, trying to smile.

'Anyt'ing? What name anyt'ing? You can pour concrete? You is a mason? You do carpenter work? Eh? Eh?'

'Ah never do it before, y'know, sah, but –'

'You can lay brick?'

'An can do anyt'ing, sah, jus' gi' me a break!'

'How you mean give you a break?' There was anger in the man's voice that Ivan didn't quite understand. 'Leave de place, man.'

'But Ah can do it, you know, sah. Ah only need a chance.'

'How you mean you can do it? You ever do it yet?' He was shouting. 'Ah say leave de place. Leff' de place, man. We need experienced people here. Don't bother waste my time. Next.' He peered into the face of the man behind Ivan. 'You again – don't I run you away yesterday?'

'Is not me, sah,' the man began to whine as Ivan walked away. [...]

(ii) The suburbs

[...] He didn't like the place where he was. Street after street lined on both sides with forbidding hedges or walls. Gates with spikes jutting up, chained and locked; silent sentinels eloquent with hostility, unapproachable. In one afternoon he had come to hate and fear dogs, to see them in a new light. They hurled themselves against the iron gates with a frenzy that was incomprehensible to him. Why would people want to live with such savage animals? Then someone would open a door or peer suspiciously from behind the iron bars which were inevitably present on every window.

'What you want?' In reply to his courteous and suitable 'Good afternoon, mam.'

'Stan' back from the gate. The dog will tear you up. Come, Brutus.' And Brutus wagging his plump rump and bounding like an overgrown puppy would obey, sweet as milk.

Nobody said 'good afternoon'. Nobody spoke in other than a cold, and for some reason that he couldn't understand, hostile tone, as though he were personally guilty of some offence against them. Sometimes, uncalled, the dogs ran along the fence barking and snarling, often in their fury snapping at the plants, until they ran out of yard and the task would be taken up by the 'Brutus' in the next yard.

The feeling that his presence was unwanted, alien, and despised, was as inescapable as it was depressing. He knew he had a right to walk the road and look for work, but his progress was nerve-wracking and hurtful.

This gate was open, hanging ajar. His first pleased surprise gave way to apprehension. Did it mean that there was nothing between him and one or more of those wolf-like creatures? No – if they had those kinds of dogs, the gates would have to be shut. Or would it? Anyway, he didn't see or hear a dog. A yard apparently without dogs and with a gate open? He started to knock, hesitated. Why not go in – maybe if he could talk to someone? He looked at the yard. It was well kept; almost certainly they had someone already an' the damn dog was probably watching, licking his teeth and waiting for him to take that one step that would put him out of reach of the safety of the street. The garden was where a dog could be sleeping too. Too big with lots of bushes. He stood in the open gateway and stared at the house. It was so big, so substantial, so beautifully painted. No – he'd better knock! He had an unobstructed view. For the first time he was not peeping between the bars of a locked gate, or through a hedge or over a wall. Jesus, this is what rich mean. Everything so clean, so fancy, so expensive. He took his first step, paused, then another. Nothing happened; he advanced well down the drive, his eyes fixed on the verandah. It was shady with green ferns on stands, it seemed a cool and delightful place in the hot afternoon. He realized that he was walking with a kind of apologetic tip, placing his battered shoes gently on the gravel walk, as though by a visible diffidence of posture and step he would negate the boldness of his presence. When he realized this, he forced himself to quicken his pace and place his feet down more firmly.

He could see a woman on the verandah. She was reclining on a rattan settee, her back turned towards the road. She was intent on something she was doing and didn't hear him approach. She was not white. But he couldn't think of her as black either, though there was not much difference in their colour. *He* was black. *She* was rich.

He stands and watches her. She is wearing a loose shirt and well-pressed slacks of the same material. Her clothes are spotless. Her hair is oiled and styled and there is not a lock out of place. She seems cool and fresh. She is painting her nails. She is perfect. He clears his throat diffidently. She starts up and nearly spills her nail polish on the gleaming tiles of the verandah.

'Excuse, mam . . . Good day, mam?'

'What you doing here?' Her voice is not perfect. It is sharp, not at all gentle on the ear, there is an unpleasant tremor in it.

'Ah looking work, mam.' He doesn't have to work to make his voice humble. He is intimidated by the opulence of the house and the conspicuously elegant grounds. He tries to smile.

'How did you get in here?'

'The gate was open, mam, so Ah come to see if –' His tone is even more self-effacing while trying to be hopeful.

She hasn't said no to the work. She looks at him – a hard, appraising glance – and seems less startled. 'Close the gates when you leave. I have no work for you.' She turns her back and picks up a magazine.

He understands that the conversation is over but he can not bring himself to turn around and walk away with so curt a dismissal. 'Ah can wash your car, mam,' he calls entreatingly, though he understands that there will be no work for him here and that the tone of his voice will make no difference.

'My husband has that done downtown,' she snaps, looking up with a frown which arches her symmetrically plucked brows and threatens to crack the make-up on her cheeks.

'Ah can tek care of the garden,' he says quickly.

'We have a service for –'

He cuts her off with 'Ah can do anyt'ing, *anyt'ing*, mam.'

'Look. You better go! There is nothing you can do for me, *nothing*. You understand that you taking a chance? We have two Rhodesian Ridgebacks. They could tear you to pieces.'

'Well den, beg you a ten cent, mam . . .'

'I don't believe in young healthy boys begging – that's what's ruining this country. Beg, Beg, Beg. You should be ashame – go try to make something of yourself. And lock the gate behind you, too. Go on.'

She watches him walk away with a certain defiant deliberateness. 'Who left the gate open?' she shrieks at the servants in the house. 'Those people really getting bold though, eh? Imagine how the boy look at me, like 'im want to beat me if I didn't give him work! You know the gate must be locked at all times!' she shouts. 'Next thing you know someone break in and kill us all in our sleep!'

(iii) 'The Harder They Come'
Jimmy Cliff

Well they tell me of a pie up in the sky
Waiting for me when I die
But between the day you're born and when you die
They never seem to hear even your cry
So as sure as the sun will shine
I'm gonna get my share now, what's mine
And then the harder they come
The harder they fall one and all
The harder they come
The harder they fall one and all.
Well the oppressors are trying to keep me down
Trying to drive me underground
And they think that they have got the battle won
I say forgive them Lord they know not what they've done
Cause as sure as the sun will shine
I'm gonna get my share now, what's mine

Chorus
And I'll keep on fighting for the things I want
Though I know that when you're dead you can't
But I'd rather be a free man in my grave
Than living as a puppet or a slave
So as sure as the sun will shine
I'm gonna get my share now, what's mine

Chorus

(i) and (ii) Extracted from *The Harder They Come*, Pluto Press, London, 1980, pp. 166–8, 170–2. (iii) From the lyrics of 'The Harder They Come', by Jimmy Cliff, ICPS 9202, Island Music Ltd and original soundtrack recording on Island Records Ltd.

NOTE
[1. Since its independence from Britain in 1962 Jamaican politics have been dominated by increasingly bitter and violent competition between the conservative Jamaican Labour Party (in government 1962–72, and from 1980), and the more radical People's National Party led by Michael Manley (in government from 1972 to 1980). The pervasiveness of conflict between the two parties and its significance for the lives of the poor is conveyed in this passage by the critical role of the 'party henchman' in hiring workers for the building site, at a time when the Labour Party was in office.]

14 Autobiography of an Urban 'Marginal': Miguel Duran

JUAN RUISQUE-ALCAINO and RAY BROMLEY

Editors' introduction

This account was edited from thirty hours of interviews with 'Miguel Duran' in 1976 and 1978 which were part of a research project on the urban poor in Cali, the third largest city in Colombia with a population of well over a million. The interviews were directed to obtaining information on work and income opportunities. The following description of the *Zona Negra* is drawn from Ruisque-Alcaino and Bromley's introduction to this 'occupational [auto]biography', and we reprint some of their comments on it at the end. The explanations in brackets in Miguel's account are theirs, and they also tell us that '[the] bottle-buyer's name and most other names in his autobiography are pseudonyms chosen by us to protect both the innocent and the guilty'.

The *Zona Negra* (literally 'black zone') referred to is 'a high-density, low-income zone just east of the city centre in Cali . . . [and] famous as the main concentration of poor people's crime and vice in the city and as a red-light zone and skid row. . . . It would be unfair, however, to portray the *Zona Negra* simply as a concentration of vice, crime and squalor, though this portrait is the norm both in official discussions on the *Zona Negra* and in its coverage in the Cali press. The area also has a remarkable concentration of small manufacturing and repair enterprises and of wholesaling and retailing establishments, including several major grain and processed food warehouses and most of the wholesalers and retailers of second-hand goods in the city. The *Zona Negra* is particularly important for the trade in old bottles, newspapers, scrap iron, clothing and footwear, and is the main focus for these goods in the whole city.'

---

1. My name is Miguel Duran and I am just 38 years old. I was born in the *barrio*[1] Saavedra Galindo in Cali, when that *barrio* was right on the edge of the city. (It is now about one-third of the way between the city centre and the urban periphery, reflecting Cali's rapid growth since 1940.) My parents were married and had four children, three boys and a girl. I was the youngest. My eldest brother left home before I was even five years old and I don't know what has happened to him. My second brother, Luis, was about 11 years older than me. He went to secondary school and then became a jockey at the Cali Racecourse till he was dismissed from the racecourse for taking bets to make horses lose. Then he sold newspapers on the streets and potato crisps in the football stadium for a bit, before he took off for Venezuela. He left Cali about 1965 and I haven't heard of him since. My father used to work for the Municipality, operating a pneumatic drill for the Public Works Secretariat. He retired a long time ago. He's still alive and is over ninety now, but though he's still in Cali we never see each other. My mother

had a newspaper stall in the street and my sister just used to hang around with her or stay in the house.

2. My mother put me in the Saavedra Galindo primary school, but I didn't even complete a whole year. As my mother sold newspapers she got home late to feed me. So as not to go hungry, I sucked up to the teacher so as to get a free school meal. From each class they took four boys for the restaurant; those who worked hardest. They put me up from first grade to second grade and I began to write in ink. When we were about to finish the year, my mother died, so my father asked me 'Do you want to keep going to school?' and I said 'No father, I don't want to go to school any more, I've learnt to read and write, why learn more?' My father went and found another woman. My eldest brother had already gone to Bogotá and Luis left home disgusted at my father and didn't return. When we completed the nine days of prayers after the funeral, my father left the house with my sister and they went to live with the woman that he had found. I was left alone in the house, though I was only six or seven years old then. My father even took most of the furniture and clothes out of the house and sold them to neighbours. The house was a big one. It still exists, but I never go there now. I never visit my father, as we don't get on with each other. Anyway, he doesn't live in the house, he just rents it out.

3. I lived there in the house on my own for a bit, then I found some other boys for company and they came to the house. They were layabouts and used catapults. My mother didn't used to let me go with those boys. They went to shoot at chickens and had a good aim. I even became a crook through going with them. We shot chickens in the head – pow – they fell, and we stuck them in bags and sold them to restaurants. In the restaurants they bought each chicken for six to eight pesos,[2] which at that time was an awful lot of money for a boy. We bought wine and *aguardiente* (literally 'Fire-water'; an alcoholic spirit made from sugar cane) and a box of *Pielroja* (Colombia's most popular brand of 'lower-class' cigarettes) and matches and rice and cooking fat, and we would go and get drunk in that house and cook stolen chickens. I ran out of money and so I used to go with the boys from the house to Jotagomez and Tia (two of the main supermarket firms operating in Cali) to steal. We went in and stole screws and sold them to the fences in the *Zona Negra*. There are lots of fences in the *Zona Negra*; you can take anything and they'll buy it. So I wasn't short of money with those boys and I began to go round following a teenage girl who was known as 'crazy Eneas'. ('Odd' or 'eccentric' poor women in Cali are often nicknamed *la loca* –literally mad or crazy – if they are aggressive, loud-mouthed and ignorant.) Eneas was bad-tempered, carried a knife, and acted like a man. When she realized I was a good thief and knew how to use a knife, she got to like me. So, by the time I was eight years old, I was going round with a prostitute. I was a *gamin* (the Colombian colloquialism for 'street urchin'; an orphan, cast-out or runaway boy who lives on the streets), though I was more a solitary type than a member of any regular gang.

4. I was just a layabout. I saw other petty thieves who were big – sixteen year olds and twelve year olds – and of course I wanted to do the same as them. I got wrapped up in the Central Market with all those thieves and prostitutes. I wanted to get a room to live in; at that time rooms were cheap –six pesos for a night. Then Eneas asked me if I would like to live with her and I said yes. So I went to my father and told him I wasn't coming back to the house again. My father asked me why I wasn't going to school and I told him that I was drinking and smoking cigarettes. And my father said 'All right, you go where you like and I'll close this house.' Then I told him that I had become a petty thief and had a woman and he

put his hand on his head. 'What I'm going to do with you is this; as I work for the Municipality, I'm going to give you to the Municipality so that you can sweep up and carry things in the workshop. I'll buy you a pair of trousers and a shirt every week and I'll give you pocket money to go to the cinema.' And I said, 'Father, I don't need it, look,' and I took piles of money out of my pocket. I told him again that I wasn't coming back and I left.

5. Why were those people so dumb? It was easy to rob. Those people (rural migrants to the city) came to open their eyes here in Cali. They were incredibly dumb and humble. At mid-day you could rob people like crazy around the Central Market. So I went to live with Eneas and I started pickpocketing (*la cosquilla*; a pickpocket is known as a *cosquillero* or *carterista*). Eneas told me to go and work with a man called Madera, so we worked together. He would push and shove people in the street and I would stick my hand into their pockets and steal things. Then the police hit me – pow – and they took me to the police station. They searched me and – pow – to the cells; the 'Pavilion of Minors'. I was about 10 years old then and as it was a first offence, they let me out after a few days. So I changed profession and I became a *caimanero* (someone who steals from ladies' handbags). You work with a partner who gets ahead of the woman, then stops, and when she tries to get round him, you come up behind her and – pow – you hit her and grab her handbag. So I stole like crazy till they got me again. And they put me in that pigsty the Pavilion of Minors and then they wouldn't pardon me again, and they sent me to the Reformatory (near Buga, about 75 km north of Cali). From then on I stopped using my proper name and started using a variety of false names. I escaped and eventually I got back to Eneas in Cali.

6. Eneas was about 19 and was a hell of a thief. We had great times with her, but no sex. I went back to stealing, and the next day the police got me again, and – pow – into the Pavilion of Minors and – pow – back to the Reformatory in Buga. There they caned me and shaved my head and took my clothes. Eventually I escaped again, but in escaping I twisted my arm and my elbow became swollen. I managed to get back to Cali and I went to Eneas and she bathed the arm in hot water. Then, after two days, they put her in jail for five to ten years for attacking and wounding someone. I sold all my things and hers to pay the rent and I went back to thieving, though my arm was agony. Eventually I moved to a different lodging run by a homosexual called Manuel who used marijuana and had lots of 'pretty boys'. I must have been about 14 then. In the next room, there was a black woman from Chocó who had run away from her husband. She cured my arm, though it's left permanently bent. I started to sleep with her. She was hard-working and sold in the Market; I would steal cases of tomatoes for her to sell. Then her husband came and took her away and I was left alone, living from theft. They sent me to the Reformatory again; they were frightened of me there, and they tied me up in a cell.

7. I was a *cosquillero* and a good one at that, and a *caimanero*. Then, later, I got hooked on pickpocketing pens; Parkers and Shaeffers – all those fine pens that they used to use here. Then from *plumero* (pen thief), I changed profession to *escapero* (sneak thief). I used to go into the shops behind the public to steal. Sometimes I used to buy a pile of newspapers and walk around selling them as a cover for stealing. One day, in front of Jotagomez, there was a watchmender working on a little table with a display cabinet by the side. I managed to get my hand into the cabinet without him seeing me and stole a watch. When I got the money for that watch, I was almost killed. I started drinking because then a watch was worth a hell of a lot of money and a girl who used to have a soft spot for me called me a son-

of-a-bitch and a queer. So I hit her with my fist and she pulled a knife and stabbed me in the stomach, cutting the veins and hitting the bone. They tied me back together in the hospital.

8. In those days, I used to sleep the nights in the charity house run for *gamines* by Dr Riascos. That house only lasted about six years till it was closed when Riasco died. He was a great benefactor and really took an interest in poor kids. They used to let us sleep there and sometimes they gave us food, but we were free to roam around the streets in the daytime. They even made me a 'foreman' of a dormitory.

9. I used to go to Puerto Tejada (a town about 30 km from Cali) every Wednesday to steal, because the weekly market there is very good. You know, it's not so bad to steal – a lot of rich people do it. They open a shop and sell things for twice what they bought them for – and they have the cheek to call that robbery 'business'! Then there are the hoarders and speculators – what a good way to steal!

10. When I was still a minor, they sent me to the main Cali jail (known as *El Rastrillo*); they were such bastards in that jail that they put me in the men's courtyard. Once you went into that courtyard nobody protected you; you had to be a corrupt son-of-a-bitch like them. They put me in a group where they put the young, 'pretty' ones, and most of them were homosexuals. Then they sent me to the Alaska Colony (a penal colony on the *Cordillera* west of Buga, a town 75 km north of Cali) and put me on road building. I was there for two years, then later back again for six months, then on 90-day and 60-day arrests. I carried on robbing in Cali when I wasn't in the Reformatory or the Cali jail or the Alaska Colony. I spent most of my teens and early twenties in penal institutions for one offence or another; generally robbery or selling marijuana. Occasionally I earned an honest living. I sold newspapers for a bit and then I sold cakes and sweets for a woman. She used to sell cakes and sweets on the street and she gave me some of her stock to sell for her. I used to go round with two baskets of cakes and sweets and she used to pay me a ten per cent commission for everything I sold. Well, I soon got bored with selling and I could never keep off robbing for long.

11. I became an *atracador* (a street thief who uses violence to rob), working with a big negro nicknamed 'Chute'. He was the projectionist in the Cinema Cali, which used to be by the market. At one stage, we even thought of going straight in partnership. We built a rickety old hand-cart and we started to carry loads to and from the Central Market, but we mainly used the cart as a cover for stealing. We would take sacks and boxes from the warehouses and stalls and slip them onto the cart when no one was looking. Once we stole a box of chocolate and we were just splitting the money between us after selling it when – pow – the police got us. Well, they confiscated the cart and the money and sent us to the Pavilion of Minors for a few days. We never saw the cart or the money again; they stole it from us. A few times I bought fruit or vegetables and sold them on the street, but I never kept it up for long. Robbing came more easily to me, though whenever I got out of prison I felt very nervous and frightened about robbing.

12. The main honest job I had while I was in my teens was playing drums for a piano-player who worked various bars and dance-halls around the *Zona Negra*. I learnt to play drums by hanging around the bars, watching drummers and practising on their drums when they would let me. Each bar had its own piano and drum-set, so the musicians needed no instruments; they just went round from bar to bar asking for work. Well, I got friendly with a piano-player called Alberto Gutierrez and I played with him on-and-off for a couple of years. Then one day he was poisoned by a prostitute. He lived but he never recovered; he became like a child

and didn't even know where he was. About then there was a big municipal persecution campaign on the bars and dance-halls around the *Zona Negra* and the old *Zona de Tolerancia* and the work for musicians just dried up (the *Zona de Tolerancia* was the traditional 'permitted zone' for brothels and prostitution, to the north of the *Zona Negra* and overlapping with it; it was abolished in the 1960s).

13. When I was about 18, I killed a man in a knife fight. His nickname was Mono Cagado (literally dirty, fair-skinned man) and he worked with me on some sneak thefts. One day I crept into the store of the Everfit shop and stole a big case of clothing. I carried it out onto the street and passed it to Mono Cagado who was waiting with a taxi. He went off with the case in the taxi, while I ran off down the street happy at the success of the robbery. Anyway, Mono Cagado didn't come to meet me. About a week later I ran into him. He was wearing clothes from the case stolen from Everfit and said he had sold the rest and spent all the money on drink. Of course, I was furious, and pulled a knife and stabbed him. He pulled a knife and lunged at me, but he missed. I stepped back and he fell forwards and died soon afterwards. I ran away, but the police arrested me in a lodging house after a woman from the house gave me away to escape imprisonment for possessing drugs. I swore I was innocent of the murder and after 19 days the police set me free for lack of evidence. So I got away with it.

14. When I was 19, I found a girl called crazy Rosa. She sold intestines there in the Central Market. I used to steal in the market, especially from the hand-carts that went to and from the shops. I stole chunks of meat, boxes of *Pielroja*, boxes of lavatory paper and bags of rice. I even stole from Rosa. Well, I got to know her and eventually I seduced her. I lived with her on-and-off for nine years, but most of that time she spent waiting while I was on one prison sentence or another. They got me again and again for robbery and for selling marijuana. As I was older, they sent me to the new Villanueva Prison in Cali, and to the Aracuara and Acacias Penal Colonies in the jungle (in the eastern lowlands of Colombia). They were tough places. A lot of prisoners were beaten up and even killed, some by guards and others by their own cellmates. You know what's really wrong with the prisons. They taught me nothing except fighting, more vice and crime. They should educate people and find jobs for them when they get out so that they've got no reason to go on committing crimes. I was a criminal because I was poor and ignorant and didn't know any better way to make a living.

15. When I got out of jail, I always went back to crazy Rosa. I was cruel to her and I used to hit her a lot. The last time I was in jail was in 1961 when they sentenced me to a year and a half for stealing a bicycle. When I got out of jail for the last time, I got Rosa pregnant and she had a baby boy that we called Jimmy. Anyway, I continued to mistreat her and we separated. She's got at least three other kids by different men, but I haven't seen her for years now. Jimmy's 13 now. He's an *atracador* and is following in my footsteps. He's in the Reformatory for Minors, and I think they're teaching him some useful things there. He comes to see me sometimes.

16. When I got out of prison in 1962, I took charge of a lodging-house called La América. It's been demolished now. The owner had known me for a long time and he asked me whether I thought I was capable of running that brothel. I said 'Yes' and took the job. The owner didn't care about how the place was run; he just came for his money every day. I had to pay him 400 pesos per day. I kept a note of the rooms and who had paid. At that time a *rato* (the term used for sexual intercourse) cost three pesos for the room plus what the prostitute charged for herself. I had about five women downstairs in the doorway to attract the men. They brought the

men upstairs and charged directly for their services; all I took was the three pesos for the room, I didn't charge the girls anything. I kept the rooms clean and made sure that no one robbed or attacked the clients. It was a rough house, with women from Buenaventura. Chocó and all over the place. When I saw a woman who had recently arrived in Cali I tried to get her to corrupt her. Of course, we didn't just have rooms for *ratos*; there were also people who stayed a long time, mainly prostitutes, homosexuals, thieves and dealers in stolen goods. To make more money, I sold marijuana. It was good business. I used to buy a half-pound for 400 pesos and make thousands of *papeletas* (tiny quantities each wrapped in a piece of paper) to sell at 50 centavos. There was a lot of police persecution and I was always having to hide the marijuana away, but it was an easy way to make money. I used to stay in the lodging-house all day and go out drinking in the evening. When I went out I used to leave a negro called Uldarico in charge of the place. He eventually died of consumption from staying up at night so much. Anyway, when I got back from drinking or the cinema at midnight, he gave me the money that he had collected for the rooms and for the marijuana that he had sold. But he swindled me a lot on the *ratos*, pocketing some of the money for the *ratos* for himself when he should have given it all to me.

17. Some little *gamines* (street urchins) began to come to La América. One came with his box to shine shoes, another begged for food round the restaurants and others went to collect paper (to accumulate paper and sell it by the kilo to paper-buyers, who pass the paper on to other wholesalers and to the large paper factories, who then recycle this paper). They were a gang of about 11, and they wanted to sleep in the lodging-house. I rented them a space on the floor at the back and I charged them a peso to sleep there in a line. Well, from then on I started to get angry with these kids, wasting their youth and all dirty. One day I said to them: 'Here, the one who doesn't get money, who doesn't rob, and who doesn't change his clothes, can't stay; pass me that box, pass me those sacks!' And I broke the box and took the sacks (that they used to collect paper in). Well, one soon arrived with some shirts that he had stolen, then another arrived with some shoes, then another with a shopping basket with some groceries in it. I kept a cupboard full of things that they had stolen; they stole on the street and I used to steal from them in the lodging-house; I used to give them any price I chose. Then they started to get clever and mean and stopped bringing the best things to me; they started selling the good things out on the street. Those *gamines* have turned into heavyweight *atracadores* now; I still see some of them around the streets from time to time.

18. I got to know Socorro, the girl I've lived with for the last 11 years, there in La América. Cecilia, her mother, came to Cali from Florida (a town about 42 km away), with two daughters, Socorro and Lucia. Frankly I didn't have any bad intentions, I just took pity on them. I put them to live in a room in the lodging-house and told them to buy a case of tomatoes and to get up early to sell them in the street by the Central Market. They didn't have any money to buy the tomatoes, so I lent it to them. I didn't even notice the daughters for quite some time. Then, eventually, I took a fancy to Socorro, I gave the two girls food and they got fatter and prettier. Socorro was only twelve when, one day, I seduced her right there in the lodging-house. Her mother was furious, though she's long since forgiven me. Anyway, I was offered the custody of another lodging-house, so I moved away with Socorro to get away from the mother.

19. When I moved to the new lodging-house with Socorro, I formed a gang of burglars – only four, but good ones. They stole whisky and silver plates, and food-mixers and pressure cookers; they brought things every day from those rich neigh-

bourhoods. But everything was swindled from us by old Alonso the fence; the one who's got the pawn-shop. He was once kidnapped and they got one-and-a-half million pesos for him. He used to swindle us and threaten us all the time.

20. One day on the street, I saw a man taking some shoes from one of my gang and I went up to him and told him to give the shoes back. He refused and pulled a knife, so I pulled my knife out. We fought, he gave me this cut here, and I stabbed him in the stomach. He still suffers and has a tube inside him, but by a miracle he didn't die.

21. One day the police were doing a house-to-house round-up (a *recogida*). So I closed my lodging-house that day; they were carrying everyone off in lorries. I blocked the door and refused to open it to the police. When some of my people got back the next night, they paid for their rooms. All of them looked frightened and many left. A policeman I knew told me that the Police Captain was furious that I hadn't opened the door the night before and that the F2 (the Colombian special police – more-or-less equivalent to the US FBI) were going to come to get me and would take me out to the countryside to kill me.

22. I got scared, so I went away and got a job running a different lodging-house beside a bar belonging to the same owner. Then a man shot one of the prostitutes, a woman called Rosita – shot her dead and ran. The police came and took the body and the gun. The dead whore had no family; she was on her own here. She had been very good to me, and used to give me cigarettes and whisky. I had 300 pesos so I went to the hospital (where the police autopsy was performed) and claimed the body. I paid 100 pesos for them to tidy up the body and to put her in a 900 peso coffin, on which I paid a 200 pesos deposit. Then I brought the corpse back; what a good corpse – I made a lot of money out of that dead whore. I arranged the wake and put out a collection plate. Everyone who came to the wake contributed. I arranged and paid for the funeral and burial, renting a car and two buses for the people who went. Burials were cheap in those days – only 120 pesos. Anyway, I made 1,800 pesos out of that funeral. Rosita was a bit old, but she kept her body in good condition and the men used to rain down on her – she was so randy that she would sometimes do 20 or 21 men in a day. She made a lot of money.

23. Well, not long after the business with Rosita, I gave up administering lodging-houses. Socorro and I moved into a rented room near the Central Market. I worked as a night-watchman for a bit, guarding some houses near the Market, but the owners were slow to pay up and I didn't make much money. I also worked with Luis for a few months, selling potato crisps in the football stadium. Because he had been a jockey, Luis had important contacts who fixed it for him to sell in the stadium and he fixed it for me. Sales in the stadium are a monopoly and you have to have friends in the Sports Council to fix it for you to work there – it's a mafia.

24. I've lived with Socorro all the 11 years since we met. She has made me into a new man. I used to be wild, but she reformed me. After Rosita's funeral, a half-brother of Socorro's called Watusi turned up. Watusi's a nickname, but no one ever uses his proper name. He had been a sugar-cane cutter in Florida, till one day he decided he couldn't stand it any longer. He came to us exhausted, penniless and hungry, asking us for help. Well, I told him he'd have to find a way of earning a living, especially as Socorro and I were having to support Cecilia, who's often sick with asthma. Well, we made a long hand-cart and we started to work together with the cart. We called the cart 'Born to lose' and painted the name on it. The name was to show that we were nobodies and that everything in our lives had been wasted. We started off selling fruit, but it didn't sell well. A lot shrivelled up or rotted in the sun and much of the left-over fruit from one day didn't keep till the next. Sometimes we didn't make any money; we actually came out losing.

25. Then we started to transport and buy and sell scrap metal. But I got fed up with pulling the cart, so I left Watusi working with the cart and went back to robbing. I started petty theft, and I was better off. But I watched Watusi, he didn't get so much money but he came satisfied to the house, while I got home frightened and bitter. So I said to Watusi 'I'm going to start working again', and the next day we got up early and went a long way into the rich *barrios* and started buying and we made 60 or 70 pesos between the two of us by 3 p.m.; we split it, but it wasn't enough because we had to pay rent and Watusi never helped with money for his mother – we needed to cook more food because his mother used to eat with us. The other sister, Lucia, had run off with a man to Tumaco (a city in the extreme southwest of Colombia), so she wasn't contributing anything. So I said to Watusi, 'Brother, the best thing is that we split. You carry on with the cart and I'll go and get another cart.' So I went to a bottle wholesale-buyer I knew in the *Zona Negra* called Pedro, and he told me that he hadn't got a cart to lend. So I said to him 'I'm desperate, brother, I want to work, I want to do something.' So he asked me if I would like to run his *depósito* (store) and sort bottles for him.

26. So I started sorting bottles, putting bottles of the same type together; medicine bottles here, perfume bottles here, cooking oil bottles there, and so on. If the bottle was damaged, I spotted it. I learnt the many different types and sizes and how to pack them so that they won't break. Pedro paid me 40 pesos a day – he's very vice-ridden; everything that he makes each day he gambles, or spends on drink, or he gives it to women – present of 200 and 300 pesos. I said to him: 'Hey Pedro, I wish you would help these *frasqueros* (bottle buyers) instead of giving all that money to women. You could pay them five or ten centavos more for each bottle; if you did, they would look after their bottles more carefully and would bring more to you.' He listened to me and raised the price on all bottles by five centavos and more *frasqueros* came to him, and he made more money. He could make 9,000 or 10,000 pesos from the sale of a big load of bottles, but in a few days he was broke again and owing money on his rent. The landlord threw him out from the store, so we shifted to another room nearby. I worked like mad to get that business going. It was me who ran the warehouse; I was the one who bought and sold; I even paid the *frasqueros*: I had to receive, sort and sell the bottles and get money to lend to the *frasqueros* next day. Everything that was profit, I gave to Pedro. I worked five years for him, but I made no progress, he wouldn't even pay me 50 pesos a day. He said he wouldn't pay me more and he got angry with me. So I said 'OK we won't work together any more. This hand-cart is yours and for the time that I have worked for you, I'm going to take the cart.' And he said 'OK, take the cart' and I said 'Right, here's your store brother; tomorrow you lend me money to start working with my cart.' The next day I went, he lent me money, and I started to work as a *frasquero*. But his business started to go downhill; he couldn't run it as well as I could.

27. In the house where we rented a room, there was a woman called Margarita who made *rellenas* (black sausages) and the business went well for her. She liked me and Socorro. I got clothes and shoes for Margarita and she said to me 'Why don't you put Socorro to work'. Socorro didn't know how to do anything. She's not bad looking; well dressed, she could work anywhere. So the woman offered to teach her to make *rellenas* and to cook them. I said it was all right, so Socorro learnt how to make *rellenas* and went to sell them in the Floresta Market, while the other woman went to sell in the Alameda Market. I had a radio and I sold it for 160 pesos and I sent her to buy the two big pots that we would need to cook our own *rellenas*. Then we needed the big tray which cost 75 pesos. So I grabbed two pairs of

trousers and went to pawn them and got 50 pesos and 25 pesos. Then I gathered up some rags and took them over to a tailoress who worked over the road; she lent me another 25 pesos. So we bought the big tray and got up at 2 a.m. to go and buy all the ingredients for *rellenas* in the Porvenir Market. I had got the urns with plastic tops to carry the blood and we got all the ingredients and went back to the house. But we had no charcoal; at 4 a.m. with all our money invested! So I had to go out to the warehouse and find Pedro and he bought the cart back from me for 200 pesos. I got charcoal and we even burnt the boards off the bed to fuel the fire. We cooked everything and feasted on the left-overs, but then I had no cart to shift the pots of *rellenas*. So I went to Euclides, another bottle wholesale-buyer who lived nearby, and explained to him that I had sold my cart to Pedro and had nothing to work with. So he lent me another cart and 100 pesos to buy bottles with. I went back to our lodgings, we put all the pots on the cart and we headed down to the Market. That day Socorro spent 207 pesos on ingredients and made 95 pesos profit. We did pretty well, and after a few weeks we bought a radio again. I got the trousers back, and we got new boards for the bed. But the *rellena* business didn't last long. The cost of the ingredients rose rapidly, and customers wouldn't accept price rises, so Socorro ended up selling less and making virtually nothing out of the sales, till she gave up the business altogether.

28. Over the years, since the *rellenas*, Socorro has worked hard. She has sold *chontaduros* (a tropical fruit) on the streets. She has gone round the houses getting odd jobs as a washerwoman. She even worked as a servant for a family in the *barrio* Santa Helena for a couple of months till she was assaulted by the crazy degenerate son of the family. Mainly, Socorro has worked washing bottles in a bottle wholesale-buyer's store and that's what she does now.

29. Then in 1969 Cecilia got two plots in an invasion[3] in La Unión (Unión de Vivienda Popular, a low-income *barrio* on the eastern periphery of Cali). We looked after her food and things and she took her tarpaulin and stakes to the invasion. I had tried twice to make a claim in invasions in the mid-1960s, once in the *barrio* Asturias and once in the *barrio* Villamar, but both times I was thrown off – after all that staying up at night and getting bitten by *zancudos* (large mosquitos with a particularly irritating bite)! Anyway, Cecilia was successful and built on one plot and sold it. Then she built on the other plot and we all went to live there. I bought a bicycle so as not to have to ride in those smelly, overcrowded buses. Then Watusi bought a bike for 200 pesos, stolen of course, and we swopped wheels, took a few things off, and repainted it. We had a corner lot in La Unión; hardly anyone went down there as no cars could reach it. I got a friend and got a table, and we started to form a gang on that corner. It got like a gaming house. We built up to eight or nine tables with betting on dominoes. Everyone went there to enjoy themselves. No one really lost because the bets were only 10 or 20 centavos each. This continued till we left La Unión.

30. While we were living in La Unión, I found Diego, the little boy that we have – he's good looking and intelligent and does everything I tell him to do. He's white, with light hair; he's the child of good people, but they left him like rubbish in a box. I was working when I saw a box by the roadside and went to put it on the cart. I opened it; he was all thin and had been crying a lot; the rubbish truck would have got him soon and that would have squashed him up like a dead rat. I took him to La Unión and he looked very sick, as if he was going to die. I took him to my mother-in-law and got a bottle from a neighbour and bought milk and fed him. Gradually he got better and he's grown up a bright little kid. Diego's three now and is just like our own child.

31. For a bit, while I was living in La Unión, I tried going out to the rural towns and villages to sell old clothes and shoes that I had collected with the cart, or that I had bought from the clothing and shoe traders in the *Zona Negra*. Going to sell in the country used to be good business, but not these days. You used to be able to put up a stall where you liked, but now you have to bribe some lousy *Alcalde* (mayor; local political officer) or Police Sergeant 100 or 200 pesos to get a permit and to pay someone else 30 or 40 pesos when you put up a stall. The trips cost a lot in busfares and lodging and most rural people are so poor that they can't afford to pay a decent price for the clothes. Some of them were so pitiful that I even gave clothing away to them. So, I made virtually nothing out of those trips to the countryside and I soon gave them up.

32. I never liked La Unión. It was so isolated and far from the centre. There were an awful lot of negroes there; people who breed like rabbits, and go hungry, and don't look after the kids. They just leave their kids out on the street and the kids turn into *gamines*. I used to drink a lot in La Unión and I used to give away a lot of money. There were always hungry children and people complaining that they hadn't even been able to make a pot of *aguapanela* (unrefined sugar boiled up with water and *canela*, orange or lemon flavouring, and drunk hot or cold; the poor man's 'milk' in Cali). And we lived right by the main sewer, the great open ditch that comes down from the rich *barrios*. At one or two in the morning, it stunk so much that you felt drunk; from there we got insects, vermin and diseases of all sorts. There was a lot of sickness and we had to go a long way to get water. There were a tremendous lot of *zancudos*.

33. What finally got me sick of La Unión was the business with the horse-and-cart. It started when a guy tried to sell Watusi the metal undercarriage and wheels of a cart – the big carts that are pulled by a horse. Watusi liked the idea; we could buy more bottles and paper with less effort with a horse-and-cart than with a hand-cart. Watusi bargained him down to 800 pesos for the undercarriage and he arranged to sell his bike for 300 pesos. Then he came to me and persuaded me to go halves on the whole business. I sold my bike for 150 pesos and all the pots and tray that we had bought for the *rellenas*. Watusi sold his radio and then we had enough to go and buy the undercarriage. We dragged it to the house and the next day we went to a man in the *barrio* Villanueva who made carts. We told him we had a good undercarriage and asked how much he would charge to buy the wood and build the cart. He offered to do it for 1,800 pesos and we bargained him down to 1,200 pesos. We sold almost everything in the house to get that 1,200 pesos: a bed, four pairs of trousers, some shirts and blouses, the cooking stove, a pile of spoons that I had collected, some glasses and an old Japanese lamp. I had to threaten that cart-maker before he would do the job, even though we paid him in advance. Anyway, he finished it, and Watusi and I pushed and pulled that cart by hand all the way from the *barrio* Villanueva to La Unión. We arrived exhausted and then we had to pull down part of our fence to get the cart onto our plot. We spent the rest of the night arguing about how we would buy a horse. The next day we went to look at several horses on sale; 2,000 pesos, 3,000 pesos – impossible prices. Then we found a man with an old mare in foal; after some bargaining, we agreed on a price of 800 pesos. The problem was how to get the 800 pesos. I went to see Pedro and threatened him, saying that I worked for him for five years and the only thing he gave me was the hand-cart – I threatened to complain about him to the Ministry of Labour because he hadn't paid me a minimum wage or registered me for social security, and he gave me 500 pesos towards the cost of the horse. We still lacked 300 pesos, so we sold Watusi's hand-cart for 150 pesos and

then stripped all the roofing tiles off the house and sold them for 185 pesos. We gave the extra money to Socorro and her mother and told them to cook rice and potatoes and eggs to celebrate our getting the horse. So we went and got the horse, then we remembered that we had no reins and collar. We asked the original owner of the horse if he had the reins and collar and he offered to sell them for another 200 pesos. We had no money left and nothing that we could sell to get money, so we took him to our *rancho* (rustic-style hut/house) to show him where we lived and persuaded him to let us have them on credit so that we could earn the money by working the horse-and-cart. We called the mare Dartagnana and the cart 'This is my Cross'; we never guessed what a crucifixion that horse-and-cart were going to be. Well, we worked 23 days with the horse-and-cart and things went well. We gathered quite a lot of bottles and papers and scrap iron and got some more money by shifting earth and various cargoes of potatoes and grain. We paid for the reins and collar and even managed to replace some of the things we had sold to get the horse-and-cart. But the mare was getting very tired and thin; she didn't have many teeth and found it difficult to eat grass, so we gave her a bucket of molasses mixed with water. We decided to give her a few days' rest and Watusi and I went and borrowed a hand-cart and started getting bottles and paper with the hand-cart.

34. One day, while we were resting the mare, I got into a knife-fight and got a stab-wound in my leg – it cut my veins and I had terrible fevers and shivers for days. I stayed in the house while everyone else went out to work; Watusi pulling the borrowed hand-cart, Socorro washing bottles in a *depósito* in the centre and Cecilia selling tomatoes on the street. One day, when everyone had got back from working, we gave water to the mare and put her out to graze by the sewer, then we all went to sleep for the night. The next day the mare had vanished. We thought she had been stolen to be sold to be slaughtered and cut up as food for the animals at the zoo. I started working with the hand-cart again, though the leg was still giving me hell. Well, about a week later a mechanical excavator came to clean out the sewer and one of the neighbours' kids came to tell me that it had dug up the body of a horse like our mare. We went down to look, and it was the mare. Someone had given her a great *machete* cut on the neck and had pushed her into the sewer; some enemy of ours who was jealous of us having a horse-and-cart. Well, we were ruined. Then, to crown it all, a few days later someone stole the cart while we were asleep overnight. I went round the horse-and-cart men in the centre asking them where they knew of a cart for sale, and they told me of a newly-made cart on sale in the *barrio* Villanueva. Well, I paid one of them to take me there; it was a little hut belonging to another horse-and-cart man *(carretillero)* called Emilio, who has a lame leg and had known me for quite some time. I banged on the door and out came a woman who said that Emilio wasn't around. She looked frightened and when I told her the cart was mine she didn't argue. So I went back and got Watusi and Socorro and Cecilia and we pulled the cart by hand back to La Unión again. Then we decided to sell it. We found an Indian who went to look for buyers. He brought three, but they all offered 1,000 pesos. We eventually decided to sell and after giving the Indian 100 pesos commission, Watusi and I only had 450 pesos each left from the whole horse-and-cart affair. Everything else was lost.

35. Well, after that I got fed up with La Unión. We went back to working with borrowed hand-carts and I got another bike, but Socorro and I decided to move back to a rented room in the centre. So we shifted in 1974 and Cecilia and Watusi sold the *rancho* and followed us soon afterwards. Watusi did quite well for a bit when he came back to the centre and now he has a bottle store and is a wholesale-

buyer. He started working for Pedro. Then Pedro went broke, so Watusi took about 200 pesos and 300 cooking oil bottles and started his own store *(depósito)* in a room he rents from a scrap-iron dealer. It's a big room; you can even get a cart right into it. He passes his bottles onto 'The Rat', one of the big *depósito* owners. Watusi only has two *frasqueros* who sell to him and the business is going badly. I used to sell to him when I had my own cart, but now I use a borrowed cart, I have to sell to the guy who lent me the cart. Cecilia sells *frescos* (iced fruit drinks) on the streets in the *Zona Negra*.

36. Since we came back from La Unión, Socorro, Diego and I have lived in a room in the *Zona Negra*. Socorro is 23 now and the boy's just three. We've got a bed which needs painting, three second-hand chairs, a stove and some pots, an old radio and maybe one change of clothes. What we don't have is plates. It's a little board-walled room full of woodworm and fleas and it costs us 17 pesos a day. When Diego got sick once, I took him to the hospital. They said he needed some medicines costing 138 pesos and I only had 60 pesos. So I went out and pulled up one of those great iron manhole covers that weigh 100 kilos. I sold it for 200 pesos and with that I paid the medicine and some more potatoes and *aguapanela* for the kid.

37. Socorro washes bottles in the store where I sell most of my bottles. The owner used to be a *frasquero* like me, then he became a bottle-sorter in someone else's store, then he started his own store. He's got quite a lot of money in the bank now – he even carries a cheque-book. He pays Socorro one peso for every box of bottles that she washes; that's 24 bottles. Working hard she can wash 18 boxes in a day; that's only 18 pesos – it's not fair. She's illiterate and very ignorant and she has no identity papers, so she doesn't stand much chance of getting better work. Sometimes I get her making paper bags out of old newspapers in our room. (These crude bags are used by street and market vendors selling tomatoes, grapes and some other delicate fruits and vegetables.)

38. Since we came from La Unión, I've been a *frasquero* the whole time. I sold my bike and bought a cart, but then that cart was stolen with its cargo and everything. So I started to work with a borrowed cart from another store; a terrible old cart which made you want to cry, it was so hard to pull. Well, I was pulling it one day when I saw a man and a woman getting into a taxi with various shopping baskets. They were outside their own house and were obviously going to market. Then their servant ran out and asked him for the money to pay for the milk. He stuck his hand into his pocket and took out a note to give to her; what he didn't see was that he dropped a roll of notes on the ground. Then he got into the car and they drove off. I picked up the money and headed off as quickly as possible; 325 pesos. Well, I bought an undercarriage for 200 pesos and 100 pesos worth of wood (the two long arms for 45 pesos and 55 pesos worth of boards). I had a lot of nails in the house. A friend lent me a hammer and a saw and by 2 a.m. the next day I had finished building my own hand-cart. I worked with that cart until a couple of weeks ago, when I had to sell it for 300 pesos. Socorro got sick. I took her to the hospital, but nobody would look at her. She was shivering and feverish and looked as if she was going to die. So I went to La Rebaja chemist's shop and the dispenser recommended me to a cheap doctor who gave her an 80 pesos injection and gave me a prescription for a course of injections – five more at 60 pesos each. She's asthmatic you see, just like her mother. Well, she's had the treatment and she's more-or-less better now, but I had to sell the cart to pay for the injections.

39. If you have your own hand-cart and buy with your own money, you can sell to the store that will give you the best price, but if you have to borrow a cart and

the day's buying money, you have to sell to the store that lends them to you and accept the prices they pay. The guy I get the cart from is a bastard. I work with the cart from 6 a.m. to 5 p.m. and when I get to him at the end of the day, he takes the cart inside the store to unload while he leaves me outside. He hates anyone coming inside. So he swindles me on the count of the bottles and the weighing of the paper and metal; it's humiliating not having your own cart. He lends me 200 pesos at the beginning of the day and I use that to buy with. At the end of the day he discounts the 200 pesos from what he pays me for the bottles, scrap metal and paper. He gives bad prices for them, but at least he doesn't charge interest on the loan. There's a guy on the next corner who pays better prices, but who charges 10 per cent on the day's loan and 5 pesos for the rent of a cart. If you don't pay up, he goes to the police and they put out a warrant for your arrest. When they get you they throw you in jail and you have to pay to get out. The police just steal from thieves and take money for themselves. They're related to criminals like finger-nails to dirt. If I'm ever sick, the wholesaler won't even give me an aspirin; he just lends the cart and money to someone else, and refuses to lend them to me again when I come back.

40. The guy I get my cart from at present has 15 *frasqueros*. There are about 60 stores *(depósitos)* in Cali, most of them in or around the *Zona Negra*. I take my cart round Granada, Alameda, Versalles, Juanambú, San Fernando and Peñon (all middle- to upper-income *barrios*) where all those rich people live; those are the neighbourhoods where people have things to sell. But there are some rich *barrios* like Santa Rita where the police won't even let you go into the *barrio*; they're frightened that the *frasqueros* will rob from the houses. On a good day, I make 90 or 100 pesos after I've paid back the 200 pesos. On a bad day I might only make 20 or 30 pesos. I always pay back the 200 pesos. If I didn't, he wouldn't lend to me again, so I just have to go hungry and ask to postpone paying the rent if things go very badly or if anyone gets sick. We *frasqueros* don't have any form of organization and the stores won't do anything for us; they won't even give us a cigarette on Christmas Eve! The stores won't even pay us half of what they get for the things that they buy from us. They buy a cooking oil bottle from us for 20 centavos (there are 100 centavos in a peso) and sell it at 42, or even 45 centavos to one of the cooking oil factories, or if it's very dirty, to Patojito (the detergent factory) for five centavos less. They could pay us 25 centavos, couldn't they? After all, it's us who have to tramp around to get the bottles. They buy a kilo of newspaper for three pesos and sell it for 6.20, 6.30 or 6.40 to the paper factories. Surely they could pay us four pesos.

41. Sometimes I buy old clothes and shoes and sell them to the clothing and shoe traders here in the *Zona Negra*. I might buy a shirt for five pesos and sell it for eight, or some old shoes for eight pesos and sell them for twelve. One thing I never do is take things out of the rubbish cans that are put out for the EMSIRVA lorries (the Municipal refuse collection service). If people see you in that filth, they won't come out and sell you anything. You can be a good *frasquero* or a good *gallinazo* (literally 'vulture'; a garbage scavenger), but you can't be both.

42. It's not my fault that I'm poor. We poor people in Cali are so ignorant and illiterate; he who has children just produces prostitute and vagabond girls and thieving boys. The rich breed children for us to serve; they breed leaders to oppress the children of the poor. A couple of weeks ago I saw a wage-worker that I know who hadn't been paid for two and a half months. He was going round with a sack scavenging in the garbage, his hands full of blisters and cuts from digging ditches for water piping; indebted right up to his soul to the shops, and that day he

had nothing to eat. What did he do? He went and tore a watch off someone's wrist and sold it to a fence in the *Zona Negra* for 200 pesos; then he filled his sack with food. Life makes people bad and corrupt; that man was a good man and now he's bad. Lots of people are stupid, illiterate animals because they haven't had any education. If you treat a child like a good person and bring him up right, he'll be a decent citizen, but if you bring him up like a ruffian from childhood, he will live like that all his life.

Postscript

In April 1978, the second author re-interviewed Miguel on several occasions, visited his house, interviewed Socorro, Watusi and other members of their family, and interviewed various *frasqueros* and owners of *depósitos*. These interviews were mainly intended to verify and clarify the interviews conducted in 1976, but it is also worth noting some of the changes which occurred between 1976 and 1978.

Early in 1977, Miguel changed his mind on the pros and cons of living in La Unión and bought a small plot in the invasion where Cecilia had previously had her houses. He built a one-room *rancho* (shack) on the plot and moved down to La Unión with Socorro and Diego. The main reason for moving to La Unión seems to have been the irritating burden of daily rent payments in the *Zona Negra*. In spite of avoiding these payments, however, 1977 was a particularly difficult year for the family and Socorro even became a *frasquero* for six months, borrowing a hand-cart from a *depósito* owner and pulling it round the streets. It is extremely rare for women to work as *frasqueros* (there are probably no more than five female *frasqueros* in the city) and the adoption of this occupation for a few months led to ridicule on the part of many male *frasqueros* and proved to be physically exhausting for Socorro. By the end of 1977, she had returned to washing clothes and bottles as her two main income sources. Watusi closed his unsuccessful *depósito* in 1977 and returned to working as a *frasquero*.

Comments

[Miguel's] house and general living conditions would certainly place his household in the poorest 10 per cent of Cali's population . . . [and he] is, in many senses, a fairly typical member of Cali's 'disreputable poor', those members of the urban poor who have been involved, at some stage in their lives, in petty crime and vice and who have engaged in *gaminismo* (being *gamines*), prostitution, begging or garbage scavenging. His life illustrates some of the linkages between these activities and also the extent to which they are intermixed with more legal and reputable activities. It also illustrates how diverse income opportunities are combined to support an individual and his/her household and how almost all but the very youngest members of a household (the under fives) contribute something to the household budget.

[. . .] Miguel's autobiography serves to illustrate the weaknesses of two conventional 'caricatures' of the poor; that the poor are poor *simply because* they have too many children and that the poor are poor because they *all* don't work hard or show initiative. Miguel only has one child of his own (Jimmy, para. 15) whom he never had to support, and one adopted child (Diego, para. 30) whom he has supported since 1973, hardly a large family by any standards. Watching Miguel and Socorro working, and talking to them about their work, there is no doubt that they work very hard to make a meagre living. They are far from underemployed in terms of hours worked or effort expended, though clearly they are under-remunerated in relation to average incomes in urban Colombia. The degree of effort, sacrifice and joint commitment that was put into the *rellenas* enterprise (para. 27) and the acquisition of the horse-and-cart (para. 33) was enormous, yet in each case the effort came to nothing. Indeed, the horse-and-cart episode was an economic setback from which they have still not fully recovered.

[. . .] Most importantly, Miguel's autobiography illustrates the continuously precarious nature of enterprises, work, and even existence itself, for the very poor. Poverty is not only associated with low incomes, but also with lack of savings and capital, meaning that 'reserves' are very limited, even taking account of what can be obtained through sales, pawning and appeals to friends and relatives. Severe instability of work and incomes, and even of health and housing, are common characteristics of the poor, and are typical of 'the poorest of the urban poor'. Poverty is not simply a condition of insufficiency or deprivation, but also one of insecurity and instability.

Extracted from 'The bottle buyer: an occupational biography', by Juan Ruisque-Alcaino and Ray Bromley, in Ray Bromley and Chris Gerry (eds), *Casual Work and Poverty in Third World Cities,* John Wiley and Sons, Chichester, 1979, pp. 185–215.

NOTES

[1. District in a city or town; unless qualified by an adjective (e.g. 'rich') it usually refers to a working class or poor urban locality.]

[2. Approximate exchange rates for the Colombian peso at five-year intervals during the main period of Miguel's account were: 1951, £0.14; 1956, £0.14; 1961, £0.05; 1966, £0.03; 1971, £0.02; 1976, £0.02.]

[3. One strategy for the poor to cope with housing shortages is by taking over vacant areas of land, often but not always on the periphery of cities. These 'invasions' are usually organized by groups of families. The authorities often clear them again but it can also be politically expedient to recognize the squatters and even to provide them with services such as water and electricity.]

15   Small Engineering Workshops in Howrah

M. P. GHOSH

Editors' introduction

The 'city of Howrah' is effectively part of Calcutta, a major industrial city that is the capital of the state of West Bengal, and one of the principal centres of political and intellectual life in India. In this reading we encounter, physically and socially, a very different Calcutta from that inhabited by the 'middle-class bureaucracy' referred to in Reading 5. Ghosh provides a graphic picture of an area given over to 'informal sector' industry, and of conditions inside its workshops. The scenes

described, with local variations, are encountered in many of the more
industrialized cities of the Third World, where 'informal sector' engineering
workshops are usually involved in a dense network of 'horizontal' linkages with
similar establishments and 'vertical' linkages with larger-scale industries.

Belilious Road, with its teeming small and tiny workshops, had once earned the
city of Howrah the name, 'India's Sheffield'. Those small-scale industries which
had once flourished are now engaged in a life-and-death struggle to merely
survive. But even in their present miserable state, some of the older *mistrys*
[artisans] of Belilious Road retain their unique skills.

As one walks along the crowded Belilious Road teeming with small factories and
workshops on both sides, the first impression is one of complete anarchy and
absolute squalor all round. Dirty and narrow alleys branching out from the main
road, which itself is little more than a narrow street; open stinking and choked
drains; tottering sheds unsystematically huddled together in miserable clusters
housing small industrial units. A moulding unit is situated right amidst a cluster of
a few turning shops; a precision grinding works is almost choked with the heat and
smoke of the surrounding forging units. In the different workshops there are all
kinds of machines – lathe, capstan, shaping, milling, punching, slotting,
grinding; but there is an utter lack of systematic co-ordination and planning. Yet,
behind this appearance of confusion and anarchy there does exist a kind of co-
ordination – the Bililious Road type, one might say – which eludes the
inexperienced eyes of a newcomer.

This special type of co-ordination is confined to small groups of workshops the
owners of which are bound to each other by many extra-economic relations and
loyalties. For these petty conglomerates of small workshops – these joint families,
so to say – caste, localism and the forces of tradition were and, in some cases, even
now, are more important than business considerations and hard economic
realities. For example, the owner of a turning shop would have his press jobs done
at a ballpress half a mile away simply because the owner of that press was a
member of his community or hailed from his village. A precision tool maker would
have his shaping jobs done from a particular workshop because the owner of that
workshop was his 'uncle', i.e., a dear old friend of his late father. But hard
economic realities are gradually forcing many of the owners of these tiny workshops into a reluctant submission to the laws of the market.

Working conditions in these workshops are simply horrifying. In a dark and
smoky shed measuring 20 ft × 15 ft there are likely to be up to ten lathes and
capstans with hardly any space for a person to move between them. All the
machines are linked by a primitive device to a rotating shaft overhead which in its
turn is driven by an electric motor. The workers move about in between and
underneath the whirling belts with perfect ease, apparently unconcerned about the
dreadful consequence of even the slightest error in their movements. The
machines themselves are often as dilapidated as the tottering sheds in which they
are installed. Equipped with substandard and sometimes broken tools, the worker
has to struggle with his old and worn-out machine for up to fourteen hours to eke
out a miserable living for himself and his family. Often enough a worker would be
bending over his machine and operating it with his left hand while his right hand
keeps a firm hold over the half-broken tool post which would otherwise shake
violently. Accidents are all too common; and the single panacea for all minor

injuries (minor, according to the Belilious Road standards) is mercurochrome, popularly known among the workers as *lal oushudh*.

Such miserable working conditions should, one may reasonably suppose, constitute a fertile ground for militant trade unionism. But here again, the typical Belilious Road type of relationship between the owners and their workmen has stalled all the efforts on the part of trade unionists of all shades. Often the owner is an 'uncle' or a *dada* to his workmen (or vice-versa) and an appearance of close social and family ties is maintained between the two – including exchange of visits on festive or ritual occasions. The owner in many cases being little better off than his workers, it is difficult to arouse in the latter feelings of 'class hatred' against their 'bourgeois' employer.

But even without labour problems, the very existence of these small units is in danger. If the big industries face labour troubles, these small ones face the problem of chronic shortage of capital. The wages of the workers are miserably low and so, in most cases, are the profits. These small units secure orders from established factories which thrive at their cost; but the small units themselves have to engage in stiff competition to secure such orders, often being forced to quote low rates and thus further bring down their own profits.

On [. . .] top of all this, chronic and widespread loadshedding[1] has dealt a mortal blow to these industries. During the better part of the day the machines lie idle. Loadshedding has left its indelible mark on both the men and the machines. While the machines gather rust, the men are sullen and irritable. The area, once vibrant with life and activity, now wears a look of despair and desolation.

Reprinted from the *Economic and Political Weekly*, vol. 15, no. 50, 13 December 1980, p. 2083.

NOTE

[1. 'Loadshedding' is the term used in India for the rationing of the supply of electricity.]

16   Beedi-workers of Nizamabad

Editors' introduction

Beedis are a type of hand-made cigarette, rolled from tobacco leaf and tied with thread without the use of paper. They are bought by smokers who cannot afford machine-manufactured cigarettes (the great majority). As well as being a consumption item of the poor, they are produced by one of the poorest categories of factory workers as the following account vividly details. The *beedi* industry is the second largest provider of employment in India after agriculture, with estimates ranging between four and five million workers, of whom 400,000 are in the state of Andhra Pradesh (AP). It becomes clear from this account that 'industry' here refers to a mode of organizing labour in production rather than to any distinctive form of technology. The 'labour process' in *beedi*-making requires no 'inputs' beyond the leaf and thread, and the dexterity and stamina of the workers themselves. In some

places in India it is done at home on an 'out-work' basis with bosses or intermediaries supplying the raw materials. In the case of Nizamabad described here it
is presumably more profitable for the *seths* (bosses) to crowd the workers, who are
mostly women, into 'factories' so as to maximize the hours worked and to
supervise their labour more closely.

Of the four major beedi-producing districts of Andhra Pradesh – Adilabad,
Karimnagar, Nizamabad and Medak – Nizamabad leads both in employment
and production. It employs 1.5 *lakh* out of the 4 *lakh* beedi-workers in these four
districts and produces half the total number of beedies.[1] Beedi making is
practically the only industry in the district, which is one of the most backward in
the state. Literacy is only 21 per cent compared to the state average of 29.9 per
cent; among women it is a bare 12 per cent compared to the state average of 20
(these are 1971 figures). Ninety-five per cent of the beedi workers are women and
97 per cent of them are illiterate. This combination of factors tells its own story.
The reason for the concentration of beedi-making in a district which is not a major
tobacco producer, and is not even as well placed with regard to beedi leaf (locally
called *tuniki* leaf) as the heavily forested Adilabad, is historical. With the decline in
traditional weaving industry, the *padmasaalis* (weavers) migrated in search of work
to neighbouring Maharashtra; the women of the caste picked up the beedi trade
there and on their return home formed a ready-made labour force for the beedi
industry.

   This is probably also the reason why almost all the beedi *seths* [bosses] are, in
currently fashionable language, outsiders. Most of them are Gujaratis and a few
are Maharashtrians. However the main complaint against them is not that they
are 'plundering Andhra's beedi wealth to enrich other regions' but rather that they
have made unashamed use of the combination of factors detailed above to enrich
themselves. Detailed figures, taking all costs into account (excepting excise),
provided by the AP Beedi Workers' Union indicate a gross profit rate of about 100
per cent.

   An account of how the *seths* have enriched themselves should be of interest. The
major complaint of the beedi workers is that the leaf provided to them by the *seth*
for the purpose of rolling beedies is never adequate. While the workers find that
1,000 big beedies require 1,000 gms of leaf and 1,000 small beedies 800 gms, they
are given only 800 and 700 gms, respectively. Even out of the leaf that is given,
invariably a part is spoilt and unfit for rolling beedies. If such leaf is used to roll
beedies those beedies will be rejected entailing a loss for the workers since payment
is on [a] piece-rate basis. Thus every day the workers have to buy leaf to
supplement what is given and to replace spoilt leaf. When some activists of the
Stree Sakti Sanghatana, a Hyderabad-based women's organization visited Nizamabad the women workers mentioned this 'leaf problem' as their biggest problem.
However, they do have a few other problems. If a worker is not able to roll her
quota of beedies before nightfall and has to stay on in the factory after 6 p.m. she is
charged some beedies as *maaf* (compensation) for the electricity provided by the
seth. In many factories the workers themselves have to buy the thread to roll the
beedies with; and in those factories where payment is not made daily but weekly or
fortnightly, workers are charged about Rs 3[2] per week or fortnight (as the case
may be) for the card on which account of the leaf supplied and beedies rolled is
kept. What all this means is that while on paper a worker who rolls about 800 to

1,000 beedies per day (which is the norm) may take home about Rs 5 to 6 (this incidentally, includes bonus as well as compensation for not giving annual paid leave as required by the Beedie and Cigar Workers Act, 1966), the actual monthly earnings come to barely a hundred rupees per worker.

And yet, beedi rolling is far from being a secondary occupation for the women workers. The Sanghatana activists found that on the contrary beedi making was actually an obsession with the women. They make beedies, think beedies and talk beedies. The Beedi and Cigar Workers Act lays down a maximum of nine working hours (Section 17): The women actually spend only six hours at the factory, from 12 noon to 6 p.m.; but after that they bring home the leaf for the next day's beedies and spend the rest of the day wetting the leaf and laying it out to dry. Next morning they spend perhaps two or three hours on house-work and afterwards sit down to cut up the dried leaf. By noon they are back at the factory to start the new day's work. In the process their children are badly neglected and are as unkempt as the houses themselves. In most places these days it is customary for even the poorest to at least enrol their children in school, even if they are sent to school only when there is no work to be done at home. But Sanghatana activists did not find a single (female) child of a beedi worker attending school. They stay at home to do the work their mothers cannot do. And once they are sufficiently grown up they go to the factory to 'help' their mothers. It is true that the aforementioned Act prohibits child labour (section 24) but if children insist on filially helping their mothers, what can the poor *seth* do? And if, in the process, the *seth* also acquires well-trained new recruits whose training pays for itself, is he to be blamed?

We have been using the word 'factory' in a rather loose manner; it generally consists of an ill-ventilated room into which workers are crowded without much space for anybody to move around. Indeed, the frames of the Beedi and Cigar Workers Act do not seem to have felt that there is any need for anybody to move about. For Section 10(2) of the Act, which speaks about overcrowding, lays down that there should be 4.25 cubic metres of air space per worker, allowing a maximum upward extension of 3 metres. Allowing that, we have about 1.4 square metres of floor space, that is to say about 1.2 metres lengthwise and breadthwise, which is certainly just sufficient for a worker to squat, along with leaves, tobacco, rolled beedies and a can of drinking water that the management is supposed to provide the workers with but which the workers, who know better, bring with themselves from home. However, even when the government is generous with air space the *seths* know how to get around it. A state government act requires that the factories should be at least 12 feet high. That they certainly are. But six feet above the floor the clever *seth* erects a false floor with a hole in the middle to climb on to it and effectively makes two factories out of one.

There are many more provisions in the Beedi and Cigar Workers Act, like Section 12(1) that demands urinal and lavatory arrangements, Section 14 that asks for canteens and creches and so on. It is unnecessary to take these seriously for even bigger organized sector factories do not always provide such things. Section 37(3) of the Act says that the Maternity Benefit Act, 1961 applies to beedi workers. The reality is that during that period the women are 'allowed' to purchase leaf and tobacco from the *seth* and make beedies at home. The upshot is that they not only endanger their health but earn less in the bargain, for the occasional concessions their unions have wangled from the *seths* apply only to factory workers. The weekly holiday, compulsory under the same Act, suffers the same fate. The annual paid leave, to be given at the rate of one day per 20 working days [section 26(1)] has been adjusted against some trifling increase in the wage rate. Overtime is not only not paid but, as explained above, the workers themselves have to compensate for the current charges.

The Beedi Workers Welfare Fund Act, 1976 (together with the Beedi Workers Welfare Cess Act, 1976) provides for the collection of a cess from the management to 'provide for medical, educational and recreational facilities', and to give a 50 per cent grant to the factories which are required to run dispensaries, etc., for the workers. We have already spoken about the kind of education their children are receiving; as for medical facilities, not a single factory has any and the government, while dutifully collecting the cess from the management and asserting that 'the common main dispensary shall be so situated that none of the establishments or factories ... is more than 15 kms away from it' (Beedi and Cigar Workers Welfare Fund Rules, 1978, section 29(2), (iii)) has set up just one mobile dispensary for the whole of Nizamabad district and that dispensary too has not been functioning for some time now. This is to be seen against the fact that beedi work is known to cause diseases as serious as tuberculosis.

This appalling state of affairs is not attributable entirely to the backwardness of Nizamabad. An equally important factor is the mode of functioning of what is being referred to these days as 'Congress culture'. Until his recent death in a car accident that put an abrupt end to a career of extraordinary political opportunism that took the form of perpetual 'dissidence', Finance Minister G. Rajaram ruled Nizamabad as his pocket-borough. The beedi *seths* were his good friends and so was Ananta Reddy, the INTUC leader of the beedi workers.[3] No wonder that the beedi industry saw very few struggles and little real improvement in the working and living conditions of the workers until 1975, when the AP Beedi Workers Union was formed. Since then the workers have been fighting not only the *seths* but also that state, in the form of the police. During the recent month-long strike in March–April the police in Nizamabad town indiscriminately beat up the workers and their sympathizers. One Sattemma, a middle aged woman, and her schoolgoing daughter were severely beaten with *lathis*,[4] taken to the police station and kicked around with booted feet. (Photographs of their lacerated skins, published in the Union's bulletin, stand evidence to this gruesome treatment.) The Press too played its role by quite irrelevantly bringing in the alleged 'extremist' connections of the Beedi Workers' Union (it is affiliated to IFTU). The strike itself ended with nothing better than a promise from the labour minister to look into the workers' grievances which related to supply of adequate amount of leaf, increase in wages and implementation of the provisions of the Act. Another important demand, not included in this list but essential if the nine-hour working day is to be anything better than a farce, is that the leaf must be cut by the management before being supplied to the workers. Beedi workers of Ahmednagar district in Maharashtra too have raised this demand.

Reprinted from the *Economic and Political Weekly,* vol. 16, no. 32, 8 August, 1981, pp. 1305–6.

NOTES

  [1. One *lakh* = 100,000.]
  [2. Rs 18 = £1 (1981).]
  [3. INTUC: Indian National Trade Union Congress, associated with Mrs Gandhi's Congress Party.]
  [4. *Lathis*: long sticks or staves carried by the Indian police.]

17   The Sekondi – Takoradi General Strike, 1961

RICHARD D. JEFFRIES

Editors' introduction

Ghana, formerly known as the Gold Coast, was the first colony in Africa to achieve independence, in 1957. For this reason it acquired enormous political significance in Africa in the late 1950s and the first half of the 1960s, much of that significance attached to the person of Kwame Nkrumah. Nkrumah had broken away from the middle-class United Gold Coast Convention (UGCC) in 1948 to form the Convention People's Party (CPP), which became the prototype of the 'mass' political parties involved in the movements for African independence. The CPP consolidated its position in a series of elections in the 1950s to form the first independent government in 1957, by which time various opposition groups (including leading figures of the old UGCC) had combined to establish the United Party. All these parties are referred to below.

The potent contemporary symbolism of Nkrumah's Ghana as heralding a 'new dawn' in an Africa free from colonialism, together with the economic stagnation, corruption and recurrent political crises of the years since independence (including Nkrumah's overthrow in 1966), give Ghana a particularly sharp focus for examining struggles arising from frustrated hopes and aspirations. The latter provide the theme of a brilliant novel by the Ghanaian writer Ayi Kwei Armah *The Beautyful Ones Are Not Yet Born* (Heinemann, 1969). The following piece describes and interprets the reactions of one section of Ghanaian workers as manifested in the Sekondi–Takoradi general strike of 1961. That action encapsulated a great deal of history in that most of those involved were Fante people from southern Ghana with a tradition of resistance to colonial rule, and who also constituted a key group of workers in the colonial economy. The economy of Ghana as established in the colonial period (and as it still prevails to-day) was geared to the export of raw materials – crops and minerals – for the world market, a pattern in which transport workers like the railwaymen and dockers of Sekondi–Takoradi perform a critical role. They have, by African standards, a long history as a stable working class whose militancy was well established under colonialism and has continued since independence.

One of the recurring elements in the turbulent history of Ghana since independence has been the actions of workers to gain a better life for themselves. For example, the mineworkers of the Ashanti Goldfields engaged in a series of bitter strikes from 1968 to 1972, in which miners were killed by police and army actions against them. One of the conclusions of Richard Jeffries' analysis is that militant trade unionism in Ghana has 'been extremely popular not only with the unionized workers themselves but also with large sections of the non-unionized urban masses who looked to it for expression of radical criticism of government in the absence of an effective representative opposition party'.

In September 1961 the railway and harbour workers of Sekondi–Takoradi staged a seventeen-day strike against the Nkrumah government's July Budget, a strike in which, according to well-informed commentators, 'the Government saw its very existence implicitly challenged', and which 'drastically altered the entire character of political activity in Ghana'.[1] The strike leaders were consequently imprisoned for periods ranging from five months to four years, and prohibited from further office-holding in the Railway Union. TUC control over the union was made more tight and direct. Of more general significance, the strike lent urgency to a house-cleaning process within the Convention People's Party, on Nkrumah's instructions, to guard against 'bourgeois' elements. Later in the year a one-party state was established.

The seriousness of the government's reaction was partly due to suspicion of a United Party plot to excite such disturbances throughout the country and so bring down Nkrumah. But, as the President appeared to realize in giving the strikers an assurance of future changes in government policy and conduct, United Party subversion, while certainly an important facilitating element in the strike action, did not itself adequately explain the fact, aims, or significance of rank and file mobilization and solidarity. Some of the strike leaders ('branch' officials in distinction from the national executive, which tried to avoid involvement) were certainly in touch with United Party representatives before and during the strike, and received money which they used to enable the market women to supply food to the strikers. But these branch unionists, and the market women also, had their own aims and grievances, independent of the United Party interest, and mobilized the rank and file around issues which had, and had to have, nothing to do with subversive 'party politics'. For most of the rank and file were still vaguely pro-CPP rather than supporters of an elitist United Party which held little personal or ideological appeal for them, and knew nothing of United Party involvement.

The formal reason given for the strike, and certainly the cause of much resentment, was immediate economic grievances, the particular, sectional nature of which appears, superficially at least, to lend support to the labour aristocracy thesis.[2] The skilled railway and harbour workers objected to the introduction in the July budget of a compulsory savings scheme, which would involve a five per cent deduction from the wages of those earning more than NC.336 [approximately £160] per annum (most skilled workers earned slightly more than this), and a property tax, to be levied on larger than average sized houses (i.e. two rooms and a hall) – that is to say, measures which would hurt many of them but few of the unskilled workers or unemployed directly. Moreover, Ghana's farmers were being required to make even greater sacrifices in the cause of national development, and the skilled workers could not honestly claim to be so economically desperate as to merit exemption from the government's austerity measures. The most reliable statistics available suggest that Ghana's skilled and unskilled workers enjoyed substantially improved living standards by 1961 relative to a decade earlier, and they were accustomed to the regular seasonal rise in food prices which coincided with the strike action. An explanation of the strike in narrowly economic terms would seem, therefore, to imply quite exceptional unreasonableness on the part of the strikers; and it would appear more likely that the militancy of their reaction – the staging of an illegal strike for seventeen days in the face of detention of leaders and threats of military intervention was clearly an intensely militant act – and the enthusiastic support they received from the unskilled workers, market women, and even some of the unemployed in Sekondi–Takoradi, derived rather from the wider significance these economic issues assumed in the context of the politics of the national labour movement, and of widespread popular opposition to the direction of development of the CPP regime. Implicit references to these wider issues were contained in the precise grounds on which the strike leaders criticized the budget.

The property tax, so they argued, would inhibit private building which was much needed in consequence of the CPP regime's failure to provide sufficient low-cost housing, and, if levied on 'family houses', would indirectly hurt the lower-paid workers and unemployed who depended on extended family charity for their accommodation. Implicit in this charge was a protest against party favouritism and corruption in the National Housing Corporation, which had recently taken over the administration of two new housing estates built in Sekondi–Takoradi supposedly for the lower-paid workers, but had allocated them instead to those who could afford to bribe NHC officials, party big-wigs, and even Accra-based MPs and their girlfriends. Secondly, they objected to the compulsory saving scheme on the grounds that, since it was a new and ideally voluntary form of taxation, 'the people's consent should have been obtained'.[3] Implicit in this objection was an expression of lack of confidence in Parliament and in the leadership of the TUC which had failed to press the rank and file's demand for negotiations with the government on the budget. It is worth noting in this context the history of opposition, sometimes riotous, to 'arbitrary' taxation in the southern coastal towns of Ghana, and the wide significance 'tax protests' had thereby assumed.[4] The symbolic issue in the 1961 strike was a protest against the increasingly oligarchical and authoritarian style of CPP government, and was clearly articulated in the strike leaders' threat that, 'If Parliament did not give way to the demands of the people they would disband that body by force.'[5]

The issues in the 1961 strike extended beyond immediate economic grievances, therefore, and beyond even trade union affairs narrowly defined: though somewhat paradoxically, the 'new structure' of the Ghana TUC, established by the 1958 Industrial Relations Act, was from the start the central issue for the strike leaders. This involved wider questions concerning the nature of the CPP regime, since it was the railway workers' conception that the TUC, or national labour movement should, ideally, be especially concerned to check degenerative elitist tendencies in the political system as a whole. As will later be shown, this conception had informed their struggle against the post-1954 leadership of the TUC, in which the 1961 strike was essentially the showdown. Three years earlier, in 1958, the strike leaders had organized a splinter union, the 'Loco-Electrical', with the support of more than half the railway and harbour workers, outside of, and in scarcely veiled opposition to, the 'new structure', but had been compelled to rejoin the mother union and the TUC by a subsequent amendment to the Act. They had objected not to the principle of a single powerful trade union centre, but to the lack of adequate consultation with 'working unionists' involved in the formulation of the 'new structure' – it was the brainchild of 'party careerists', as the railway workers regarded John Tettegah, Joe-fio N. Meyer, and the other TUC leaders, men with little experience or supporting base in the old trade union movement which had developed from the shop-floors of Sekondi–Takoradi – and to the excessive degree of centralization and party control it entailed.[6] Certainly this seemed likely to frustrate the 'Loco-Electrical' leaders' own political ambitions, and to curtail their autonomous powers and responsibilities as trade union representatives; but it was also, as they argued to the rank and file, a certain recipe for top-level corruption and unresponsiveness to the membership's demands. Even if the TUC leaders succeeded, through their close ties with the party, in securing substantial economic benefits for the workers, which in 1957–61 they undoubtedly did, it was of overriding importance, these railway unionists insisted, to fight to maintain trade union democracy and independence in view of the pattern of growing corruption, oligarchy, and authoritarianism which characterized the CPP regime.

In explaining why the Sekondi–Takoradi railway workers took the lead in 1961, we have therefore to explain more than their relative organizational ability to do so. Certainly, their concentration in the two large industrial installations, at Takoradi Harbour and Sekondi Location Workshops, made for easy communication, in-depth organization, and a strong sense of power through solidarity; their relatively high educational level ('middle-school') facilitated awareness and articulation of the wider issues; and their relative job security, as skilled workers, made strike action the more easily contemplated. But also, in contrast to, for example, the mineworkers, who were situated in relatively isolated rural locations, the railway workers' residential integration in the urban centre of Sekondi–Takoradi enabled them to maintain close social ties with other socio-economic groups, and afforded them opportunity for first-hand observation of many aspects of CPP rule and identification with the grievances of the 'common people'.

In addition, or rather as a reflection of this structural situation, they had developed during the nationalist-Independence era a union political culture especially sensitive to corruption, elitism, and authoritarianism, and stressing their own vanguard role in protesting such tendencies in government. Others have remarked on the importance of this cultural heritage of the railway workers, but their description of this as one of 'conventional trade union practices', with 'an economist ideology', is seriously misleading.[7] The railway workers' political structure is more accurately described as one of 'urban populism', and the 1961 strike is best conceived as a familiar form of conflict between 'purist' rank-and-file and 'revisionist' leadership within a popular movement.

Railway union 'populism'

'Populism' is here [defined . . .] as a style of popular participation rather than a systematic ideology. It involves, however, subscription to two cardinal principles: (a) [. . . it] 'identifies the will of the people with justice and morality', (b) 'the desirability of a direct relationship between people and leadership, unmediated (or certainly 'unobstructed') by institutions'.[8] Such style of popular participation, it is observed, are generally accompanied by a high valuation of the virtues and culture of the uncorrupted, simple folk, and a converse distrust of the wealthy, over-educated, idle, parasitic, and fundamamentally corrupt urban elite.[9] The social structure is conceived dualistically in terms of an elite–mass division and opposition. Often, populism is a form or style of nationalism, in which the native elite are seen as the stooges of an external imperialist power. The populist leader is generally a charismatic figure, and often characterized by a 'strong man' image and by acceptance of violence as a legitimate means of effecting political change. On assumption of power, however, the leader is likely to be faced with an especially acute form of the familiar problem of 'institutionalizing' a new, and in some ways inevitably disappointing, order. Increasing separation of leadership from rank and file and attempts to defuse the movement and substitute control for orderly development are likely to be seen as a 'revisionist' betrayal, particularly in view of the vagueness and/or diversity of the movement's positive policy aims. The Sekondi–Takoradi railway workers' brand of nationalism as expressed in their leading role in the 1950 'positive action' strike, and the nature of their subsequent disillusionment with the CPP regime, were very much to this pattern.[10] They were organized, inspired and led on this occasion not by their official union executive but by Pobee Biney, a charismatic rank-and-file leader, nicknamed 'Let Go The Anchor', who held no official position in the main Railway Union (though he was, in 1949–50, president of the Enginemen's Union and vice-president of the Gold Coast TUC).

Biney's leadership was crucial, firstly in the sense that the prior development of the union had been by no means unswervingly in the direction of populist political involvement. Since the Second World War years, when the union had been reorganized on the advice of the Colonial Labour Department, the Union Executive had been dominated by ex-officio clerical staff representatives, who generally favoured a policy of peaceful negotiation and separation of trade union affairs from politics. The skilled and semi-skilled workers, who had been responsible for the original establishment of the union and constituted a majority of the total railway labour force, became increasingly dissatisfied with the ineffectiveness, and, as they saw it, political irresponsibility of this policy. On three occasions in 1947–50 the strong man, Pobee Biney, rose to lead them in unconstitutional but successful 'direct actions', which, implicitly at first and then in 1950 explicitly, challenged the legitimacy of the colonial government structure.

In fact, Biney did more than simply act as a spokesman for rank-and-file discontent. In addition to re-amalgamating the Enginemen's Union with the main Railway Union to attain greater solidarity, he built up a reputation with the whole rank and file for human approachability and bold representation of their grievances, inspired them with something of his own courage and scorn for the colonial authorities, and educated them in a radical Nationalist ideology. By 1950 his substantive leadership and control of the rank and file was so assured he was able to declare and organize a virtually hundred per cent solid political strike without the active support of the official union executive (the union president resigned in fear of government reprisals) and without even calling a mass meeting.

Biney's ideology,[11] expressed in rousing speeches at union mass meetings, and at the nationalist rallies he organized in Sekondi, might best be termed 'African socialist'. He attacked the evils of colonialism on the grounds not only of economic exploitation but also of its destructive effect on the traditional culture and social relations, the sense of brotherhood of the Ghanaian people.[12] The true 'people' he defined as 'the common people', distinct from the elite of lawyers, civil servants, and other collaborators with the colonial regime. He derided the latter's cultural separatism, their 'white African' dress and manners. He was therefore strongly opposed to the United Gold Coast Convention and its leadership of 'lawyers who would not risk their wigs for the sake of the common man', and totally unsympathetic to the view, prevalent among Railway Union and TUC officials in 1949–50, that staging a strike in support of 'positive action' would be to confuse trade unionism with party politics and to misrepresent those workers, mainly clerical staff who favoured the UGCC rather than the CPP.

This did not mean he wished to 'marry' the Ghanaian labour movement to Nkrumah's Convention People's Party. In the first place he was wary of Nkrumah's Marxist–Leninist ideas and later came to attack the regime's ideologizing as 'that Soviet"ism" nonsense which has nothing to teach us about Socialism'. Secondly, Biney's emphasis on the vanguard role of the organized, enlightened workers in leading the Ghanaian people to achieve their independence involved the corollary that they should continue to act thereafter as defenders of the Nationalist Movement's aims, checking degenerative tendencies in the party-become-government. This implication became clear from his behaviour after the 'positive action' strike and the CPP's accession to a share of government power: and it was the consistency and idealistic aggression with which Biney acted out his ideology, relatively indistinctive in itself perhaps, that earned him a legendary status in Railway Union political culture surpassing that of Nkrumah and infusing and defining the process of railway worker disillusionment with the Nkrumah regime.

Biney was detained towards the end of the 'positive action' strike in January 1950, and, on his release in 1951, was nominated by the CPP for the Assin constituency in the Legislative Assembly elections; but, unlike so many others, he did not proceed to sell out to the Party, or pursue his personal advancement.[13] Rather, he became rapidly dissatisfied with Nkrumah's failure to help revive the TUC (virtually destroyed in consequence of the 1950 strike and government reprisals), with the slow and petty procedures of parliamentary party politics, the discipline expected of back-benchers, and the debilitating effect of all this on party momentum and idealism. His persistent criticism of the government for doing little for the workers and common people brought him Nkrumah's displeasure, and termination of his Legislative Assembly membership after only two years. He then returned to help reorganize the Railway Union, but his dismissal from the presidency was engineered within the year by CPP loyalists on the Executive Council. He then took various jobs but appears to have spent a great deal of his time in Sekondi bars, loudly voicing his disillusionment with the Nkrumah government's slide into elitism, corruption, and 'nonsensical' ideology. It is said that Nkrumah tried to bribe him with gifts and offers of jobs to restrain his criticism, but, though he accepted some of these, and in the 1960s became a Government Security Officer, he did so 'merely to keep body and soul together', and refused to perform his so-called duties. Throughout this time, including his spell in the Legislative Assembly, he remained in touch with the common people of Sekondi–Takoradi, maintaining a simple house in Sekondi, and dressed always in a cheap traditional cloth and pair of sandals.

This background helps provide insight into the very real idealistic element in the 1961 strike action. The CPP's rejection of one of the few nationalist leaders who had remained faithful to the original ideals of the movement, consistently and courageously speaking up for 'the common people', came to symbolize for many railway workers the failings of the Nkrumah regime. Biney's embodiment and articulation of 'pure' nationalist ideas lent definition and contrast to CPP 'revisionism'. But Biney's influence was also more direct than this. During his presidency of the Railway Union in 1954–55, he had helped organize an attempt to overthrow the incumbent TUC leadership, and had recruited to positions of officialdom in the Railway Union men especially sympathetic to this aim and to his own populist style and ideology of union leadership. These followers were prominent among the middle-level officials who led the 1961 strike. In 1955–61 they had been, in a sense, continuing the struggle in Biney's absence.

Nevertheless, it would be mistaken to attribute excessive independent influence to the personality of Pobee Biney. In the first place, railway worker populism derived encouragement from a tradition of 'common man' political participation in the Fante coastal towns of Ghana. The majority of skilled railway workers, including Biney himself, originated from Elmina or Cape Coast, where they were members of Asafo companies, semi-military organizations of the commoners as distinct from the elders and chiefs. During the first half of the twentieth century the Asafo companies were frequently and centrally involved in political disputes over the legitimacy of particular chiefs and their policies, and, sometimes implicit in this, over the institutional reforms the colonial government sought to introduce. Stylistically, the Railway Union's borrowing of Asafo cultural elements can be seen in the use of an Asafo gong-gong, an Asafo battle-cry ('Kryo-be' – 'Prepare yourself for the coming struggle'), and, more generally, in the military atmosphere of many mass meetings of the union, with speakers trying to outdo each other in bravado. And the traditional legitimacy of 'common man' collective participation in the politics of the Fante states perhaps helped provide subjective justification for railway worker self-assertion in national politics, similarly rationalized as opposing autocracy on behalf of the people. In the 1961 strike more particularly, the Asafo influence is apparent from St Clair Drake's on-the-spot account: 'Red head-bands and arm-bands were in evidence everywhere; they were symbols worn in former days by Fante tribal fighting men to mean, "We are ready for War".'[14]

Secondly, the continuing vitality of this cultural heritage, and the influence exerted in turn by Biney's 'spokesman of the People' conception, derived from their correspondence to the rank-and-file's empirical perception of their situation in the national socio-economic and political structures, and the close inter-dependence of their own interests with those of other sections of the urban masses. A brief consideration of this structural position vis-à-vis other urban groups will also help to explain the support the strike received from virtually the entire Sekondi–Takoradi community.

The social structure of Sekondi–Takoradi and the elite–mass gap

St Clair Drake and L. A. Lacy's account of the 1961 strike emphasizes the widespread support it received within Sekondi–Takoradi: 'By midweek practically every activity in the port was closed down. Municipal bus drivers had joined the strike, as had the city employees who collected the sewage daily. Market women dispensed free food to the strikers at municipal bus garages and other strategic points ... There was an air of excitement and pride throughout the city ... Morale was high ... The railway workers were heroes.' Interviews conducted in 1971 suggested that even some of the unemployed participated: 'The support we received from all the people here was so tremendous, we realized we could not back down even if we had wanted to. Many who weren't workers, our unemployed brothers and sisters, for instance, came on the demonstrations. People felt it was a burning issue to the community.'

Sekondi–Takoradi, it must be emphasized, was and is, more than any other Ghanaian city, a predominantly working-class community, dominated both numerically and in terms of general ethos by lower-paid manual workers. The 1955 Population and Household Budget Survey estimated that 90 per cent of earnings in Sekondi–Takoradi came from wage-employment, compared with 67 per cent for Accra and 22 per cent for Kumasi. In 1961 the skilled and unskilled workers employed in the Railway and Harbour Administration constituted almost a quarter of the city's total male labour force of 43,000. Another quarter were employed as skilled or unskilled workers by the City Council, the various government departments (e.g. Public Works, Posts and Tele-communications), the shipping companies, or in one of the several manufacturing industries located there. At least 12 per cent were unemployed, and the proportion of elite elements was very small.[15] In so predominantly a working-class community, many of the unemployed looked to their worker fathers or brothers for assistance, and were therefore directly dependent on the workers' financial capacity for the continuance of this social welfare function. Similarly, the market women and small businessmen relied very largely on the trade of the workers, and had an indirect, but clearly perceived, interest in the financial fortunes of the lower-paid workers and in the politics of the TUC. This close economic interdependence was paralleled on the social and cultural levels by the integration of most workers in the main residential centres of Sekondi–Takoradi, and by the numerical predomin-ance of workers in the majority of associations and meeting places.

In addition to such pragmatic considerations, the unionized workers and other groups among the urban masses were united by a common sense of social injustice and equally important were not significantly divided by socio-economic differen-tiation among themselves. Saul and Arrighi suggest that 'wage workers in the upper stratum' (i.e. including skilled workers) 'receive incomes 3–5 times those received by wage workers in the lower stratum' (i.e. unskilled workers).[16] This is simply not true of Ghanaian workers, and more particularly of the railway and harbour workers. Skilled workers have received, on average, almost twice as much as unskilled workers; and this differential has generally been considered justified by the skilled workers' education and training, and by the fact that, being relatively job-committed southerners, they normally have wives and children to support in the city unlike most of the northern migrants who provide the majority of the unskilled labour force.[17] In turn, the skilled railway workers have consistently concerned themselves, in their major wage campaigns and strike actions, with raising the wages of unskilled workers rather than merely securing improved conditions of service for themselves. While the skilled workers have been, in a sense, privileged relative to the unskilled and unemployed, this has not been, judging from interviews, the commonsense view of the Sekondi–Takoradi unskilled and unemployed themselves.[18] The difficulty experienced by skilled workers in making ends meet to support a style and standard of living which includes little beyond the basic necessities is obvious to all. The skilled workers' economic and social distance from the middle-class proper – school teachers, middling businessmen, middle-rank executives – has been, and still is, both considerably and highly visible.

Of far more doubtful legitimacy than the unskilled–skilled worker differential, therefore, has been the scale of differentials between these lower-paid workers and the middle and higher executives in government service. Apart from the minor reforms introduced by the Lidbury–Gbedemah award of 1952, the Nkrumah government did nothing to reduce the gross inequalities in the wage and salary structure inherited from the colonial civil service. This was one of Biney's principal charges against the regime. The intensity of resentment at the continu-ance of such inequalities could not be doubted on the evidence of interviews: e.g.

> It all depends on cheating. There are so many people being paid fat salaries without working. I didn't go to school but I know my trade. If an educated man comes along and he's given more pay than myself I have to challenge the Government and find out what is happening.

Even more infuriating was the excessive wealth and conspicuous consumption of politicians owing their positions, originally at least, to the votes of the common people. In the 1961 strike action the common people of Sekondi–Takoradi looked to the more highly organized and articulate skilled workers to express their resentment at this growing elite–mass gap.

President Nkrumah himself, it should be noted, recognized this. Earlier in the year, when preparing for the necessity of an austerity budget, and considering the likely obstacles to its popular acceptance, he had publicly criticized the 'self-seeking tendencies' of some members of the party 'who by virtue of their functions and positions are tending to form a separate new ruling class.' This was 'working to alienate the support of the masses and to bring the National Assembly into isolation.'[19] On September 29, recognizing that the Sekondi–Takoradi strike had revealed widespread disbelief in the effectiveness of such warnings, the President took more drastic action to implement his 'dawn broadcast'. Six ministers were to resign and to surrender part of their property to the state, among them Krobo Edusei, infamous for the gold bed episode.[20] To this degree at least the 1961 strike was successful and its significance appreciated in governing circles.

The growth of an elite–mass gap, governmental corruption and authoritarianism were, however, apparent in other Ghanaian cities, indeed probably more visibly so in Accra and Kumasi than in Sekondi–Takoradi. Why should the people of Sekondi–Takoradi prove especially sensitive to such tendencies and ready to unite in protest against them? Two main reasons might be given. Firstly, it would seem likely that general structural factors tend to generate strongly anti-elitist and anti-corruption attitudes among Ghanaian workers, and especially skilled manual workers. For they, unlike some clerical and administrative executives, enjoy few opportunities for benefiting from corrupt practices, or gaining promotion through patronage, while suffering directly from managerial and governmental corruption, to which they tend to attribute government's lack of finance for raising wages. Earlier in this paper the similarly pernicious effects of corruption in the National Housing Corporation were noted. Moreover, government employees, and private employees also to the degree that they recognize the impact of government wage policy on their own wage scales, have a direct financial interest in maintaining democratic processes and opposing authoritarianism in government-management; though other factors making for an anti-authoritarian orientation are probably equally important, the literacy of most skilled workers, for example, and their socialization in democratic values in the unions. Further, the skilled workers' position in the socio-economic structure, between the unskilled and unemployed, on the one hand, and the middle-class proper, on the other, is a highly ambivalent one, involving a strong aspiration to bourgeois status, to which they feel entitled by virtue of education and training, but at the same time intense resentment of the excessive wealth of the elite which is the most obvious cause of their own impoverishment. For these general structural reasons, then, lower-paid manual workers are especially prone to develop critical attitudes to elitism, authoritarianism, and corruption, and the peculiarity of Sekondi–Takoradi among Ghanaian cities consists, from this perspective, simply in its overwhelmingly working-class composition, and the prevalence of a strong proletarian ethos in the community as a whole.

But in 1961 these sources of special disillusionment with the Nkrumah regime were compounded by more particular communal grievances. Although they had played a crucial and courageous role in the nationalist struggle, the people of Sekondi–Takoradi felt they had gained little from Independence compared with Accra, with its fine new roads and plush hotels; and now their major source of livelihood, the harbour at Takoradi, seemed likely to be severely devalued by the government's construction of a new harbour at Tema, some fifteen miles from Accra. What little had been provided them in the way of new facilities, the new housing estates, for example, had been plundered by CPP officials. More important than the objective extent of exploitation, or deprivation, perhaps, was the feeling that their voice was not heard nor were their interests represented in Accra because of a steady diminution in the channels of communication and influence between Sekondi–Takoradi and the central government during the 1950s.

In consequence, there was a pronounced communalistic element in the 1961 strike and the railway and harbour workers' populist consciousness. The despised elite were the 'big men' in, or from, Accra: the 'common people', the people of Sekondi–Takoradi and the Western Region. This sense of communal, and regional, deprivation was still apparent in 1971, as the following remark by a railway worker illustrates: 'We Westerners, especially, the government never minds us, yet we have all these industries, bauxite and gold and things, and we work much harder than all those office-workers in Accra, drawing their fat salaries. If they don't look out, it will be another Biafra.' Such openly communalistic sentiments are atypical and even frowned upon in Railway Union political culture, but the Accra–Sekondi–Takoradi dimension has certainly served to intensify the railway and harbour workers' sense of social distance and conflict between the 'big men' and the 'common people'.

Extracted from Richard D. Jeffries, 'Populist Tendencies in the Ghanaian Trade Union Movement,' in Richard Sandbrook and Robin Cohen (eds), *The Development of an African Working Class*, Longman, London, 1975, pp. 261–80.

NOTES

1. St Clair Drake and L. A. Lacy, 'Government Versus the Unions: the Sekondi–Takoradi Strike, 1961', in G. Carter (ed.), *Politics in Africa: 7 cases*, Harcourt, Brace and World, Inc., 1966, p. 68. The majority of unionized workers in Sekondi–Takoradi participated in the strike at one stage or another, but the skilled railway and harbour workers gave the lead and stayed out by far the longest.

[2. The 'labour aristocracy thesis' puts forward the idea that industrial workers with relatively secure, skilled and well-paid jobs form a 'privileged' stratum in Third World countries where modern industry employs only a small proportion of the labour force. As a result, it is argued, such workers have an interest in the preservation of the *status quo* similar to that of business groups, professionals and civil servants, rather than any identity with unskilled casual workers, urban 'marginals', or the mass of the peasantry. A well-known statement of this position can be found in the article by Arrighi and Saul cited in note 16 below.]

3. Interviews with the strike leaders. In clarification of the point about the Housing Tax, many of the unemployed, and some of the lower-paid workers, did (and still do) pay little or no rent for accommodation in the houses of richer relatives. If these houses were to be subject to taxation, so it was argued, their owners would be inclined to demand rents of such dependants, or even to eject them and let rooms instead to tenants who could afford high rents.

4. The most notable instances of violent opposition were the October 1931 tax riots in Sekondi and Cape Coast.

5. Drake and Lacy, 'Government Versus the Unions', p. 99.

6. Bulletin of the Joint Council of Railway Unions, 8 Sept. 1958, Railway Unions Archives.

7. Drake and Lacy, 'Government Versus the Unions', p. 115. ['Economism' refers to the ostensible preoccupation of workers and trade unionists with immediate issues of work

conditions and pay, rather than with the wider social and political factors that affect their lives.]

8. Peter Worsley, 'The Concept of Populism', in G. Ionescu and E. Gellner (eds), *Populism, its meanings and national characteristics,* Weidenfeld and Nicolson, 1970, pp. 243–4.

9. Some of the literature on populism emphasizes its specifically rural location and orientation, and would deny applicability of the term to urban movements, conceiving the people as the urban as well as rural lower strata. This seems to the present writer [. . .] unnecessarily specific. In this particular case, for instance, the traditional society and culture were urban, that of the Fante coastal towns.

[10. In 1950 Nkrumah launched a campaign of 'Positive Action' to accelerate the struggle for national independence; as part of this the Gold Coast TUC called for a general strike against the colonial regime. The latter's response was to jail a number of CPP leaders, but the CPP won a resounding victory in the general election of 1951 and Nkrumah was released from prison to form his first government. The effects of the 1950 general strike on the TUC were disastrous, and it effectively disintegrated with disputes between different unions and leaders throughout the 1950s, as noted on p. 133 above.]

11. This interpretation of Biney's ideology is based primarily on oral sources, and therefore presents the way his ideology was generally understood and/or has been remembered. Phrases in quotation marks are frequent sayings attributed to him, translated from the Fante.

12. Biney's concern for the traditional culture did not extend to support for the continued political authority of the chiefs, whom he characterized as 'our little gods of times past, now become messenger-boys of the Colonial Government'.

13. The interpretation of Biney's career presented here is that current among the railway workers, rather than an attempt at historical objectivity. While this legend does appear to correspond closely to the historical reality on all empirical points, alternative interpretations obviously are possible on such matters, as, for example, the reason for Biney's dismissal from the Legislative Assembly and the Railway Union Presidency. Party and trade union officials claimed at the time that this was because of his excessive drinking and rude demeanour. It might be noted that Biney's drinking exploits were not necessarily a disability in the eyes of the railway workers, who rather applauded them as a 'strong man' trait; also, that Biney's downfall did coincide closely in time with the expulsion from party and trade union hierarchies of two of Biney's close and political ideological associates, Turkson Ocran and Anthony Woode, for alleged communism.

14. Drake and Lacy, 'Government Versus the Unions', p. 98.

15. 1960 Population Census of Ghana, Government Printer, Accra, 1961.

16. Giovanni Arrighi and John S. Saul, 'Nationalism and Revolution in Sub-Saharan Africa' [in Ralph Miliband and John Saville, *The Socialist Register,* Merlin Press, London, 1969,] p. 135.

17. On the relatively high job commitment of Ghanaian skilled workers see Margaret Peil, *The Ghanaian Factory Worker: Industrial Man in Africa,* Cambridge University Press, 1972, pp. 101–3. Takoradi skilled workers appear to be more committed than those in other Ghanaian cities, however, with 68 per cent of those surveyed by Peil having been in their job for longer than five years.

18. This brief and, unfortunately, simplistic summary of prevalent attitudes is based on open-ended interviews with a sample of 90 railway workers, and informal conversations with several hundred workers and unemployed primarily in Sekondi–Takoradi but also in Accra and Kumasi, in May to November 1972.

19. Dawn Broadcast, *Evening News,* 3 Apr. 1961, p. 2.

[20. When it became known that Krobi Edusei had made his wife a present of a gold bed.]

18 Interview with Luís Inácio da Silva ('Lula')

President of the Sindicato dos Metalúrgicos de São Bernardo do Campos

Editors' introduction

The Brazilian economic 'miracle' of the 1960s and 1970s was a process of unprecedentedly fast industrial growth, which combined massive investments by multinational corporations with strict social and political control by a series of authoritarian regimes following the military seizure of power in 1964. The state and city of São Paulo played a leading role as a 'growth pole', and within São Paulo the automobile and associated industries (in the metalworking, electrical and engineering sectors) expanded especially rapidly.

Under Brazilian trade union legislation, dating from the 1930s and 1940s, the state determines which union can operate among particular categories of workers in a particular area. That union then has sole rights of recruitment and organization, with its activities subject to strict state control. The Metalworkers Union of São Bernardo do Campos, one of the 'boom' industrial zones south of the city of São Paulo, represents all metalworkers in that area, including the majority of auto industry workers. In March 1978 there were 125,000 metalworkers in São Bernardo, of whom 65,000 worked in five large auto plants. Union membership ranged from around 45 per cent to just over 30 per cent for hourly-paid workers.

Before the strikes of 1978 the Metalworkers Union of São Bernardo, under the leadership of Luís Inacío da Silva, popularly known as 'Lula', had built up an effective organization particularly through the work of its *diretores de base*, members of the Union Executive who were full-time organizers in the factories. As a result the union was well placed to play a leading role in the wave of strikes that followed the initial action of day-shift toolroom workers in the Saab–Scania plant on 12 May. During May much of the southern industrial belt of São Paulo was affected by total or partial stoppages, in which workers attended the factories but refused to operate the machinery. Subsequently a whole series of strikes occurred throughout 1978 in other industrial areas and in public services.

In the course of the strikes from 1978 to 1980 with which he was closely associated, Lula was deposed by government intervention in the running of the trade unions. He then devoted his energies to the *Partido dos Trabalhadores* (Workers Party) which he helped to establish at the end of 1979, and which was permitted under the cautious reforms of the *Abertura* ('opening') introduced by President Figueiredo. Lula was subsequently tried under the National Security Law and sentenced to three years' imprisonment, but is still politically active in conditions of considerable insecurity while the latest of a series of appeals against his conviction awaits a hearing.

The interview gives some idea of the complexity of strategic, tactical and organizational questions confronting a large industrial working class and its leaders, in the face of laws operated by an authoritarian regime which aims to prevent independent trade unionism. In this situation the pursuit of 'economistic' demands concerning wages (see Reading 17, note 7) means that the legal and political conditions of any kind of effective presentation of workers' demands themselves become an object of struggle. Lula's concern with direct and democratic organization of the working class is expressed in an ambivalence about party politics at the end of the interview, although party political work has become his main area of activity since he was deposed from union office by the government.

Much of the information provided here is derived from an illuminating article by John Humphrey which gives substantial details about the nature of recent trade union struggles in Brazil and the conditions in which they have taken place.[1] Humphrey argues that their employment in a fast-growing, capital-intensive modern industrial sector does not make auto workers in Brazil a 'privileged' stratum, insulated from the harsh conditions faced by other workers. On the contrary, he suggests a combination of factors which explain why these workers' struggles have inspired working-class organization and action more generally.

What comparison can be established between the present workers' movement and that of a few years ago?

Today's worker movement is not too different from that of a few years ago. What has changed some are the basic ideas of some union leaders who believe that the unions should become independent once and for all and who have tried to apply this with the rank and file in their sectors. This was not the case before 1964, when we knew that many movements were started for partisan reasons, many times for the benefit of those in power or for those who were not in power but who desired to be.

Some unions began to insist on the necessity of our fighting our own battles, since we didn't need the interference of outsiders. The workers, they said, ought to learn to win on their own and should judge their own strength and learn how important they are in the process of the development of their country. And I think it has really happened. It is not that we are going to stand back and clap or celebrate the laurels of victory. However, we understand that the strikes which took place since May 12 (1978) have shown that there is a greater class consciousness on the part of workers. Workers have ceased to believe in many things that deceived them for a long time. They had believed, for example, that the governments could do many things for the working class, because the pseudo-benevolences of Getúlio Vargas were still firmly implanted in workers' minds.[2] The worker believed that the political leadership was elected to do something for his benefit, even though it was not composed of workers but of managerial people and other members of the elite.

Today the worker does not believe in that any more. Today he believes more in his own strength. Maybe it is just that we believe in our own strength to solve our immediate problems. But I think that this is the basic difference between the workers before 1978 (not to speak of going back to 1964) and those of today. The worker started to see that the people talking about freedom and using the term 'working class', were in fact far removed from him. After having been massacred for a long time, workers started to believe that they could resolve their own problems.

What comparison do you see between the 'wage recovery'[3] fight and the recent work-stoppages?

It's very difficult to talk about the 'wage recovery' because it gives the impression that we are praising our own (metalworkers) union in São Bernardo. When we started the movement for the wage recovery, I remember that from the beginning we were discredited by our fellow union leaders. They were saying that we were going to pull rabbits out of hats and were just doing a lot of yaking [*sic*] without any results. We talked with the workers in meetings and through our newspaper, and we said that the most important thing was not the 34 per cent raise demand but the restoration of union freedom, the lack of which had caused the wage theft of 1973 and 1974. Then, through the fight for wage recovery, we had to attack the government wage policy and the union structure openly, sensitizing the worker. We were able to use, in capital letters, in all our materials, the word 'ROBBERY', to say that in a certain period the government lied to the Brazilian people about the so-called 'miracle'. This 'miracle' happened specifically because of the exploitation of those who are the most exploited in this land, the working class.

All of this alerted the worker and put him on guard. I have already said through some newspapers that the most opportune time for the strike would have been, in principle, at the time of the wage recovery struggle (in 1977). They didn't come out on strike because there as yet was no base of support for the strikes. So we could have called a strike, but it would have died an early death. But I think that the struggle for wage recovery was the cause of the strike of May 1978. It was this strike that alerted the working class about what we call the 'wage squeeze', about the wage robbery, and about the government's lack of understanding of the working class.

We also should not forget to talk about the wage level awarded by the government. In the wage decision[4] this year (1978), the union decided to take a position of demystification of the government's wage decision, showing the worker that everything that the government had claimed up to then (May, 1978) was lies; everything was done to deceive the working class. It was necessary to show that even if we called a meeting about the wage level, it did not matter if 500 or 20,000 workers came since everything would remain the same, because it was the government that decreed the new salary index. I remember that at that time we were misunderstood because of many workers' lack of consciousness. The union did not ask for a particular salary index (higher than that decreed by the government) and many workers said: 'Lula wants to screw us. He did not ask for anything, and we are not getting a wage increase.'

We then came out with a news bulletin explaining to the worker that the reason for not asking was to show them that the solution to their problems was not in coming to the union meetings to participate in a collective-bargaining wage agreement, but the solution was to be found inside the factory, standing in front of the machine. At that time there was a company executive who was saying that he would not give in to pressure. This gave me an opportunity to reply that negotiation could only take place if there were pressure. Without pressure I don't believe that at any time the managerial class would agree to negotiate with us. I had already experienced this because I had talked to more than 40 factory managers and none of them conceded a thing. But when the machines stopped, they gave in.

After all that preaching, on May 12, when the workers received the first paycheck with the salary readjustment, they noticed that pay in advance had been deducted, that some companies even cut overtime pay, and that some workers received their envelopes with zero money, only with deductions . . . Then, what was the alternative for these workers except to strike? To work the whole month and get to the end and then get nothing . . . Thus the conclusion the working class arrived at was that it had to take a chance.

And I can guarantee you that everything started with the 'wage recovery' campaign. The wage recovery was the big weapon, and everyone could have used it. Those who didn't, did not because they did not believe in it. And it seems to me that it can be used for some time. I even said that with a bit more freedom we could recover not just 34 per cent but 68 per cent, because the fundamental question is the lack of liberty. And it has to be won, it can't come through law.

Lula, there are those who say that the strikes took on a spontaneous character . . .

I already explained some of the reasons for these strikes. There are many people trying to be the 'father of the baby'. Many people think that the strike occurred for this or that reason. The strike had only one thing which was its father: the stomach of the working class. I don't feel put down when it's said that the strike was spontaneous. I put forth the thesis of spontaneity, and I would die to defend it. It was a spontaneous movement of the working class which felt its salaries were more devalued than ever. The worker would arrive home and would find his woman asking for money to buy food, and he did not have it. That's when the workers decided to strike.

What I can say is that the metalworkers' union of São Bernardo and Diadema was in control of all the strikes. We had control to negotiate and to tell the worker to go back to work, to say that he should accept the agreement – and this was not the case in other unions. What impressed me deeply about the strike was the workers' confidence in the union. And I think that this was for a good reason: this was the result of the concerted work over five, six, and seven years. For the first time I started to believe in words. I think that if you start to throw many ideas at the head of the worker, eventually he will accept them. And I think that this was the reason the strikes developed with great spontaneity. The union was careful not to put out any bulletin and to avoid distributing clandestine ones. We made about ten official statements which were published in all the newspapers showing the worker that he should not be influenced by many of the things that they tried to put in his head. I think that the movement had great merit and it was victorious. It was not the victory that we expected, but it was a victory the workers needed to feel – the taste and feel of winning. From then on everything became easier because the worker started to believe in himself.

Do these strikes indicate, in some way, the collapse of the present union structure?

I think that these strikes already started the collapse of the current union structure as well as the present strike law. We always said, here in the union, that the legality of the movement would come from the movement itself. If it was victorious, it would be legal; if it wasn't, it would not be legal because we wouldn't have won anything. Almost everybody recognizes the archaic nature of the current labour-union structure. It was constructed when there were hardly any workers in Brazil . . . It was made around 1939 and it couldn't last. Today's Brazil is not the Brazil of 1939: it's a developed Brazil, with a city like São Bernardo, for example, which can be compared with the large industrial centres of the world, and it cannot be submitted to a legislation which attracts the interests of the multinationals to the extent that labour is cheap and that the union structure is tied to the government. The only thing we want is the freedom to fight with capital without making any distinction between national and multinational capital, because the national companies are in no way better than the multinationals. But, if we can't get the right to fight on an equal footing, it will always happen that a few make a lot but that most earn very little.

The union leaders should not assume the responsibility of resolving the problems of the working class; they must have the guts to say that the union is bound and castrated and that it's the worker who will resolve the problems.

Going back to the strike of São Bernardo, to what extent does emphasizing what you call the 'spontaneous character of the strikes' impede the work of long-term organizing of the workers within the factories? What importance do you give to this type of organizing? Isn't it important that the workers be constantly mobilized from the inside of the factories so that they may act collectively early-on toward the resolution of their problems?

Look, I think that there was organization. It was the most organized worker's movement that I've ever seen. It is very difficult to keep a group of workers organized. I think that you have to 'pluck up heart' to keep a working class organized as one whole.

The term 'factory commission' is being bandied about as if its creation depended on one man, for example, Lula. It doesn't depend on Lula, but on the workers' consciousness. And we know that there are dozens and dozens, not of factory commissions per se, but of groups of workers, highly politicized and prepared, that at any moment could be fired from the factories. Then what we understand is that the factory commission inside of the present structure places the worker's neck in a noose, and because the commission cannot be recognized, they must be clandestine. The guy cannot be too visible or he will be fired. We must fight for job tenure because if it existed, these factory commissions could develop much more easily. But without a job guarantee ... And clandestine work is difficult. Besides, I think that union struggles must be in the open.

What our union demands is that there be one man in each section of the company responsible for union work and that he be given a guarantee against being fired. Each department of a factory should have a man from the union. Then we could count on at least 600 or more union delegates doing union work.

In these strikes, for example, if you asked us to identify the (factory) commissions, we wouldn't have a way to do it. We were approached by various groups of workers here in the union office to give them some orientation about how to act. At that point we came out against the formation of factory commissions and in some companies where they appeared we tried to abolish them. Why? Because the problem was everyone's, not the problem of only a handful. If we could have a commission representing the majority of the workers, they would have their necks in a noose. Why? Because in negotiations with the boss, should the boss give a negative answer, the commission would have to say: 'Listen people, there won't be any raise and we'll have to continue our strike.' Now, who is responsible for the work-stoppage in the eyes of the boss?

Almost all the factories tried to create factory commissions, but they were not set up because the union did not want them. In São Paulo, for example, at the 'Metal Leve' plant a commission was created and an agreement was signed. Who could guarantee that Mindlin (the manager) would give job guarantees to these people and that 80 per cent of them won't be out in the street next year?

In any case, do you recognize that the work of those workers with highest consciousness in the factories, even though it was developed under the table, was important for the spread of the strikes?

It was important. The work of all the conscious workers is important. I am going to tell a story. On the first day of the strike at the Mercedes (plant), a commission of machinists looked for me and demonstrated a high level of consciousness. The machine shop at Mercedes halted and the management went to talk with the machinists. The machinists said: 'look, we do not want to talk with you guys, and we are not telling you what we want. The union will tell you what we want when they get here.' So then the union went there to lay out the demands.

We previously had held a series of talks here at the office, because I think that when you talk to an assembly of a thousand workers you have less chance of putting something in their heads than if you talk to a group of 25 to 30. The possibility of their absorbing what you have to say is much greater in a small group. So without having to get approval from anyone, the union decided, for example, in the week before the first of May to have a series of talks at the union's school. At these more or less 900 workers attended. These were the most politicized, because it is the people who are studying who can see the situation most clearly. Talks were about unionism, etc., and they gave the workers a better orientation.

As a result of all this, a group of workers came to us and said: 'The union taught us that negotiations are only possible when the machines are stopped. O.K., at Mercedes, they are stopped. And we want to negotiate now.' We even kidded the guys: 'We were kidding, and you guys took what we said too seriously.' So you can see that among the metalworkers is a group of very conscious workers.

The proof of this is that, after we had a meeting with the workers at Volkswagen, scores of workers stayed here in the hall waiting for me, and when I went out to talk to them, the drift of the people was the following: 'Lula don't make any agreements because it is we who have to win this fight. We know that legally the union cannot assume responsibility. Therefore we do not want you to go there to fight for us. What you have to do is to keep encouraging and pushing us to continue fighting.' For me, this is a high level of consciousness, you know?

I myself have condemned many union leaders who tried to assume a paternalistic position in relation to the working class. I think that the union's job is to show the working class the truth, to show them that the union is there to assist, but that the union cannot do shit for the working class, except in individual cases. But in the group sense we can do very little for the worker. So the union's role is not to assume the responsibility of resolving the problems of the working class. It's to have the guts to say that the union is tied, is castrated, and that it's the workers who will resolve the problems. No more lies for the working class. I think we showed that if you tell the truth to the workers, you get fast action. You have to show him that he is being exploited and that it is he who must resolve his problems instead of continuing to believe in the union. Unfortunately, there are few leaders trying to tell this truth.

There are those who feel that it is possible to propose the formation of a coordinating committee of factory commissions outside of, and independent of, the unions. Do you find this viable, especially in the present conjuncture?

I think that something must be clear. I try to be realistic even though that doesn't please many people. Truthfully, if you look all over Brazil, you might not find more than three factory commissions.

I don't refer to the commissions formed by members elected by the whole factory, but to groups of workers.

There are groups of workers. Where there are five workers, there will be a group. And there could be two workers with an idea of helping in something. But to go from that to recognizing this group as a pro-union factory commission is stretching it a long way. When I was in the company where I worked, we had a group of workers who got together and discussed things, and I never considered this group a factory commission. In my view, the factory commissions inside of a free labour-union movement would have to remain subordinate to a broad coordination by the union. I think the union must be seen as a representative of the worker. We cannot propose freedom for unions and at the same time want commissions parallel to the unions.

Are you in favour of tying the factory commissions to the union under the present union structure?

There is no doubt that I do favour that. And if there is a worker who does not believe in his union, it's up to the worker to get rid of the union leader.

The way I see it is as follows: in a company with, for example, 50 sections, it should have 50 elected union delegates. This of course would be in a different union structure. This way you could have a union convention made up entirely of union delegates. Now for me, the union delegate would only be of value if he is elected. It's not right for me to become a member of a factory commission just because I want to. I think there must be an election, and the worker must choose someone based on a particular programme. These delegates could choose the union leadership. They would be the guys who would be in daily contact with the workers, talking about their problems, and in all their statements they would be representing the workers of their section. You could have meetings with the delegates of a particular company to discuss the specific problems of that company, and once a month we could have a general meeting of the delegates to take a united position for the metalworkers as a whole. Otherwise we could have the most diverse types of commissions, perhaps even bringing harm to the working class.

Lula, I insist on going back to the former question. Given the limitations that distort the Brazilian system, isn't it important, at least in certain cases, for the workers in many companies to have coordination outside the union?

No, I think that position is not valid. Now, if there is a legally constituted union to represent the workers, what must be done? We must bring into the unions the best elements that are in the factory. I think that the union can orient the working-class struggle without the union leadership going out and preaching. Imagine that you are fighting to have a free student organization. Imagine that you set up the free student directorate and that each class then set up a student commission parallel to the student organization which did not follow the policy of the official organization. So then what was the student directorate established for?

I think we must show the worker what the Brazilian union structure is, so he can start fighting against it. He must know that it must change because it is no good. But the union must orient the worker.

But then you face a big risk. If you have a directorship that is not combative or ends up being co-opted by the authorities, the present structure means that you can't do anything until the next election. Certainly during this period this directorship would contribute to the disorganization of the workers. On the other hand, you mentioned that in various companies there are groups of conscious workers. Wouldn't it be a guarantee for the workers if such groups had a central group elected by them, which could support the union in a strong way, but if the union was not responsive, the group could continue to act independently from the union?

But I think we are saying the same thing. With or without a commission, I think that the worker should only support the union when it (the union) is correct. Now only the worker must change the Brazilian union structure, and it's a question of changing the union leaders. That is, if we understand that democracy is the wish of the majority. If we understand democracy as an imposition by the minority, then ... The union always had and will continue to have conditions to orient as many groups of workers as may wish to be oriented. I think the worker also is to blame for electing his leadership badly, even though the leaders lied a great deal to the working class and the working class did not have clear explanations.

I understand that there can be as many commissions as there are groups of workers functioning inside the union – either to pull down the leadership of the union or to make the leaders work harder, you know. But, I repeat, it must be done inside the union if we want to change the character of unionism, because the person who decides things in the union meeting is the member. If, for example, there are 1,000 workers from various groups, and these people decide to change the rules of the game, they go and change the rules. What we need are the conditions for these people to start participating.

Now, I can guarantee that at least here in São Bernardo there are no organized (factory) commissions. What existed was the consensus of a class and people in leadership positions in some factory departments, but they do not set up factory commissions individually on their own. Here at the union there are various examples of that. I tell the fellows: look, you who are there with your fellow workers twenty hours a day, start a factory commission. But the people want the director of the union to set up the commission. With the fellow workers that I have talked to here at the union, the impression I get is that it is very difficult for them to take the initiative because they have no job security, and they are afraid of losing their jobs.

So we have to keep our feet on the ground. I am certain that there are many workers, not in a position to form a commission of twenty, but who meet in groups of three or four, and exchange ideas every day. And these workers do things normally in accordance with the orientation received from the union. Now there are many people who speak out on their own behalf but give the impression that they are speaking for everyone ... And then when you meet with the guy, you ask him: 'Hey, man, where is your commission? Do you have one?' He will tell you he doesn't, because it is very difficult to start one ... What you can do is use action by the union to provoke the worker and force him to take a position. Sometimes it is necessary to slap the guy in the face because some people only respond this way.

What happened with the Brazilian worker is that for a long time he was conditioned to look to someone at the top to do everything for him because he felt he was impotent, weak, poor, miserable and, that up there, the people with power were capable of doing something for him. The politicians always said that they had the solution for problems, that the workers should trust them, and that everything would be resolved inside congress, etc. The truth is that the politicians say they cannot do anything because of the special laws that weaken the legislature. But before 1964, there was no special legislation and they also did nothing. What did these people give the working class? What was changed in the union structure? What did the working class gain during Juscelino Kubitschek's period – and he was considered the great Brazilian statesman? Nothing. It did not change because it was never in the interests of those in power to change. And Mr João Goulart? He also did nothing to change the union structure.[5]

Look at what is happening now. There are many people applauding the *Frente Ampla* (broad front) which is coming. Why should I applaud? What does it offer me? If the thing is born from the top down and if it comes with marked cards, the only thing left is the right to applaud. I want them to show me a programme. I want to see the *Frente*'s programme. Who is the candidate for President? Euler Bento, Magalhães Pinto?[6] I saw the programme by Euler in today's *Folha de São Paulo* and did not see anything interesting. Let's discuss a programme with a group of workers, with a serious group of union leaders. But having the elite work out a programme and wanting us to accept it, is not right.

I stated some reservations when the demand for a constituent assembly was put forth because I was afraid of repeating the history of the 1946 Constituent Assembly and that again the workers would be submitted to a constitution made by the elites.[7]

How does the working class look at the fight for amnesty, for a constituent assembly, and for democratic liberties? What do you think today really mobilizes the working class?

Let's start with the democratic liberties. I think that this demand is important not only to one or other group of Brazilian society, but to all groups. I expressed some reservations about the demand for a constituent assembly because I was afraid it might repeat the experience of 1946 and that we workers would be subordinated to an assembly controlled by the elites. I think the constituent assembly could be valid if all sectors of Brazilian society participated.

As for amnesty (for people accused of political crimes, or stripped of their rights), I believe that in good conscience, no citizen could be against it. And I go further than amnesty for just the politicians thrown out of office and deprived of their political rights. I support the amnesty that the working class needs: the right to live with dignity, because the working class is the eternal prisoner, the eternal thrown-out-of-office; it doesn't participate in anything in this land except in the process of production. So I defend more emphatically a broader amnesty which would give the working class what belongs to it. This is why people are frequently confused, because it's not just a question of amnesty for political prisoners and people deprived of their political rights. I think it is legal to cancel a person's political rights if it is done by the courts in a legally constituted regime with civil rights, where it is determined that a person acted wrongly and must pay for it. But I'm against depriving people of their rights arbitrarily. In conclusion, I am in favour of these demands as long as they involve the proportional participation of the working class.

How can the working class participate in the struggle for democratic liberties? What level of organization and what kind of weapons does it have to enter in this fight?

This question can be answered in a few words. I think the level of organization was demonstrated by the working class in the recent strikes. I also feel that the working class has more power than any other segment of Brazilian society. It just needs to be alerted to take certain positions, and it will take them.

Should the labour movement work by itself, or should it try to establish relations with the other sectors of the Brazilian opposition like the student movement, the medical interns' movement, the bank workers, etc.? If it should establish these relations, how can they be made concretely?

I have maintained the following: to participate in a movement that is outside of labour before participating in our own movement would be to do the impossible; it would be putting the cart before the horse. The type of freedom that we workers want, if it is the same type of freedom that the students want, that the middle class wants, that all groups want, then I think it will be impossible to refuse the common aspirations after each specific struggle has developed. The biggest problem for the workers today, what motivates them today, is wages. Obviously we must start by fighting for wages. Once this problem is partially solved, we must move to other types of struggle. What cannot happen, for example, is for me to stop fighting for salaries, which is what interests the working class, and go and demonstrate in the Largo de São Francisco (a large square in São Paulo where human rights demonstrations are held). Then I would be running away from reality. I cannot stop fighting for wages in order to join the interns' struggle.

I feel everyone can contribute to restoring normality to the country. What cannot happen is that the SBPC (Sociedad Brasileira para o Progresso da Ciencia – the Brazilian Society for the Progress of Science) start to give contributions at the factory gate; nor should the worker contribute to the SBPC office. I think each one should keep his or her own struggle.

Today people are already talking about reconstructing parties, including the establishment of a workers' party. What do you think about this?

I think that the participation of workers in politics can be independent of political parties. But it depends on the worker having someone elected to defend his right and his principles. I believe that we have arrived at the moment of forming a party of the working class which does not need to have only workers. What we cannot do is put the owner of a company in the worker's party, because he will never support legislation in our interests; he will do what interests him. But there are many people who are not workers – liberal professionals, intellectuals, etc. – who identify greatly with the working class and who could participate in a workers' party. What should be important in this party is that the workers should be the majority, the coordinators and the determinants in the party.

I feel that we are not too far from having this party. There is a gradual evolution of the working class. Today, at least in Sao Bernardo do Campo, there is a group of new workers who will not be as submissive as in the past. And these people, more than ever, ask for freedom for political participation. In the meantime, I think that it is impossible to create anything until after the November (1978) elections. In the next elections, the role of the working class is to choose a party to vote for and within the party to choose the candidates that best represent its interests. I believe that later some other union leaders will come forth to concentrate on structuring something which belongs to the working class.

Reprinted from *Latin American Perspectives*, vol. 6, no. 4, 1979, pp. 90–100; translated by Mauri Garcia and Timothy Harding from the Portuguese original in *Cara a Cara*, vol. 1, no. 2, 1978.

NOTES

1. John Humphrey, 'Auto workers and the working class in Brazil', *Latin American Perspectives*, vol. 6, no. 4, 1979.

[2. 'Populist' President (or dictator) of Brazil from 1930 to 1945, and from 1951 to 1954 when he committed suicide.]

3. The *reposição salarial* [wage recovery] campaign involved 'Lula's' union taking the government to account after it was disclosed that the salary increase in previous years,

authorized by the government and supposedly based on the increase in the cost of living, had been based on deliberately falsified cost-of-living figures which had underestimated inflation [. . .]. The union demanded a 34 per cent wage increase to compensate [. . .].

4. The *dissidio colectivo*, or wage-increase decision, was decreed by the government based on its calculation of inflation. Before 1964, such a *dissidio* was the result of collective bargaining, but under post-1964 law it became a government decree [. . .].

[5. Kubitschek was the President of Brazil from 1956 to 1961, and was succeeded by Goulart whose term of office ended with the military coup of 1964.]

[6. The *Frente Ampla* was a moderate coalition established to contest the presidential election of November 1978, in opposition to João Baptista Figueiredo, the candidate of the official party of the military junta, the *Aliançã Renovadora Nacional* (ARENA). Magalhaẽs Pinto, a civilian supporter of the junta, unsuccessfully sought the nomination of ARENA and changed sides to the *Frente*. The latter eventually fizzled out after Figueiredo won the election and took office as President in March 1979. General Euler Bento was the presidential candidate of the *Movimento Democrática Brasileiro* (MDB), the only other political party allowed at that time.]

[7. The Constituent Assembly of 1946 was part of a movement to democratize political life following the overthrow of Vargas, but achieved little for the working class, hence 'Lula's' scepticism about the calls for another Constituent Assembly in Brazil in 1978.]

Editors' introduction

In the period of the economic 'boom' initially stimulated by reconstruction after the Second World War, the economies of the advanced capitalist countries overcame their labour shortages by recruiting vast numbers of migrant workers from poorer countries. It is estimated that between 1945 and 1975 fifteen million people, mostly from the Mediterranean countries including Turkey and North Africa, settled in northern Europe. They were migrant workers and those of their families who were able to accompany or follow them. In the United States by 1975 approximately one half of the unskilled labour force of twenty-five million people was composed of legal and illegal immigrants who had arrived since 1945, mostly from Mexico, the Caribbean and Latin America.[1] The labour shortages of Britain in the 1950s and 1960s were resolved by encouraging immigration from the former colonies of the Caribbean and the Indian sub-continent.

Holland imported migrant workers in the 1950s for large industries such as coal, steel and textiles. Subsequently many immigrants were also employed in smaller industries and in the service sector, where their uncertain legal status and rights, making them cheap to hire and easy to fire, suited employers. In 1967 a recruitment agreement to supply Holland with Moroccan workers was signed by the governments of the two countries. As the long post-war 'boom' started to turn into recession in the early 1970s the Dutch government began to regulate more strictly the numbers of 'guest-workers' in the country, some of whom were illegal immigrants – those most vulnerable to the pressures of labour recruiters, employers and the state. The restrictive measures introduced were directed at the workers themselves rather than at those recruiters and employers who had encouraged, and profited from, their entry into Holland.

A set of new regulations in 1975 stimulated further the organization and activities of immigrant workers against the daily harassment and insecurity to which they were exposed. The campaign against the new regulations led to the formation of the Committee of Moroccan Workers in Holland (KMAN), and crystallized around the case of 182 Moroccan workers who faced deportation. These workers confronted not only the Dutch authorities, but also faced hostility from their own government which maintains surveillance over the political activities of Moroccans in Europe. The Moroccan embassy in The Hague made it difficult for members of 'the 182' to renew or to obtain valid passports, one of the conditions of continued residence in Holland. The three-year campaign of 'the 182' was conducted in the face of protracted political manoeuvres and bureaucratic contortions by the Dutch government; the tactics of the campaign included a series of hungerstrikes in mosques and churches, and mass demonstrations and petitions which attracted an increasingly broad range of support from Dutch people and organizations. On 17 October 1978, the third anniversary of the first hunger strike, the Dutch parliament ruled that 'the 182' could apply for residence permits.

Here we reprint a collective statement issued by 'the 182', and individual statements by two of the hungerstrikers.

(i) Statement of 'the 182'

With the regulation measures the Dutch government decided not to punish the illegal employers but us, their labourers. We had to bear the brunt, while we have often been exploited in a disgraceful manner by those bosses, who think only of more profit at the cost of our blood and sweat. A large number of labourers could not prove that they were in Holland before November 1974, whilst they had been working here for years already. We, the 182 Moroccan hungerstrikers, are a part of them. We have united to fight for our rights and we have continued the struggle [...]. It has already lasted 3 years: in November 1975 we began with a hunger-strike in the churches in Amsterdam, Utrecht and The Hague and now, in August 1978, we are again on hungerstrike in the church of De Duif in Amsterdam. We feel supported by a large number of Dutch people and organizations who give us their support and solidarity. Therefore we can continue, in spite of disappoint-ments, because when there is a lot of support, there is hope of a victory.

With our action in De Duif we reject the decision of the Dutch government, we declare our anger about this unjust treatment and we have a safe place for those Moroccans of the 182 who are being sought by the police to be evicted.

We refuse eviction, we keep demanding:

A RESIDENCE PERMIT FOR THE 182.

Because who will guarantee us that nothing will happen to us in Morocco when we have been evicted, and no one will know about us anymore? Who guarantees us bread for our children? Who guarantees us work in a country where thousands of unemployed are begging? It is now five weeks that we have been in De Duif, demanding a decision. We fight our battle for a residence permit for the following reasons:

The regulation measures are unfair.

The measures are directed *against the employees* instead of the employers, who use our labour.

The most important witnesses – the labour recruiters – cannot be heard. They demand that *we* show, with legal proof, that we worked here, whilst the recruiters keep us in illegality.

Because they do not want us to know that they have exploited us.

We have, just like the comrades who *do* have an employers' certificate, the right to a residence permit. We have been here many years and not for nothing. Dutch industry profits mostly by our labour. We refuse to be treated constantly as a labour force which has no rights. Through our labour we are part of Dutch society. Holland must also give an answer to the question of the risk we run when we return to Morocco because of our actions here. Holland cannot let us go back to Morocco frightened and uncertain about our future. We have the right to a residence permit. We demand it now.

A large part of the Dutch population are behind our action: democratic political parties, the trade unions, the churches, and a continually increasing number of solidarity organizations. Also a lot of people come to De Duif to give us their support. De Duif is the centre of our action.

Clearly the Dutch people do not want us to be robbed of our rights and evicted, because the ultimatum has run out for some of us twice already.

We also get much support from actions which have taken place in the last few weeks in some 15 places in the Netherlands. We clearly do not stand alone in our struggle. Secretary of State Haars will have to reply to the general demand alive among the Dutch people: a residence permit now for the 182.

But Secretary of State Haars does not wish to go into any of our arguments. At first she even refused to discuss the matter with us. She refused to change or reconsider her decision. But under pressure by the Dutch people she could not go through with her decision to evict us.

With the Council of Ministers she took the decision to refer our case to the State Council. The intention of this strategy is obvious: Secretary of State Haars took care that the case was put off, in order to let the solidarity of the Dutch people run its course, then we could be thrown out of the country without much fuss.

The Ministry of Justice, responsible to Secretary of State Haars, has not handed in to the State Council all documents concerned with our case. That fact alone makes us doubt her proclamation that she does not possess enough evidence on the risk we run if we would be sent back to Morocco now.

The delaying tactics of Secretary of State Haars place us in a position in which we are put under even more moral pressure. The uncertainty in which we have been living for 3 years already is now becoming a torture.

We do not know what will happen to us in the Netherlands or Morocco. We no longer have any income, because we had to leave our jobs to fight for our rights. We feel responsible for our families in Morocco. They ask where the money is that they need in order to exist.

We have already been in the church for five weeks and do not know whether the decision will come tomorrow or in 2 months' time. But our reply to Secretary of State Haars and all her manoeuvres remains clear:
WE CONTINUE UNTIL WE HAVE A RESIDENCE PERMIT.

(ii) Individual statements by two hungerstrikers

'By Democracy I understand real freedom' – *hungerstriker from Utrecht*

I left Morocco in the first place to work and to earn money. I myself am single. I come from a family of 10 children, who are largely dependent on what I earn here. My parents are very poor. In Morocco the situation is hopeless for poor people. You can only look forward to a decent job when you have been to school and have diplomas, but that is only for a very small part of the population, the bourgeoisie. The circumstances you have to live under in Morocco when you are poor are indescribable. When you have got a family with 5 children and are unemployed, you are entitled with your family to a kind of social benefit of f26.[2] Corruption is unlimited. If you need an official document from a civil servant, for example, a copy from the marriage register, it will cost you a minimum of f500. For the most miserable service from the authorities you'll have to bribe a civil servant at least f2,500 to f3,000.

Ben Barka[3] made a kind of estimate in 1962, from which he drew the conclusion that so much money is owing to the government from taxes on phosphates, and agricultural (multinational) industry that it should be possible to give every head of the population daily an amount of f50. Who takes all that money? In any case not the unemployed with his 5 children and his benefit of f26 per month. I have heard that everything has become terribly expensive in Morocco because of the war.[4] Vegetables and coffee have become nearly impossible to afford. The rents in particular have gone up enormously in recent years; for a room you pay f50 per month, without gas or electricity. Besides there is the political angle. You are not free to enquire about what is happening in society around you. Any opinion against the authorities is always dangerous. I participated in the first hungerstrike in Utrecht because of hopeless anger. I could not show the police an employers' certificate, because I worked illegally for a labour recruiter. I thought this terribly unfair. That man has exploited me dreadfully. I worked very long hours for hunger wages, all this illegally, without being in a national health scheme. He went free, because I could prove nothing and I was supposed to leave the country.

The first hungerstrike certainly has yielded a number of positive things, such as an extension, so we could stay in Holland until the decision of the Council of State was known. We did get a kind of legal recognition. If we were without work, we could sometimes claim benefits from social services. The support we got from sympathetic Dutch people was very important. After the hungerstrike, when we were able to stay, it has been hard to survive. We did not get work permits. Because of this it was difficult to find work.

In the past year I have had 3 different employers. I worked for a while for a cleaning agency, on the market for a private employer, and also for agencies. The last three months before I got my benefit I worked in Woerden in a factory, 5 days per week from 6.00 am to 8.00 pm for f1,200 per month.

The last six months I have had some benefits from social services. I would love to educate myself. I have tried very hard to go to school. Through someone from the labour exchange I succeeded in the end. I could only stay for 15 days though – then the head came and asked for my work permit, and I had to leave again. At the moment the situation seems hopeless. I have been informed by the police that I'll have to leave the country on 1st August. My benefits have been stopped. I had to give up my room because I had no money. Therefore I came to Amsterdam, to my comrades. I tried at first to find work, but now I am participating in the action and begin to hope again. I notice that we get a lot of support from Dutch people.

The decision of Mrs Haars is and remains inhuman. Apart from the fact that there is nothing for us in Morocco, our group runs a political risk there because we fight for our rights. She ignores the report of Amnesty International. She knows full well what risk we run. It has nothing to do with justice or something like that. Netherlands and Morocco are on the same wavelength, they have the same interests. They have agreed for some time that we would not get a permit, because they don't want to upset each other.

If you ask me whether Holland is a democratic country, I have to say no. It is in fact in the same situation as in Morocco, only people here are much better off. By democracy I understand real freedom: freedom to be able to inform yourself, to have an opinion, to lead your own life, to choose your education and work, to support your family. In the Netherlands all this is not for us foreigners, but it is also impossible for many Dutch people. Everything remains much more hidden here than in Morocco. On the other hand I have here at least the illusion that there is a future – that you might be able to make something of your life. By refusing us a work permit after we have worked for so long in Holland, have learned Dutch, made friends, they destroy us. We are in something of the same situation as the Moluccans.[5] Mrs Haars talks about justice, equality before the law, and compassion. She might mean something by that, but that has little to do with us. Therefore this action, therefore we fight for the right which *does* concern us, our group and our Dutch comrades.

'I have much to lose' – hungerstriker from Amsterdam

I have been in the Netherlands for four and a half years. There was not enough work in

Morocco. Moreover I was very dissatisfied with the political situation in my country. I have come to Europe in the hope that there would be more freedom. And that is indeed so. At the beginning of 1974 I came to Holland. After 3 days I had already found a job. When the regulation measures were introduced I went to my employer to ask for a certificate to prove that I was already working for him before November 1974. He refused and sacked me straight away. I then found out that I had worked illegally and was therefore not entitled to benefits.

In those days the KMAN, the Committee of Moroccan Workers in the Netherlands, organized actions against the government measures. I once got a pamphlet announcing a meeting and I attended. At this meeting the situation of the labourers who could not get an employers' certificate was discussed. The decision to go on a hungerstrike was taken by 182 Moroccans who otherwise would have to leave the country. The hungerstrike started in the Mosque and was continued after 5 days in the Moses and Aaron Church (Amsterdam). This action lasted 4 months, until February 1976. When we left the church we had obtained an extension and the promise that the matter of the employers' certificates would be further looked into. I then got benefits from social services and found work again in June 1976.

In July 1976 Zeevalking (then Secretary of State for Justice) decided that our applications for residence permits would be refused again. We could appeal to the Council of State. We went to see our lawyers and decided to appeal. This case went on for 1½ years. In April 1978 came the definite refusal. So we could not get a residence permit. The present Secretary of State, Mrs Haars, promised to look at all our dossiers, and to have discussions with Amnesty International about a report of theirs concerning the situation in Morocco and what would or could happen to people who returned to their country after having been active in politics abroad [. . .]. In spite of these promises 6 Moroccans had been deprived of their passports with the summons to leave Holland before 1 August 1978. I have hopes that Mrs Haars [. . .] will reverse the decision of the Council of State. The action will not end before this has happened. If I had to go back to Morocco I would certainly expect trouble. I am politically active in Holland and as this is a punishable crime in Morocco I'll probably be imprisoned.

In all countries where Moroccans are employed you find members of the *Amicales*, a group formed by the Moroccan government with the aim of keeping a check on compatriots abroad, so that they won't even be aware of different political forms. These *Amicales* check whether one becomes a member of a trade union or a political party. If this happens, he can then be picked up by the police when he returns to his country.

For all the 182 there is no guarantee that nothing will happen to them when they return to Morocco. Moreover there is no work in that country. A large part of the population is unemployed. Another part of the population is doing well and an even smaller part is rich (about 5 per cent). People who work for the Moroccan government are doing very well. Of the political parties [in Holland] the PvdA (Labour Party), PPR (Radical), PSP (Pacifist) and CPN (Communist) are behind us. All groups working for foreigners are in solidarity with us – Amnesty International, FNV [Federation of Dutch Trade Unions] and other trade unions, students' organizations, IKB [Dutch Council of Churches], Amsterdam lawyers' collective, Moroccan Committee of the Netherlands, all democratic Moroccan organizations in Europe and last but not least the people of De Duif, who have granted us use of their church. All these groups support our action. Apart from my job, I do cultural and social work with Moroccan labourers in Holland. I do this as

an active member of the KMAN (Committee of Moroccan Workers in Holland). I
fight against the presence of the *Amicales* in Holland, also in the context of the
KMAN. I am anti-fascist and therefore in solidarity with every democratic
Moroccan organization in Europe.

I have much to lose in Holland: all the people I got acquainted with, my work
for the KMAN and everything I have built up in these 4½ years. If I stay in
Holland I am going to learn Dutch well. And then I am going to study. I will go on
fighting the Moroccan regime and the presence of the *Amicales* in Holland and in
Europe. And of course I will remain an activist in the KMAN.

Translated by Gavin Hudson from a special issue of the *Bulletin of the Committee of
Moroccan Workers in Holland*, 1978; made available to us by David Seddon and
published here in English for the first time.

NOTES

1. Robin Cohen, 'Migration, Late Capitalism and Development', address to the
Development Studies Association, University College, Swansea, 1980 (unpublished).
   [2. About 4 florins = £1 (1978).]

[3. Mehdi Ben Barka was the leader of the Union Nationale des Forces Populaires, a left-wing
political party formed in Morocco in 1959. It gained support from the trade unions and
enjoyed considerable political success until a period of repression began in June 1965 when
King Hassan assumed direct rule. Ben Barka himself was kidnapped and murdered in Paris
in 1965. This caused a political scandal in France where there was widespread suspicion
that his murder was the result of collusion between the French Secret Service and Morocco's
Minister of the Interior and 'strong man', General Oufkir.]

[4. In January 1976 when Spanish forces left the former colony of Spanish Sahara, the
territory was jointly annexed by Morocco and Mauritania. Since then a war of liberation
has been waged by the POLISARIO movement to establish an independent 'Saharan
Democratic Arab Republic'. Mauritania has since withdrawn from the conflict but
Moroccan troops continue to fight in the disputed area, which is very sparsely populated
but rich in phosphates and other mineral deposits.]

[5. People from Molucca, formerly part of the Dutch East Indies. Many of them settled in
Holland, where they feel themselves to be an oppressed racial minority.]

Part Three

Women's Struggles

Introduction

Little of the documentation on peasants and agricultural and urban workers includes information or analysis concerning how their problems and struggles specifically affect women. One reason for this is a manifestation of women's subordination itself: men are more literate, usually 'represent' the family to the outside world, are more often in positions of leadership and are more easily accessible to interview. While researchers and activists are remedying this through recording and publishing the experiences of particular groups of women, there remains a lack of general accounts of struggles which integrate analysis of sexual divisions as well as class relations. This section highlights the additional struggles confronting women peasants and workers because of their gender.

The readings in this section have been ordered as follows. First, we illustrate some of the conditions faced by women engaged in agricultural production, whether as peasants (Readings 20(i) and (iii)) or wage workers (Readings 20(ii), 22 and 26). We also include an interview with a woman leader working in a producer cooperative (Reading 23). A number of the readings bring out the difficulties of earning a living in the rural areas; they show why women migrate to towns and what kinds of employment are open to them there (Readings 24, 25 and 26). Readings 27 and 28 (and Reading 16) concentrate on the conditions of urban dwellers and the ways they earn their living through informal sector activities (see introduction to Part II) or wage employment. Our final reading expresses the views of a proletarian woman as wife and women's leader. The readings portray not only economic conditions but also mechanisms through which women are subordinated ideologically and culturally and which give rise to different forms of struggle.

A universal mechanism of women's subordination operates through the sexual division of labour. At the most general level, this division is manifested in the family through women's role as child bearers and rearers and through all the activities of maintaining the home which are combined in the concept of 'domestic labour'. Domitila de Chungara (Reading 29(i)) describes her daily domestic grind as the wife of a miner and cynically notes: '. . . in spite of everything we do, there's still the idea that women don't work . . . that only the husband works because he gets the wage.' But as all the readings show, poor women in the Third World rarely, if ever, just do domestic work. Women also earn an income whether through producing food on their farms, through wage work or producing and selling commodities. As Reading 22 points out, women are thus subjected to 'double work'. Readings 22, 23, 26 and 29 all illustrate how women combine domestic work with earning a living either to supplement family income or to provide entirely for the family. The division between the two spheres is, however, often blurred. On peasant farms (Reading 20(iii) for example), the household is the unit of both production and consumption. Women's work in cultivation is as necessary to maintaining and reproducing the family as their domestic labour. The blurring of these distinctions is not just a phenomenon of peasant agriculture. The *beedi*-workers in Reading 16 carry out part of their industrial work in the home and even take their children with them to help them in the factories.

The other way in which women's subordination is made most apparent is through relations between the sexes, in marriage and the family. As many of the readings show, this is double-edged: on the one hand, women are subjected to forms of male domination within the family itself; on the other, marriage and family relationships are often unstable which imposes an economic and psychological burden on women who are usually left to care for the children. An example of the first is in Reading 28: forms of control exerted by her husband and his family have negative economic and social consequences for Tarabai when she asserts herself within the marriage. Reading 23 illustrates the ways in which husbands prevent their wives' independence and again how self-assertion can lead to the disruption of family life. Almost all the readings illustrate the instability of marital relations and its impact on women. For many peasants, rural and urban workers, the material conditions for marital stability do not exist. For example, the Mozambican song (Reading 20(iii)) and the poem in Reading 21 are on the theme of 'desertion' by migrant husbands. Instability is also reflected in the casual liaisons that characterize many family relations, particularly between those who are often on the move looking for work (Readings 9, 14 and 26). Social and cultural factors are also involved: desertion and divorce often result from men going off with other women ('He got an attack of hot-headedness', Reading 23) or other forms of (usually socially determined) dissatisfaction ('"She can't have a son, let's marry our son to a different woman"', Reading 28). Economic and cultural factors can make married life as hard for women as desertion and single motherhood. 'Tarabai almost spontaneously bursts into a mocking song about her husband . . . and then . . . turns to me and says, "Gail-*bai*, don't marry. Don't marry"' (Reading 28).

The sexual division of labour is manifested in a specific way in the kinds of work that women do to earn a living. While this differs between societies, there is always a division between men's and women's work. An example of the sexual division of labour in agriculture is given in Reading 22: '. . . men's work is ploughing, cutting ears of corn, collecting the crop, carrying it away, collecting leftovers for cattle. Women's work is winnowing grain from chaff, weeding, picking cotton and removing the seeds, sowing.' In Reading 20(ii), hoeing was regarded as women's work. That some women were later allowed to cut cane reflects how occupational roles can change when there is a shortage of male workers. Women who cannot earn sufficient income in the rural areas and migrate to the towns for limited periods of time, or even permanently, usually find themselves working in personal services. Some women turn to prostitution as a way of earning a living (Readings 24 and 25) and this can often improve their economic security, if not their social status, in their place of origin (Reading 24). In Reading 25, prostitution is even seen as an improvement on the lot of the peasant's wife, described as 'Days without meat, without sugar, and without songs,/The sweat and dirt of hard work.' Many urban women do not have regular wage employment and rely on their own initiatives in the informal sector to get by. Such an example is the Annapurna women (Reading 27) who commercialize their domestic skills and make money through cooking for single migrant men. Those who do have waged work are often employed in menial tasks in the service sector, like the street cleaners of Pune (Reading 28), although as Reading 16 illustrates, they can also provide a ready source of cheap labour for factories.

As many of the readings indicate, the 'outside' work that women do is usually paid at even lower rates than men receive. The *Dalit* women in Bori Arab (Reading 22) complain that their wages are less than those for men, and Aída Hernández (Reading 23) describes how, even in the context of a cooperative, women are paid different rates for the same work. Low wages and gender differentials in wages are likely where there are more workers than jobs, where there is no effective legislation against differentials linked to gender and where the workers themselves are not organized. In the case of women, it is generally assumed that they are not the main wage-earners (although often they are the main or the *only* wage-earners) and can therefore be paid low wages. The wage paid to men is often called a 'family wage' (although in the Third World even these wages are extremely low, particularly among migrants, because it is assumed that they have economic support from other members of the family who remain in the rural areas). A 'family wage' assumes that the work required to maintain and reproduce the family (i.e. domestic labour) has no costs. A statement encapsulating the effect on women of the 'family wage' is made by Domitila: '. . . the miner is doubly exploited, no? Because, with such a small wage, the woman has to do much more in the home. And really that's unpaid work that we're doing for the boss, isn't it?' (Reading 29(i)).

Inequalities manifested in family relations and the sexual division of labour are reinforced through cultural and ideological factors. This means that the *forms* of women's subordination differ both within and between societies even though the *effects* are similar. The role of culture and ideology is illustrated in many of the readings through particular aspects of relations between the sexes in which forms of male domination are apparent. We have already mentioned the restrictions on mobility and activity that husbands, fathers and brothers often impose on women and what may happen to those who transgress the norms. These mechanisms of control (as well as the ways in which women try to avoid them) can be both subtle and contradictory. Such an example is Reading 24 where women ensure their economic security through prostitution. While this is frowned on ('The women of Yumbe are nothing but harlots'), productive activities normally allowed to women could not provide them with the independent income and limited freedom gained through prostitution. In general, men mediate or control women's independence within the home and their contact and participation in public life. One example is the reluctance of the Bombay trade unions to help the Annapurna women: '. . . trade unions with a predominantly male membership, are rarely sensitive to the problems of women' (Reading 27). Women like Aída Hernández and Domitila de Chungara (who both learnt their leadership skills from male comrades) tend to be exceptions. As Aída explains: 'The problem is not only that the men don't want to give them responsibility, but also that the women don't want to take it' (Reading 23).

While confronting many common problems, women cannot be seen as a homogeneous group. The readings illustrate how the different struggles they face are determined not only by gender but also by class, caste and ethnic group. Various kinds of response to particular conditions of existence can be identified. There is the individual 'solution' which may have become institutionalized, such as the women who become prostitutes in Yumbe (Reading 24) and who have the implicit support of their female kin. The beginnings of a quest for unified action are illustrated in the conversation of the women of Bori Arab (Reading 22). Some women have made their way into existing organizational structures (Readings 23, 26 and 28). Others have become part of women's organizations (Readings 20, 27 and 29). The domestic and reproductive role of women determines to a large extent the ways in which they can organize themselves on a collective basis. Moema Viezzer, who published Domitila's account, remarks that the Housewives' Committee 'is an organization of women who live from permanent domestic labour and who believe that they can win their liberation through indirect struggle connected with production'.[1] Overcoming isolation and atomization is one of the most difficult problems that women have to confront. Domitila herself sees the women's struggle in Bolivia as integral to that of the working class as a whole. She is therefore conscious of the ways in which women are divided as well as united. When a member of the Mexican delegation to the International Women's Year Tribunal approaches Domitila and says, '"Let's speak about us, señora. We're women"', Domitila, recognizing the upper-class origins of the women, replies, '"Is my situation at all similar to yours? ... We can't, at this moment, be equal, even as women, don't you think?"' (Reading 29).

NOTE

1. Moema Viezzer, 'El Comité de Amas de Casa de Siglo XX: an organizational experience of Bolivian women', in *Latin American Perspectives*, issue 22, Summer 1979, vol. 6, no. 3, p. 85.

ALPHEUS MANGHEZI

Editors' introduction

The three interviews below describe the conditions faced by rural women before and after the independence of Mozambique. The first two deal with aspects of the use of female labour under Portuguese rule. One looks at the forced cultivation of particular crops (see also Reading 4(ii)). As this was carried out by peasant households on their own plots, most of the additional work involved fell on women whose husbands and other male relatives migrated to work in the mines of Rhodesia and South Africa (see Reading 12). The shortage of male workers in agriculture meant that women were also employed on plantations. Our second interview is with a woman who worked on the Nkomati Sugar Estate at Xinavane, established in 1913/14 by a British company. Alpheus Manghezi notes: 'After its foundation, it was faced with very stiff competition for labour from well-established labour recruiting giants such as Wenela [Witwatersrand Native Labour Agency] and the Caminho de Ferro de Moçambique [Mozambican Railway Company]. Its own recruiting policy was aimed at capturing both voluntary and *chibalo* workers [see Reading 4(i)]. Information gathered in 1981 suggests that because of the chronic male labour shortage in colonial Mozambique, the company started recruiting female labour from the 1940s onwards. According to [...] an ex-employee of the company [...] it was mostly widows, divorcees and deserted women who came to Xinavane in ever-increasing numbers in the 1950s.'

Labour migration to South Africa has continued since independence, propelled by the need for a cash income that the peasant agriculture of southern Mozambique has been unable to provide. This is itself an effect of the 'vicious circle' of labour migration and agricultural stagnation. In recent years, however, South Africa has greatly reduced the quotas of workers it is prepared to employ from an independent Mozambique. Women remain the principal agricultural producers and our third interview highlights both continuities and changes in their living and working conditions since independence. Luisa Agosto Mbatini runs the family farm herself for much of the year while her husband works as a miner in South Africa. The interview describes her work as an agricultural producer and also brings out aspects of her married life (forcefully illustrated in the work song that introduces the interview). Luisa tells of some of the ways in which cultural patterns are gradually changing as a result of the liberation struggle and the policies of the FRELIMO government. The FRELIMO women's organization, Organização da Mulher Moçambicana (OMM), was established in 1972 during the course of the armed struggle for independence and today plays a leading role in attempting to improve the position of women in Mozambique.

(i) Women are forced to grow rice

[In the district of Manjacaze, Martha Chissano, aged 54, was interviewed about cotton and rice cultivation in that part of the country.]

In Manjacaze, everyone was obliged to cultivate either cotton or rice, no one was forced to produce both crops at the same time. However, there was discrimination against women because on top of all this, women had to give free labour to *regulos* [local chiefs] on demand, and women without husbands and spinsters were singled out for this purpose. As we all carried identity cards, the *regulo*, working through his sub-chiefs and police, was always in a position to know which family had not paid their hut tax. [. . .]

What of the two crops did you cultivate?

I cultivated rice for Makupulani, our *regulo*. Just before the harvest foremen were sent to every rice plot to make an estimate of how much rice each cultivator was likely to reap from their plot, and on the basis of that estimation these foremen would hand you the number of sacks you were supposed to fill. . . . If you failed to fill those sacks at the harvest, because they had over estimated your crop, then they would . . . accuse you of having hidden some of the rice for your own personal consumption. We were not allowed to consume any of the rice we cultivated – we had to deliver every grain of it to the authorities, and then went to the shopkeepers afterwards to buy our own produce if we wished to consume any of it.

The cultivation of rice caused us great suffering in the land of Makupulani. On one occasion a number of women, myself included, were rounded up and brought before one of the *regulo*'s sub-chiefs for questioning as we all had failed to . . . cultivate our plots on time. The reason why most of us fell behind, as everyone knew, was that none of us had any ox-ploughs and had to cultivate the very tough and sticky river-bed soil with our hoes. Some of the women had fallen behind due to illness, but all these valid reasons were rejected out of hand by the chief who then ordered us to lie down on our stomachs to be whipped with *sjamboks* [whips made of rhinoceros hide] on our backs.

Were there other methods of punishment . . .?

. . . The authorities sometimes organized a *tsima*, that is, they got together a group of people to . . . cultivate your rice plot but without your consent. For a *tsima*, you have to provide food and drinks for the people you have invited to 'help' you, and the authorities, having invited a group of workers for you without any consent from you, would pass the responsibility for the food and drink on to you. The population [under] Makupulani eventually reached a point where they could no longer tolerate this oppression, and secretly sent some men to Lourenço Marques [now Maputo], to the office of the Governor General to report the situation . . . A white officer was subsequently sent to Manjacaze to investigate some of the complaints, and a public meeting was held at Makupulani's home. All the *regulos* of the district were present. The *regulos* and their chiefs stood solidly behind each other in their denial of . . . the charges. . . .

In the end, however, . . . one of the sub-chiefs decided to let the cat out of the bag. This chief . . . stood up and testified against the *regulos* and his fellow chiefs. The white officer then decided to ask the population to testify, and I was one of those who rose and spoke against the *regulos*, telling him that we were being made to toil for long hours in the fields, that they robbed us of our crops and chickens for

THEIR OWN PRIVATE CONSUMPTION, AND THAT THEY GAVE US CORPORAL PUNISHMENT WHENEVER WE PROTESTED AGAINST THE . . . ABUSES AND HUMILIATION WE ARE MADE TO SUFFER IN THEIR HANDS. WHEN THE OFFÑCER CHALLENGED ME TO PROVE MY ALLEGATION, HE MADE THE MISTAKE OF ASKING ME TO POINT OUT ANY OF THE MEN WHO I HAD CLAIMED [. . .] assaulted me. It was a mistake because when I pointed this man out, the latter, to our surprise, did not even try to deny my accusations but, on the contrary, he stood up and made a clean breast of it. He said he had beaten me up because I was naughty and did not attend my rice plot properly. The white officer, again to our great surprise, ordered the immediate arrest of this man. Mbhahane, the man who had assaulted me and other women, was put under arrest together with two other men who had also been exposed, and sent off to Sao Tome.[1]

When did this happen?
This happened in 1950. [. . .]

How old were you when this happened?
I was 24 and I had one child.

Where was your husband at the time?
He was on the mines in Joni [Johannesburg].

Did he know what was happening to you when all this was taking place?
I kept him informed – I wrote to him regularly and told him of all the problems, we were facing here at home. You see, after the events I have just described to you, there was another private meeting of the chiefs of Makupulani where they decided that our family should be expelled from the *regedoria* [local chiefdom] because we were said to be agitators who were likely to create more problems in the future. Faced with this serious threat, I . . . wrote an urgent letter to my husband . . . to return home to deal with this situation himself. With the support of some members of the community, my husband was able to prevail upon the chiefs to reconsider their decision – the threat was not carried out in the end.

[Martha Chissano is now responsible for organizational work in the OMM.]

(ii) Women plantation workers

[Alda Mulungu, aged about 45, relates her own work experience of Xinavane where she worked for several years.]
[. . .] My husband died and left me with two small children to care for and . . . I decided to go to Xinavane to look for work. This was in the 1950s, and I left my children under the care of my mother.

What type of work did they give you when you first went to Xinavane?
It was hoeing.

Were there many other women employed at Xinavane when you first went there?
There were many, many women when I was there. [. . .]

Was there accommodation available for female workers in the compounds of the plantation?

There were dormitories for women who came from long distances, and we slept four to eight women in each dormitory, providing our own bedding and the company providing the food. The women who came from neighbouring areas went back to their own homes in the evening. Some of the women who came from far afield were at times able to arrange accommodation with relatives or friends who lived in the neighbourhood because they did not like the hostel atmosphere in the plantation.

Did they provide you with any work clothes?

We made our own work clothes from sacks.

How much did you earn?

When I first went to Xinavane I earned 5$00[2] per day, then 10$00, and after that 15$00 per day; we got an increase every year.

What other tasks were assigned to women workers apart from hoeing?

At the time when we were paid 5$00 per day . . ., women were confined to hoeing. With the raising of the wages some women were selected and given the task of cutting and loading the sugar cane previously a male domain. It was at this point in time that women were provided with a pair of shorts for the first time as work clothes.

Was there any discussion with the women before they were issued with these shorts?

In those days the bosses never held meetings with the workers. The only time when we were ever called to a meeting was when the bosses had decided to raise the wages from 15$00 per day to 25$50 per day. The manner in which this was done made the workers suspicious because it was not common to get a wage increase without a demand from the workers. This offer, therefore, was rejected by the workers who, instead, demanded a much higher increase. . . . Our demand was for a wage of 150$00 per day. To this the boss retorted: 'if the company were to pay you (labourers) that sort of wage, what do you think the machine operators and office clerks would demand in turn?' And we replied: 'who do you think is more valuable to the company: . . . those of us who toil in the fields or the . . . office workers?' [. . .]

By this time the situation was becoming very militant as we continued to press for a higher wage increase. . . . With our hoes raised high, we threatened to prevent people from continuing with their work. The boss tried to defuse the tense situation by asking for a postponement of the meeting to the next day to allow time for rethinking, and appealed to everyone to return to work; but we refused to go back to work [wanting . . .] to know when the answer to our demand would be forthcoming.

The boss promised to return with an answer the next day, but we still refused to return to work that day and went back to our hostels instead. . . . When the boss reappeared on the afternoon of the third day . . . it was with an offer of 60$00 per day, plus another 5$00 per day as a Christmas bonus. This wage increase was accepted by the workers without any further discussion.

[. . .]

How was it possible that the workers who were presented with an offer of a wage increase without any previous consultations were able to give a unanimous response to the bosses?

There were 7 different compounds in the plantation, but I don't know if there had been rumours about the imminent offer of a wage increase, and if therefore, there might have been some clandestine meetings before the day the offer was made.

Who were those who spoke out on your behalf during the big gathering with the big boss?

It was the 'bossboys' who did most of the talking, but the attack on those who tried to go about their work while the meeting was going on was led by the women with their hoes.

Were you one of those women?

I led the 'assault' against the gatekeeper when the latter tried to allow a lorry driver to pass through.

Were all 'bossboys' males in those days?

They were all men in those days, but later women were selected as gang leaders over women workers.

(iii) The life of a migrant's wife

[Luisa Agosto Mbatini led the following work song 'I waste my energy' after which she was interviewed.]

Leader: Hei! women, my energy is wasted.
Chorus: My energy is wasted; it is wasted.
Leader: When I build a home
Chorus: My energy is wasted; it is wasted.
Leader: When I plaster the hut
Chorus: My energy is wasted; it is wasted.
Leader: Won't you weep for me?
Chorus: My energy is wasted; it is wasted.
Leader: When I cultivate the fields
Chorus: My energy is wasted; it is wasted.
Leader: When I cultivate peanuts
Chorus: My energy is wasted; it is wasted.
Leader: When I plant mandioca
Chorus: My energy is wasted; it is wasted.
Leader: They have thrown me out
Chorus: My energy is wasted; it is wasted.
Leader: He has left me
Chorus: My energy is wasted; it is wasted.

At the close of the song, one of the women makes the following appeal to the 'woman concerned': 'Your husband has not deserted you (on purpose), it is the white men who are responsible for this! Stay where you are even when you have to suffer. Remain there and till your fields and take care of your small children! This is the advice which we fellow women give you and this is based on experience – [. . .] we have suffered too. It does not mean that your husband has deserted or left you; he is the victim of the white men's ways (of life). He will return and find you here!'

How did you meet your husband?
I had seen him around before because he is of this area.

Does that mean that you had met him before, talked to him and you fell in love with him?
He came to my home (laughter).

Did he come to your home and talked to you there?
Yes, yes.

Before he came to your home, you must have met and talked, not so?
He knew me because his home is not far from mine.

You must have met before, talked and looked at each other properly!
No! (laughter)

You are not telling the truth!
He came to my home (big laughter).

So he came to your home and said that he was in love with you – did the family accept him?
They did not.

Why did they reject him?
They said I was too young.

They said you were too young because you were then 14 years old!
[. . .] I told my mother that I loved this man, and insisted on getting married to him.

And then?
She refused, and then I left and came to live with him.

Had your husband already built these houses?
Yes, and his wife had deserted him and gone to Beira.[3]

So your husband had been married before, and his wife had left him and gone to Beira!
Yes.

Did they have any children?
They had one child.

Did she take the child with her when she left him?
No, the child is here; she has gone to school.

How old is she?
She is 15.
[...]

Did your husband [. . . give] lobolo[4] to your family?
No.

Did he not? Has he paid now?
My mother did not accept his *lobolo*. You see, I have no father and who was going to receive the *lobolo*? My mother did not want anyone else to receive my *lobolo* and therefore she did not allow my husband to give *lobolo*.

Your mother took this decision by herself, but what did you feel about it?
What could I have done? There was no one to receive the *lobolo*.

Did you want your husband to pay lobolo?
Yes, he should have given a 'gratification'[5] [...] did he pick me up from the footpath?

You felt that he should have thanked your mother [. . .]?
It is okay because he takes care of her now.
[...]

How long have you been living here with your husband?
Since 1974.

Do you have any children?
No.

Is it a problem?
The children 'refuse to come!'
[...]

How long has your husband worked in Joni?
He has been working for a long time – he was already working when I came here.

Do you know how many contracts[6] he has already completed on the mines?
I don't know the number of contracts he did before I came here, I only know the contracts he has done since I came.

How many?
This is his fourth contract.

Does he send money regularly – how often?
I don't receive money every month, he sends it at intervals [...].

Does he send the money by post?
He sends it by returning *maghayisa* [miners].

What about this [...] house – was it already constructed when you came to live here?
It was built after I came.

I can see now that the house is not yet completed – is it because of a shortage of cement, etc.?
We have no cement at all.

How big is the house?
Two bedrooms and a sitting room.

And the other house [...] was it built when you came?
Yes, it was there.
[...]

What particular problems do you face when your husband is in Joni?
I have had no problems. I just work in the fields and stay and wait for his return.
He will find me here when he returns!

Do you have lots of work in the fields – do you have big fields?
Well, we do not have seeds. We do have fields but we have no seeds!

Is it not possible to buy seeds from the shops at Homoine with the money from your husband?
There is none in the shops – where shall we find seeds?

Does your husband have cattle?
We have no cattle.

Has he never bought cattle?
No.

So you cultivate with the hoe! Do you have pigs?
I have a young one.

One only?
Yes.

When your husband is home, do you work together in the fields or does he prefer to sit around saying 'well, I am a ghayisa [miner], I have worked hard in Joni and now must rest!'?
We work together – he also works.

How long does he normally remain at home when on leave?
Between four and five months, but never six months.

Do you mean that you work together during all this time when he is home?
Yes, we work together.
[...]

Do you attend celula[7] *meetings regularly?*
I do.

Since FRELIMO arrived, it is being said that women must be liberated. What do you think about that?
I think it is a good thing.

Why is it a good thing?
Because men have [...] stopped doing those things which our fathers did.

Which things were those?
(Laughing) – our mothers say that they used to be whipped with *sjamboks* and sticks but this does not happen to us. Even when you are whipped, it is done more gently, and you are beaten up only for something you know you have done wrong. (everyone laughed)

Has your husband ever beaten you up?
My husband has never beaten me up.

SOURCE
See Reading 4.

NOTES
[1. Penal colony in Portuguese territory off the coast of West Africa.]
[2. The currency is the *escudo*; then about 100 = £1.]
[3. Second city, port and railway terminal for Zimbabwe.]
[4. Bride-price usually paid to the father of the family on the marriage of daughters.]
[5. FRELIMO changed the *lobolo* to a 'gratification' – a form of 'thank-you' present.]
[6. In South Africa contracts are from 12 to 18 months.]
[7. Local meetings of the party (FRELIMO).]

Editors' introduction

This poem is a poignant expression of the feelings of a woman whose husband is working as a migrant labourer in Europe. Not only does it capture in a different mode some of the problems voiced by the Mozambican woman in Reading 20(iii), but it reflects the other side of the struggles of the migrant workers themselves (Reading 19): the distress experienced by their wives and families.

*   *   *

Germany, Belgium, France
and Netherlands
Where are you situated?
Where are you?
Where can I find you?
I have never seen your countries, I do not
speak your language.
I have heard it said that you are beautiful,
I have heard it said that you are clean.
I am afraid, afraid that my love forgets
me in your paradise.
I ask you to save him for me.
One day after our wedding he left,
with his suitcase in his hand, his eyes looking ahead.
You must not say that he is bad or aggressive;
I have seen his tears, deep in his heart, when he went away.
He looked at me with the eyes of a child;
He gave me his small empty hand and asked me:
'What should I do?'
I could not utter a word; my heart bled for him.
The henna[1] is dead in my hands.
Germany, Belgium, France
and Holland:
I ask you to save him for me, so I can see him once a year.
I knew him in his strength which could break stones
I am afraid, jealousy is eating my heart.
With you he stays one year, with me just one month
to you he gives his health and his sweat,
to me he only comes to recuperate.
Then he leaves again to work for you, to beautify
you as a bride, each day anew.
And I, I wait; I am like a flower that

withers, more each day.
He writes me that his hand will not
remain empty, but my heart tells me
that it's not true.
He hides the truth for me so as not
to hurt me.
But he knows not that I share his despair,
that I am jealous during his absence of ...?

Germany, Belgium, France and Holland:
I have heard it said that you are beautiful,
and good.
He gives you his health and his power,
with you he stays one year,
with me only one month.
I am afraid that he forgets me.
The henna is dead in my hands.
I ask you: give him back to me.

Source: See Reading 19, p. 158.

NOTE

1. Henna is a plant dried for its red-brown colour. Normally it is used for the hair. During the honeymoon the bride makes figures in her hand with henna, which disappear after a while.

22   'Women have to do double work'

GAIL OMVEDT

Editors' introduction

There are three pieces from India in this section, each portraying various aspects of the problems of low-caste women, and the struggles they give rise to. The readings focus on the themes of:
(a) the double day: the problems of combining domestic labour with earning a living;
(b) the nature of women's work: the sexual division of labour in agriculture (and differentials in wages) and in ways of earning a living in the towns;
(c) the problems of struggle, including forms of organization relevant to the different social conditions and activities of specific groups of women.

The author of Readings 22 and 28, Gail Omvedt, is an American sociologist who lives in India and has conducted extensive research there. The travels and meetings that provided the material for her book took place in 1975, and the extracts that we reprint here centre on issues of caste, tribe and class with particular reference to women of 'scheduled' (or 'untouchable') castes and of tribal minorities.

Caste is a hierarchy of spiritual and social ranks established in the beliefs of the Hindu religion. This hierarchical system is expressed both in a series of rules and rituals concerning purity and pollution, and in a related social division of labour. The former legislates which kinds of contact between different castes are permitted and which are forbidden (for example, in relation to eating together and to marriage). This is reflected in the naming of castes and sub-castes by the occupations they traditionally pursued in the social division of labour, some of which are indicated in Readings 20 and 28 (see also Reading 16). The permitted social transactions and contacts between castes are known as *jajmani*, which specifies a necessarily unequal (because hierarchical) 'reciprocity' whereby lower castes perform agricultural labour and/or a range of personal services for higher castes in return for payment in kind and patronage or 'protection'. The details of the caste system and its local variations are complex, but in broad terms there is a strong correlation between the ritual and ideological status of different castes and the contours of material and social inequality that we associate with the notion of 'class'.

'Tribes' are ethnically distinct minorities, presumed to be descendants of the indigenous population of India at the time of the arrival of the Aryans (about three millennia ago), who evolved Hinduism. The tribal people occupied hilly and forested areas, and their lack of legal title to their traditional lands has facilitated their expropriation by others. Today many 'tribals' are landless and migrate to find seasonal work as agricultural labourers. The constitution at India's independence in 1947 contained positive discrimination measures to improve the position of scheduled castes and tribal peoples but the effect of these measures has been slight for the majority and they have helped only those with professional education and careers (in government service, for example). Because scheduled castes and tribal peoples experience sufficiently similar conditions of exploitation and social and ideological oppression, Gail Omvedt refers to them by the common term *Dalit* (see Reading 22). This term has entered the Indian political vocabulary in much the same way that 'Black' (as in 'Black power') came into the language of American politics in the 1960s.

Class in rural India is determined primarily by access to means of production such as land, tools and animals, and command over labour. While size of land-holding is one significant determinant of class position (including the differentiation of rich, middle and poor peasants), another is the extent to which owners of land can employ labourers, and on terms advantageous to themselves. This depends on how many people, lacking adequate (or any) means of production for household agriculture, are forced to work for others. Land reform programmes in India in the 1950s and 1960s attempted to abolish large-scale and absentee landlordism and various forms of bonded tenancy associated with them. These measures, combined with the increasing commercialization of agriculture (including the introduction of 'Green Revolution' and other new technologies) frequently resulted in the eviction of customary tenants and the dispossession of poor peasants (as shown in Reading 5). The net effect, therefore, has been an increase in rural unemployment, and the rural 'reserve army of labour', and in migration to the towns in search of a living (although some forms of bondage continue to exist, for example, the *saldars* referred to in Reading 22).

The women described in these readings belong to the exploited classes of rural and urban India. Their class positions are combined with the inequalities of caste and gender. This powerful combination – and concentration – of inequality is seen in the lives of the agricultural workers of Bori Arab (Reading 22), and in the urban context in the lives of the street cleaners of Pune (Reading 28). In Reading 27 the only reference to caste is that male workers will only eat food cooked by women of a compatible caste. At the same time, these Annapurna women of Bombay can earn a living only by pursuing a 'traditional' woman's task and selling its product. The same is true of the *Dalit* women of Pune who are street cleaners, an occupation that is prescribed both by their gender status and the inherited caste services of 'untouchables'.

The different types of social division connected with caste and class (forms of social inequality combining features that existed in India before the expansion of Europe and those developed through colonialism and capitalism) thus have particular consequences for women. From Reading 22 it is apparent that rural low-caste women might be less restricted and more mobile than higher-caste women, if only as a result of economic necessity. (An important element of superior social status among men is the ability to keep 'their' women confined within the home.) In the case of the street cleaners of Pune, the fact that they are wage-earners with relatively secure jobs (thanks to a high level of unionization) makes them desirable wives for *Dalit* men. Because of their material conditions, low-caste women are less able to observe the ideal forms of contact and purification laid down by Hinduism, and have relatively more flexible marital arrangements. The struggle of the divorced woman in Reading 28 to establish herself economically and to be an active trade unionist shows, however, that self-assertion easily leads to marital conflict and can rebound on the woman in all areas of her life. In this case, the initial source of friction was partly that the woman was the main wage-earner (*transgressing* the ideal status of women), and partly that she had not borne her husband sons (*failing to fulfil* the ideal role of women).

Another aspect of the subordination of women is that the leaders of organizations are usually men, even where women are being organized. The male orientation of trade unions is underlined by Mira Savara in Reading 27 where the Annapurna cooks were perceived as a sort of 'class enemy' by male trade unionists before the decisive intervention of a woman union activist. Between them these three readings show some of the complexities of social divisions in India, and how the configurations of caste, tribe, class and gender determine the kinds of work that women do, as well as indicating some of the struggles that they engage in to improve their conditions and the types of organization such struggles employ.

Bori Arab: village on the sun-baked plateau of central India, with little to distinguish it from hundreds of thousands of other Indian villages except that I have decided to visit it for my first encounter with agricultural labourers. Bhimrao, a young union organizer friend, whose home it is, tells me about Bori Arab during our bus ride.

'There are about 4,000 people. They grow corn, millet, vegetables, some cotton. It's mostly dry land, like the rest of the area. There are seven big landlords who own about 500 acres each, they are Marwaris, the merchant caste. Yes, they live in the village, though some own land in other villages too. Two of them have cars, one owns a factory. It's a cotton ginning factory with about 300 workers, both men and women, who have to work twelve hours a day for three and a half rupees.[1] There are a few middle peasants, including one Dalit, who have about fifty acres. That's not very much when it's dry land . . .'

He pauses as the jolting bus swings aside to pass a bullock cart. Outside, in the early morning air with the indefinable smell of cowdung fires still mingling with other odours, I can see men and women at work in the fields, bicycles moving down the road, an occasional stunted tree on the rolling land. Inside people jostle us, women in faded saris, peasants with turbans wrapped around their heads carrying tins of grain or bundles of goods tied up in dirty cotton cloth.

'About half the village people are landless. They include all sorts of castes and communities – tribal people, Muslims, Banjaris, Mahars or Dalits, Telis, Kunbis, Marathas. Before, many of them were tenants, but after land reform the big landlords managed to keep most of the land and throw out the tenants, and now all of them work as wage labourers.'

Mahars are the biggest ex-Untouchable caste in the area, and have almost always been village servants and agricultural labourers. But they have been well organized as a group, and converted en masse to Buddhism many years ago in disgust with the Hindu religion which ostracized them. Now many of their angry young educated people call themselves *Dalits* or 'down-trodden', much as young Negroes in America began to use the term 'Black'. My friend Bhimrao is a Dalit, from an agricultural labourer family of this village. *Banjaris* are another low caste of the area, traditionally casual labourers. *Telis* were traditionally oil-pressers; now most are peasants. *Kunbis* and *Marathas* have been the main landholding peasant caste of the state, and in most villages many of them are among the richer peasants who have benefited from land reform and the technological developments known as the 'Green Revolution'. In Bori Arab, however, they seem to have been victims of the growing impoverishment and class polarization of the last decade.

This is the Indian caste system, so complicated in its ramifications and so much a source of fascination for foreigners. But I have come to search the depths of an even older form of social inequality: the position of women.

'Every landlord has about seven *saldars*, labourers hired on a yearly basis who are almost bound serfs. They are at his beck and call every hour of the day; their wives serve the landlord's family too. The rest work on daily wages. No, they're not much in debt, they're not tied to the landlords, they're casual labourers, with men and women both getting whatever work they can in the fields. Their wages are low because there's no other work available. They have to take what they can get.'

I am going to Bori Arab because I want to meet rural women. In the two months since coming to India in December 1974, I have met and interviewed housewives, students, women factory workers and middle class employees – but always with the feeling that I have to get away from the towns to get at the heart of things. The old cliché is true: the villages are the source. After 150 years of colonial rule and three decades of independence, the fate of Indian women is still tied to the land.

I know the statistics practically by heart. Most Indian women do not get jobs outside the home, but of those counted as 'workers' by census takers, 50% are agricultural labourers, which means they work for wages in cash or kind, and 30% are cultivators, which means they work on family-owned land. Of the rest, most are employed in which is called the 'unorganized sector', which means they are casual labourers doing unskilled work at inadequate wages on roads or construction projects, or working as domestic servants. Only 6% of all working women are in white collar or factory jobs which employ large numbers of people and are likely to be unionized.

And there is so much variation in this as in other things in India! In the north, very few women work outside the home, even in agriculture. Elsewhere, in the hilly 'tribal' states and in the south and west, work participation is higher and women make up nearly half the agricultural labour force, a major portion of the work force in the rural areas.

What is the reality behind these figures? Part of it, I feel, is that where women do get work outside the home they are likely to have more social independence and near equality with the men of their class. Where they do not, where they are bound to the home, they are at the mercy of the traditional barriers, of servitude in the home, of dependence on men, of customs like dowry and arranged marriages, of the vows and fasting and particular religious observances assigned to women. Among the middle sections in India, from white collar families to factory workers,[2] women may have overwhelming work burdens, managing the home, dealing with continually rising prices and the tedious tasks of preparing food where nothing comes 'ready-made' – but it is not the kind of work that gives them independence.

But among the lowest classes, especially in the rural areas where women do contribute to agricultural production and have land or work of their own, their toiling life seems to mean more social freedom. I know that low caste women have customary rights to divorce husbands and remarry whereas upper caste and middle caste women can hardly dream of this even today, that they move around more freely, that they talk to their husbands and brothers more on a level of equality . . .

If they have land and work of their own, that's the problem. Both land and work are vanishing in India. Landlessness is rising, and job opportunities are declining, so that where 33% of all workers were women in 1901, only 20% are women today. Correspondingly, where the very lowest caste and tribal women may have more traditional freedoms, the subordination of women seems to extend far into the society. And I know other figures [as I noted in passing in the Introduction]: that the sex ratio in India is now 107 men for every 100 women, and that this gap is increasing, and that it means simply that girls die at every age more than boys, and that the simple cause is that girls do not get as much food and medical care as boys. And in a country where food and medical care are in absolute shortage among the poor, this difference is a matter of life and death.

I know of stories which dramatize the fate of women very much like those I can see through the bus window stooping in the fields or carrying burdens of grass. In Bihar in the north, where feudal traditions are stronger, Mary Tyler[3] has told the stories of poor women she has met in prison, women in jail for defying their families and trying to marry men outside their caste, women forced to sell their meagre oil and soap rations in the jail to save money so they can give a feast for village elders after being released in order to regain their caste status which has been degraded by sharing a jail cell with who-knows-who. Mary writes of an old woman who had killed a daughter made pregnant by the village headman's son simply because she could not face the total ostracism of the village (and was ever after haunted by it), of another woman jailed for aborting the child of a man who had forced himself on her. And I know the story of the ex-Untouchable women of the district of Uttarkarshi in the state of Uttar Pradesh, where researchers found that families who were tied in debt-bondage to high caste landlords would have their daughters – treated as slaves by these landlords – sold into the prostitution network in Bombay. Such women, when interviewed, were cynical about legal or social work solutions: 'Buy freedom for our men, give them land and only land. It is these green fields which will contain our girls. Nothing else can.'

Land. From the rich rice-growing district of Thanjavur in the southern state of Tamilnadu comes a different kind of story. Here the land is worked by agricultural labourers who are also ex-Untouchables or Dalits, but through years of organizing under communist leadership they have freed themselves from serfdom and fought for higher wages. Women, nearly half the wage workers in the state, were prominent in the struggles and strikes. Then, in 1968, in the village of Kilven-mani, in the midst of one such struggle, the landlords collected a gang of 200 thugs and marched on the Dalit settlement at night. The men ran, the women and children who couldn't fled into one of the huts. And the landlords and their men burned this hut down with the rest, barricading the doors and forcing those who tried to escape back inside. In the morning it was discovered that 42 people, mostly women and children, had been burned to death in Kilvenmani, one of the most notorious atrocity stories of recent India.

But the story did not end in 1968. The labourers continued to fly the red flag and cling to their union. And the women in subsequent years became involved in a women's association where, according to Mythily Shivaraman, one of its organizers, 'their capacity for leadership was really developing; they saw this as their own.' And in December 1974, about the time of my arrival in Bombay, the Democratic Women's Federation held its first state conference twelve miles from Kilvenmani. Of its 27,000 members, nearly half were the women agricultural labourers of Thanjavur, and it was the women of Kilvenmani who marched the miles to plant the flag that opened the conference.

The poor rural women of Uttar Pradesh and Bihar in the north appear as victims of a brutal social order, the agricultural labourers of Thanjavur as fighters against such oppression. Were the women of Bori Arab victims only or fighters too? In this state of Maharashtra I know that rural low class women almost always do field work, and the upright, often confident, and sometimes fierce, bearing of such women seems to testify to their vigour. They don't have the look of people beaten down by hopelessness. But Bori Arab itself has had no history of organization at all, no attempts at labour unionizing in the ginning factory or the fields, no 'communist' propaganda of militant equality. Waves of change have rolled over India, but Bori Arab seems to be one of those villages barely touched by the storm of the national movement[4] or Gandhism. Yet there has been the militant Dalit liberation movement led by Dr. B. R. Ambedkar,[5] who was the most famous Untouchable leader of modern India, the one my friend Bhimrao is named after. And there have been new cars bought by the rich, a single small factory, and the new schools which, after all, have produced from agricultural labourer families children like Bhimrao, who went to college and got thrown out for taking part in a student agitation.

But how much has this touched the women of Bori Arab? What will they have to say?

When the bus finally pulls into the village, it is nearly 11 a.m. We step out into one of the dusty, nondescript villages that seem so typical of India, with people hanging around the bus stand and nearby tea stalls. Merchants sit in their shops and stare as we walk past; off to the right is a school and what is probably a village council building set back from the road in a compound flanked with trees and a few flowering shrubs. We head off into a wide street, down winding stony lanes, past small baked-mud houses with children squatting or playing in the dust, an occasional goat tethered to a stick, a chicken squawking across the road, one or two mangy dogs slinking around. This is the Untouchable quarter, still called by its age-old caste name, Maharwada. 'Where there's a village, there's a Maharwada,' is the Marathi[6] equivalent of saying, 'Where there's a city, there's a slum.'

About twenty-five women are gathered already in the small yard surrounding Bhimrao's hut. They are mostly middle-aged, wearing faded red or green saris, some made of two or more pieces stitched together, a few younger women, children hanging around the outskirts, and one or two young men. All are people who did not get work today or who chose not to go to the [fields] out of the excitement of a proposed meeting with a foreigner. In some ways these women seem as different from the middle class women of the cities as they are from me. Even their saris are different from the smooth, unwrinkled synthetics of the cities. They wear them differently, with the end pulled over their heads – some would say out of tradition-alism, but it protects them from the burning sun – and with the longer bottom part pulled between their legs so they can move freely in the fields. These women call the shorter sari of the middle classes a 'round sari', and say that they can't work in it.

What is your life like? What do you think about your country? These are the things I want to know. But we begin concretely: what time do you get up in the morning and what do you do? And it doesn't take them long to get over whatever hesitancy or shyness in speaking may be there. One woman, Kaminibai, a strong, independent-looking woman of indefinable middle age, emerges as the main speaker.

What is their work day like? They get up at 5 a.m., get water from the well, collect cow-pats for fuel, cook, clean the floor, take their baths, wash clothes and then go to the fields at 8 or 10 a.m. They work until 6 p.m. – on the days when they can get work – and then return for cooking and household duties until they finally go to sleep at 9 or 10 p.m. Sixteen hours of work a day – we add it up together – and for this the landowners pay them 1¼ to 1½ rupees.

'What do the men get?'

'Two and a half rupees for light work, three for heavier work.'

What is the difference in work? Kaminibai tells me: men's work is ploughing, cutting ears of corn, collecting the crop, carrying it away, collecting leftovers for cattle. Women's work is winnowing grain from chaff, weeding, picking cotton and removing the seeds, sowing. This is the normal division of labour in India; it only has to be added that women generally apply fertilizer where this is used and do the work of rice-transplanting in rice areas.

'What do you eat?'

'Bhakri – jawari bhakri or lal bhakri.' This means a coarse, tortilla [pancake]-like bread made of millet and sometimes of American milo (sorghum) which is often imported and sold or given to the poor.

'And vegetables?'

'Vegetables – what shall we tell you?' says Kaminibai. 'If we have vegetables we can have spices but no salt, or salt but no spices, such is our poverty! There is no work. Some collect twigs, some collect wood and sell it, or use it for fuel. What can we do? We are poor . . .'

They complain of the lack of work. Sometimes they get it, sometimes not, about two or three days of work a week. If they don't get work, they often just lie around and try to sleep because there is no food and they have no strength to do more. They can't eat, they say; all have become beggars these days because prices keep rising while wages remain stagnant.

Why do men get more pay? 'Do men work sixteen hours a day?' I ask. 'No,

women have to do different work from men, with a *leave*'[7] (Kaminibai uses the
English word here to mean 'work break'; many such words have crept into the
language even of these rural women) 'between 4 a.m. and 9 a.m., just to go to the
fields and come back at 6.'

'This year is International Women's Year – do you know that?'

'They don't know anything of that,' says Bhimrao, and we try to explain,
saying that the leaders of all countries have agreed that women are oppressed and
should have equal rights, that women all over the world are organizing to win
these rights, that women in the cities of India have had huge marches against
rising prices.

'We know nothing, *bai* [woman],' replies Kaminibai. 'We can't read, we
can't write, we can't do anything. If you say to sit someplace we sit there, if you
say sleep someplace we sleep there, such is our work. We are *jungli* people.' *Jungli*
means 'rural, uncivilized'. There is a bitter awareness of deprivation in this.

'There should be demands for *jungli* women too,' I say.

'Yes, there should be demands. You make an attempt – we will follow you.'
Bhimrao and I explain that one person can do nothing, that there must be a united
effort. He gives an enthusiastic pep talk about a 'union'; he has been working for
the last several months as a union organizer.

'Unity? How can we have unity? There is no united opinion among us. If I
don't go to work, someone else will go, and I will lose. There is no unity among
us! The farmers, though, they have unity.' And the discussion of unity that follows
excites them and illustrates again the awareness born of desperation, the sense that
the poor have for the importance of unity, and their initial feeling that it is
impossible.

I return again to the issue of the particular problems of women. So far they have
not picked up on this too much; economic issues seem primary. But what follows
shows that ideas have been germinating.

'Another question. About divorce. If your husband goes, can you take another
husband?'

'Oh yes,' says Kaminibai immediately. 'We can take another. Two, three, no
matter. We can take out a licence if we want, or not.'

'Ask Rukmini,' says someone else. So I ask Rukmini, a young and vigorously
beautiful woman, to tell her story. Yes, she says, her husband left her several
months ago and since then she has lived with her sister and worked alone. Is that
all? 'Can't you take another husband?' I urge.

'No,' she says, then pauses, giggles. 'There is a guest ...' The women all
laugh. There seems an ambivalence about the high caste standards which define
such liaisons as immoral. They recognize the standards, but seem to want me to
know that they take them lightly, that they are not really helpless. I press the point:
'You go out, you earn, so if one man goes it doesn't matter, you're independent.'
Rukmini grins and agrees. Neighbours may talk, she says, but it doesn't bother
her.

'It seems that in your agricultural labourer community there is more equality
between men and women than in the higher communities!'

'Yes, yes,' they say.

'But is there male supremacy?' I ask. I use the Marathi term *purush pradhan*
which I have heard from others, but it seems too literate and 'sanskritized'. I
wonder if they understand.

At this point Bhimrao feels the need to intervene and goes back to the issue of
wages. 'Yes, there is male supremacy. Still, during the days of government relief

work during the famine,[8] they got equal pay. But in the work they do in the
fields, men get more daily wages and they get less, and the reason for that is that
men's work is heavier, more toilsome. Women's work is different –'

'– but women –' I begin.

And then Kaminibai burst in:

'– have to do *double* work!' (And again an English word!) 'We have to do the
housework and when the housework is finished we have to do the field work and
when the field work is finished we have to take care of the children, we have to do
all the work! Suppose someone is thinking like this, some reader-and-writer, let
him sit down and write an account: what sort of work has to be done, what sort of
work the men do, what work we do. I am ready to tell you. What do men do? They
get up, they take a bath, they eat some bread and go to the fields. But understand
what their duty is: they only do the work that is allotted to them in the fields. They
only do one sort of work –'

She pauses for breath and I say that, in the US [United States] also, women
who work outside the home get less pay than men and also have to work in the
house without pay.

'Oho! That is the case here too. We remain without pay. If it would have been
paid we would get *double* pay! If housework were paid it would go to the women!
Are you men listening? Admit it! If there is competition about housework we
would defeat them completely.'

The second shift, the unpaid shift, the double burden of women. And wages for
housework! Did anyone say there weren't some universal issues of the women's
movement?

We go on. What about dowry? 'Is there dowry among you?' I know that in
some low castes there has been instead the custom of a small brideprice (where
the husband's family pays money to the bride's family), though many have been
switching over to dowry in recent years under the impact of the prestige of high
caste customs and the lesser importance of women as workers.

'Dowry, yes,' says Kaminibai. 'Gold chains, horses, cycles, money, wrist-
watches . . .'

'You know,' I say, 'that in the Indian constitution dowry is supposed to be
illegal. Untouchability is illegal, dowry is illegal, there are rights but in reality –'

'There are no rights. Yes, that is correct.' Kaminibai is the perfect lower class
cynic about democracy on paper.

'It's written in the constitution,' says Bhimrao. And in fact, in legal terms,
India has full equality and more guaranteed rights for women than most countries,
including equal pay, maternity benefits and so on for women workers.

'It's written, but it's not like that.'

These women, as Kaminibai shows throughout our talk, have a tremendous
ambivalence towards education, towards what is 'written' and towards 'readers-
and-writers' who have control over this magic. It is something that represents the
aspirations and promises of a better life, but it also represents the continuing
betrayal of those promises and the departure of the educated elites who leave their
people behind in the villages.

'When you go to work, do these other people – Kunbis, Marathas, Telis –
practise casteism against you?' This is from Bhimrao, who is as preoccupied with
the horrors of caste as I am with the oppression of women.

'They do, but we don't have to bother about that. We have our own pots and
drink from them, we don't bother. We are not going to drink water from their
hands. Now they don't do it much.'

Water is the ultimate symbol of casteism. For these village women, the idea of eating together and marrying with other castes is beyond the realm of possibility; the concrete reality of caste in daily life is the refusal of caste Hindus to share water with Untouchables. In most of India's villages there are still separate wells. Kaminibai isn't bothered by the difference too much; but there have been cases of drought when caste Hindu denial of the use of the common well to Untouchables has resulted in death.

What about the effects of caste on general class unity? 'What do you think, with Kunbis and Telis and all other agricultural labourers, is unity possible?'

'No. We need unity, but it won't be. If we Buddhists don't go to work others will go and then we will fall. What can we do? If our own leaders[9] go ahead, of course we'll follow them, but they stay behind, they sit in their houses, so where can we go? And if there's some money the big people eat it up. They eat up the votes. They take the money, we give votes, but we remain starving . . .' The bitterness of a corrupt democracy, at its worst, is the bitterness that the poor themselves see none of the benefits of corruption.

'New leaders are needed,' I venture.

'Yes, leaders of pure metal!'

'Like Ambedkar?' throws in Bhimrao.

'Yes, he was great, but there's none like that now. Now they want *dhotis* of 50 rupees and their wives want saris and we have to endure rags.'

What about Indira Gandhi? Has having a woman prime minister made any difference to India's poor? 'Some people feel that women in India must have more rights, that you must have made some progress.'

'Not at all, not at all, not even one anna in a rupee [i.e. about 6%]. She's doing politics and it's all right, it's not for us, our life has not changed.'

'You're being sarcastic,' says Bhimrao.

'You can take it that way. I'm talking out of anger. But it's not false. They've done nothing for us, there's no happiness for us.'

'In the time of the English – was that government better than this one, or not?' asks Bhimrao.

There is a chorus: yes, yes. Kaminibai elaborates: 'We were small then, *bai*, but we were getting everything, grain, food, everything. Money was less but our stomachs were full. Tell me, if there is no grain, if there is nothing for our stomachs, what have we to do with the state? Nothing at all. We condemn it. Because we are miserable, we say the state is miserable. Isn't our life miserable? Then, whatever it does it does for them, it does nothing for the poor. So tell us . . . we are expressing our sorrows to you, but up to this day no one has come to ask us about our sorrows.'

'But, in the time of the English, wasn't there more casteism?'

'Now it's better, about 4 annas in a rupee' (about 25%).

Bhimrao tries to ask if India really does have independence, to talk about economic dependence, foreign ownership of factories, neo-colonialism.

'What can we understand of that? We don't know how to read and write, we have no information at all about the country, about who runs the factories. We have no information. Only that we don't get anything, that our wages are less, that our food and clothing are insufficient, that everything we get falls short, only *that* we know and try to discuss. If I had been educated I would have been a leader. But, as it is, I am only a bull for a festival.' What Kaminibai means is that she may be ceremoniously honoured on one day out of the year, as bullocks are covered with bright blankets and paraded around, but must slave as a lowly drudge the rest of the time.

Women like Kaminibai have, after all, been touched by the waves of social change that have swept unevenly but tumultuously over India. They are not the poorest of the poor. There are people worse off, men and women driven out of their villages completely for lack of even the most meagre work, labouring elsewhere on construction projects for a pittance and tied down to the contractor by endless debt, camping under trees or in open-air small town markets as their only 'home' for years on end, with no question of educating their children, no question of dowry because they have no money at all. Women like Kaminibai are only near the bottom, they have some kind of village home, occasional work, perhaps a tiny piece of land and a living community around them.

More than this, they have a long experience of promises, promises from the government of better lives, promises from the leaders of their own caste of human dignity and achievement. And many of these promises have centred around the dream of education. Children of these agricultural labourer families do go to school in the village and some go on to high school and even college. Some of these graduates are returning to work in the fields because no other employment is available. One young girl in this group is a high school graduate and still working in the fields, though for her it seems all the school has done is to give her a middle-class shyness to replace the fierceness of the illiterate women. Women like Kaminibai are the ones passed over by education and mobility. Their field work has not changed, they have not seen the new products of the factories in their houses, but they know that there are things that they don't have and they know that there are things that they don't know, and they are angry about it.

They are even ready to be cynical about me. For when someone raises a question about why an American woman should come to talk to them, Kaminibai replies, 'Now she has come, so she'll do something for us, perhaps for one anna in a rupee, forget about the other fifteen.'

Bhimrao takes my side. 'She's going to study the conditions of women here and whatever obstacles there are to building an organization, how to overcome them, in what way to build it, she'll write something –'

'Yes, but will she write to us? She'll write something worth reading and writing, but it will be in thin small letters and we won't be able to read it, not at all, there will be no profit or loss to us.' (General laughter.) 'Is this true or false, *bai*, what I am saying to you? Understand, we will show our difficulties to you, you send from there some paper, and some educated person, some children, will read it to us, and we know nothing, whatever they tell us or explain to us we will understand. If we even have the time.' [...]

Extracted from *We Will Smash this Prison! Indian Women in Struggle*, Zed Press, London, 1980, pp. 9–18.

NOTES

[1. 18 rupees = £1 at this time.]
[2. i.e. those with regular employment.]
[3. English woman who spent five years in a Bihar jail, accused of being involved in the organization of a violent uprising.]
[4. i.e. for independence from Britain.]
[5. Contemporary of Gandhi, who urged Untouchables to convert to Buddhism to 'place themselves outside' the Hindu caste system and thereby gain self-respect.]
[6. Language of Maharashtra.]
[7. i.e. while women get up at 4 or 5 a.m., they do not go to the fields until 9 a.m. and there they work until 6 p.m.]
[8. Food for work programmes referring to the famine which started in 1971.]
[9. i.e. community leaders.]

23 Conversation with Aída Hernández from a Peruvian Cooperative

AUDREY BRONSTEIN

Editors' introduction

In 1968 a coup brought a reformist military government to power in Peru. As part of its programme a Land Reform Act was passed in 1969 which placed maximum limits on the size of landholdings and confiscated the estates of absentee landlords. One of the ways in which peasants could establish a claim to this land was to set up agricultural producer cooperatives.

These cooperatives have a contradictory character. On one hand, they are organized collectively and, despite various problems, have stabilized agricultural employment and improved the conditions of life for those working in them. On the other hand they have to behave as capitalist enterprises in a capitalist economy. They tend to restrict their membership and to enjoy privileged access to resources at the expense of those peasants who are not members. Although cooperatives often employ casual workers (paid at lower rates than cooperative members) local wage opportunities for peasants have declined and the men have to engage in longer distance migration to find jobs. This has intensified the work burden of women who are left behind. Membership or non-membership of cooperatives has therefore become a factor of differentiation among those who gain their living from the land.

The following interview shows that it has been possible for impressive mobilization to take place in the cooperative sector. Aída Hernández played a leading role in the establishment and subsequent development of a cooperative with a successful record in fruit and dairy production. The cooperative farms the land of a former *hacienda* (estate) which was seized by peasants in the late 1960s. Aída's own progression from president of the cooperative to membership of the Executive Committee of the Peruvian National Federation of Peasants was itself unusual. Women still have a subordinate role in spite of the general material gains that have been made. As Aída explains, women have to struggle for equal pay and an equal say in management given that ideological and cultural factors bind them to the home preventing their full participation.

How did you join the cooperative?
I have always worked here in the fields, when it was a 'hacienda', before the co-operative, before the Agrarian Reform. And in 1968, when we had all the problems, I began to see the strikes, and the stoppages. At the beginning, even though I was a member of the union, I didn't think it was that important. I didn't

understand. But then, each day, I saw more and more, and I began to realize what it all meant to fight together against those who were exploiting us. And I realized what it meant for each of us to belong to the fight . . . and I had a clearer vision of what the union could do, and what each of us could do if we participated. [. . .] The battle for the land began in 1968. My husband and I separated then. He was already a member of the union, but our problem had nothing to do with that. It was completely independent. He got an attack of 'hot headedness', and went off with another woman.

But I went on. I had left my children with my mother and father, and I carried on with the struggle. And I became a leader of the union, and then a delegate to the valley federation. And I carried on struggling and finally became president of the union, but because of certain political ideas and problems, I was removed. Some members of our group didn't agree with my ideas, and they denounced me, and with some help from the government, they had me removed. But then they really got angry, because I went on to become a leader in the national Federation of Campesinos [peasants] – for all of Peru. And I carried on fighting . . . always fighting.

But then I said to myself that I wasn't going to get involved any more. That I had had enough of people denouncing me. But, you know, when you are a leader, you always have that inside of you, even though you say you don't. You carry it with you in your blood. And I remember one of the battles, here, when the police were after us, and we were throwing bombs, and they were beating us . . . there was no way to say, 'No, I won't carry on.' And as a woman, I had to carry on. I have always tried to represent the women – the campesina [peasant] women – wherever I went. [. . .]

And I work here as a full member of the cooperative. And I earn my money, and do whatever work has to be done. First I was working in the factory, packing oranges, then in the fields in the tree nursery, and lastly, they put me in the children's nursery, where I worked in the kitchen. And then I was working, cleaning the nursery. Now the day of the meeting, last month, I was elected to work on the electoral committee. So I have special permission to do this, and leave the other work. When I finish with this committee, I will go back to my regular work. I have never done this before, and I wanted to learn about it. [. . .]

What do you think is the greatest problem for the campesina woman?

It has a number of aspects. One is that many times, the women can't go out to do things, because they are completely tied to the house – washing, cooking, and looking after their families. Another problem is the lack of understanding amongst many of the husbands. 'I am a man,' they say. 'I can go out, but you (the woman) can't.' And the women, themselves, actually believe that we, the compañeras [sisters], are inferior beings . . . that the men are superior. And those women that do work in the fields, during the week, do have a lot to do in their houses on the weekends.

But the problem as I see it is that the women are not organized, and don't have any awareness of the fact that they have the same rights as the men. Of course, the men do some things . . . going out drinking, staying out all night . . . we aren't going to do those things. We are women; we aren't going to wake up at dawn in a canteen [bar]. But participation . . . being leaders, and assuming responsibilities . . . that we can and should do, equally with the men.

But from the beginning, women are not accustomed to doing this. From the time they are born, in school, in the house, women are taught to be submissive. They are taught to dedicate themselves to the wishes of their fathers and husbands.

The problem is with the women themselves. They say, 'No, because my husband . . . no, my children . . . no, how can I . . . no, because the men are there. . . .' And they believe they are worth less. And I am always saying that women have equal rights with the men. We have our papers, our voting cards . . . everything to prove we are equal.

What would you do if you were president of the country?

Ah, that is a question that makes me . . . it gives me some difficulty . . . I don't know how to answer.

But I do know that the women need to organize, so they can change. They need to prepare themselves politically. Because until women have political awareness, we won't be able to do anything. And that is true of anyone . . . man or woman.

Before . . . I was the same as all the other women . . . I didn't really think about things. But then I began to see the problems more clearly, and I learned a bit about politics . . . although I'm not in any political group, but I understood a little about what different people say. And I realized that if we stay in our ignorance, we will never change anything. And I asked some of the compañeros [comrades], and they explained a number of things to me. As I said earlier, I have always gone to many different parts of Peru, and each time I talk to the compañeros, and I learn. And I tell the women that they must come out, and talk, and see, and above all, participate without fear.

But before the women can change, they have to get rid of the prejudice that they have had for a long time . . . year after year . . . about men and women . . . and all the social prejudices, too. We aren't going to be free that quickly.

Have you ever thought that it would have been better to have been born a man?

No . . . because I believe that as a woman, I have the same rights as a man, and whatever a man can do, I can do as well. I don't feel inferior to any man, not in work, or in anything. A man works to maintain his house and family . . . so do I earn the money to feed my children.

I have 4 children . . . and now that they are bigger, they help me. My daughter helps me in the house. But when they were small, they were all studying. In the holidays they would help me. It used to be difficult, but I would say to myself, 'I can do it; I have to do it.' I believe that you can manage anything if you really want to . . . *querer es poder* (to want to is to be able to). And that is what I used to tell my children. I would say to them, 'We are going to do this, but I need your support. If you help me we can build a wall.' And now we are fixing our house. In spite of the fact that I am a woman, without a man to do it for me. But we are fixing the roof, and painting, doing everything that has to be done.

What do you think about family planning?

Here there are many families who have a lot of children. There are others who only have 2 or 4. Because in reality, people here don't want to have big families . . . for economic reasons. They can't maintain them or educate them. Another reason is that there isn't enough work here for all the young people, and a lot of them leave.

Some people use contraceptives . . . pills and injections. Others have their own methods of looking after themselves. The husband and wife have to be in agreement, whatever they use. I think that with some families, yes it is a good idea, because the women who are working ... if they have children, year after year, they can't work. It is better if they have some kind of control. Because if not, the children suffer. Here, the mothers can leave their children in the nursery but in other places there is nowhere to leave them.

I think a good number for a family is 4 ... 4 children. I had 3, but I wanted to have 4 ... that is why I had the last one. If you have more, when it comes time for them to go to school, you can't afford the shoes, uniforms, and the other things they need. And the land that we have won't support so many people. The men also feel this way ... it is very hard for them if they have 6 or 7 children. [...]

Your children ... what kind of life would you like for them?

Well I hope my oldest daughter doesn't get married until she is older ... until she is about 25 years old. I don't want her to get married too young or too old. And I hope that she marries a good man, who respects her, and who, above all, is political ... who understands that there must be an understanding between the husband and wife, and who believes that the wife must participate and be strong. The most important thing is that he must be a worker. And his family ... they should have 4 ... no more and no less. Because if you only have 2, and one dies, you are left with only one. And three is an unlucky number ... I don't know ... I think it is a bad number. All the time I had only 3 children, bad luck followed me. I don't really know where I got the idea that 3 is a bad number, but I feel that it is. [...]

Do you think it is important for women to have work outside their duties in the home?

Yes ... it makes you stronger. I think you are more 'full of life', and you learn more ... even more than the work you are doing. You feel more able to do other things, and you have more experience. Every day, you can talk to people ... in an office or in the fields. You talk to the other workers about many different things – about what is happening in the work. And your understanding of things can change, because other people have different opinions. But the person who is in the house all day, who doesn't have any other work, never leaves ... and never has an understanding of what is happening in the world. Many women never leave their houses. Reality frightens them.

A woman doesn't really have what you could call 'independence'. She must always do whatever her father, her husband, or her mother tell her. And she, herself, doesn't try to do anything to educate herself ... to find her own liberation. I talk with the women, and they say to me that there is nothing they can do ... that's the way it is. And they feel even weaker because of that. And because the men work 6 days a week, and on Sundays, they go out, to a movie, or to get drunk. But the women work all the time and can't go out. But I ask, 'Why can't you say that you are going to visit your mother? Why can't you say that you are going out?'

But, unfortunately, they can't. They say to me, 'If I say I am going out, my husband gets annoyed with me, and then the problems start.' But I have always said I was going ... and I went. When I was with my first compañero [companion/ husband], I would say that I was going to visit my mother. And he would say, 'You aren't going there, because your mother has a canteen, and you will come back drunk.' And I would say, 'Look, I said I was going to visit my mother and I am going. She is my mother, and you aren't going to stop me from seeing her.' And I went. And he said, 'If you go, you will have to find somewhere else to live.' But why should I find somewhere else to live . . . it was my house. And so I went to see her. And he wouldn't talk to me for one or two days. But I didn't care. I hadn't said or done anything wrong. And then one Saturday, I said that I was going to go to the movies, and he shouted, 'No, you aren't going to the movies.' And I said, 'You go to the movies. Why can't I go? There is nothing wrong with going to the movies. You aren't going to have me under your thumb like a slave . . . working all day, at night, looking after the children, and at the weekends, washing, cooking.' And I went.

But most women would never say that . . . only the really aggressive or strong ones. Most of them stay at home washing, cooking, ironing . . . doing everything. That is the life of most women. [. . .]

What do you think influenced you to become a leader?

I don't know. The only thing I know is that I have always wanted to see and learn. I'm not afraid of life . . . I have never been afraid . . . not even in front of my father when I was a little girl.

My mother was always raised at the point of a fist, or a blow. She has had a very sad life, and has been very oppressed. She was an orphan when she was 9 years old. And she always tried to raise us in an old-fashioned way . . . or the way she was raised, but I have always shown a certain kind of independence. And she never used to like it, but she couldn't change me. And I'll probably die this way. I won't change.

And my children, even they say, 'Don't go . . . don't leave.' But I say to them, 'Look, I have to go to this meeting in Lima, for my work. I will leave Saturday and come back Sunday.' And I tell my oldest child, my daughter that she is in charge of cooking and looking after the others. I tell her to keep the door closed, and not to let the others wander all over the place, and that I will be back on Sunday. And I go, and they are alright. [. . .] They have their duties and their independence. I don't want them to be dependent on me. One day I'll die, and I won't be coming back. They have to learn to be independent, to know their own worth, and to manage for themselves. Even though they are young, they have to learn. [. . .]

Who do you think needs a 'capacitacion' (preparation, training) more . . . the men of the women?

Both of them need it. Everyone here needs it. The only thing that we have had really, is an understanding and explanations and training about what a cooperative is. But it stopped there. I have always said that we should give the women jobs and things to do that will prepare them more. There is a long, hard job to do so that women, not only here, but all over Peru, learn how to feel different about themselves, and what they can do . . . not just to be able to do more work, but also to take on responsibilities and participate in their communities like equal human beings.

The women here do come to the meetings, and they have their vote. It is the place where most of them participate. After that there aren't many who have any responsibility . . . one woman is on the control committee and another woman is on the administration committee, but that's all . . . only two women out of the whole cooperative (about 600 people). The problem is not only that the men don't want to give them responsibility, but also that the women don't want to take it.

The women here also earn less than the men. [. . .] Some women do earn more than the men, but that is because for that work, the pay is more. For example, my brother works in the section where they fumigate the plants, and I work in the children's nursery. I earn more with the overtime that I get, than he gets working the basic hours. But in the basic wage, for example, packing oranges, the men earn 10 soles [2p] per hour more than the women.

And in one of the meetings, I suggested that the women should earn the same as the men. 'We do the work equally,' I said. 'The only thing we don't do is drive the lorries.' But they said, 'No, how can we pay the women the same as the men. The men are worth more. The men have to be paid better than the women.' And so we have those basic inequalities. And if the women can't get paid the same as the men for equal work, they will never feel equal. We also have a discrimination that I think is wrong between the full workers, and the casual workers, whether they are men or women. The full members get more. So even there, we have men exploiting men. That didn't change with the Agrarian Reform. The cooperative, like the boss [of the hacienda] carries on exploiting the poor workers. [. . .]

Have you ever thought of trying to work somewhere else?

Well, last year, I thought of stopping all my work here . . . all my political work. I was so tired of hearing my name everywhere, and everyone always calling for 'Aída Hernández', here . . . and 'Aída Hernández' there. And I told people that. But this electoral committee is new for me. I haven't been on it before, and I wanted to see what I could learn from it. That is why I accepted to do something again. Because you know, without the experience of being a leader, and president, even for the little time I did it, I wouldn't have learned anything.

But I think you should stop, after you have been a leader for a while. If you are always a leader, doing the work of a leader . . . you need a rest. But, more important, you get to expect certain things, or you get used to working on a certain level. You should stop, go back to the earth . . . to the people, you forget what it is like. You should give other people a chance, and you should start again from the bottom, just so you don't forget what it is like . . . what you are fighting for.

Extracted from material collected by Audrey Bronstein and printed in full in *The Triple Struggle*, War on Want Campaigns Ltd in association with War on Want, London, 1981.

JANET M. BUJRA

'There are some women here who don't want to be married, they don't want husbands, they prefer to do their "work".' (Yumbe man.)

'Perhaps Tima has gone to search for men – there are no men here.' (Yumbe woman, speaking of another who had migrated to Mombasa.)

'There is also a sense in which the prostitute's role is an exaggeration of patri-archal economic conditions where the majority of females are driven to live through some exchange of sexuality for support.' (Kate Millett, *Sexual Politics*: 123.)

'Sexual politics' is not a subject we usually associate with rural communities, where, it might be supposed, the relationships between the sexes are grounded in time-honoured custom, and where patterns of (male) authority are well-established. What I want to explore here is one instance where male–female relationships are overtly antagonistic, and to suggest that this has its basis in the local political economy and in the dialectical relationship of that economy with broader patterns of changing political and economic power.

My interest here is in 'sexual politics', not so much in the sense appropriated by K. Millett, whose arresting study concerns itself mainly with the *cultural* weapons developed by men to assert male dominance and to denigrate and restrict women to passive and subordinate roles. I am here more concerned with the 'institutional weapons' forged by women to enlarge their freedom of social manoeuvre, and with the extent to which these are effective.

Yumbe,[1] with which this study is concerned, is not a populous village, having only just over a thousand inhabitants. It is one of a group of villages on a remote island lying off the northern coasts of Kenya and mainly occupied by Swahili-speaking Muslims. The island used to be a prosperous export enclave in the commerce of the Indian Ocean, acting as an entrepôt for ivory, copra [dried coconut kernels] and timber in their passage to Arabia. Now it is a backwater on the extreme periphery of the post-colonial economy. Its communications with the mainstream of that economy are poor indeed, but it nevertheless produces copra, cashew nuts, and some cotton and simsim [sesame seeds] for the world market. In its way the local peasant economy is highly 'developed', undoubtedly a reflection of its more prosperous past. Private individual ownership over land producing high income export crops is a basic principle of the economy, with consequently quite considerable socio-economic differentiation amongst the population. In the precolonial period when slavery was an on-going institution, the richer men of the village cultivated their land with slave labour, whilst the poorer men had to cultivate for themselves. With the emancipation of the slaves in 1907,[2] slave labour was no longer available. Today the ex-slaves are indistinguishable from other poor men in the village, being by and large subsistence producers with a marginal surplus for sale, and generally indebted to richer farmers in order to cultivate at all. Poor peasants are here poor because they own no land, and exercise only *use* rights over plots on common land growing annual crops (largely for subsistence). By contrast the rich farmers in the community owe their prosperity to their *ownership* of land, yielding profitable products such as copra and cashew nuts. With the surplus accruing from such production, the wealthiest of them go into petty commerce, shopkeeping and moneylending.

The women of Yumbe are in one respect fairly typical of women anywhere, in being more or less effectively excluded from access to the vital economic resources and political positions of their society.[3] In a formal sense, women in Yumbe are mere chattels and dependants of men, and men accordingly speak of them in a manner of contemptuous dismissal: 'Only men know what is right and sensible.'

Women are not wholly passive recipients in this man-made social context however – they attempt to elbow out an effective sphere of action for themselves. Although Yumbe men are formally allowed by Islamic law to take four wives, women who will agree to such an arrangement are very few. If, as L. Tiger and R. Fox affirm, 'polygamy has to do with power rather than sex',[4] then clearly, for women to refuse to cooperate within polygamous unions is also a statement about power relations between the sexes.

Divorce is in fact frequent in Yumbe, and it is often instigated by, though it cannot be effected by, women. On divorce it is the husband who is forced to seek residence elsewhere, because in Yumbe it is women who own houses rather than men. Divorced women can and do support themselves for considerable lengths of time, at first by reliance on help from female cohorts and on the meagre earnings which accrue from local occupations open to women; in the last resort by emigration to Mombasa as prostitutes. In this capacity they may earn considerable sums, far exceeding the paltry incomes of male labour migrants (who are mostly forced to accept work as lowly paid unskilled or semi-skilled workers). Sometimes these women are lost to the village altogether; more often however they return home regularly, investing their earnings in building a house in the village, buying gold ornaments, holding public feasts and assisting relatives.

Concerning the activities of women as prostitutes, men are more or less powerless. In some senses the dividing line between sharply demarcated sex roles is obscured in this situation, with women, like men, acting as free sexual agents, independent earners of income, and initiators of economic and social activity. Men express their uneasiness at this state of affairs, with more than a touch of hysterical exaggeration, when they say: 'The women of Yumbe are nothing but harlots.' And although they roundly condemn such 'harlotry' in principle, in practice there are few men who would refuse an invitation to a feast paid for by prostitutes, or a remittance comprising 'illicit earnings' from Mombasa.

Women in this context then, though very far from achieving equal consideration with men, at any rate continually undermine the comfortable self-assurance of unquestioned male chauvinism. In so far as we can describe their activities as rebellious, these women have created certain institutional arrangements with which to back them up.

One may critically ask what can possibly be learnt from the analysis of women's behaviour in one small village in Africa. I would argue simply that in most discussions of development, women – who after all comprise half the population – are often ignored. At best they may be considered as a 'conservative' element, inhibiting and opposing change. This may mean little more than that they have no option but to continue as they have always done. On the other hand, attempts by women to make a radical break with traditional patterns are not always to the liking of men, and may not even be in their own long-term interests. It is important therefore to consider women's options in and reactions towards their changing environment, and to understand the pressures to which they are subjected.

More specifically, it can be shown that the attempt by women here to gain a measure of economic independence through prostitution is not a unique phenomenon. In all the towns of East Africa (and not of course only there) the economic opportunities available to women who have no formal education or skills are negligible. Even petty commerce, the resort of many women in West Africa, is here effectively in the hands of others.[5] For many women in urban areas, prostitution is the only viable way to get along. I have elsewhere tried to show the background to and consequences of this fact for Nairobi.[6] Women appear to have come to Nairobi for individual reasons but in response to generalized social disturbances. What is perhaps unusual about the case of Yumbe is that the migration of women from a single area is on such a scale that it cannot be ignored in any analysis of *local* social organization.[7] There are probably other areas in Africa of which this is true; the point is that we do not know very much of the rural background to the phenomenon of urban prostitution.[8]

What I shall attempt to do here then is to understand how prostitution is accommodated within the local socio-economic context of Yumbe, but also to suggest to what extent it is a response, within a wider perspective of historical trends, to the changing politico-economic realities facing this area. Within this framework it would appear that the reaction by women is in its way socially innovative, even whilst it does not achieve genuine independence for them. Operating within the harsh limitations imposed by their sex and economic standing, these women have acted 'to create as much living space as possible'.[9]

The labour migration of women

Although the broad outlines of my analysis of sexual politics could be generalized to most of the island's villages, Yumbe is said to have the largest number of women away earning a living as prostitutes. Since my argument here will be that it is the option of prostitution which is the key to understanding the character of sexual politics in Yumbe, we may start by looking at the extent of the phenomenon there. In 1965 there were almost half as many women absent from the village as there were women resident in Yumbe itself (namely 168 compared with 350). The number of male migrants away was only fractionally higher than that of women (172 compared with 276 resident adult men). For both men and women, Mombasa was the most likely venue of migratory activities, though a few migrants were also to be found in other East African urban centres. Mombasa, the main port of Kenya, is over 250 miles away from Yumbe, and requires a lengthy journey taking generally two days.

Some of the women who were absent from Yumbe were married, either to Yumbe migrants or to men they had met in Mombasa or elsewhere. Sixty-three per cent of the women were however unmarried, and the vast majority of these were divorcees. Most of these women (they numbered around a hundred) were earning a living as prostitutes. Of those women at present resident in Yumbe,

12% had migrated independently in the past, spending periods of between one year and twenty-five years away. There were many more women who had visited Mombasa for periods of less than one year – some of these went merely to visit relatives, but a certain proportion may be considered 'failed migrants'.

By and large the migrant labour of men does not contribute significantly to the village economy. Most men who migrate are unmarried or divorced. Occasionally they are accompanied by their wives; very few men leave wives behind since they say women cannot be trusted to remain faithful to absent husbands. Consequently men send remittances to Yumbe irregularly if at all, and those who are successful labour migrants often settle permanently away. By contrast the migration of women to Mombasa is much more Yumbe-focused in that prostitutes invest their income in building and repairing houses in Yumbe – houses in which they can live independently during the periods when they are in Yumbe, and to which they can retire in their old age.

In Mombasa prostitution is a highly profitable business if a girl is young and pretty. In 1965 I was told that such a girl might earn between £50 and £100 or even more per month.[10] An older woman would earn much less of course – but in spite of this some Yumbe women continued to pursue this occupation until they were in their late forties or early fifties.

Within Yumbe itself women may also earn small sums by sleeping with men. Although village people refer to this by the same term *(malaya)*[11] as prostitution in Mombasa, it is a good deal more ambiguously so. There is no defined category of women in Yumbe who act only or always as prostitutes; 'prostitution' is more in the nature of a temporary phase between marriages for some women. At any one time in Yumbe there are a high percentage of divorced women, some of whom may make themselves available to men. Adultery is also frequent in Yumbe, judging from the regularity with which it is given as a reason for divorce. The sexual activities of women within either of these contexts may be described as *malaya*. This is why it is possible for men to say: 'All the women in Yumbe are *malaya*.' At any one time however there are also a handful of women in the village who more openly receive 'customers', and are well known for this. Even such women may at any time marry.

Secondly the status of the 'payment' itself may be ambiguous, since it may be more in the nature of a 'gift' from a man to his lover than a purchase of sexual services. In so far as straightforward payments are made, they are said to be much lower than the rates in Mombasa – estimates ranged from as high as Sh.5 to less than Sh.1.

In Yumbe, this state of apparent sexual licence (of both men and women) goes hand in hand with a marked avoidance of the sexes in public and with a constant social emphasis on the dependent state of women. The public arena is solely the preserve of men here, whilst women are restricted largely to the domestic sphere. This is succinctly symbolized on the occasion of public feasts. Whilst men are seated outside and served first with food, women guests are concealed inside the house of the host and must wait until the last man has eaten and gone before they are served.

Similarly prostitution here is hidden and concealed, not openly acknowledged or flaunted publicly. Women going to Mombasa say they go *kutembea tu* 'just to walk around', whilst others may say of them that they have gone *vivi hivi tu* 'just like that'. Whereas men privately speak with contempt or resentment of these activities of women, women's attitudes are either neutral or defiant. There is rarely an occasion when the matter is confronted openly. The activities of prostitutes within

Yumbe itself are however more controversial, because these entail direct competition between women themselves for the sexual attention of particular men. Some of all this emerges dramatically if we look more closely at the case of one Yumbe prostitute:

Sometime during July 1967 a girl called Kitina came home to visit her parents. She had been in Mombasa for almost a year, earning her living as a prostitute, and had been highly successful. Kitina was a very pretty, fragile-looking girl. She was only in her early twenties, but this was already her third visit to Mombasa. She had been married off, before puberty, to a visiting teacher from a town more than 150 miles away from Yumbe. After a time the teacher returned home, taking Kitina with him. She was very unhappy, and it was not long before she ran away, back to her parents in Yumbe. She was thereupon divorced by her husband. Soon after this she went to Mombasa for the first time, staying for two months then coming home. During her stay at home she was married by her paternal cousin, Issa. The marriage had not lasted for more than a few months when they quarrelled and Kitina was divorced for the second time. Undaunted she returned to Mombasa, this time staying for four months and pursuing a life of prostitution with success. She came home again for a rest, but agreed instead of returning to Mombasa to remarry her cousin. This time she became pregnant, and remained in Yumbe until her child was born. The baby died a few months later and soon Kitina had quarrelled again with Issa, forced a divorce and returned to Mombasa.

This time she did even better and it was almost a year before she came home again. She arrived back in Yumbe with conspicuous evidence of her success – a matching set of bedroom furniture, transported all the way from Mombasa, which had cost her £50. In addition she herself was dripping with gold – ear-rings, necklaces, bracelets, rings and watch – as well as two golden teeth. She also had an extensive wardrobe of new dresses.

She was not the only attractive young Yumbe girl to be visiting from Mombasa at that time, and within a few days the whole village was chattering about those goings-on. In particular a series of quarrels was set in motion after certain men of the village visited Kitina and another of the girls and then boasted of the outcome. It was not long before their wives came to hear of this, and they began bitterly to upbraid their husbands and to pour forth verbal abuse on Kitina and her friend for having 'stolen' their husbands.

A small knot of women gathered at Kitina's mother's house, eager to hear the gossip at first hand. Kitina's mother reacted nervously to all the publicity, 'People are saying this and that, and accusing this one and that one. . . .' Kitina sat serene, smiling to herself, and then, in response to a question by one of the women, said defiantly, 'So much talk in Yumbe, you can't do anything. I shall be glad to go back to Mombasa.' It wasn't true that she had had all the men mentioned – some indeed had come, but not *all those*. Kitina flashed her two golden teeth, and pressed her hands (bedecked with seven gold rings) together. 'Too much talk here altogether. In Mombasa I don't accept our men [as customers]; my customers are Europeans or Indians. They are willing to pay Sh. 100 a time, but our men want it for Sh. 5.' She would return to Mombasa and not remarry for at least a year, she asserted.

At least one man 'divorced' his wife as a result of these affairs but he returned to her a few days later.[12] Kitina toned down her boastful talk and began to organize the building of a house on a plot adjoining that of her parents.

Whilst few Yumbe prostitutes are as successful or as audacious as Kitina, there is much in this case study that typifies the general pattern. In particular it can be seen here how the option of prostitution makes the divorced state economically tolerable, even profitable, and makes house ownership a viable possibility if it has not been achieved in other ways. In a sense it is the ultimate explanation for sexual politics in that it allows women metaphorically to thumb their noses at men, to choose their time for marriage, and to select their partners in marriage. At the same time it is clear that it puts a premium on youth and physical attractiveness, and a women with neither will have far less room for manoeuvre.

Historical trends: prosperity and decline

In 1922, the Annual Report of Lamu District (of which Yumbe is a part) noted that both men and women were leaving the area to go to Mombasa.[13] On 21 September 1931, the European District Commissioner visited Yumbe on a tour of inspection. Upon completion of his visit he noted, in a book which was kept in the Headman's house, that: 'They (the Headman and his assistant) complained of a large emigration of the female population to Mombasa, and of the abandonment of many houses and plots in the town (Yumbe).'[14] The comment is tantalizingly brief and no further details are given, but at least this is written evidence indicating the length of time women have been migrating from Yumbe. Oral evidence, whilst less reliable, suggests a similar longevity for the phenomenon. Thus a Yumbe man who had spent many years working away from the village said that in his youth (in the twenties) both men and women went to Mombasa, but not on the same scale that they do now. He remembered that he and thirty or so other men had wanted to send a petition to the Governor demanding that women from their area be prevented from staying in the town unless they had a husband there, but nothing came of it. In the sixties there were elderly women in Yumbe (and some already deceased) who had spent many years in Mombasa in their youth, and hence it would appear that the labour migration of women has been going on for at least fifty years, and probably began around the end of the First World War. As we shall see, the appearance of this phenomenon coincided with a period in which the area was undergoing serious economic decline.

Very little is definitely known of the precolonial history of this area – as Chittick says, 'the sources are meagre, often corrupt, often half-myth'.[15] Only the broad outlines of political history are clear – that the island experienced a succession of alien suzerains, Arab, Portuguese, Zanzibari, and finally British, but in practice enjoyed a good deal of local autonomy owing to the lack of effective communications. It seems probable however that in the days when the island was a node in a commercial network linking the east coast of Africa to Arabia (and to a lesser extent India), the local agricultural economy was merely an adjunct to wider patterns of trading activity. The most important trade goods were slaves and ivory; obversely it was slaves who carried out the bulk of local cultivation.[16] In this kind of mercantile economy men with capital to invest could go in for commerce themselves, or finance others to do so. In addition men found employment as sailors in the Arabian bound dhows or in those engaged in coastal commerce. Thus, directly or indirectly, the people of the island derived their livelihood and their prosperity from trade. When trade declined – as it apparently did during the Portuguese period – the local economy stagnated; when it revived – as for example during the great era of slave-trading in the 19th century – the economy enjoyed a phase of plenitude and growth.

With the increasing influence of Britain in the area in the latter decades of the 19th century – and especially with the outlawing of the maritime slave trade from 1873 – the whole *raison d'être* of traditional trading patterns was destroyed. The final blow came in 1907 when slavery as an institution was abolished, and the slaves began either to cultivate for themselves or to drift away from the area. The colonial period saw a complete refocusing of commercial activity, with the expansion of Mombasa as a port of exit for Ugandan peasant and Kenya settler agricultural produce. The northern coastal region suffered a marked decline. Writing of the first decade of the 20th century, C. H. Stigand commented that: 'Most of [the settlements of the northern coast] seem to be decreasing in population, and most have declined very seriously in point of prosperity in recent years. In the old days they seem to have possessed no industries and their source of wealth must have been derived almost entirely from dealings in slaves. The freeing of slaves has reduced most of the freeborn inhabitants to a sad state of poverty, and moreover those with property and coconut *shamba* [farms] find it difficult or impossible nowadays to find sufficient labour to attend to the needs of their plantations.'[17] Although Stigand does not make this clear, the net loss of population suffered by the area was Mombasa's gain, as men went in search of new opportunities. This drift of population was to continue for many years.[18] Thus whereas in the precolonial period the migration of men as traders and sailors might be considered as a factor contributing to the island's prosperity, in the post-colonial period migration was an index of its decline.

In the absence of written historical evidence it is not easy to determine the situation in which *women* found themselves in periods of affluence compared with periods of decline. One is forced back into speculation, informed where possible by contemporary memories of the past. Nevertheless it is clear that at least two features of the era of prosperity must have been influential in determining the conditions of women. The first was the fact that this was a slave-owning economy, the second was the maritime nature of that economy.

In many parts of Africa one is accustomed to find women bearing the burden of all but the heaviest agricultural work, but in Yumbe women do not cultivate at all. Only an economy with an effective surplus can without detriment withdraw half the active population from production.[19] Thus it would seem probable that this phenomenon is a legacy of a slave-owning and trading economy where the women of slave-owners were in effect living evidence of conspicuous consumption. Not everyone in Yumbe was a slave-owner of course – oral history suggests that around half the freeborn families in the village owned slaves, but a general prosperity may have prevailed to enable even families without slaves to subsist on male labour alone. Contemporary memory portrays this as a period when only slave women went out openly, whilst freeborn women remained modestly indoors, and spent their hours 'plaiting each other's hair'. For slave women, of course, the situation was somewhat different, and some of these women were certainly engaged in agriculture. Even in this case however, it is said that female slaves were more likely to be occupied in domestic tasks than in cultivation.

It is clear that in such an economy freeborn women were utterly dependent on the prosperity of male relatives. With the onset of economic decline then, it would be surprising if the situation of these women did not suffer drastically. One did not have here the phenomenon found in so many other parts of East and Central Africa, where, when men absented themselves as labour migrants, women were left to cultivate. Since women here did not cultivate at all, the consequence of a large exodus of males was a contraction of the local economy.[20] Without slave labour, mainland agriculture (always dangerous at the best of times due to the incursions of Somali raiders) was often abandoned. With the emigration of men to Mombasa, the area of Yumbe farms, where land is individually owned and where trees are grown, diminished quite markedly, with many acres reverting to bush. The men who left were not only potential (or in some cases actual) husbands; they were also vital providers of the necessities of life. It seems likely then that this was the context within which women also began to migrate in search of economic security.

One may also surmise that in a maritime milieu, some women would have followed along the paths trodden by men even in the precolonial period. Certainly in the main ports of East Africa and Arabia, where small communities of people from this area were to be found, there were women as well as men. Most of these probably came as wives or daughters, but there may have been others who arrived independently or who were abandoned there to fend for themselves as best they could. It could thus be that the contemporary migration of women is merely a new and expanded version of an old pattern.

Mombasa

Whilst the northern coast of Kenya suffered a serious economic recession in the first few decades of the century, Mombasa was experiencing a phase of rapid growth. With the building of the Uganda railway with its terminus in Mombasa, and the development of the port of Kilindini, the town enjoyed a period of commercial prosperity which led to a marked expansion in its male population. Although East African operations in the First World War had only a marginal effect on the coast, they nevertheless served to accentuate a process already under way – namely the disproportionate growth of Mombasa relative to other coastal centres.[21] There was an influx into the town of men attracted by economic opportunities – Asian and Arab traders, Indian labourers indentured to build the railway, upcountry and coastal peoples in search of work. Moreover this disproportionate growth of Mombasa was to continue between the wars, and to be further advanced by the activity of the Second World War, when boom conditions were experienced by local commercial and business interests. It is hardly surprising that in this context the services of prostitutes found a ready market.

The Yumbe women who migrated to Mombasa at this period were well placed to take advantage of this demand. Firstly, they were strangers in the city, and hence to some extent able to disregard the restrictive rules placed upon local Muslim women. At the same time, they were able to capitalize upon local male sexual preferences, which put a premium on fairness of skin and straightness of hair. (The people of the northern coast are very mixed, ranging from those who are very light-skinned and 'Arab'-featured, to those who are dark-skinned and more African in appearance.) The demand for sexual services was in fact so great that Yumbe prostitutes were able to operate a discriminatory pricing system so as to obtain the highest rewards from those with the most money, and on the whole to avoid the poorest (i.e. African) customers. They tended to operate from particular locations of the town – especially Mwembe Tayari, Majengo and Makadara. All these were older locations in which they were amongst fellow Muslims of a similar cultural background – people who would be likely to come to their aid if trouble arose. They did not parade themselves openly but generally operated through pimps who searched for customers and brought them to the woman's house. Very often the pimps were homosexual males: they took their cut, and were influential with, but did not directly control the women concerned.[22]

The halcyon days for Yumbe prostitutes in Mombasa were during and just after the Second World War, when the port was full of British soldiers and sailors, and business was excellent. In those days, it is said, Yumbe prostitutes earned vast amounts, and expended a good deal of their income on financing grand weddings and public feasts: 'Nowadays the Navy [i.e. the Royal Navy] has gone, and weddings are not what they used to be.' One old lady, now in Yumbe, but who had been in Mombasa during this period, was said to have become so prosperous that she wore pure gold ornaments on her shoes. There was of course another side to the story of this period. An elderly woman remembered that the British soldiers ('Johnnies') used to go around beating up prostitutes, and that they had knocked out the teeth of one Yumbe woman, and raped other women who were not prostitutes.

In Mombasa today prostitutes from the coast are under pressure of competition from upcountry African women who have moved into the town in increasing numbers, and who operate more directly and audaciously. Meanwhile the traditional customers of coastal prostitutes (Europeans and Asians) have declined in numbers. In spite of this, Yumbe women are still loath to take African customers. In 1965, they charged the highest prices to Europeans (Sh.40 to Sh.60, or even more for a whole night), and rather less to Arabs and Asians (Sh.20 to Sh.40). When they were forced to accept African customers the price was even less (Sh.5 to Sh.10). By and large however they avoid African customers, even those who offer a large amount of money.[23] Nevertheless the pressure of competition has led to younger prostitutes more openly frequenting places where they are likely to find potential customers, such as dance halls and bars. Some of them learn a few words of English and they may even drink alcohol – a very shocking thing in the eyes of local Muslims.

If in the early decades of the century women migrated to Mombasa as a reaction to the decline of an economy within which they were mere dependants, one may reasonably ask whether the same factors operate today to perpetuate this pattern of migration. I think it can be argued that this is indeed the case, as we can see if we considered contemporary configurations of production and property in Yumbe.

Production and property

In the agricultural economy of present-day Yumbe, women play only a very minor part. In particular the work of cultivation is considered to be unquestionably a male activity. Women's attitudes on this question can be summed up by one who pointed at her genitals and said: 'We women cultivate here: that is enough.' On the other hand it should be pointed out that apart from their domestic and reproductive activities women do play a significant *ancillary* role to male production, whether as family labour or for payment. They help in the transport of produce from the farms to the village, they weave strips of matting which are later sewn into sacks for the transport of produce, they make roofing materials for houses and they do some basic processing of crops – sorting cotton, removing tamarind seeds from their sticky shells, drying and grinding maize and so on. Men may also carry out these tasks, but they generally do so only if they are old or sick or temporarily unable to cultivate for some reason.

A woman who has to rely on these activities for her sole subsistence however – that is, one who is not fed and provided for by a father or a husband – will find herself in extremely strained circumstances. In 1965 a woman could earn about Sh.1 per day from such activities, and with this she might just survive, though at the most meagre level. We shall see the significance of this characteristic of women's work in Yumbe when we come later to consider the question of divorce.

Since Muslim law does not exclude women from inheriting land, one would expect to find some women owning land even if they did not cultivate it themselves. In the apportionment of inheritable property women heirs receive one share in relation to every two shares allotted to equivalent male heirs. Nevertheless whilst 31.5% of Yumbe men were landowners in 1965, only 5.4% of women (that is, 19 women) were similarly placed. (In addition there were four absentee women owners.) In understanding the reason for these figures we have to recognize that a whole series of *de facto* accommodations to local social reality intervene here between Muslim theory and social practice. In particular it is argued that in any distribution of inheritable property, 'women take houses whilst men inherit land'. The reasons given for this (by both sexes) are twofold. Firstly, since women do not themselves cultivate, they can only effectively *use* land if they can obtain male labour to work on it. Secondly, it is said that 'it is important for a woman to have a house'. Why this is so we shall see presently – the point I wish to make here is that where there is a house to be inherited, male heirs generally waive their rights to a share of it.

Consequently, if a woman inherits land she will often simply sell her share to the male heirs. If they are unable or unwilling to purchase her share (or if, as sometimes happens, a woman is the sole heir), then she must find some way of cultivating the land or it will simply revert to bush. This is in fact what seems to happen in many cases. Thus three of the women have land which boasts only a few ancient coconut palms, and is otherwise indistinguishable from the surrounding bush. Unless legal claims are activated[24] and some rehabilitation carried out, such plots may enter the pool of common land, free for all on which to grow annual crops. Mere legal ownership of land is less important than the ability to invest capital to make it productive. Few women in Yumbe have access to the sums required.

When a woman does not sell out to male heirs she must organize male labour to work on her land. For about three quarters of the women landowners a son, a brother or a husband fulfils this role. The ambiguities of such a situation are obvious however – it is very easy for the relationship between owner and cultivator to be transposed into one where the cultivator, rather than being an 'employee', simply becomes responsible for maintaining the owner. Ownership thus becomes translated into dependency, and in time even the legal differentiation of roles may be forgotten. This is especially so since male relatives are in any case potential heirs of the female owner, and their cultivation of the land gives them a strong *de facto* claim to its ultimate ownership.

On the other hand a woman who has no call on such male labour is in an even more difficult position, for it is not easy to employ labour in Yumbe. With the end of slavery men no longer wished to cultivate for others, and with ready availability of common land,[25] they might scrape a subsistence living without doing so. Most labour here then is family labour, and even this might be grudgingly given – a son prefers to cultivate on his own account rather than work for his parents.[26] In 1965 only 5.8% of the adult male population were working as paid agricultural labourers. Wages were in the order of Sh.3 to Sh.5 per day, and although this is a fairly small sum by local standards, few women could afford to pay it regularly in addition to finding the capital required for running the farm. Seasonal temporary labour might be more within their means – when it is readily available. Only four of the women landowners in fact employed labour, and most of them had come to an arrangement whereby they shared the profits with the labourer rather than paying him a wage.

Considering all these problems it is not surprising that women are not eager to inherit land; nor are they quick to invest earnings from prostitution in buying land. On the other hand, it is only ex-prostitutes who are likely to have sufficient money with which to purchase land: all the three women who have bought land here are ex-prostitutes, each having spent many years in Mombasa. One of these worked her farm by employing temporary labourers, whilst a second 'employed' her grand-daughter's husband on a shared profits basis. The land of the third was cultivated by a husband whom she had married after her retirement to Yumbe (see the case of Mwana Amina 'K', below). What may happen however when an ex-prostitute buys land illustrates the common dilemma of women landowners.

Maryam Kingi spent twenty years in Mombasa and made a lot of money. In addition to building a house in Yumbe she also purchased land, but land which required a good deal of work and investment before it could be made profitable. She came to an arrangement with her brother whereby he would cultivate the land for her. After a few years however he 'persuaded' her to give it to him outright (people in the village say that he 'appropriated' it). Now he merely provides her with food.

It can thus be seen that, given certain ideological imperatives (and in particular that women do not cultivate) women in Yumbe have limited access to the productive resources of their economy, and are generally dependent on men for the basic needs of life. And if, instead of owning farms, women own houses, it has to be emphasized that (since the renting of living space never takes place here) houses, unlike land, are not productive assets.[27] So why then is it 'important for a woman to have a house'?

'Serial polygyny' and the ownership of houses

In spite of the fact that in 1965 there were almost as many women absent from Yumbe as men, there existed a marked demographic imbalance between the sexes in the village, with 1.2 adult women to every adult male.[28] Lowie has argued that 'polygyny is the obvious mode of readjustment to a preponderance of women',[29] but in Yumbe in 1965 there were only two polygynous marriages out of 186 extant unions. In general this is a 'solution' which Yumbe women are not prepared to accept – when a man suggests taking a second spouse their response is usually, 'first divorce me'. Women say that they cannot share a husband with another woman. In the only two cases extant, the women concerned insisted on living in separate houses, thus creating an extra financial burden for their husbands.

This being so, it is evident that at any one time many women in Yumbe will be without husbands. In fact in 1965, 40% of the women were divorcees or widows, whilst an additional 6% were unmarried girls. (This should be compared to 19% of males divorced or widowed, and an additional 12% of men as yet unmarried.)

If polygamy is rare in Yumbe however, what is sometimes described as 'serial polygyny' is the common pattern here. Roughly two thirds of the marriages contracted in Yumbe end in divorce,[30] most in the early phase of marriage, but some after many years of living together. The majority of Yumbe adults have therefore been married more than once, and there are some who have married and remarried innumerable times. Since Yumbe people are Muslims it is men who divorce women; women cannot divorce men. To effect a divorce is relatively easy for a man: he simply finds two men to bear witness that he has three times told his wife, 'I divorce you.' Although an aggrieved wife has no such easy recourse, women in Yumbe will rarely endure a marital situation in which they feel they have been wronged. Such a woman will simply ask to be divorced – and for most men such a demand could not be refused without masculine loss of face. Alternatively the wife may make life so uncomfortable for her husband by being uncooperative or avoiding his sexual advances that in the end he finds he can do nothing else but divorce her.[31]

After divorce it is rare for a husband to claim any children of the marriage. In general the children stay with the wife and she brings them up as best she can. Occasionally men contribute to the maintenance of their children by earlier marriages, but this is by no means a general rule: women say that men 'discard' their children. The net effect however is more paradoxical; namely that many men find themselves supporting the young children of their wives' *previous* marriage (or marriages). Almost a third (31.7%) of those married couples who have young children living with them have children of the wife's earlier marriages as well as their own.[32] (By contrast only six men – 4.6% – have living with them their children by preceding marriages.) There are of course in addition many divorced women temporarily without husbands who have young children to support.

Men blame women, and women men, for the frequency of divorce in Yumbe. Generally people attribute marital discord to adultery. Thus one man said: 'The wives of this place are always after men: it is their habit', whilst another asserted that he did not like the mentality of Yumbe women: 'Behind your back they are always looking at other men and going after them.' Women however have a different story to tell: 'Men are never satisfied with one wife; they are always on the lookout for someone else. And naturally if a wife comes to hear of this she tells her husband, "divorce me".' Whatever the truth of the matter, the fact that for men alternative spouses exist in abundance must surely influence attitudes to marriage.

Next to accusations of adultery, quarrels with in-laws are probably the most frequent cause of divorce in Yumbe. This is one of the consequences of the fact that it is women who own houses here rather than men (86.5% of Yumbe's houses are in fact owned by women). There are three ways by which women may obtain houses. Firstly, as we have seen, they may inherit a house (generally from their mother or other female relative, but occasionally from a male kinsman). Secondly, they may build a house – but since building requires capital it is generally only prostitutes who are able to build houses. The third way of obtaining a house is by gift – usually from the husband. The husband builds a house which he then gives to his wife. He will usually do this only if the marriage seems to be more or less established.

The rule that women rather than men own houses has two effects. It means that when a man marries he has to move out of his mother's house and into that of his wife or her mother (or some other female affine). More than half (54.3%) of the married men in Yumbe are therefore living with their affinal kin. Similarly, when a man divorces his wife he is the one who has to move out and generally he returns to the house of his mother or his sister. Households in Yumbe are thus typically composed of a core of permanently settled women with their children, plus isolated and temporarily settled men.

One can see, as it were, two centripetal tendencies at work here. Ideally a man would like to be in firm control of a group consisting of his wife and children, and later his daughters and their husbands. In such a situation he is not threatened by his wife's ownership of the house and may even give her a house he has built. It is a different proposition however, for a man to marry into a house where he is faced with a strong and united group of female affines, the most formidable of which is probably his mother-in-law. This situation is fraught with potential friction.

Although strong and stable male-focused households are to some extent a function of one stage in the life cycle of domestic groups, they can only occur if marriages persist in spite of the built-in factors precipitating discord. Landowner-ship is to a large extent the key to effective male control, since it is the product of the land which allows a man to organize and provide for his family with authority. It is notable for example that all the males who themselves own houses (13.5% of the house-owners) also own land, and in general a man with land is likely to establish his own household rather than live in with his wife's relatives.

If land is the ultimate security for men, women put their trust in the close knit group of mother, sisters, grandmothers and daughters, if possible all residing under one roof. The symbol of the woman's ideal is therefore a house where she can live together with her female kin. A woman who has neither house nor co-residing female kin will always work towards achieving this end, because without one and/or the other she has no security. On the other hand the co-residence of loyally united groups of related women presents a threat to the stability of the marriages of the individual women involved.

The effect of marital instability on parent–child relationships is very evident in Yumbe. Mothers and daughters are in general very close and mutually sup-portive. In addition they may live in the same household throughout their lives. The relationship of a mother with her son is more ambivalent: there may be hostility between sons and their mother's husbands, and in any case sons leave home when they marry. A father has more tenuous relationships with both sons and daughters in a broken marriage, and this is undoubtedly the reason why sons prefer to cultivate for themselves rather than for their fathers.

Sexual politics in Yumbe: divorce and the option of prostitution

Although women in Yumbe depend very markedly on the economic activities of men in order to live, this does not make them submissive or acquiescent marriage partners. On the contrary they are defiant, quick to take offence, and very ready to demand to be divorced. One can only explain this paradox in terms of women being able to fall back on alternative arrangements, which may, at least tempor-arily, substitute for the economic security of marriage. To some extent these are to be found in women's work, although as we have seen, such work produces only a meagre income. In addition the existence of groups of co-resident female kin now comes into its own as a mechanism for mutual aid – although ironically what this often means in practice is that a divorced woman merely transfers her dependence from her own husband to the husband of her kinswoman. This transfer is, however, mediated through the institution of female ownership of houses.

But in the last analysis, it is almost certainly the possibility of earning a viable living as a prostitute which allows women to reject unsatisfactory marital situations. At the same time, the fact that women may exploit their sexuality for gain, and thereby earn a certain measure of freedom from male control, is an ever-present threat to marital stability. Thus it is within the context of marital relations that the option of prostitution must be considered.

Up until their first marriage young women are restricted and subject to the control of their parents. (It is perhaps ironical that it is women rather than men who uphold and enforce these restrictions on unmarried girls.) Although these days many young girls find ways of escaping these restraints, it is unheard of for an unmarried girl independently to leave Yumbe for Mombasa. Prostitutes are without exception women who have already been married.

In 1965 Mwanahawa was living in her mother's house with her mother, her grandmother, her mother's husband, and two young brothers (one by her mother's present husband, one by a third marriage of her mother's). She was married to a man named Somoebwana, but the marriage was very unstable. Twice, whilst Mwanahawa was pregnant, she and her husband quarrelled and he left. (Her only explanation for this was that 'Men here are very stupid!') He returned to her after the birth of the child and the marriage continued, though shakily. After several more months however, Mwanahawa was finally divorced. A year later she had left for Mombasa, leaving her small child with her mother. 'Now she accepts any man,' commented her mother with resignation.

This is a pattern of events which is often repeated in Yumbe. Occasionally a divorce may even be forced by the woman running away to Mombasa, as happened in the following instance.

Ali Mohamed was married to a girl, Zamzam, of whom he was inordinately fond. She however was cool towards the marriage. She became involved with another man and asked Ali for a divorce which he refused to give her. Finding that she was trapped in an unhappy marriage, Zamzam ran away to Mombasa, where after a while she became a prostitute. Ali was thereby forced to divorce her.

The option of prostitution is not however equally open to all women who are unhappily married. One factor which clearly influences the incidence of migratory activities amongst women is their fertility. Women with several small children cannot so easily leave for Mombasa as those with none or only one or two. The fertility rate in this district as a whole appears, however, to be very low, whilst at the same time the mortality rate for children in their first year is very high.[33] Thus although people in Yumbe do not use contraceptive devices (such not being locally available, and in any case regarded as sinful), the number of women who have very large families is not as great as might be expected, and many have very few or even none at all.

A woman with one or two small children will generally leave them behind at first if she intends to earn her living independently in Mombasa. Very young children would be a hindrance to this goal, and would necessitate her employing someone to look after them whilst she works. After settling down however, she is likely to fetch older children so that they can go to school in Mombasa. Some children are however left permanently in Yumbe. In 1965 there were twelve women in Yumbe taking care of their daughters' children, and one caring for her sister's daughter's child. Altogether there were seventeen children involved, eight of whom were illegitimate. One woman had two daughters working as prostitutes in Mombasa; she meanwhile cared for the two illegitimate children of one of them and the legitimate child of the other (born before her mother left for Mombasa). If a woman conceives in Mombasa she generally comes home to bear her child and will leave it in Yumbe at least whilst it is small:

Timalale was married briefly, quarrelled with her husband and was divorced. She then went to Mombasa where she became a successful prostitute. In 1964 she already had one illegitimate child who was about four years old and whom she kept with her in Mombasa, employing another woman to look after her whilst she worked. Then she again became pregnant and returned to Yumbe to bear her child. She stayed with her mother's sister, herself a retired prostitute. Tima's own mother was in Mombasa. A few months after the apparently half-Chinese baby was born she returned to Mombasa. During 1965 the child became desperately ill and died. Timalale arrived too late, when the baby was already dead. Her grief was overwhelming, but other women were critical: 'It's not proper to cry so much [because it implies that one questions God's will]. Why does she cry so? Even now she is pregnant again.' Timalale stayed on in Yumbe to await the birth of her third illegitimate child. After it was born, in October, she became determined to return with it to Mombasa. She said she could not think of leaving it behind after what had happened to her other child. But by December she had set off again for Mombasa, and the child remained with her mother (who had by this time herself returned to live in Yumbe).

This case exemplifies the way in which the close knit female kin group can operate as an instrument of mutual support within the context of migratory activities. It also raises the issue of illegitimacy. It cannot be denied that there is a certain stigma of shamefulness attached to illegitimacy here. Children born out of wedlock are referred to as *wana haramu* 'forbidden children', and this is a term of abuse, if rarely used openly. But certain social mechanisms exist to obscure the harsh reality of a child with 'no father'. Such a child may be called 'the son/daughter of "Abdallah"', or it will be given a name implying that it in fact has a legitimate father. Illegitimate children take their social status from their mothers and may inherit from them.

Of the children under fifteen in Yumbe, 6.2% were illegitimate – more than half of these would appear to be the products of prostitution in Mombasa, whilst some of the others seem to have been born of 'prostitution' within the village context. Considering the extent to which women migrate here, the degree of illegitimacy does not seem to be very high, even granted that some of the children of prostitutes are with their mothers in Mombasa. Men say that prostitutes do not use contraceptives, and it is rare for their customers to do so. Timalale at least said that she did not do anything to prevent conception, and no woman in Yumbe would think of aborting a child. Children, even when illegitimate, are welcome. Nevertheless, many of the women who have stayed for long periods in Mombasa would seem to be relatively infertile. Of eighteen women who had spent more than ten years in Mombasa but who were now more or less 'retired' in Yumbe (the majority being past child-bearing age), five had no living child, four had only one, and only three had more than three children. There were, however, only three with illegitimate children. Most of the children born to these women appear to be the products of their earliest marriages in Yumbe, rather than of their life as prostitutes. This cannot be satisfactorily explained, although it is possible that venereal disease has affected the fertility of these women.

The incidence of labour migratory activities amongst Yumbe women is influenced by a further factor: namely local wealth differentials.[34] One might reasonably have anticipated that it would be women in the most distressed economic circumstances who would be most likely to leave the village, but this is not so. Although economic straits may in some cases propel women into prostitution in Yumbe itself, migration to Mombasa requires financial resources to which poorer women may not have access. The journey takes at least two days, and in 1965 cost about Sh.30. Although most people have some relatives in Mombasa with whom they can stay initially, a person needs a little money to keep her or himself going until he settles down and begins earning an adequate income. In the case of prostitution it seems likely that some expenditure on attractive dresses and cosmetics would greatly improve a woman's chances of success. It is difficult for the poorest women in Yumbe to obtain enough cash for such expenses. A woman from a rather better-off family however may have been able to save a little money from working at women's tasks. She may have jewellery she can pawn or sell. She is almost certainly in a position to borrow money from other women (or men) for the journey.

On the other hand the daughters or sisters of the richest men in the village are least likely to migrate. Generally these women are married to men of equivalent economic status, and such marriages have a better chance of stability. Their husbands can afford to adequately feed, clothe and house their wives and children, so that quarrels at least over such matters are less likely to arise. These men are thus more likely to be in firm control of their dependent womenfolk and to attempt action against those who 'shamefully' go their own way. Even here however they are not always successful, since other than economic factors come into play to propel some women into earning a living by prostitution:

Rukiya Zuberi came from a well-off family in Yumbe, and her brother was also a religious officiant in the Friday mosque. In 1965, she was already married to her fourth husband although she was still in her mid-twenties. In her first marriage she had borne a child which died. Rukiya's second marriage was to a man who worked away from Yumbe, and who visited her infrequently. She lived in her elder sister's house, their mother being long since dead. She became pregnant, but was divorced after a quarrel in which she accused her husband of adultery. The child was born a few months later. Rukiya's third marriage was a 'secret' affair with a man of the village, and it lasted only a week.

At this point Rukiya attempted to go to Mombasa, leaving her small child with her sister. She got only as far as the next town, however, when her brother caught up with her and forced her ignominious return. Not long after this she was married to a man from another village, but she herself continued to live in Yumbe with her sister, and so she rarely saw her husband. In 1965, she was visibly chafing at this situation and claiming that her husband did not support her properly. ('If you want anything from a man in this place you have to take him by the ear.') She had also heard tales that her husband had taken another wife.

By 1967, Rukiya had long since been divorced, and this time had succeeded in reaching Mombasa, where she was said to be living, 'any old way' (*vivi hivi tu*, here a euphemism for prostitution).

In another case, the daughter of one of Yumbe's richest men was forced into a marriage with her cousin. Neither she nor her cousin wished for the union, and the young man divorced his wife after five days. She thereupon ran away to Mombasa and stayed there for six months working as a prostitute. In the end her father sent his son to Mombasa to fetch her back. She agreed to come, and a more acceptable marriage was arranged for her, though to a man of considerably lesser standing.

These examples of attempts by well-off men to assert male authority over women may be compared to the case of an elderly man in less fortunate economic circumstances whose daughter had been many years in Mombasa. He came to tell his female neighbours that he had received some money from his daughter. After he had left one of them said disparagingly: 'His daughter has no husband, she is a prostitute. But of course, if she sends him money, he is happy.'

Sexual politics in Yumbe:
social acceptance and economic security

Although no one in Yumbe would argue that prostitution is anything but sinful, returned prostitutes are by no means social outcasts. On the contrary they receive a surprising degree of social acceptance, as the following case indicates:

Hawa Loo had spent twenty years in Mombasa, having gone there initially after she was divorced by her first husband. In Mombasa she remarried, but was again divorced and has since worked as a prostitute. She has never borne a child herself. Several years ago her sister died in Yumbe, leaving one child who later became ill with polio. Hawa took the boy to Mombasa where he was successfully treated, and she has looked after him ever since. In 1965 he was eleven years old and she came back with him to Yumbe so that he could be circumcised. From her savings Hawa provided a huge feast to celebrate the boy's circumcision. She spent something like £50, and the feast was attended by around one hundred women, and double that number of men – including all the most important men of the town, and some from other villages.

This was not an isolated case – during this same year the mother of Timalale, whose case was described above, also gave a public feast to celebrate the circumcision of two of her illegitimate children and four other boys, the sons of relatives. Again a vast amount of money was spent (by local standards) and all the locally important men were present. In inviting such men to feasts, and in securing their willing attendance, such women maintained their good public standing, irrespective of what men said about them behind their backs.

Nor are such women unacceptable as marriage partners, though on the whole returned prostitutes, unless they are still quite young, do not often remarry. Of eighteen women who had spent more than ten years in Mombasa, only two were married in 1965, although a further two entered into brief marriages in the course of the year. This is to be understood more in terms of their age and the fact that they are mostly past child bearing however, than in terms of any particular stigma attached to their past activities. It could also be that in so far as these women have savings and security they prefer their independence to the married state. Where they do marry it would appear to be more for expediency than for any other motive, and to relate to the fact that women do not cultivate. One woman described it as 'marrying for food'. In one exceptional case however, the retired prostitute who remarried had invested her earnings in land:

> Mwana Amina 'K' is an elderly woman who has never borne a child. She spent several years in Mombasa and is believed to have earned quite large sums of money there. She is also rumoured to have pocketed for herself money collected for a dance society which operated in the town many years ago. She bought a piece of land, which, though not very large, is fairly profitable. Mwana Amina then married a man of the ex-slave category who, like her, had no living close relatives. She herself was a freeborn woman, so that such a match, in local eyes, was most unfortunate. To impute motives here would be speculative, but in effect, Mwana Amina, by marrying a man with no wealth of his own, and of inferior status, ensured herself labour for her farm and continued control over its products.

Although some women settle permanently in Mombasa – they may marry or live with their grown up children there – the goal of those who return must be to guarantee a comfortable old age for themselves in the village. The two most important aspects of this are ensuring the support of kin and building a house if they do not already own one. Thus 11.5% of Yumbe's houses are owned by women *at present away*, and all but four of those women who have long-term migrancy experience own their own houses (three of the exceptions are still living in houses belonging to their mothers which they will presumably inherit). One woman has even built two houses.

Returned prostitutes also use their savings to help relatives – help which may, in the future, be reciprocated. Most of this effort of course goes into supporting and maintaining their own close female kin and their children. They are generally enthusiastic about sending their children to secular schools in the hope that they may better themselves (partly this is a reflection of their stay in Mombasa, where schools have been established for much longer, and are taken for granted, whereas in Yumbe there is still religious antipathy to the government school on the island). They may pay fees for the children of other women relatives, and can generally be relied upon to assist in the case of illness. One had paid for her brother's wedding. The case of Hawa, above, and of Timalale's mother, provide instances of support to kinsfolk – support which could stand them in good stead in the future.

Cases where returned prostitutes have invested savings in directly productive assets are more rare. But three of these women had bought land, in spite of the problems already noted. One of these had in addition built a water tank, from which she sold water, whilst another had opened a small shop with her savings (she was the only woman in the village to attempt shopkeeping).

There was one returned migrant whose case is the exception that proves the general rule that women who earn money from prostitution use it to ensure themselves security in old age:

> Batuli Dhee had spent more than 25 years in Mombasa and had been a highly successful prostitute, by repute very popular with Europeans. It was said – with what truth I do not know – that Batuli's mother had also been a prostitute in

Mombasa and had died there. Batuli spent all her earnings on good living and conspicuous consumption, and returned to Yumbe more or less penniless. She had never borne a child and had no living close relatives. Since she had built no house she had nowhere to live. In 1965 she was around seventy years of age and was occupying a semi-derelict house belonging to a woman living in Nairobi to whom she was very distantly related. In order to live she had to go round with a bowl into which charitable people would put food. People regarded her with pity – but pity mixed with contempt at her lack of foresight.

Kitina said of the life of a prostitute: 'When you are young and pretty you do well, but when you are old you may end up begging, like Batuli Dhee.'

It will now be clear that in relation to the situation of Yumbe women, prostitution is simply one of an inter-related set of social facts, the most important of which are the economic dependency of women, female house-ownership, marriage residence rules and marital instability. My argument here has been that the labour migration of women must be seen within the socio-economic context of production and property relations within the village, but also as a response to general historical trends of economic decline affecting the area of which Yumbe is a part.

Equally importantly I have been trying to illustrate the fact that without equivalent access to productive resources, and without active participation in the productive processes of their economy, women cannot gain an equal footing with men. They are forced back to utilizing their sexuality as their sole resource. The option of prostitution, and the mechanisms which have developed to make this option viable, certainly allow them to be defiant in relation to men, to reject submission within an unhappy marriage and to refuse the status of second wife. But in the long run their actions are defensive rather than offensive.[35] They threaten the authority of men but do not suggest any radical alternatives to women's dependency here. And as Millett comments: 'To be a rebel is not to be a revolutionary. It is more often but a way of spinning one's wheels deeper in the sand.'[36]

Reprinted from *Cahiers d'études africaines*, 65, xvii (1), 1977, pp. 13–38.

NOTES

1. This is a fictional name, as are all names in case histories. In order to protect the identity of the individuals involved here I have purposely obscured the precise location of the village and the specific delineation of the people. The present study arose coincidentally out of research carried out in the area in 1965–66 with a brief return visit in 1967. I am indebted to the University of London for the award to me of a Postgraduate Studentship which made this research possible. My interest at the time was in political factionalism, not in the situation of women, so the material which I have on this subject emerged by chance rather than by systematic investigation. Some at least of the inadequacies in the analysis which follows should perhaps be attributed to this fact.

2. See A. I. Salim, *Swahili-Speaking Peoples of Kenya's Coast: 1895–1965* (Nairobi, 1973): 100.

3. Since the rest of this essay devotes itself mainly to economic and family patterns, it is perhaps important here to specify the dependent character of the role of women in politics in this area. No political positions of leadership are held by women, and women do not attend political or public meetings. They are significant however when it comes to counting heads in an election, and women can be quite active in recruiting support amongst other women for candidates to whom they are related. See J. M. Bujra, *An Anthropological Study of Political Action* (London, 1968), Ph.D. thesis.

4. L. Tiger and R. Fox, *The Imperial Animal* (New York, 1971): 108.

5. Internal trade patterns – as opposed to externally directed trade – were ill-developed

in the precolonial period. Later, during the colonial period, petty retail trade in Kenya was dominated by Asians and Arabs; see Salim 1973: 135. Mutiso speaks of oral traditions of Kamba women traders (G. C. Mutiso, *Kenya: Politics, Policy and Society,* Nairobi, 1975: 250) and in the colonial period Kikuyu women became active retailers of agricultural products. But coastal women have never really practised trade to my knowledge.

6. See J. M. Bujra, 'Women "Entrepreneurs" of Early Nairobi', *Canadian Journal of African Studies,* 9 (2), 1975: 213–34.

7. The earliest women to settle in Nairobi, by contrast, would seem to have been isolated individuals who had more or less irrevocably broken their rural ties by their activities in town and had established themselves permanently there.

8. See however A. L. Richards and P. Reining, 'Report on Fertility Surveys in Buganda and Buhaya', in F. Lorrimer, ed., *Culture and Human Fertility* (Paris, 1952). The urban aspect of Bahaya prostitution in East Africa is discussed by A. Southall and P. C. W. Gutkind, in *Townsmen and the Making* (Kampala, 1957): 82–3.

9. E. Genovese, *Roll, Jordan Roll: The World the Slaves Made* (New York, 1974): 125. Genovese is writing of slaves in the American South, but there are suggestive parallels with the situation of women. See also K. Millett, *Sexual Politics* (London, 1971): 348.

10. In 1965 Kenya currency was at par with sterling.

11. *Malaya* – a 'prostitute'. *Kufanya malaya* means 'to practise prostitution'.

12. It would be more accurate to say that he 'repudiated' his wife, since he did not go through all the formal stages of divorce, and hence was able to return to her without loss of face (this is called *kuregea* 'to return to').

13. Referred to by Salim 1973: 136.

14. The notebook has been preserved in the old headman's house, and I was able to examine it in 1965.

15. N. Chittick, 'The Coast of East Africa', in P. L. Shimmie, ed., *The African Iron Age* (Oxford, 1971): 93–125, see p. 108.

16. Copra (the product of coconut palm plots on the island), and mangrove poles (cut by slaves from the fringes of the island) were both exported; in addition grain crops, grown on the fertile mainland opposite the island, were undoubtedly sold to provision trading expeditions, if they were not also exported. The main exports were slaves and ivory; imports consisted of cloth, household utensils, beads and firearms, which were traded down the coast and up the Tana River. J. E. G. Sutton (*The East African Coast,* Dar Es Salaam, 1966, Historical Association of Tanzania, Paper 1) and N. Chittick (1971) both give brief and critical reviews of what is known of coastal history, and of the participation of the coast in Indian Ocean trade. Salim (1973) has a fascinating and detailed account of the slave-owning economy of the coast.

17. C. H. Stigand, *The Land of Zinj* (London, 1966): 149. This book was originally published in 1913 and was based on several years of travel in East Africa. Stigand describes the small settlements of freed slaves which were set up on the mainland after emancipation (p. 171).

18. See, e.g. Salim 1973: 194, who notes that in 1933, 'The population of Lamu District was estimated at about 17 per cent less than at the end of the war.'

19. Drawing on the work of Greenberg (1946), Lewis notes that: 'In some Hausa areas women have discontinued their traditional farming duties on the conversion of their menfolk to Islam.' (I. M. Lewis, ed., *Islam in Tropical Africa,* Oxford, 1966: 50.) Although the people described here are also Muslims, I do not think this is the explanation for women not cultivating. The potentiality for withholding female labour must already exist within the scope of an economy: Islam merely symbolizes in the ideological sphere what is possible in the realm of reality.

20. One might have anticipated that ex-slave women at least would have cultivated for themselves after emancipation. This however does not appear to have happened. Except for isolated individuals, ex-slave women now became as dependent on male labour as were freeborn women.

21. For details of this period see Salim 1973: 155.

22. Writing of the period around the late fifties, Wilson commented that: 'Organized intimidation, graft, gangsterism, protection money and so on – the evils which are usually

associated with prostitution – simply did not exist in Mombasa.' (G. M. Wilson, 'A Study of Prostitution in Mombasa', in 'Mombasa Social Survey', unpubl. ms., no date.) In general Wilson's account tallies with that I have given here.

23. Racial stereotypes and attitudes are another legacy of the slave-owning era: see Bujra 1968.

24. Thus a certain woman in Yumbe accused someone else of encroaching on land which she said she had inherited from her father. When the old men of the town got together to discuss the case, they upheld her claim, although with some doubts – the piece of land in question had not been cultivated within living memory.

25. One must always keep in mind the net population decline in the area.

26. This may be better understood in the context of family instability (see following section).

27. A house may be sold and, depending upon its mode of construction and state of repair, may fetch anything from £10–£100. But there was no real market here for houses, and only one house was sold in 1965 (the transaction was between two men). Women occasionally use their houses as security for loans and there was one case in 1965 where an ex-slave woman asked a rich farmer to take her house on her death in lieu of paying her funeral expenses. Ownership of a house can thus at least give a woman credit-worthiness.

28. This demographic imbalance is marked in all except one of the villages on the island, and is presumably related to past patterns of migration and emigration of males.

29. R. Lowie, *Social Organization* (London, 1950): 118.

30. According to the register of marriages and divorces kept in the District offices since 1951, 59.7% of marriages contracted and registered by Yumbe men between that date and 1957 had ended in divorce by 1965. Although there is a legal obligation to register marriages, not all do so, and very short-term marriages are unlikely to be registered. Nevertheless the figures are indicative.

31. The customary bridewealth payment *(mahari)* is here £12, and it is promised on the occasion of marriage. In very few cases it is actually paid however. In only 16% of registered divorces had the total sum been paid to the woman; in most cases nothing was paid. To some extent this is explained by the fact that many women voluntarily forfeit the payment in demanding the divorce. An additional payment, for the costs of the wedding, is more generally made, but in second marriages this is rarely more than £5.

32. This does not mean that the other 68.3% of marriages with small children were necessarily more stable. Earlier marriages (of either husband or wife) may not have been productive of children, or the children may have died or be already grown up. In addition the children of some of these men's earlier marriages are living with their mothers.

33. Low fertility rates may be a reflection of the incidence of venereal disease, but this is by no means certain. With regard to infant mortality: during the period March 1965 to January 1966, when I kept my own records of Yumbe births and deaths, 36 children were born whilst 26 died [i.e. 26 of the 36 died within the first year].

34. Assigning a cash value to all production here (i.e. including production for subsistence) we find that at one extreme 4% of the adult male population had incomes of £600 and over per annum, whilst at the other end of the economic hierarchy, one third of the male population had incomes of less than £50 per annum.

35. It has been suggested that female-centred kin groups are generally 'of a predominantly defensive nature' (R. Morpeth and P. Langton, 'Contemporary Matriarchies: Women Alone – Independent or Incomplete?', *Cambridge Anthropology* I (3), Apr. 1974: 35). In this analysis I have tried to show that such groups are more than this, in that they also threaten marital instability and provide support for alternative arrangements. But in a more general sense, women's responses here may indeed realistically be seen as a defensive reaction to their deprived and dependent economic and social status.

36. Millett 1971: 349.

BERBER SONG

Editors' introduction

This song reflects some of the sentiments expressed in Reading 24. In contrast to the realism articulated by the prostitutes in the previous reading, however, this song idealizes prostitution. The image of the seductive flower in line 27 can be compared with the flower that withers away in the lament of the Moroccan woman in Reading 22.

Poor naïve young man, stop hassling me!
I came to the village to visit my parents,
Not to look for a husband – God preserve me from that!
And soon I'll go back to Azilal,[1] if God so wishes it.
You say you want me to be your wife
After just one night of my love making.
Well, I know how long your desire would last!
And what can you offer that's sweeter than freedom?
Come on now, don't give me that look
To try to shame me in my profession,
My profession, thanks to which you enjoyed yourself so last night!
What other life could make me happier?
And you, who beg me to be yours alone,
What can you give me, tell me that, naïve young man?
Days without meat, without sugar, and without songs,
The sweat and dirt of hard work,
The dung of the stable, stinking clothes,
And that awful smoke in the dark kitchen,
While you're off on the mountain, dancing the dance of the rifles?
And you'll keep after me, all the time
To bear boys, boys, and more boys!
Can't you see I'm not made for all that?
No, let me go back to the market in Azilal.
You're wasting your time, this pleading is making me tired.
Why should I work here, for you,
When there they load me with presents and silver?
I'm like a flower with a seductive scent
That only blossoms for a pleasant reason,
To receive, when it chooses, each night and each day,
The freshness of the dawn, the caress of the sun.

Recorded from a recital by Mririda N'ait Attik in the Tachelhait dialect and reprinted here in English translation from E. W. Fernea and B. Qattan Bezirgan (eds), *Middle Eastern Women Speak*, University of Texas Press, 1977.

NOTE

[1. Town at the foot of the Haut Atlas mountains in Morocco.]

26 Testimony of a Guatemalan Woman

LUZ ALICIA HERRERA

Editors' introduction

The majority of Guatemala's population are small farmers growing staple foods such as maize and beans. The main earnings of the country's economy, however, come from export crops such as coffee, cotton and sugar. There is also commercial ranching and an expanding extraction industry in nickel and oil. The oil finds in particular have given rise to serious conflict over land tenure and land use in northern Guatemala.

Commercial agriculture employs some permanent wage labour, but there is also a diminishing 'colono' system where peasant farmers are given the use of plots of land in return for labour service on the landlord's farm. (The family in the following testimony may have been in this position.) Commercial farming increasingly relies, however, on seasonal wage labour engaged through 'contratistas' – labour contractors. The bulk of the peasant population, mostly descendants of the Mayan Indians, live in the Central and Western highland areas but engage in seasonal migration, particularly to the southern coastal region, to work as wage labourers. The indigenous workers referred to in this account were Indians and likely to be contracted labour. (The indigenous population has suffered the double oppression of exploited labour and racial discrimination since the time of the Spanish conquest.) The family of the woman in the testimony, by contrast, lived in the coastal area, and we can infer from her reference to 'indigenous workers' that she herself is not of Indian origin.

The history of the woman in our reading exemplifies the many ways in which poor people struggle to earn a living (see also Readings 9 and 13). Permanent workers in agriculture or industry account for only a small proportion of the workforce.

The political history of Guatemala is an important factor in understanding the woman's attitude to joining a union: why she might be risking her life. There has been severe repression of any signs of opposition to the military-backed government in Guatemala since the coup against the progressive regime of President Arbenz in 1954. This repression has been carried out by both the army and paramilitary organizations and has affected primarily urban workers and peasants, although political leaders, lawyers and other professionals have been assassinated. At the time of the account, daily killings of workers and peasants, whether organized or not, were a fact of life.

Women have, however, not only had to confront the possibility of repression by the state for joining a union but also resistance from their husbands and families. Often, militant women are unattached or separated. '. . . if the Guatemalan working woman does not participate more actively in the labour union movement it is because her male fellow-workers continue to think that a woman's place is not in labour union activism but in the home.'[1] The exigencies of the current political situation in Guatemala have probably forced that to change. Since this account, there has been increasing polarization of classes in Guatemala through armed opposition to the repression of the working class and the peasantry. A recent analysis of a guerrilla column showed not only that it was predominantly Indian but that 30 per cent were also women under eighteen.[2]

[. . .] I was born in a little village on the southeast coast. I was fifteen when we moved to a parcel of land far away, still on the same south coast. My mother was a widow. There were four children, three girls and a boy. In the new place where we went to live, my mother established a little restaurant. We cooked for thirty people. We also picked cotton. My mother, my thirteen-year-old sister, and I would get up at one in the morning to do the household chores: cook corn [maize], make tortillas [small pancakes made from maize flour], prepare the food and clean the house. At 6 o'clock all was ready, and at 7 a.m. we would take the bus to the cotton fields. I used to go with my sister to a plantation that employed between 150 to 200 cotton pickers, men and women.

On the plantation, an active picker would pick 100 to 150 pounds of cotton. My sister and I would pick 100 pounds between us and be paid one cent per pound. We would take our own food with us. When it rained, we would work from 8 a.m. in the morning to 3 p.m. in the afternoon. If the weather was very humid, we would work from 12 noon to 3 p.m. in the afternoon.

It is hard work under the hot sun on a cotton plantation. The women wore hats to protect their heads from the sun. There would be many of us women with the sack of cotton tied to our waists. The foreman and the labour contractors made sure that the workers kept their attention on the picking and tried to keep them from establishing contact with their fellow workers.

Sometimes, when we were picking cotton, the airplane would fly over us, spraying insecticide, and the majority of the workers would get poisoned. We had to hide the water and food so that the poison wouldn't get to them.

The foremen were rough and would make the women use the plough by themselves if they left some cotton behind. They treated us badly and humiliated us. The indigenous workers [i.e. Indian] were treated even worse than other workers. They were given only tortillas and beans to eat. Indigenous workers were forced to weigh their cotton on a different scale, undoubtedly to pay them less. The indigenous workers came with their whole families to work – wives and children. The children were only five years old when they began to pick cotton.

Working on the plantation, I was angry about earning so little. Working under the hot sun all day and for so little pay! The foreman and the labour contractors who took advantage of us thought they were kings. A man from the village – a contractor – hired the rest of the workers from the village to do the picking. The foremen were also exploited people but they chose to be on the side of the bosses. We would get home from work at 6 or 7 p.m. and after that feed the other workers – about thirty people outside of our family. Then we would do the dishes and start to cook corn all over again. We would cook 25 pounds of corn a day.

'Serious work. Get up, get up, it's time.' That's how my mother would wake us up. So short was the night! We would go to bed at 10 p.m. the evening before and get up at 1 a.m. in the morning. At that time, I was fifteen years old and my sister was thirteen; since we were the eldest, we were made to do the hardest work. We also worked on the little plot of land that was given to my mother. On it, we would plant corn, *maicillo* (millet), and chile [chilli] for everyday use. Sometimes we would sell the little bit that was left. For us, there were no Sundays, no good times. Only weeks of work.

In 1963, through a friend, I got a job working as a babysitter and maid in Escuintla. I worked there for five years. The first six months they paid me seven *quetzales* a month[3] to take care of a little girl from 7 a.m. in the morning to noon when the woman of the house, who was a secretary in an office, would get home. It was a big responsibility, and I really didn't know how to take care of little children. The lady decided that since I was very affectionate with her little daughter, she would pay me 12 quetzales a month. Then she raised it to 20 quetzales a month. This was clear money for me since they gave me other things that I needed – shoes and clothes – and I sent the money to my mother. I worked in this house for five years. The little girl is now thirteen years old, and when she sees me, she says I am her second mother. 'You took care of me and my mother didn't,' she says.

After this job I returned to my mother's place in the village. The three of us sisters separated from my mother because she was with a man who didn't like us. We rented a tiny house. With a little money that my mother gave us we started a store, and, there in the house, my sister (since she is a dressmaker) had her sewing machine, and we continued with the little restaurant, just we three. There we had thirty mobile military police and the people who passed by on their way to the *fincas* (ranches) for customers. The three of us lived happily. We earned very little, just enough to eat, more or less dress, and shoe ourselves.

After that, I came once again to work in Escuintla, in a soft-drink stand. There I worked only for room and board. During this time I had the stupidity to run off with a boyfriend. He studied in the capital [Guatemala City] and his parents paid for him to stay in a boarding house. From the soft-drink stand, I went with him to the capital. I lived a year and a half with him. We lived, on what his parents sent us, in a small room that didn't have a place to cook so we bought our meals. I put up with this difficult situation for a year and a half. I went to work in a clothing factory. I was a seam-gatherer. It was my job to gather and trim. I earned four quetzales and twelve cents weekly. I didn't know how to sew on the electric machines. There were times when I worked extra hours and then I would earn twenty quetzales a month. But I didn't continue in the factory because he didn't like me to work. At the same time, what we had didn't cover anything. I became so desperate that I went home to my mother in the village, once again.

My boyfriend fought with me a lot because I didn't get pregnant. 'You'll never have a child; heaven knows what things you do' [he would say]. Well, it was just my bad luck that the month I left him I was already pregnant, but neither of us knew it then. Once when I was with my mother, I noticed how I was, and I told my sister and she told my mother. And my mother caused a big uproar. My mother did not like the boy and she was angry at me. My mother threw me out of the house on my own. I went to a friend's, the one with the soft-drink stand and told her my problem, and I worked with her for room and board.

After two months, my mother arrived to look for me and took me back to the house. I returned to the house and in the state I was in, no one would give me work. An uncle told me, 'You can't work in a bar anymore.' I told the problem to a neighbour who had a *nixtamal* (the dough used for tortillas) mill. She let me go there and grind for one quetzal a day. I felt very tired and worn-out working there. Everyday my belly grew larger. My friend found some women who would buy tortillas from me each day and she ground my corn without charging me a cent. Daily, I ground twenty pounds of corn, made and sold the corn. After that, I washed clothes for people, did embroidery and needlework, and bought small clothing to sell with the earnings of the needlework. My stepfather would say: 'I will not maintain someone else's children,' and my mother would get angry with me.

I sent a message to my boyfriend about my pregnancy, and the response he gave was that the child I was about to have was no child of his, and he wouldn't pass me one cent – at least until the child was born. My son was three months old when my boyfriend came to see him with his mother. They came with the idea of taking him away from me but, like the majority of mothers who struggle to keep their children, I wouldn't give him up.

My ex-boyfriend had married another girl and he wanted to keep me as his lover. He only arrived to see his child when he was drunk and never even brought him candy. One time he even arrived with a revolver, threatening us from the window. My sister and I threw him out and punched him. Not until my son was three years old did I manage to convince his father to recognize him. I did it because children need to carry their father's name.

My son didn't like his father. Because he is not with us, he would say. He would notice that other fathers would bring their little children home from school. I've told him everything, and he doesn't like his father. 'Because he was bad with us, because of that, I only love you,' the child would say to me.

I began working for the revolution some time ago. My stepfather was from a peasant organization. Aside from the fact that he was bad with us sometimes, when he was in good humour, he gave us advice and we began to collaborate with the organization in the countryside. I, working as a babysitter, already collaborated.

He [my ex-boyfriend] did not think like me. He is a teacher but he doesn't understand the necessity of organizing the workers. He didn't know that I had those views and when he realized it, he told me not to get involved in anything that was bad for me. I told him that as long as I lived, I would continue struggling for an organization wherever I was and that there were no limits on where my commitment might take me. 'You believe in a struggle that will never triumph, one that won't ever even end,' he would say. I went to work in a factory again, and there, convinced that I should stay, joined a union. I have some friends who say I am crazy, that I shouldn't get involved in these things. And all I am going to get in return is unemployment or death. But I feel even braver when they tell me that I am going to end up dead. Also, it makes me want to know things I haven't known before.

I have had a lot of serious problems, but I have never been afraid. They have taken away my job ... I think about my son. But he tells me: 'If my mother dies, I will stay with the *compañeros* (comrades). ....' The compañeros are from the *sindicato* (union). Therefore, thinking about the welfare of my child has not kept me from organizing. Sooner or later we all have to die. It might be in some accident. My little boy already is aware of everything and I have taught him how one survives here. He already pays attention to the movements of the police . . . and advises us of them. [. . .]

Translated by Maria Alice Jacob from the Salvadorean journal, *Estudios Centro-americanos* (1978) and extracted from 'Testimonies of Guatemalan Women' in *Latin American Perspectives*, issue 25/26, Spring/Summer 1980, vol. 7, nos 2 and 3.

NOTES
1. Maria Amalia Irias de Rivera and Irma Violeta Alfaro de Carpio, 'Guatemalan Working Women in the Labor Movement', in *Women in Latin America*, an anthology from *Latin American Perspectives*, 1979, p. 162.
2. Concerned Guatemala Scholars: 'Guatemala: Dare to Struggle Dare to Win', New York, 1981, p. 54.
[3. One quetzal [= £0.50].]

27   Organizing the Annapurna

MIRA SAVARA

Editors' introduction

This account tells of the way in which women in the informal sector of Bombay have commercialized an aspect of domestic labour – preparing food – and organized themselves collectively to finance their production. (See also introduction to Reading 22.)

Introduction

One of the greatest problems facing workers in the informal sector is their lack of an organization to improve their social and economic status. Given the operating conditions of the informal sector, the traditional form of workers' organization – the trade union – is inappropriate, so different forms of collective organization have to be sought.

This article describes a recently formed organization of women in Bombay, who by extending the scope of their traditional domestic chore of cooking, offer eating facilities to male migrant workers whose families remain in the countryside. The organization is called Annapurna Mandal [Association] (Annapurna means 'Goddess of Food') and currently has 5,000 members. The basic function of the organization is raising bank loans on a group guarantee basis for individual Annapurnas to run mini-restaurants in their own homes. This frees them from reliance on the traditional money-lenders who charge interest rates of up to 150 per cent per annum. The group of women that stands guarantee for the individual loans constitutes the basic building block of the organization.

Women in the informal sector in India

Women participate in the production process both by producing goods and services for sale, and also by performing domestic functions within the household, which are an essential part of the economy as a whole. The growth of industrialization usually splits these two types of economic activity – the home becomes the private sphere in which women's work is primarily related to the maintenance of the family members, while in the external or public sphere they work for others for a wage.

However, in India, the separation between wage work and domestic labour is not so well defined, and a vast and significant sector of the economy exists where the home – the site of household labour – coincides with the site of wage work. The advantage of this is that it allows a woman a more flexible time schedule for the performance of her domestic and wage labour. The disadvantage is that it knits her even more tightly into the relations within the family and home, leaving little opportunity for her to build a wider network of social relations.

Women who work in their homes fall into two broad categories. First, there are those who take in work put out by a company or a subcontractor – such as assembly work, production of handicrafts, *bidi* making, food processing. Though at first sight these workers may appear to be self-employed, in reality they are involved in a disguised form of the capital-wage labour relationship. In such cases, the organization of workers into trade unions has been difficult but possible.

The second category of women can more accurately be described as self-employed. The Annapurnas, women who feed workers other than their own family members for payment, provide an example of this.

Cities in India are, and have been for several decades, overwhelmingly male, since it is primarily men who migrate there in search of jobs, leaving their families behind in the villages.

Table 1   Sex ratio in seven Indian cities, 1971

	females per 1000 males
Calcutta	636
Bombay	716
Delhi	806
Ahmedabad	833
Bangalore	874
Kanpur	769
Poona	885

Source: Govt of India, *Towards Equality*, Report of the Committee on the Status of Women in India, Government Central Press, 1977, p. 13.

The migrant male city-dweller must find alternatives to the functions previously performed by the female member of his family. One of his most basic needs is for cheap and wholesome food, but eating out in conventional restaurants is expensive, so a worker has either to cook for himself or to look for a cheap alternative. Such an alternative has evolved in Bombay where women in working class areas (either wives of workers needing extra income, or women whose husbands squander most of their income on drink) feed 16–20 workers in their own homes for a fixed amount per month. The men not only share the same social background as the women but in a large number of cases are relatives, or of the same caste, or from the same village as the woman or her husband. The arrangement can therefore be seen as a variant within the working class of the institution of the family, a significant difference being that this variant is extended to those outside the family network, and can thus be commercialized. Traditional relations which within the family imply duties and obligations, are here replaced by commercial relations of buying and selling. It is precisely this commercialization of relations which introduces conflict into the 'extended family'.

The Annapurnas

From a survey of 100 Annapurnas (Sherov 1979) it was found that 76 per cent of the women were married, three per cent single, three per cent separated and 18 per cent widows. [. . .]

Of the women's husbands, 82 per cent had some form of employment, while 18 per cent were either unemployed or retired.

The study found it difficult to get accurate estimates on family income. However, the majority of the married men (60 per cent) worked in textiles, where in 1979 the lowest paid textile worker earned approximately 450 rupees[1] a month. With no separation between the household economy and the enterprise, women found it difficult to estimate their earnings, since the money made from their customers was always spent on buying the ingredients for the next meals, from which the woman's family was also fed. Thus if a woman has a family of five, and she also cooks for 16 workers, the payment received from these is sufficient to feed her family as well.

The majority of the women were illiterate (73 per cent), 17 per cent had had four years of education or less, the rest more than four. Thus the Annapurnas did this work because their educational qualifications did not qualify them to aspire to the more organized factory work, because they were single, or because their husbands did not earn enough to maintain the family.

The women generally live in one room in the *bustees* (a multiroomed slum dwelling). The day starts early, usually by 5 a.m., the first chore being to queue and then bring water from the street standpipe, and store it against the day's needs. Where there is running water in the room, it is usually available for only an hour at a time, so it also has to be stored.

Then there is the daily shopping for vegetables; grains and pulses being bought every two to three days. Women buy retail because their customers, many of whom are temporary workers, pay as and when they get money, so they can rarely put aside enough money to buy in bulk.

All the work of shopping, preparing the meals, serving and washing up is done by the woman herself. She may be helped by younger daughters or a daughter-in-law. Sometimes a young girl is hired to do one task, usually the washing up, or to help throughout the day. The women usually cook on kerosene stoves, which presents considerable difficulties because kerosene is rationed, and buying it involves lengthy queuing. When there is a shortage (a very common situation) they have to cook on wood *chulas* [stoves], which involves extra work and, worse still, having to tolerate the thick smoke which fills the small room.

It is commonly assumed that a woman who works at home is the mistress of her own time, and that therefore her pattern of work is more relaxed than that in a factory. However, the Annapurnas worked literally all day, from 5 a.m. to 10 p.m. at night. Since there was no fixed time during which the men came and ate their two meals, the women had to spend all the time at home, keeping food hot and serving the men, who trickled in at their convenience.

Problems of the women

The women complained about the long hours of work, and the fact that they never got any time off during the day to get out of the house, nor any holidays. Their main grievance, however, was the rate of interest charged by local grocers (150 per cent annually) on credit for buying daily provisions, which effectively meant that the women were permanently in debt. Very often they did not know the extent of their debt, nor how much interest was being charged, since the majority of them were illiterate. Only the grocer-moneylender kept any records. Having once taken credit from a grocer, the women were bound to buy only from him, which prevented them from shopping around and buying at the cheapest price. The women felt this allowed the grocer to overcharge for items. Sexual harassment was not unknown. In one case a young and good-looking Annapurna woman who was deeply in debt was forced into having sexual relations with a grocer so as to ensure continuance of supplies. According to a woman activist in the area, this practice is probably quite widespread.

Another problem was that each woman worked alone, and bought food alone so that each woman in a sense formed her own work universe. She was in no way economically or otherwise related to the thousands of other women who were doing the same work and facing similar problems. There was also little cooperation between the Annapurnas. The clearest example of this was when a customer who had not paid an Annapurna for a month switched to another one: this led to confrontations between the two women rather than with the customer, and to bad feelings between the women, rather than collaboration.

The third problem area related to the nature of the work. The women wanted the government to give them gas or kerosene on a priority basis and to buy grains and provisions in bulk, which would lower the cost of the food and improve its quality. They also wanted a regular day off so that they could have some social life of their own.

The birth of the Annapurna scheme

In the Parel-Dadar area of Bombay, the heart of the textile industry in India, trade union activism has had a long history. What was the union's response to the Annapurnas' problems?

Although they were aware of the existence of this large group of women, they did nothing to organize them for a number of reasons. Firstly, the organization of scattered individuals, as in the case of Annapurnas, poses practical difficulties. Secondly, trade unions, with a predominantly male membership, are rarely sensitive to the problems of women. But most important, in the case of the Annapurnas, trade unionists view the Annapurnas not as workers, but as people who were antagonistic to the workers' interests, as exemplified by this comment by a union member: 'The women charge the workers too much, and don't give them good food. Moreover, they take money off the workers.'

However, in 1973 an event forced Prema, a woman trade union activist for many years, to re-examine the way she had looked at the Annapurnas. As she said:

I saw the problems of these women for the first time during the 42-day strike in the textile industry in 1973. During the strike I became aware that these women continued to feed the workers despite the fact that the workers had no income and thus could not pay the women for the food they ate. The women were pawning their mangalsutras (a necklace worn by all married women and considered sacred), and their utensils, to raise the money to feed the workers. I came to know the interest rates women were paying to buy grain. Till then I had never looked at the problems of these women. The women, quietly, without any fanfare, were enabling the men to continue their struggle, encouraging them to hold out till their demands were met. And yet their own problems were never taken up.

The main problem was to get the women out of the clutches of the moneylenders. Working through the banks, which had been nationalized, was an obvious first step.

We decided that we would not try to get loans for individual women. Instead, a group of 15 women had to get together so that a gradual building up of an organization occurred.

This step was crucial in differentiating this programme from the usual loan-giving programme, in which a relationship is established between an individual and the loan-giver. Here each woman gets a loan individually, and has to return the loan individually to the bank, but the loan is guaranteed by the group. Thus members of the group are accountable to each other, and if one woman defaults, the entire group is penalized. For the banks it is a means of bringing community pressure to ensure repayment of loans. For the women it means breaking out of an isolated individualized existence, and relating in a positive way to other women doing the same kind of work.

At first the women were reluctant to form a group despite the fact that the banks charged only four per cent interest annually. This was due both to their fears of forming any type of relationship with formal institutions, and to a rumour campaign started by the moneylenders, which suggested that there would be regular government inspections to ensure that the women were not carriers of infectious diseases; that they would have to start paying tax; that family planning would become compulsory. Most of the women were scared off and did not come forward to form the first group.

Eventually however, a group of 14 women was formed, composed of wives of workers active in the union movement, who were persuaded by their husbands to try the scheme, and women who were at the point of financial desperation, and thus willing to take some risks. Prema's 25 years of union work was of crucial significance, since she was well-known in the area. The women felt that unlike other social workers who came and went, Prema would always be there to look after their problems.

The first application was prepared after continuous discussions for four days and nights, and submitted in 1975. After six months, the scheme was approved, and each woman received Rs 1,000. Once the scheme was seen in practice, and it was recognized that there were no government checks, nor forced family planning, the news spread and in three years the scheme embraced approximately 5,000 women in Parel-Dadar.

The banking scheme

The purpose of the Multiservice Scheme of the Bank of Baroda was to provide investment in the so-far neglected and unsophisticated sectors of the economy by giving unsecured loans, thereby improving the standard of living of the clientele and generating more employment. A loan was available only to those whose family income fell below Rs 3,000 a year. As security, the goods purchased with the loan were mortgaged to the bank, or group guarantees were accepted. As part of the Scheme, the bank simplified its procedures. Application forms were shortened and made available in vernacular languages with only one document to be signed. To help the mostly illiterate borrowers to know how much they were repaying, stamps specially printed in different colours for different denominations were used as receipts. Monthly repayments were collected by agents who came to the borrower's home. To avoid the burden of paying the loan instalments in one lump sum, borrowers were asked to deposit daily, weekly, or fortnightly, a portion of their earnings into a savings account; on fixed days each month the amount accrued was transferred to the borrower's loan account. Not only were these procedures less complex, but the operational cost to the bank was only one third of the regular cost.

How the organization functions

The Annapurna Mandal has been registered as a Society and a Trust; only recipients of loans are entitled to membership of the Mandal. The 5,000 members elect a 60-woman committee which meets once a month to take decisions regarding the operation of the society. Besides Prema, the originator of the programme, only two other committee members are outsiders. The rest are Annapurnas themselves

Members are grouped into 11 local centres [each] of which has a committee of women members. Since a large number of the Annapurnas are illiterate, a few male volunteers are recruited for filling out forms, writing, and keeping accounts.

Instead of getting women from outside the area, from the educated middle class to fulfil these functions, the decision was taken to accept the help of men from working-class families, since they are known to the women, and they can help in other ways in community work. Moreover, educated women from outside are often irregular and stand apart from and outside of the community.

A woman who needs a loan comes to the committee with her request. The committee checks the number of workers she feeds, the economic condition of the family, and whether the woman will be able to pay back regularly. Once the committee is satisfied on these counts, she is asked to wait till another nine women have applied, and a group can be formed. Once she has received the loan she has to follow the savings and repayment plan outlined above. On a fixed day each month, a collector from the bank visits each centre for repayments; a worker's home thereby becomes the bank's temporary office, and business is transacted in a relaxed atmosphere.

Each member of the Mandal pays a monthly contribution of Rs 1 to cover administrative costs and overheads. So far, Prema's house has served as the organization's office. Since efforts to get office space from the government have so far been unsuccessful, the Mandal now proposes to buy its own premises, one third of the money coming from the women's donations and the balance from bank loans.

Impact of the scheme

On the economic side the gains are that the women are no longer in debt to grocer-moneylenders, and are able to spend the extra income on basic necessities, or on improving their *bustee* room.

Equally important is its social impact, with participation in committee meetings, entertainment programmes, and in the bank scheme leading to greater confidence among the women. In the words of Leelatai, an Annapurna and also Vice-president of the Mandal:

Ninety-nine per cent of the women were illiterate, but now they can sign their names. Earlier they showed no motivation for education – today they are showing a desire to learn to read and write, to count and keep accounts. This is because it is related to their work and the women recognize its necessity and worth. Education is not something external, but something needed in everyday life. We are planning to start night classes soon.

Women have also started becoming more assertive within the family. Earlier, wife-beating was not uncommon. Now women say 'You can go and drink but you have no right to beat me.' Often they do not let the man back into the house. Before, if a woman behaved in this way to her husband, other women would criticize and ostracize her. Now that the women meet regularly, this sort of criticism has lessened.

Another interesting side-effect has been the women's response to the family planning programme:

The women are coming forward voluntarily to have sterilizations done. They are beginning to control their own bodies as they begin to gain more control of their lives. Another reason is that previously they could never find the time to go for an operation since it meant a month's rest which they could not afford. Now with a lump sum of money in their hands they can hire help for a month while they recuperate.

With encouragement from the Mandal and the banks, women have started to save and many have savings (of approximately Rs 200) in their own name for the first time in their lives. Competition between those involved in the same trade has begun to break down. Now, when a worker tries to change his eating place without paying, he is asked where he used to eat. The new Annapurna then checks whether all debts have been cleared. Cases of conflict or confusion are taken to the Mandal to be sorted out.

Conclusions

The Annapurna Mandal organization has succeeded against heavy odds. The nature of the women's work keeps them isolated from each other, and as self-employed workers, organizing within the traditional trade union structure is difficult. The fact that the women often sell services or products to members of the working class introduces an element of conflict between themselves and their worker customers.

In spite of these constraints, the experience of the Annapurna Mandal shows that it is possible to organize worker-housewives. And considering the tasks and the jobs that the Annapurnas do, an extended form of housework, it is possible that the experience could be the basis for organizing housewives *as housewives*. It is essential to develop new and different forms of organization amongst women, but these can only sustain themselves on a long-term basis if they materially benefit the women in some clear way.

From this analysis of the history of the Mandal, it is clear that two things were essential before the organization could be born: first, a woman with both the vision to break away from the accepted way of perceiving the problem and the courage, foresight and dedication to guide the programme through its difficulties; second, a small number of women from the community who were prepared to take a bold step.

The insistence on developing an *organization* of women was essential in making the scheme more than just a loan-giving programme to help individual women with their problems. Essential to developing a sense of community out of the existing isolation was the idea of having groups as intermediaries between the banks and the women, of having women from the area take on all responsibilities, and of gradually expanding the women's own potential.

However, there are still many limitations to the programme: working conditions have not been improved and the Annapurnas still work day after day in smoky kitchens for long hours, without any day of rest. Once the Mandal has acquired premises, it is hoped to open a cooperative wholesale store so as to provide cheaper and already cleaned grains which would substantially reduce the women's hours of work. The organization has yet to develop welfare schemes such as maternity benefits and health coverage, but a programme of regular health check-ups is planned once premises are obtained.

Regular holidays are still not possible, though occasionally Annapurnas do leave their homes to attend meetings, demonstrations, or entertainment programmes, but this gives rise to complaints from the customers, who have to serve themselves: having secured fixed hours of work and regular days off for themselves, they fail to recognize the legitimacy of similar claims on the part of those who serve them. The Mandals have not been able to draw out the implication of the worker role of the Annapurnas, and the workers continue to expect them to act as surrogate housewives. An examination of the nature of housework would help to convince them that housework is *work* like any other (and should have fixed hours) and not a woman's duty. [...]

Reprinted from the *Bulletin of the Institute of Development Studies*, vol. 12, no. 3, 1981, pp. 48–53.

NOTE

[1. 18 rupees = £1.]

REFERENCE

Sherov, Nancy, 1979, *A Study of Bank Loans on Annapurnas*. Financed by the Multiservice agency of the Bank of Baroda, unpublished MSW thesis, College of Social Work, Bombay.

28   'The Union is Our Mother'

GAIL OMVEDT

[...] Returning to Pune[1] after Bori Arab is like coming to another world. Originally an old political-educational capital that is now a major industrial centre, the city of Pune seems full of cosmopolitan turmoil and modern conveniences in contrast to the dusty barrenness and sleepiness of the countryside. At its heart the houses and palaces that represent the centuries-old heritage of grey-eyed Brahman aristocrats surrounded by the maze of streets of merchants, carpenters, brassmakers and all the artisan servants; beyond that the wide expanse of the newer upper classes with their tree-shaded bungalows and broader, straighter streets; beyond these the three- and four-storeyed apartment blocks of the bank, insurance company, lower-level clerical class, interspersed with the hutments of the poor. Beyond these, again, the deceptively sleepy reaches of the military cantonment, home of Christians, Parsis[2] and majors on one side; and on the other, in green fenced-off compounds, Vulcan Laval, David Brown, Sandvik, Traub-India, SKF, Kirloskar-Cummins – British-, German-, Swedish-, American-, Japanese-collaboration factories,[3] surrounded by the huts and hovels of workers, inadequate housing on the cleared land of former villages. Old elites, new elites, soldiers, workers; and interspersed with all the tiny shops, roadside stands, hutments, vegetable and fruit sellers, shoe repairmen, bicycle tyre pumpers, the Indian paraphernalia that fills what in more settled countries would be sidewalks; and on the roads the buses, handcarts, trucks, bicycles, motorscooters, motorcycles, motor rickshaws, and pedestrians who walk on the street because there is no room on the sidewalks.

Pune has all the appearance of a booming industrial city. Yet women have very little place in this development. They are to a small degree in the banks, the offices and the universities and colleges (but these are part of old Pune), and they are to be found in large numbers in the streets: middle class women shopping, visiting temples, strolling with their husbands in the evening; students going in clusters to coffee houses and queueing for buses; working class women striding through the streets with babies on their hips; construction workers carrying their pans and tools on their heads; housewives and servants carrying bags or large tin cans filled with grain on heads or hips. But women are not to be found in the new factories. With perhaps the minor exception of electronics assembly plants where young girls squint over delicate parts, industrial jobs are a male preserve in India.

Who are women workers, then? They are casual labourers and domestic servants; they are construction workers toiling under the hot sun on the new apartment buildings rising for the middle classes; they are workers who roll *bidis*, the small native cigarettes, for twelve hours a day in stuffy, crowded fume-filled rooms with babies on their laps. And, they are the street cleaners: the largest group of employed women in Pune – and the largest single organized work-force of women that I meet during my stay – are the municipal workers, the sweepers.

In Pune, when the streets are filling early in the morning with women bustling to buy early food, when the milk sellers make their deliveries, when windows are thrown open in the middle class apartments and the poor wander from their huts to nearby open places that serve as public latrines, the sweepers can be seen in the streets, stirring up the dirt and dust and scattered refuse of the day, shoving it to the side of the road, gathering it into round baskets, brooms whisking as they walk bent over, brooms flying . . . .

'We make the city clean: then why should we be considered unclean?' is the age-old cry of street sweepers in India. For these women and men who clean up the dust and dirt and excrement of towns and villages are Dalits or Untouchables, performing an updated version of their traditional caste service. In earlier days (and still in many small towns of India) their job included clearing out the 'night soil', pulling basins out from under latrines, carrying it on their heads, dumping it in stinking garbage carts. Now, with modern plumbing universal in Pune, this is not a major part of their job, though one group of city workers does take care of public toilets and nearly all those employed to clean apartment toilets are still Dalits. The majority of city employees simply clean the streets. Yet they are still all Dalits by caste, and the majority of them are women. Only the truck driving and hauling is done by men; the women are the sweepers.

These women are militant unionists. Municipal street sweepers were among the first workers in India to organize themselves; their attempts began in the nineteenth century. The Pune workers formed a union in 1930, first under the leadership of men of their own caste, then switching to a communist-led union that was more militant and less corrupt. They have won steady pay rises and a fair amount of permanent status, as well as benefits that include maternity leave, sick leave, two saris a year and city-provided housing. Consequently, where sweeper families once found it difficult to find husband or wives for their children – because even other Untouchables tended to consider those who performed the traditional duty as degraded – now their children are desirable mates indeed. In these days of stagnating employment, their well unionized positions are considered good jobs, and sons and daughters-in-law will inherit them. So the sweepers are women with some status, some financial independence, often the main support for their families; women who walk the streets they sweep with the oddly lilting yet dignified gait of the lower class workers of Pune.

But what does this economic independence really mean to the women? I am interested in learning about the sweepers, and my friends in the union want to find new ways to involve and mobilize the women. And so a meeting in the union hall is arranged.

I come with a student helper and Leela Bhosle, wife of union leader A. D. Bhosle, an activist herself and a friend of some of the workers. As the women in colourful red, green and blue saris crowd into the hall, the union activists preface the discussion with an ideological talk in which they – not I – throw out the new ideas about women's place, women's rights, the injustice of women having to do double work. It is a new and somewhat amazing experience for me to hear such whole-hearted espousal of *stri-mukti*, 'women's liberation', from male leaders, but it is a pattern that will be repeated later. The initial reaction of the Left to this concept, especially among those close to the masses and concerned about real organizing, is by no means the unbelieving ridicule often seen in the West; the resistance is there in more subtle ways, but this is now beside the point in this first 'meeting on behalf of women's year'.

We start the questions. What is their work like? Do they get the same pay as men? Yes, they say, due to the union: and also, due to the union, the supervisors don't dare to trouble them much. (This contrasts with the common tendency for women workers to be harassed sexually.) How many hours a day do they work? The count begins at 5.30am, when they rise, dress, and, after a cup of tea on the way to work (a proud right: to buy tea independently), gather at the work site for the morning 'sign-in', to 9.30 or 10 at night when they are finally able to sleep. In between are all the usual tasks of child care, shopping, cooking. And do men help at all?

Here there is general laughter. This is hardly the *dharma* (hereditary religious duty) of the male race! 'We may be tired, worn out, sick, still we have to drag ourselves up to do these things!' At this point Leela throws out a challenge – 'And when you come home dragging your feet to find not only your husband but even your children sitting around and tossing out orders for a glass of water – don't you get infuriated?' They laugh again, responding but sceptical.

What about child care? 'Where do you leave your children when you go to work?'

'Under a tree, in a basket, or some little girl takes care of them. Then anything can happen – some get burned by the fire, some fall and break their heads, something or other goes wrong. Don't we also feel love for our children? But we don't have time for love. There are no facilities.' So they complain, and the fact is that whatever promises and programmes there are for child care facilities, nursery schools and day care centres reach only a minority. The vast work of child care in India is done by relatives, but there are not enough grandmothers to go around, and no provision at work sites.

(And Leela comments: Such is the life of the poor who make things comfortable for the upper classes. Those rich women and men who sing the praises of 'family life' build their own daily comforts on the sacrifices of millions of ruined families!)

The big question I want to ask has to do with the attitudes of the women toward their work. But it is not adequate to simply ask 'Why do you work?' or 'Do you work for money or status or what?' This would only lead to incomprehension. Instead, taking my cue from a Bombay sociology graduate, I ask: 'Suppose your husband or son could get a job that paid 1,000 rupees, enough so you wouldn't have to work. Would you want to stay at home?'

And this provokes a tumultuous discussion. A woman says immediately, 'What do you think! Of course, why would we keep going exhausted to work? To do everything at home and then have to go to work is a hell of a life!'

There is some murmuring, then another voice rises from the back, 'Shut your mouth, woman, we aren't going to leave our jobs! It may be true our husband can get more money. We need our own life. Whether it's tobacco or betel nut[4] or tea, it may be any little thing we want, will he give it freely? And without raising his hand against us? If he doesn't behave well tomorrow, are we going to shut up beneath his blows?' And most seem to agree. 'Independence', 'respect', 'status' are abstract terms that only middle class women might relate to, but for the sweepers they have a concrete embodiment: the ability to be able to buy something of their own, even if only a cup of tea on the way to work or a small tin of chewing tobacco, the security of being able to get along alone. It is not something they want to give up.

And I want to ask about the union: Is there any neglect of women's issues? 'If you had some suggestions to make to union leaders about what kind of women's problems they might take up, what would you suggest?' But even this mild phrasing gets nowhere, for at least some of the women sense some implied insult to the union, and from the side of the room the old activist Sitabai, rising up like a gaunt wraith, strides over to shake her fist at me and close the discussion: 'The union is our mother!'

And in truth such extravagance seems to be shared. The sweepers are demonstrably loyal to their union, giving 100% participation in strikes, turning out for sit-ins, fasts or demonstrations, and coming out in numbers of 300 to 400 for the major marches of May Day and the union's anniversary. In broader strikes involving other categories of workers, who may be less ready to join the strike, many are ready to charge in, ignoring the police, and pull the recalcitrant scabs bodily out into the streets. Later, when I begin a survey of these women, I find that the union is practically the only political force in their lives. The national movement hardly touched them; they know little of contemporary political leaders. The only thing comparable to the union, for those who are Buddhists, is the movement led by Dr Ambedkar which resulted in the conversion to Buddhism; and these women will sometimes say, 'The Buddhist movement gave us self-respect, the union helps us fill our stomachs!' In any case, the sweepers are a vibrant example of the kind of union militancy of which women are capable if they are in a position to organize.

But what the union has concretely meant has to be seen in terms of individual lives, the history of personal struggles and the slow winning of dignity. The story of Tarabai, a 35-year-old divorcee with one child, may or may not be 'typical', but it shows the process of change.

Tarabai lives in Pandavnagar, one of several city-provided housing colonies for the workers. To reach it, you walk down one of the larger roads in the upper middle class section of Pune, turn past a small temple on a corner and walk down alongside a wall covered with mostly religious and a few political slogans, past fruit and vegetable sellers and construction workers coming home from work laden with tools, grass, provisions, babies, and pass a slum settlement of low clay huts with their musty smells and cowdung fires and open drains – this is Wadarwadi, home of the Wadar caste who provide so many of the construction workers of Pune. And then you come to Pandavnagar, with its rows of three-storeyed grey buildings, the paint peeling off except where some of the better-off workers have raised the funds to paint their section in bright new colours, lined up beside a central dusty yard where children play. In the evening when we come, the children shout and yell at us, women sit beside their doors gossiping and sorting rice or pulling lice out of each other's hair as they stare at us, and young boys giggle and point.

This is Pandavnagar, by working class standards high quality housing. For a minimal monthly rent, each family gets two rooms, and a bathroom and a toilet shared with the next apartment. This is almost luxurious; in Bombay equivalently paid workers are lucky to get one room with a partitioned-off bath area and a toilet at the end of the whole floor, while in the industrial suburbs of Pune workers may have to pay one-third of their salary for a single room. But – and here is the rub – not all of the 800 regular municipal workers live in their own city-provided apartment. Many, an uncounted number, sublease their flat and live in nearby slums like Wadarwadi, which may also house women who are temporary employees of the city. The reason the regular workers do this, though it is illegal, is usually to pay off debts. Practically every worker is in debt in India, and regular employees like the municipal workers have deductions owing to credit unions taken out of their pay cheques every month. Debts are incurred for a wide variety of reasons, weddings, illnesses, for any number of special expenditures, and simply for consumption, trying to support too many people on one person's salary.

For it turns out that the fate of these working women like Tarabai is highly linked to their family position. Working may give them some economic independence, but socially male domination still prevails. They are married young (from 12 to 15 or 16) and normally the husband and children they are stuck with become the determinants of their fate. If they have a working husband or son contributing to an overall family income, if somehow they don't have to support three or four adult non-workers, they can manage fairly well. But if not, if husbands and other adults are unemployed and particularly if they drink, their situation can be miserable indeed. And drink, the male's refuge from the miseries of daily life, unemployment and poverty, ravages the slums and villages of contemporary India.

Tarabai, for instance, a divorcee with no one to support but one daughter who is studying in a boarding school which gives concessional rates to low caste girls, can manage to have a cot, a radio, chairs, a cupboard to keep clothes in, a good set of kitchen utensils, and a goat tethered on a walkway outside to provide occasional milk; she is planning to buy a kitchen table-and-chair set – an aspiration to almost middle class consumption levels. Or, down the way, Sonabai, who has a large family but one that includes a working husband and a working son, can have a kitchen filled with brass vessels and cupboards and a certain amount of stored grain and two goats, and can be secure in the knowledge that her daughter-in-law, now living with her and taking care of most of the housework, will one day inherit her sweeper's job and be able to maintain her in her old age.

But Hirabai, a young woman downstairs from Tarabai, has no one to help her, only a single unemployed husband who is constantly drunk and beats her. If you enter Hirabai's apartment there is nothing to be seen, not a single piece of furniture, not a cot or a cupboard, only a piece of matting on which she sits nursing a scrawny baby. A few utensils in the kitchen; a bit of coarse millet; her existence is a struggle to survive from day to day just as much as that of the casual daily labourers in the countryside. It is very likely that soon, if she gets an offer, Hirabai will sublet her flat, the only thing she has left that she can get any money from.

So the family situation remains determinant for the sweepers; work only helps them manoeuvre a bit. Yet there are points when this manoeuvring becomes transformed into something more, into a real leap for independence. And this is why I want to hear the story of Tarabai's life, in fact why Leela and I have come to Pandavnagar.

'My name is Tarabai Namdev Sonavane,' she tells us, having passed around the tea and sitting now before the tape-recorder, a bit self-consciously but ever ready to move into the drama of a tale. 'Before that, it was Tarabai Laxman Kshirsikar – my husband's name.' Which means that she is using her maiden name, unusual even for a divorced Indian woman.

Tarabai was born in a village in Pune district, married when she was seven, and went to live with her husband 'when I came of age' nine years later. After some time she had a daughter, but no son, 'and this began to have an effect on my mother-in-law, father-in-law and all. They began to harass me and say, "She can't have a son, let's marry our son to a different woman". And they were really troubling me . . .'

By this time she was working for the city council, through her mother-in-law who was a sweeper. Tarabai worked as a kind of apprentice, 'doing my mother-in-law's work' first and then started to do the same for another woman worker, who paid her privately. In effect she was doing a major part of two women's jobs, without any official employment, and getting paid almost nothing; such arrangements are common in job-scarce India. But the second woman encouraged her to petition the city for official work, and as a result she was hired to do road repair, first for only four to five days a month, then by 1969 on a full-time basis. It was at this point, when her daughter Lata was five, that the real trouble started.

'I began devoting time to my father, who was very old. My mother and father began to come and stay with me, for a few days at a time. I was giving them grain too. Then my older brother's second marriage was arranged, and the next day I was thrown out of the house! I'll tell you how it happened. My in-laws said that it was because I was having an affair with the man next door, but really they didn't like me helping my parents.' What infuriated her in-laws was that Tarabai, already disgraced for not having produced a son, was defying the marriage bond which compels a young wife to forget the family of her birth and give all her attention, toil and earnings to her husband's family. 'A woman when young should be under the control of her father, when adult under the control of her husband, and when old under the control of her son,' wrote Manu, the Hindu 'lawgiver'. The break that comes with marriage is sharp and traumatic. A woman is considered to have no rights or responsibilities to her blood relations after that, and 'under the control of her husband' means normally under the control of her mother-in-law. But Tarabai, standing on the strength of her new earnings, was defying custom by giving money to her father and brother.

'I remember how it happened,' she says. 'We went to work in the morning, my husband and I, then my guests came and my husband and I and all of them sat and drank tea in a restaurant. My brother's new in-laws told me, "You are responsible for them now".' (That is, since her brother was at that time unemployed, Tarabai was being viewed as the family earner.) 'Then my husband said, "Tara, give me a rupee". I said "Why?" He said, "I need it". So he took the rupee, and went somewhere on his cycle, and after an hour came back, and I, my mother, father, brother were still talking and drinking tea, and then we all went to the house . . .'

What is abnormal in this situation? From a traditional point of view, many things. Indian women should not be expected to 'take responsibility' for their brother's family. Nor should they really be sitting in teashops in the first place entertaining guests. Nor should husbands ask, *have* to ask, their wives for money. Nor, going beyond this, should wives presume to ask why. But Tarabai was now the main earner in a job-scarce society. And taking tea out, normally in a shop on the way to work in the morning, has now become one of the small but valued luxuries of life of the municipal workers. And, standing on the strength of these small collective gains and her own financial independence, Tarabai, already defiant in the face of her in-laws' harassment and insinuations, provokes her husband ...

'Then we went home, and my people, my husband and the people of the house, about eight to ten of us, were sitting to eat when my mother-in-law started swearing at my father, swearing in the language of our community and saying, "You're living like a pimp off your daughter's earnings!" So I said, "Look here, if you want to say anything, say it to me, but there's no reason to talk like that to my father". Then my mother-in-law said, "Live with your father; if not, live with your brother".' (What she was implying was sexual relations in both cases.) 'On hearing this I started to cry. So I said, "We'll take this to court," but my father said, "No, your brother's marriage was illegal, and if you go to court who knows what complications there will be". And at that point my mother-in-law took all my things and threw them outside and locked the door on us.'

So they went to the bus station, where Tarabai, her brother, father, mother and daughter sat until evening, 'And no one came, not my husband nor even my mother-in-law,' she says, crying, 'I felt very bad.' But though her father urged her, she refused to go home.

Instead she slept in the bus station with her daughter and went to work alone the next morning. Then began her period of trial, working, without a home, enduring the threats of her husband who would come drunken to harass her at work, staying for a time with a fellow working woman but forced to leave that house because of the continual visits and threats of her in-laws, often taking baths with her daughter at street pumps. 'I had to wear one sari for seven days once, seven days,' says Tarabai, her indignation showing the real consciousness of cleanliness among these lower caste workers who clean the streets and latrines. During this time Tarabai didn't go to the union, of which she had as yet little experience; rather she appealed for help several times to her supervisors (the 'sahibs') but with little result. In fact, it was women who helped her – her fellow worker, and a middle class woman living in the area of her work who allowed her use of a water tap for bathing ...

Finally, after three months, Tarabai's divorce came through. 'They asked my husband, "Do you want to live with your wife?" and he said no. Then they asked me, "Will you live with your husband?" and I said no; and he was saying that I had run away with another man, and I said, "At least leave me my honour!"'

But the divorce was by no means the end of her troubles. Her angered in-laws levied a court case against her and the man next door, accusing him of kidnapping her, and Tarabai was again dragged to court, where she related her whole story and added with great indignation, 'Even people who are going to be hanged are allowed one dinner in peace, but my in-laws didn't even let my parents eat!' After this case failed, Tarabai then found she had to fight for her very job:

'After that, my husband, mother-in-law, his brother and all sent a notice to the municipality saying, "She got this job through my influence and she is no longer my wife; she's run away with another man, so she shouldn't have the job",' and Tarabai had to deal with this. What was involved here was the custom of 'inheritance rights' found in many organized working class jobs: a son has first claim to his father's position on retirement, and a daughter-*in-law* 'inherits' her mother-*in-law*'s position. What such a right does, in a way, is to provide a substitute for the pensions of white-collar employment, and the nature of the inheritance, of course, is a faithful reflection of the Indian family system, for it is the son and daughter-in-law who care for the old on retirement, not a daughter who is married off to another family.

But Tarabai, who was defying all these customs and attempting to stand on her own feet, won this fight too. All this she had done on her own, but she was developing contacts with the union, and went to A.D., the union leader, for her own next minor initiative, saying 'I want to change my name, I don't want to keep my husband's name, I want my father's name back.' And after accomplishing that, 'I've been in the union, in marches, meetings, strikes up to the present. I've been carrying on with the union as my support. Let me die under the red flag, there is no other support.'

The union, she says, is her *sansar*, her 'daily life'. But what does it all mean to her? Tarabai still can't read, and has no knowledge of the Marxist ideology that motivates union leaders like A.D. and Leela. What is the ultimate aim of all their movement and strike activity, I ask, and she replies with enthusiasm, after a period of puzzlement and a bit of prompting from Leela, that 'union rule' should come. Months later, when I meet Tarabai during a strike – the workers all sitting on an initial one day fast in demand for a bonus – she is more specific:

'How many days will you stay on strike?'

'Until we get our bonus. We will fast first, then go on strike, then face the police blows or whatever, but we will go ahead.' By now this is almost old stuff to Tarabai.

'And if the city refuses to negotiate?' I ask.

'If the city refuses! Who will do the work? Their round-sari'd housebound wives? If they refuse, the garbage will rot on the city streets. We do the work!'

'And if the police come . . .?'

'We don't care if the police come, we are fighting for our class rights!' And I ask again about their ultimate goal, and one of the more politicized workers says, the establishment of a toilers' state. What is a toilers' state? I ask Tarabai.

'Capitalists, moneylenders, all those Marwaris must go and the peasants' and workers' state must come!'

'But yesterday in the meeting you talked about women's liberation – so what is the connection between women's liberation and the toilers' state?'

'When the workers' state comes, then women's liberation will also come. It will come a little, why not? The exploitation of women will become a little less. Now who rules? – the big people, the moneylenders, the bosses, the landlords, the parasites. In this situation women's liberation is difficult!'

But if this all sounds still somewhat abstract, then compare Tarabai's vivid depictions of the arrogant ways of supervisors and the defiance by herself and other workers, the dirty drudging toil of the job of sweeping, and – above all, and increasingly – the innate superiority of women who, she is convinced, are stronger than men, coping with two jobs and various male harassments. These are not at all abstract. And my most striking memory, finally, is sitting with Tarabai and Leela in a small railway worker's house, grumbling about the ways of husbands, joking over tea until Tarabai almost spontaneously bursts into a mocking song about her husband, a satirical version of the custom in which husbands and wives use each other's name in a rhymed couplet, and then at the end, when everyone is helpless with laughter, turns to me and says, 'Gail-*bai*, don't marry. Don't marry.'

SOURCE

See Reading 22.

NOTES

[1. Also known as Poona; city in Maharashtra.]
[2. City-dwelling merchants originating from Persia and adherents of the Zoroastrian religion.]
[3. Industries involving both Indian and foreign capital.]
[4. Mild stimulant used widely in India.]

29   At the International Women's Year Tribunal

DOMITILA BARRIOS DE CHUNGARA

Editors' introduction

Domitila Barrios de Chungara was a women's leader and miner's wife in Siglo XX, the most important tin-mining community in Bolivia. It was nationalized in 1952 and is now run by the *Corporación Minera de Bolivia* (COMIBOL) which also owns and controls the camp and the services. Siglo XX has 5,000 families and has had a long history of union struggles. It has been the site of several massacres of miners by the army, which Domitila refers to in her account (29(ii)).

In one of these periods of struggle, in 1961, the union leaders were imprisoned. Their wives staged a successful hunger strike in the capital, La Paz, and then decided to form a Housewives' Committee (referred to in the account as the 'housewives' front') to work in alliance with the unionized mineworkers. It participated in the struggles of the union over living and working conditions and became affiliated to the *Central Obrera Boliviana* (Bolivian Workers' Congress). The Housewives' Committee was also involved in struggles over political rights and tried to organize women around their own problems, particularly unemployment.

The Committee faced many problems: the difficulties of organizing as housewives; lack of support, especially at first, from the men in the union; family problems when husbands were sacked because of their own or their wives' militancy; political repression and harassment from the government (Reading 29(ii) reveals the difficulties Domitila experienced in leaving the country to participate in the International Women's Year Tribunal). Here we have reprinted two extracts which describe the conditions in which the miners' wives lived and Domitila's reactions to the International Women's Year Conference.

Domitila de Chungara was forced into exile in July 1980 when the Bolivian government was taken over by a military coup. In the autumn of 1981 all trade unions were made illegal and the offices of the *Central Obrera Boliviana* were demolished. Although the mineworkers and the Housewives' Committee are not allowed to operate, meetings and elections of leaders in the mines continue.

(i) How a miner's wife spends her day

My day begins at four in the morning, especially when my compañero[1] is on the first shift. I prepare his breakfast. Then I have to prepare the *salteñas*,[2] because I make about one hundred *salteñas* every day and I sell them in the street. I do this in order to make up for what my husband's wage doesn't cover in terms of our necessities. The night before, we prepare the dough and at four in the morning I make the *salteñas* while I feed the kids. The kids help me: they peel potatoes and carrots and make the dough.

Then the ones that go to school in the morning have to get ready, while I wash the clothes I left soaking overnight.

At eight I go out to sell. The kids that go to school in the afternoon help me. We have to go to the company store and bring home the staples. And in the store there are immensely long lines and you have to wait there until eleven in order to stock up. You have to line up for meat, for vegetables, for oil. So it's just one line after another. Since everything's in a different place, that's how it has to be. So all the time I'm selling *salteñas*, I line up to buy my supplies at the store. I run up to the counter to get the things and the kids sell. Then the kids line up and I sell. That's how we do it.

From the hundred *salteñas* I prepare, I get an average of 20 pesos[3] a day, because if I sell them all today, I get 50 pesos, but if tomorrow I only sell thirty, then I lose out. That's why I say that the average earning is 20 pesos a day. And I'm lucky because people know me and buy from me. But some of my women friends only make from 5 to 10 pesos a day.

From what we earn between my husband and me, we can eat and dress. Food is very expensive: 28 pesos for a kilo of meat, 4 pesos for carrots, 6 pesos for onions. . . . Considering that my compañero earns 28 pesos a day, that's hardly enough, is it?

Clothing, why that's even more expensive! So I try to make whatever I can. We don't ever buy ready-made clothes. We buy wool and knit. At the beginning of each year, I also spend about 2,000 pesos on cloth and a pair of shoes for each of us. And the company discounts some of that each month from my husband's wage. On the pay slips that's referred to as the 'bundle'. And what happens is that before we've finished paying the 'bundle' our shoes have worn out. That's how it is.

Well, then, from eight to eleven in the morning I sell the *salteñas*, I do the shopping in the grocery store, and I also work at the Housewives' Committee, talking with the sisters who go there for advice.

At noon, lunch has to be ready because the rest of the kids have to go to school.

In the afternoon I have to wash clothes. There are no laundries. We use troughs and have to go get the water from the pump.

I've also got to correct the kids' homework and prepare everything I'll need to make the next day's *salteñas*.

Sometimes there are urgent matters to be resolved by the committee in the afternoon. So then I have to stop washing in order to see about them. The work in the committee is daily. I have to be there at least two hours. It's totally volunteer work.

The rest of the things have to get done at night. The kids bring home quite a lot of homework from school. And they do it at night, on a little table, a chair, or a little box. And sometimes all of them have homework and so one of them has to work on a tray that I put on the bed.

When my husband works in the morning, he goes to sleep at ten at night and so do the kids. When he works in the afternoon, then he's out most of the night, right? And when he works the night shift, he only comes back the next day. So I have to adapt myself to those schedules.

Generally we can't count on someone else to help around the house. What the husband earns is too little and really we all have to help out, like my making *salteñas*. Some women help out by knitting, others sew clothes, others make rugs, others sell things in the street. Some women can't help out and then the situation is really difficult.

It's because there aren't any places to work. Not just for the women, but also for the young men who come back from the army. And unemployment makes our children irresponsible, because they get used to depending on their parents, on their family. Often they get married without having gotten a job, and then they come home with their wives to live.

So that's how we live. That's what our day is like. I generally go to bed at midnight. I sleep four or five hours. We're used to that.

Well, I think that all of this proves how the miner is doubly exploited, no? Because, with such a small wage, the woman has to do much more in the home. And really that's unpaid work that we're doing for the boss, isn't it?

And by exploiting the miner, they don't only exploit his wife too, but there are times they even exploit the children. Because there's so much to do in the house that even the little kids have to work; for example, they have to get the meat, fetch the water. And sometimes they have to stand in line a long, long time, getting squashed and pushed around. When there's a shortage of meat in the mining camp, those lines get so long that sometimes children even die in the crush to get meat. There's a terrible frenzy. I've known children who died like that, with fractured ribs. And why? Because we mothers have so much to do at home that we send our children to line up. And sometimes there's such a terrible crush that that happens: they squash the kids. In recent years there've been various cases like that. And there's also something else you should take into account and that's the damage done to the kids who don't go to school because they have to run errands. When you wait for meat for two or three days and it doesn't come, that means lining up all day long. And the kids miss school for two or three days.

In other words, they try not to give the worker any sort of comfort. He's got to work it all out for himself. And that's that. In my case, for example, my husband works, I work, I make my children work, so there are several of us working to support the family. And the bosses get richer and richer and the workers' conditions get worse and worse.

But in spite of everything we do, there's still the idea that women don't work, because they don't contribute economically to the home, that only the husband works because he gets a wage. We've often come across that difficulty.

One day I got the idea of making a chart. We put as an example the price of washing clothes per dozen pieces and we figured out how many dozens of items we washed a month. Then the cook's wage, the babysitter's, the servant's. We figured out everything that we miners' wives do every day. Adding it all up, the wage needed to pay us for what we do in the home, compared to the wages of a cook, a washerwoman, a babysitter, a servant, was much higher than what the men earned in the mine for a month. So that way we made our compañeros understand that we really work, and even more than they do in a certain sense. And that we even contribute more to the household with what we save. So, even though the state doesn't recognize what we do in the home, the country benefits from it, because we don't receive a single penny for this work.

And as long as we continue in the present system, things will always be like this. That's why I think it's so important for us revolutionaries to win that first battle in the home. And the first battle to be won is to let the woman, the man, the children participate in the struggle of the working class, so that the home can become a stronghold that the enemy can't overcome. Because if you have the enemy inside your own house, then it's just one more weapon that our common enemy can use toward a dangerous end. That's why it's really necessary that we have very clear ideas about the whole situation and that we throw out forever that bourgeois idea that the woman should stay home and not get involved in other things, in union or political matters, for example. Because, even if she's only at home, she's part of the whole system of exploitation that her compañero lives in anyway, working in the mine or in the factory or wherever – isn't that true?

(ii) At the International Women's Year Tribunal

In 1974, a Brazilian movie director came to Bolivia, commisioned by the United Nations. She was travelling through Latin America looking for women leaders, to find out their opinions about women's conditions, how much and in what way they participate in bettering their situation.

With regard to Bolivia, she was very intrigued by the 'housewives' front' which she'd heard about abroad and, also, she'd seen the women of Siglo XX acting in the movie *El Coraje del Pueblo* (The Courage of the People). So, after asking for permission from the government, she went into the mines. And she came to visit me. She liked what I said and she said it was important that everything I knew should be told to the rest of the world. She asked me if I could travel. I said I couldn't, that I didn't have money to even travel in my own country.

So she asked me if I'd agree to participate in a women's congress that was going to take place in Mexico, if she was able to get money for me. I had just found out that there was an International Women's Year.

Although I didn't really believe it much, I said yes, in that case I could go. But I thought it was just a promise like so many others and I didn't pay much attention to it.

When I got the telegram saying that I was invited by the United Nations, I was quite surprised and disconcerted. I called a meeting of the committee and all the compañeras[4] agreed that it would be good for me to travel, along with one more compañera. But there wasn't enough for two of us to go. The next day I went before a meeting of union leaders and rank-and-file delegates and gave them my report and they agreed that I should participate in the event and they even helped me economically so that I could begin making the arrangements.

So with some other compañeras I went to La Paz and we looked into the details, we got guarantees, and I stayed there alone to finish the arrangements. Several days went by. It got to look like I wouldn't be able to make the trip because they didn't want to give me the travel permit.

And it turns out that some Siglo XX leaders arrived in La Paz and were surprised to see I hadn't left. So they went with me to the secretariat of the Ministry of the Interior. And they asked:

'What's happening with the compañera? Why isn't she in Mexico already? The International Women's Year Conference opens today. What's happened here? Is it or isn't it International Women's Year? Do our wives have the right to participate in this conference, or can only your wives go there?'

And they told me:

'Well, compañera, since they don't want to let you go, let's leave. Even though you have an invitation from the United Nations, they don't want to let you go to that conference. So we're going to complain to the United Nations. And not only that: we're going to have a work stoppage in protest. Come with us, compañera.'

They were all set to take me out of the ministry when the guys there reacted:

'But . . . why didn't we start there in the first place! One moment, one moment, don't get so hot and bothered. If the lady has an invitation from the United Nations, we should have started there. Where's the invitation?'

The invitation! Every single day, at every turn, I was asked for the copy. And with the experience the miners have, they'd made lots of copies of it. So of course, one copy would get lost and I'd make another. And so on. And the original, well, the leaders themselves had it, because if the first copies got used up, they could make others.

I gave them one more copy; and after an hour, more or less, they gave me my documents. Everything was okay, everything was ready. The plane left the next day at nine in the morning.

When I was about to board the plane, a young lady from the Ministry of the Interior came over to me. I'd seen her there on various occasions, hanging on to her papers. She came over and said:

'Ay, señora! So, you got your pass? I'm so happy! You deserve it. I congratulate you! How I'd like to be in your shoes, so I could see Mexico! Congratulations!'

But then, very mysterious, she went on:

'Ay, but señora, your return to the country depends a lot on what you say there. So it's not a question of talking about any old thing . . . you've got to think it out well. Above all, you've got to think of your children who you're leaving behind. I'm giving you good advice. Have a good time.'

I thought about my responsibility as a mother and as a leader and so my role in Mexico seemed very difficult to me, thinking of what that young lady had said to me. I felt I was between the devil and the deep blue sea, as we say. But I was determined to carry out the mission the compañeros and compañeras had entrusted me with.

From La Paz we went to Lima, then to Bogotá, and finally to Mexico.

During the trip I thought . . . I thought that I'd never imagined I'd be travelling in a plane, and even less to such a far-off country as Mexico. Never, for we were so poor that sometimes we hardly had anything to eat and we couldn't even travel around our own country. I thought about how I'd always wanted to know my homeland from corner to corner . . . and now I was going so far away. This made me feel happy and sad at the same time. How I would have liked other compañeras and compañeros to have the same opportunity!

In the plane, everyone was speaking in other languages, chatting, laughing, drinking, playing. I couldn't talk to anyone. It was as if I wasn't even there. When we changed planes in Bogotá, I met a Uruguayan woman who was also going to Mexico to participate in the Tribunal and so then I had someone to talk to.

When we got to Mexico, I was impressed by the fact that there was a bunch of young people talking all different languages and they were there to meet all of us who were arriving. And they asked who was coming to the International Women's Year Conference. They made it easy for all of us to get through customs. Then I went to the hotel they told me to go to.

In Bolivia I'd read in the papers that for International Women's Year there'd be two places: one, the 'Conference', was for the official representatives of the governments of all the countries, another, the 'Tribunal', was for the representatives of the non-governmental organizations.

The Bolivian government sent its delegates to the Conference. And these women travelled making fancy statements, saying that in Bolivia more than in any other place, women had achieved equality with men. And they went to the Conference to say that. I was the only Bolivian woman invited for the Tribunal. There I met other Bolivian compañeras, but they were living in Mexico.

So I had this idea that there'd be two groups: one, on the government level, where those upper class ladies would be; and the other, on the non-government level, where people like me would be, people with similar problems, you know, poor people. It was like a dream for me! Goodness, I said to myself, I'll be meeting peasant women and working women from all over the world. All of them are going to be just like us, oppressed and persecuted.

That's what I thought, see, because of what it said in the papers.

In the hotel I made friends with an Ecuadorian woman and went with her to the place where the Tribunal was being held. But I couldn't go till Monday. The sessions had already begun on Friday.

We went to a very big hall where there were four or five hundred women. The Ecuadorian said:

'Come on, compañera. Here's where they talk about the most important problems women have. So here's where we should make our voices heard.'

There were no more seats. So we sat on some steps. We were very enthusiastic. We'd already missed a day of the Tribunal and we wanted to catch up, get up to date on what had been happening, find out what so many women were thinking, what they were saying about International Women's Year, what problems most concerned them.

It was my first experience and I imagined I'd hear things that would make me get ahead in life, in the struggle, in my work.

Well, at that moment a *gringa* went over to the microphone with her blonde hair and with some things around her neck and her hands in her pockets, and she said to the assembly:

'I've asked for the microphone so I can tell you about my experience. Men should give us a thousand and one medals because we, the prostitutes, have the courage to go to bed with so many men.'

A lot of women shouted 'Bravo!' and applauded.

Well, my friend and I left because there were hundreds of prostitutes in there talking about their problems. And we went into another room. There were the lesbians. And there, also, their discussion was about how 'they feel happy and proud to love another woman . . . that they should fight for their rights. . . .' Like that.

Those weren't my interests. And for me it was incomprehensible that so much money should be spent to discuss those things in the Tribunal. Because I'd left my compañero with the seven kids and him having to work in the mine every day. I'd left my country to let people know what my homeland's like, how it suffers, how in Bolivia the charter of the United Nations isn't upheld. I wanted to tell people all that and hear what they would say to me about other exploited countries and the other groups that have already liberated themselves. And to run into those other kinds of problems . . . I felt a bit lost. In other rooms, some women stood up and said: men are the enemy . . . men create wars, men create nuclear weapons, men beat women . . . and so what's the first battle to be carried out to get equal rights for women? First you have to declare war against men. If a man has ten mistresses, well, the woman should have ten lovers also. If a man spends all his money at the bar, partying, the women have to do the same thing. And when we've reached that level, then men and women can link arms and start struggling for the liberation of their country, to improve the living conditions in their country.

That was the mentality and the concern of several groups, and for me it was a really rude shock. We spoke very different languages, no? And that made it difficult to work in the Tribunal. Also, there was a lot of control over the microphone.

So a group of Latin American women got together and we changed all that. And we made our common problems known, what we thought women's progress was all about, how the majority of women live. We also said that for us the first and main task isn't to fight against our compañeros, but with them to change the system we live in for another, in which men and women will have the right to live, to work, to organize.

At first you couldn't really notice how much control there was in the Tribunal. But as the speeches and statements were made, things started to change. For example, the women who defended prostitution, birth control, and all those things, wanted to impose their ideas as basic problems to be discussed in the Tribunal. For us they were real problems, but not the main ones.

For example, when they spoke of birth control, they said that we shouldn't have so many children living in such poverty, because we didn't even have enough to feed them. And they wanted to see birth control as something which would solve all the problems of humanity and malnutrition.

But, in reality, birth control, as those women presented it, can't be applied in my country. There are so few Bolivians by now that if we limited birth even more, Bolivia would end up without people. And then the wealth of our country would remain as a gift for those who want to control us completely, no? It's not that we ought to be living like we are, in miserable conditions. All that could be different, because Bolivia's a country with lots of natural resources. But our government prefers to see things their way, to justify the low level of life of the Bolivian people and the very low wages it pays the workers. And so they resort to indiscriminate birth control.

In one way or another, they tried to distract the Tribunal with problems that weren't basic. So we had to let the people know what was fundamental for us in all of that. Personally, I spoke several times. Short speeches, because we could only use the microphone for two minutes.

The movie *La Doble Jornada* (The Double Day), filmed by the Brazilian compañera who invited me to the Tribunal, was also useful in orienting people who didn't have any idea of what the life of a peasant woman or working woman is like in Latin America. In *La Doble Jornada* they show the women's lives, especially in relation to work. There you see how women live in the United States, in Mexico, in Argentina. There's a big contrast. But even more so when you see the part about Bolivia, because the compañera interviewed a worker in Las Lamas who was pregnant. In the interview she asked her: 'Why aren't you taking it easy since you're expecting a baby?' The working woman said that she couldn't because she had to earn a living for her children and her husband too, because he's retired[5] and his pension is very small. 'And the pension?' asked the Brazilian woman. Then the miner's wife explained that her husband had left the mine absolutely ruined physically and that all the money from the pension was spent trying to cure him. And that's why now she had to work, her children too, in order to support her husband.

Well, that was pretty strong stuff, and dramatic, no? And the compañeras at the Tribunal realized that I hadn't lied when I spoke about our situation.

When the movie was over, since I'd also been in it, they asked me to speak. So I said the situation was due to the fact that no government had bothered to create jobs for poor women. That the only work women do that's recognized is housework and, in any case, housework is done for free. Because, for example, they give me 14 pesos a month, in other words, two-thirds of a dollar a month, which is the family subsidy that's added to my husband's wage. What are 14 Bolivian pesos worth? With 14 pesos you can buy two bottles of milk or half a box of tea. . . .

That's why – I told them – you have to understand that we won't be able to find any solution to our problems as long as the capitalist system in which we live isn't changed.

Many of these women said that they'd only just begun to agree with me. Several of them wept.

The day the women spoke out against imperialism, I spoke too. And I said how we live totally dependent on foreigners for everything, how they impose what they want on us, economically as well as culturally.

In the Tribunal I learned a lot also. In the first place, I learned to value the wisdom of my people even more. There, everyone who went up to the microphone said: 'I'm a professional person, I represent such and such organization. . . .' And bla-bla-bla, she gave her speech. 'I'm a teacher', 'I'm a lawyer', 'I'm a journalist', said the others. And bla-bla-bla, they'd begin to give their opinion.

Then I'd say to myself: 'Here there are professionals, lawyers, teachers, journalists who are going to speak. And me . . . what am I doing in this?' And I felt a bit insecure, unsure of myself. I couldn't work up the guts to speak. When I went up to the microphone for the first time, standing before so many 'titled' people, I introduced myself, feeling like a nothing, and I said: 'Well, I'm the wife of a mine worker from Bolivia.' I was still afraid, see?

I worked up the courage to tell them about the problems that were being discussed there. Because that was my obligation. And I stated my ideas so that everyone in the world could hear us, through the Tribunal.

That led to my having a discussion with Betty Friedan, who is the great feminist leader in the United States. She and her group had proposed some points to amend the 'World Plan of Action'. But these were mainly feminist points and we didn't agree with them because they didn't touch on some problems that are basic for Latin American women.

Betty Friedan invited us to join them. She asked us to stop our 'warlike activity' and said that we were being 'manipulated by men', that 'we only thought about politics', and that we'd completely ignored women's problems, 'like the Bolivian delegation does, for example,' she said.

So I asked for the floor. But they wouldn't give it to me. And so I stood up and said:

'Please forgive me for turning this Tribunal into a market-place. But I was mentioned and I have to defend myself. I was invited to the Tribunal to talk about women's rights and in the invitation they sent me there was also the document approved by the United Nations which is its charter, where women's right to participate, to organize, is recognized. And Bolivia signed that charter, but in reality it's only applied there to the bourgeoisie.'

I went on speaking that way. And a lady, who was the president of the Mexican delegation, came up to me. She wanted to give me her own interpretation of the International Women's Year Tribunal's slogan, which was 'equality, development, and peace'. And she said:

'Let's speak about us, señora. We're women. Look, señora, forget the suffering of your people. For a moment, forget the massacres. We've talked enough about that. We've heard you enough. Let's talk about us . . . about you and me . . . well, about women.'

So I said:

'All right, let's talk about the two of us. But if you'll let me, I'll begin. Señora, I've known you for a week. Every morning you show up in a different outfit and on the other hand, I don't. Every day you show up all made up and combed like someone who has time to spend in an elegant beauty parlour and who can spend money on that, and yet I don't. I see that each afternoon you have a chauffeur in a car waiting at the door of this place to take you home, and yet I don't. And in order to show up here like you do, I'm sure you live in a really elegant home, in an elegant neighbourhood, no? And yet we miners' wives only have a small house on loan to us, and when our husbands die or get sick or are fired from the company, we have ninety days to leave the house and then we're in the street.

'Now, señora, tell me: is your situation at all similar to mine? Is my situation at all similar to yours? So what equality are we going to speak of between the two of us? If you and I aren't alike, if you and I are so different? We can't, at this moment, be equal, even as women, don't you think?'

But at that moment, another Mexican woman came up and said:

'Listen you, what do you want? She's the head of the Mexican delegation and she has the right to speak first. Besides, we've been very tolerant here with you, we've heard you over the radio, on the television, in the papers, in the Tribunal. I'm tired of applauding you.'

It made me mad that she said that, because it seemed to me that the problems I presented were being used then just to turn me into some kind of play character who should be applauded. I felt they were treating me like a clown.

'Listen, señora,' I said to her. 'Who asked for your applause? If problems could be solved that way, I wouldn't have enough hands to applaud and I certainly wouldn't have had to come from Bolivia to Mexico, leaving my children behind, to speak here about our problems. Keep your applause to yourself, because I've received the most beautiful applause of my life, and that was from the calloused hands of the miners.'

And we had a pretty strong exchange of words.

In the end they said to me:

'Well, you think you're so important. Get up there and speak.'

So, I went up and spoke. I made them see that they don't live in our world. I made them see that in Bolivia human rights aren't respected and they apply what we call 'the law of the funnel': broad for some, narrow for others. That those ladies who got together to play canasta and applaud the government have full guarantees, full support. But women like us, housewives, who get organized to better our people, well, they beat us up and persecute us. They couldn't see all those things. They couldn't see the suffering of my people, they couldn't see how our compañeros are vomiting their lungs bit by bit, in pools of blood. They didn't see how underfed our children are. And, of course, they didn't know, as we do, what it's like to get up at four in the morning and go to bed at eleven or twelve at night, just to be able to get all the housework done, because of the lousy conditions we live in.

'You,' I said, 'what can you possibly understand about all that? For you, the solution is fighting with men. And that's it. But for us it isn't that way, that isn't the basic solution.'

When I finished saying all that, moved by the anger I felt, I left the platform.

And many women came up to me, and at the exit from the hall, many were happy and said I should go back to the Tribunal and represent the Latin American women who were there.

I felt ashamed to think I hadn't been able to evaluate the wisdom of the people well enough. Because, look: I, who hadn't studied in the university, or even gone to school, I, who wasn't a teacher or a professional or a lawyer or a professor, what had I done in the Tribunal? What I'd said was only what I'd heard my people say ever since I was little, my parents, my compañeros, the leaders, and I saw that the people's experience is the best schooling there is. What I learned from the people's life was the best teaching. And I wept to think: how great is my people!

We Latin American women issued a document about the way we see the role of women in underdeveloped countries, with everything we felt was important to say on that occasion. And the press published it.

Another thing that I got out of the Tribunal was meeting compañeras from other countries, especially the Bolivians, Argentines, Uruguayans, Chileans, who'd been in similar situations to those I'd experienced in prisons, jails, and all those problems. I learned a lot from them.

I think I fulfilled the mission that the compañeras and compañeros from Siglo XX gave me. In the Tribunal we were with a lot of women from all over the world, and we made everyone who was represented there aware of my country.

It was also a great experience being with so many women and seeing how many, many people are dedicated to the struggle for the liberation of their oppressed peoples.

I also think it was important for me to see once again – and on that occasion in contact with more than five thousand women from all over – how the interests of the bourgeoisie really aren't our interests.

Extracted from Dimitila Barrios de Chungara, *Let Me Speak!*, Stage 1, London 1978, pp. 32–6/194–204.

NOTES

[1. Compañero here means her husband.]
2. A Bolivian small pie, filled with meat, potatoes, hot pepper, and other spices.
[3. About 44 Bolivian pesos = £1.]
[4. Sisters or comrades.]
5. As an invalid. For the majority of miners, the invalid condition is caused by silicosis.

Part Four

Understanding Struggles

ROBIN COHEN

At dusk, two Mauritian sugar-cane cutters carefully cut off the long central stem of an aloe plant. They discussed briefly the appropriate length, then determined on a piece about 15 inches long. One end was carefully hollowed out and stuffed with nearly two boxes of tightly packed matchsticks. This incendiary device, with the slow-burning pith of the aloe acting as a fuse, was strategically placed to catch the strong gusts of wind coming in from the sea, while the matchsticks were covered with a handful of wilted strippings from the cane. Back at the village the two men drank quietly with their companions in the local store. When the dull glow appeared on the hillside, they walked home. Work tomorrow. The estate-owner, one of the score of Franco–Mauritians who owned the sugar industry, had laid off many of his workers the previous day. Too much cane had been cut and there was a log jam at the estate mill. Now the burnt field had to be cut within forty-eight hours if anything was to be rescued. The sirdar would be rounding up the labourers in the morning.   (Field Notes, Mauritius, 1976)

A pungent odour streamed from one corner of Mokola market. An old woman was selling newspaper wraps of dried 'Indian Hemp' for one shilling a piece. Labourers, mainly from the Public Works' Department, squatted at the side of the road and sucked deeply on their joints. 'It is our reward for a day's work', they said.
                              (Field Notes, Ibadan, 1968)

Initially the workers' conflict with the technical manager [. . .] concerned allocated time for prayer. Some time during 1961, a worker was caught praying without permission and was penalized by a seven-day suspension from work. He was able to arouse support for his position among fellow-workers, so that an appeal was made to the Emir resulting in the worker's reinstatement along with the provision for proper prayer breaks. (The Union Secretary recalled) . . . 'I told them that we should not agree to this ruining of our religion by the company.'
                              (Lubeck in Sandbrook & Cohen, 1975: 146)

Retiring workers would inform those in the villages of their experiences and this would in turn affect the labour flows in subsequent seasons. . . . Parties who left the rural areas with some knowledge looked forward to gathering more recent information along the route . . . returning parties took considerable care to warn new workers of bad employers and in case they missed anybody making their way to Rhodesia, they took the precaution of pegging notices to various trees en route. Sometimes written in Swahili, these notes, addressed to Africans in general or individual workers in particular, warned of mines to be especially avoided. For the illiterate, a system of signs carved on trees served the same useful purpose. . . . The African names (for mines) were (also) rich in meaning. . . . most helpful of all to the prospective workers were those names which gave ready insight into management policies and practices. . . . The total absence of generosity in food and wages at

the Ayrshire mine was reflected in the name *Chimpadzi* – meaning small portion.
... And while *Chayamataka* – 'hit on the buttocks' – was hardly a name to make
the Masterpiece mine popular, the fact that the Celtic mine was known as *Sigebenga*
(a murderer or cruel person) made certain that the manager there was never
plagued with work-seekers.   (van Onselen, 1976: 234–5)

Introduction

The opening quotes are designed to highlight forms of labour protest in Africa that
are 'hidden' or 'covert' – forming part of the everyday forms of consciousness and
action by the African proletariat, but rarely systematically considered in the
literature on workers and trade unions in Africa. In general, studies of African
labour issues have been confined to the more overt forms of protest –
predominantly strikes, the struggle to unionize and to direct political activity (see
e.g. Sandbrook & Cohen, 1975).

It is virtually entirely in the context of 'closed institutions' – the mining
compounds of Southern Africa – that the most directly relevant work has been
undertaken. One account was made possible through the unlikely circumstance
that the author was a personnel officer in a Namibian mine as well as being a
doctoral student at the University of Illinois and a sympathetic observer of the
workers in the mining compound (Gordon, 1977). But while Gordon provides rich
ethnographic information, the more theoretically satisfying is the work of van
Onselen, an economic historian of the Rhodesian mines. In the concluding
chapter of his book the author maps out what he considers are the special features
of labour protest in the 'labour coercive' economy he surveys, that of the
Rhodesian mines. His comments can, however, be widened in applicability and
seen as laying the groundwork for a richer approach for the study of African labour
protest. He writes:

> In a labour-coercive economy ... worker ideologies and organizations should be
> viewed essentially as the high water marks of protest: they should not be allowed
> to dominate our understanding of the way in which the economic system
> worked, or of the African miners' responses to it. At least as important, if not
> more so, were the less dramatic, silent and often unorganized responses, and it
> is this latter set of responses, which occurred on a day-to-day basis that reveal
> most about the functioning of the system and formed the woof and warp of
> worker consciousness. Likewise it was the unarticulated, unorganized protest
> and resistance which the employers and the state found most difficult to detect
> or suppress.
>   (van Onselen, 1976: 227)

Why is it important to stress the 'silent' and 'unorganized' responses of workers?
First, such a perspective is essential where there are strong political, or other
constraints, on open organization. An interesting comparative case is that of Nazi
Germany, where despite ruthless attempts to structure the pattern of industrial
relations by the regime, Mason argues that there was a high level of worker
opposition in the form of lowering productivity, 'disguised' strikes, absenteeism,
slow-downs, demonstrations and a defiance of work-place rules (Mason, 1981:
120–137). Second, by penetrating below the level of formal organization and

activity, even where legal sanctions for trade union organization are long
established, as in the US and Britain, researchers have discovered a more
pervasive existence and more various forms of class consciousness than had
previously been adduced (Sennet & Cobb, 1973; Beynon, 1973). In the African
case, where the process of proletarianization is still incomplete, conventional
patterns of labour protest are more likely to be supplemented, or in some cases
replaced, by more subtle and more spontaneous forms of resistance to the
capitalist social relations implanted by an alien power.

The labour process and worker responses

Before examining the particular manifestations of worker resistance in Africa, it is
first necessary to specify some generic features of the capitalist labour process. It is
postulated here that the labour process under capitalism involves both the creation
of a working class and its habituation to industrial production in five major ways:

(a) The potential worker is forced to abandon [previous . . .] forms of subsistence
or income (land-holding, petty trade, craft-production) and to rely, increasingly
fully, on wages. This in the language of industrial relations' experts is known as
'labour-commitment' – a notion which typically misconceives the problem by
presenting it as if it were a matter of psychological choice for the worker. In fact, of
course, there is usually a high element of compulsion in what is more accurately
perceived of as the creation and control of a stock of labour-power (for short,
Enforced Proletarianization).

(b) Once at work, the worker has to accept the hierarchical authority structure of
the workplace – with directors, managers, gang-bosses, foremen and supervisors
installed in a relationship of superordination (Managerial Control).

(c) The worker has to adapt to the physical and psychological conditions of
employment that obtain in the workplace (Psychological Adjustment).

(d) The worker has to accept an unequal distribution of reward for the labour-
power expended (Differential Reward).

(e) The worker is forced to recognize the overall political and juridical structure
that permits, or encourages, the growth and establishment of capitalist social
relations (Political Control).

Even within the most advanced capitalist societies not all elements of the labour
process are fully commandeered by capital. In the case of Africa, one would
anticipate that the element of control would be much reduced in view of the
uneven and partial degree of penetration by capitalist enterprises. Nevertheless, it
is important to emphasize, as do the editors of a recent volume on African labour
history that '. . . the spread of capitalism even to a peripheral zone detaches man
from his product, man from his habitual environment, man from the right to
dispose of his labor-power and his agricultural goods in his own right. It is in the
scale and intensity of this dislocation and decomposition of domestic modes of
production, distribution and exchange, that the colonial presence manifests itself'
(Gutkind, Cohen & Copans (eds.), 1978).

   The elements of the capitalist labour process identified above, thus meet with a
broadly common set of responses which match, though not always perfectly or
completely, the threat posed by capital (see Table 1).

Table 1   Workers' responses to the labour process

Elements of the labour process	Characteristic workers' responses
Enforced Proletarianization	(a) Desertion
	(b) Community withdrawal or revolt
	(c) Target working
Managerial Control	(d) Task, efficiency and time bargaining
	(e) Sabotage
	(f) Creation of 'work-culture'
Psychological Adjustment	(g) Accidents and sickness
	(h) Drug use
	(i) Millenarian or other-worldly beliefs
Differential Reward	(j) Theft
	(k) Unionization
	(l) Economistic strikes
Political Control	(m) Participation in rallies, riots, demonstrations
	(n) Support of anti-status quo parties
	(o) Political strikes

Note: The tinted area is singled out for subsequent discussion.

Even a superficial examination of the table will help to further ground the initial distinction between hidden and overt forms of worker protest – categories (a)–(j) comprising the former, categories (k)–(o), the latter. But the clear lines drawn between the two sets, and within the sets, should not mislead us into thinking that real events are containable wholly within the confines of a single listed response. Let us take, for example, the vignette from Mauritius that opens this paper. Here Mauritian workers are committing sabotage, not as in the normal case to delay production and evade work, but precisely to ensure that they would be permitted to work. How is this to be explained? Given the destruction or serious decay of all prior modes of production on the island, the indentured Indian labourers and freed African slaves had, perforce, to adapt to the capitalist mode. A few ex-slaves became fishermen (*not* their previous occupational specialization) in an attempt to escape work on the estates, but nearly all the remaining workers had little alternative but to sell their labour-power merely to survive. The estate-owners, for their part, neither wanted nor needed a stable labour force – far better, they thought, to rely largely on a seasonally employed and unorganized group, with a large reserve army hovering in the wings. In such circumstances workers' protest needed to be directed towards fostering stabilization, a strategy which in other contexts has been fought under the slogan 'A Right to Work'. By way of parenthesis, it could be added that with the advance of the economic crisis in the Western world since the mid-seventies, such a slogan has acquired the status of a self-evident demand by workers in the advanced capitalist societies. However, where the capacity for self-employment or independent product still exists, or can be created, workers may well advance the slogan, 'A Right Not to Work'.

The discussion of the Mauritian example should alert the reader to the possibilities of a more complex theoretical elaboration of each category, but here the discussion has been organized by following the identified responses, (a)–(j), in sequence and illustrating them by data drawn from the African labour experience.

Workers' responses in Africa

(a) Desertion

This was a common means of escaping habituation into the capitalist mode all over Africa. Stichter (in Sandbrook & Cohen, 1975: 26) regards desertion as the 'chief mode of protest' once labour recruitment in Kenya had begun. One report from Nyanza, in 1907, said that railway workers were 'extremely apt to throw down their tools and run away on the slightest pretext'. Another from the Kikuyu area complained 'no man can run a farm with monthly relays of raw natives: labour of this kind is always capricious and liable to desert'. In 1909, 31 out of the 48 complaints received by the Nairobi Labour Office all concerned cases of desertion. A year earlier on the other side of the continent, the British were attempting to push through the Baro–Kano railway line in Northern Nigeria. According to Mason 'resistance spread and became more determined'. Mr Gill, a political officer on the railway in Southern Zaria province, reported 300 desertions from the line, while another officer complained of 800. The Acting High Commissioner counselled caution but not, of course, the abandonment of the enterprise: 'It is madness to take large levies during the farming season from pure agriculturalists like the Gwaris, far better go slow till dry weather . . .' (Mason in Gutkind, Cohen & Copans, 1978). Desertion of soldiers from colonial armies, often used as 'labour brigades', was also common, as were cases of self-mutilation to escape conscription. Both these forms of protest are extensively documented in the case of French West Africa (Echenberg, 1975). In the case of Southern Africa, a similar structure exists. Van Onselen quotes the lament of Mashonaland mine owners: 'The police use every possible effort, but the fact remains that whole gangs can, and do, abscond and are never traced or heard of again.' He goes on to show that where total contraction out of the wage-labour system was not possible, workers deserted one mine for another to try to secure better wages and working conditions (van Onselen, 1976: 230).

Colonial governments and mine owners alike responded to the high rates of desertion by attempts to control and supervise both the recruitment and mobility of workers. In the French colonies highly supervised labour was used until the 1930s. In the British colonies, Masters and Servants' Ordinances and other legislation (registration bureaux, a work certificate, called a *kipande* in Kenya, etc.) were all designed to criminalize worker mobility, and reduce the rate of desertion. In the armies of the two principal colonial powers it was a clearly recognized principle of service that a private recruited in one place should, where possible, serve out his time in another colony. As well as reducing the possibilities for flight, this strategy conferred the incidental benefit that the stranger troops fired with less hesitation in the event of riot or public disturbance. In the case of a Namibian mining compound, Gordon argues that the company's control over the workers' income and expenditure 'attempts to subject the worker totally to the goals of the organization for the duration of his employment by minimizing the worker's commitments to his outside world' (Gordon, 1977: 62).

The rate of desertion depends on the degree of control exercised, but also, more saliently, on the degree of viability that remains to the pre-capitalist mode of production. Herein, as has previously been argued, lay a contradiction for the underdeveloped form of capitalism prevalent in Africa. 'The ideal solution . . . was one in which agricultural production remained sufficiently virile to produce an exportable primary product and absorb return migrants, but not so viable that it threatened the supply of cheap unskilled labour. Such a delicate balance was impossible to achieve and may indeed be considered one of the central contradictions of the colonial political economy' (Cohen in Gutkind & Wallerstein (eds.), 1976: 161).

(b) Community withdrawal or revolt

This, *par excellence*, is a category where there is an enormous weight of historical evidence to reinterpret. Most of the colonial historical sources have rich and bloodthirsty descriptions of the early wars of 'pacification'. Usually, of course, some higher purpose is adduced such as destroying 'barbarity', 'spreading the light' or preventing 'tribal wars'. The reasons for such adventures may not be totally reducible to the need for the fledgling colonial states to create a reservoir of cheap and available labour (the colonial authorities did need to reaffirm their political power internally and against their metropolitan rivals), but this was clearly a motivating factor and was certainly the major effect of colonial wars. The necessity for the colonial authorities – especially in the areas of white settlement – to maintain an adequate labour supply is further demonstrated by the constant repetition in colonial sources that such and such a chief or headman needed to be deposed or killed for failing to honour his treaty commitments to provide labour. The local communities had two alternatives: (i) withdrawal into regions so inhospitable that the blackbirder (labour recruiter) or raiding party couldn't reach them e.g. the Pygmies or many nomadic peoples, or (ii) a communal revolt against the authority of the colonial state, its agents or its local collaborators. Examples of these forms of protest are legion, but the degree to which a protest against forced labour was the core of a communal protest has not always been emphasized. Witness however, van der Post's account of the withdrawal of Bushmen into the Kalahari:

> Everywhere, they (the Bushmen children) were in great demand as slaves because, when they survived captivity, they grew up into the most intelligent, adroit and loyal of all the former servants. Even long after slavery was abolished and until the supply was dried up their service was exacted under a system of forced labour. From the earliest days, all along the frontier, the more desperate and adventurous characters among my countrymen added to their living by

kidnapping Bushman children and selling them to labour-hungry farmers. Hardly a commando came back from an expedition without some children. . . . Many tried to escape and if recaptured, were flogged heavily for their pains. Others . . . would try furtively to signal by fires to their own people . . . and move stealthily ever deeper into the interior.

(van der Post, 1958: 48)

As to evidence of communal revolt, a recent history of the Igbo [Nigeria] documents a not untypical story. The people of Udi, who had given only a token resistance when the British first came, took advantage of the outbreak of the 1st World War to rise in rebellion. According to Elizabeth Isichei: 'It was a protest against forced labour on the roads . . . where the unpaid workers, who were expected to feed themselves, often went hungry – "sometimes they used to eat leaves". The survey of the railway line seemed to threaten their ownership of land, and herald more forced labour.' When the revolt was brutally crushed, the peace terms included the supplying of two thousand unpaid workers for the railway. After 1915 they were forced to work in the mines as well (Isichei, 1976: 134–6). In Kenya, the Giriama revolt of 1913–14, which resulted in the deaths of 400 Giriama, was a direct result of the government's attempt to use Giriama labour on the European and Arab sisal, cotton, rice and coconut plantations. Again in Kenya, the Gusii, who were asked to supply massive levies of labour often refused to work for the administration or to pay tax. Instead, many Gusii became adherents of a millenarian religious movement, the Mumbo cult, whose followers believed that the God Mumbo would allow them to live forever while their crops would replenish themselves and there would be no further need for work (Stichter in Sandbrook & Cohen (eds.), 1975: 25, 26). European depredations of African land were associated with European demands for African labour and it was for control of their own land and labour-power that such well-known revolts as Maji-Maji [Tanzania] (1905–7) and Mau-Mau [Kenya] (1952–60) occurred. In short, while many colonial historians have interpreted such events as 'wars of pacification' and for their part, post-1950s Africanist historians have seen such protests as evidence of 'proto-nationalism', the main object of the communities concerned was to resist their incorporation into a capitalist and colonial labour market.

(c) Target working

This rather old-fashioned and now largely discredited notion was first used by colonial officers to justify the payment of low wages. New workers, they argued, preferred 'leisure' to income, once they had reached a certain 'target' commensurate with their desire to purchase certain established consumer goods. A backward-bending supply curve was thought to result – the supply of labour drying up, and the return to the country speeding up, as wage levels increased. With other commentators, I have criticized this notion arguing that 'In fact the targets that workers set themselves were much more elastic than the colonial administrators realized (or were prepared to admit), and there appears to be solid evidence to support the view that wage-earners responded favourably to monetary incentives once these were offered' (Cohen, 1974: 189). However, this critique is essentially a 'liberal' notion which argues that Africans have similar economic motivations to other workers. This view needs to be supplemented by the more compelling argument that elastic targets are ultimately determined not so much by choice, as by the increasingly limited possibilities for a return to rural life. The subjectivist element in the notion of target working can, however, be usefully refashioned to explain the undoubted fact that many urban workers perceive their employment as temporary, not because they can now hope to return to the land, but because they hope to become petty entrepreneurs and independent craftsmen. These petty bourgeois aspirations are thought by Lloyd to inhibit class consciousness: 'Rather than identify with wage employment, the migrant aspires to be his real master; he sees society as a ladder up which individuals have risen to various levels of success; he does not see an irreconcilable antagonism between rich and poor' (Lloyd, 1974: 225–6). Target working is thus an important element of what Lloyd calls the 'ego-centred cognitive map' of workers. But as Lloyd concedes in theory, a sociologist cannot explain the world simply in terms of people's intentions and decisions (Lloyd, 1974: 187). In practice, there is a crucial difference between young, single men who are seeking to establish themselves and who may have a realistic appreciation of the limited possibilities of converting their savings to independent proprietorship, and on the other hand, the bulk of workers with family commitments confronting a situation of rises in rent, transport and the general cost of living. For such workers, the mythology of successful petty entrepreneurship has replaced the rural idyll as an object for escapism. Subjectively, such fantasies are part of the workers' resistance to the objective reality that most of them will have little chance to avoid selling their labour-power, whether it be in the public sector, modern industry or in the open-air sweatshops of African cities (euphemistically now designated the informal sector).

To summarize this first set of forms of resistance: to implant capitalist social relations in an area previously characterized by pre-capitalist modes, it is necessary to create and control a stock of labour-power. In Africa, this was achieved particularly violently, through wars of pacification, the imposition of hut and poll taxes, the use of forced labour, and the application of a legal code equating worker mobility with criminality. Africans responded by desertion, by withdrawal or by revolt. But acquiescence of the loss of control over labour-power and its product was inevitable, even where symbolic escape was possible. Having to accept the inescapability of wage-labour, did not, however, always mean that African workers passively accepted the conditions under which they were asked to work. It is to the forms of resistance to such conditions that attention is now directed.

(d) Task, efficiency and time bargaining

What is meant by task bargaining? Here a worker deliberately seeks either to restore his traditional skill or craft in the face of management, attempts to define job functions, or (more commonly) he seeks to reduce his exploitation by adhering overstrictly to job specifications and rules detailing his work. A 'work to rule' and job-demarcation dispute are typical examples of this form of protest – often triggered off by the managerial redefinition. Witness, for example, the indignation of an African tailor in an Indian-owned factory in Zambia who was accused of stitching a pair of trousers badly: 'If you continue to treat us like animals you will find your work in this factory becoming very difficult. I have been a tailor with Narayan Bros. for over seven years and have never during this time sewn short trousers like that pair we are talking about now.' His co-workers supported him: 'If you (the foremen) do not stop treating us like learner tailors we will walk out. Now! Now!' (Kapferer, 1972: 243). Time/efficiency bargaining is a closely related form of resistance and may be seen in the workers' characteristic and frequently successful attempts to bamboozle the time and motion men, the planner and the job-setter. The collective solidarity ('Brotherhood') in time/efficiency bargaining on a Namibian mine is well described by Gordon:

> White supervisors attribute quota restrictions by the workers to 'laziness' and point out that in terms of cash earning it is illogical behaviour since it cuts into the underground workers' bonus. Thus, it is felt that laziness must be inherent. But quota restriction, from the workers' perspective, has a logic of its own. It enables them to avoid fatigue by allowing them to work at a comfortable pace. They are thus able to establish a degree of control over their own work targets. ... Quota restriction prevents competition at the work-place which would disturb established interpersonal relationships and protects slower Brothers thus alleviating white pressure because it is believed that if one worker works harder, the white will also expect other workers to put more effort into their tasks ... walk offs were quite frequent and entailed considerable Brotherhood solidarity.
>
> (Gordon, 1977: 167–8)

As well as the reasons adduced by Gordon, go-slows may reflect the difference between rhythms of work derived from agriculture, craft production and seasonal employment and those conducive to industrial production or office routine. In his discussion of the prolonged disputes that led to the workers' seizure of the Mount Carmel Rubber Factory in Tanzania, Pascal Mihyo shows how the employer tried unsuccessfully to use the workers' committee to discipline the workers and secure greater efficiency. They responded by 'a perpetual go-slow' (Mihyo, 1975: 66, 67).

(e) Sabotage

As a form of resistance this carries time/efficiency and task bargaining to a more extreme conclusion. Sabotage is, in other words, rationally based in the determination of workers to slow down the production process and to prevent redundancies with the introduction of labour-saving machinery. Sabotage can also be seen as a means of levelling down profits to reduce inequality rather than, as in a wage demand, attempting to reduce inequality by levelling-up. A series of incidents witnessed in a Lagos plastic factory by the author (December 1968) demonstrated this clearly. After a wage demand had been refused, the workers systematically jinxed the machinery, the vats, the moulds and the firm's transport. Subsequently, when the workers evolved another strategy, deciding to occupy the factory and sell the goods themselves, they regretted their earlier enthusiasm. But there is no doubt that the initial outburst was directed against what workers perceived of as excessive managerial profits. Sabotage therefore is linked with the other forms of resistance to the differential reward inherent in a capitalist labour process.

(f) Creation of a 'work-culture'

The structure of workplace authority is also frequently undermined by the deliberate creation or amplification of social distance between the worker and manager. Frequently the creation of a contra-culture is subtle and difficult to assess even after long participant observation. In-jokes, private linguistic codes, wall slogans and the like are most common; but the creation of a work culture takes many forms. In the Namibian mine Gordon was employed in, workers had four or five names, including a 'white' name, used mainly for interaction with the management. The proliferation of names obstructed the whites. If a particular worker was sought by the management, workers would try to elicit the reason for the request. If trouble loomed the worker of that 'name' could suddenly disappear. On the other hand, some workers stuck to their indigenous names. Being difficult for the white foremen to remember or pronounce meant the worker could be anonymous and immune from singling out (Gordon, 1977: 127). In East Africa, Grillo points out that within the East African Railways an *esprit de corps* or 'corporate ethos' evolved around the use of Swahili: 'Railwaymen whatever their national background, were willing and able to use Swahili as a means of communication – even Ganda, who in Kampala tried to ignore other languages except English' (Grillo, 1973: 68). Work-songs to break the monotony of the labour and to mock the gang-boss, dances, drinking patterns all take on the character of a distinct moral universe, a private culture where, as Gordon notes, Blacks can 'be themselves' and be masters of their 'own' actions (Gordon, 1977: 102). The dialectic between 'resistance' and 'adaptation', an issue that is discussed in the concluding section of this paper, is seen most clearly in the case of a work-culture, which can act either as an insulative force, or a set of symbols to mobilize the grievances of workers. A sensitive study of the Beni dance societies, for example, shows how the symbols of white power (hierarchy, discipline, barracks, uniforms) were combined with an African-based language and music to create a new and vibrant art form which spread over much of East and Southern Africa (Ranger, 1975). Van Onselen surmises that the organization of the early mutual aid societies in Rhodesian mine compounds among workers owed much to the influence of the Beni dance societies (van Onselen, 1976: 200). At another point, van Onselen shows how mine dancing was generally approved of by the management as a means of social control and as a reinforcement for their beliefs in 'the happy tribesman', and only evoked disapprobation when the dancing took on an inter-tribal character and the organizers began to look more like an embryonic strike committee (van Onselen, 1976: 188–9).

The control that managers attempt to effect in the workplace is challenged, in sum, by four principal means: (i) attempting to repossess the definition of the task, (ii) evading or deluding management as to the level of possible 'productivity', (iii) by engaging in sabotage and (iv) amplifying social distance and creating a work-culture. The degree to which many of these actions can be considered a serious challenge to the managerial authority depends on the local circumstances. Some may be no more than pin-pricks; others, particularly cultural manifestations like mine dancing, may be envisioned by management as a harmless way of ensuring compliance. The work-culture created is, however, of fundamental importance in providing the organizing symbols around which a grievance located elsewhere may be galvanized (i.e. given appropriate leadership, organization, an 'issue', etc.).

(g) Accidents and sickness

The next set of responses are those which are normally conceived as having little relation to the labour-process itself and are often thought of as extraneous to the relations of production, even by workers themselves. A closer examination will, however, reveal that, while there may be an element of unconscious reaction involved, these forms of behaviour do indeed constitute forms of worker resistance and adaption. Take first the question of sickness and accidents. The incidence of sickness and distribution of illness and 'accidents' are, despite the verbal paradox, neither fortuitous nor randomly incurred. The type of industry, the track speed-ups by management, the particular time of the day and time of the week; if these factors are taken into account, accidents are from being accidental (see Wrench, 1974). In a like manner, morbidity is closely related to housing conditions, conditions at work, the distribution of health care, etc. Accidents and illness are, like Durkheim's *Suicide*, social facts: facts to which workers are expected to adjust. In the South African gold mines, Wilson reports that in 'the period 1936–66 no less than 19,000 men, 93% of them black, died as a result of accidents'. The white death rate was 0.97 per 1,000 men, the black death rate 1.62 per 1,000 men (Wilson, 1972a: 21, 51). By 1967, medical compensation for miners was paid at the rate of R10 million a year, but two thirds of the total went to white miners. Some diseases may be entirely confined to black workers. Beri Beri (heart failure due to lack of thiamine), for example, first extensively documented amongst young able-bodied Chinese working in Malaya, was found largely among male hostel workers in the Johannesburg mines – and barely among other workers (S.A. Medical Journal, 1972, cited by Wilson, 1972b: 186). The disease is caused by bad food and heavy drinking, particularly of the 'Bantu Beer' produced by the Johannesburg municipality – which lacks the traditional ingredient sorghum, which contains thiamine. Municipal beerhalls were the first targets of the 1976 Soweto rioters. Far from destroying their social facilities, workers were smashing the very symbol of social control and (less consciously) destroying what, it transpires, is a positively lethal form of 'nutrition'.

With regard to reported sickness, what for managers constitutes 'malingering' may for workers constitute an attempt to deny their labour-power to the employer while coping with debilitating conditions the employer has provided. Equally, accidents are deliberately (or even unconsciously) used to evade work or slow it down. The self-mutilation by army recruits mentioned earlier in the case of French West Africa, is obviously an act of volition; but accidents such as clothing caught in moving machinery, eye grit, fainting and muscular injuries have the effect of acts of resistance even where they are not consciously so directed.

(h) Drug use

Almost invariably this represents a form of psychological resistance but social quiescence by workers. Drugs tend to be used as means of 'ironing out' emotional peaks and troughs. Some stimulants, for example, the widely used West African kola nut, are taken as food substitutes simply to keep going. (Coca leaves are chewed by Bolivian tin miners for the same purpose.) More often, 'downers' like alcohol and cannabis are simply used as a means of relaxation and enjoyment – a form of compensation for an unrewarding work experience. Worker-initiated drug use as illustrated by the opening vignette from Mokola market, should however be distinguished from managerial and public provision of drug centres as in the large beer-drinking facilities in mining compounds and townships of Southern Africa. Alcohol was sometimes provided as a company store operation, but more often it was designed to prevent the recreation hours of workers being used for anything more harmful. Van Onselen recounts an interesting managerial variation. A beer brewing monopoly was granted to favoured workers as a bonus. As van Onselen points out, this increased productivity, while the reward was financed by the workers themselves (van Onselen, 1976: 169). A second example can be cited. Partly under the pressure of local wine interests, in the early sixties the South African authorities authorized the sale of alcoholic drinks (other than the traditional beer). This had the anticipated effect. During the period 1963–71, the bottle stores owned by the Cape Town Municipality recorded an increase of 500% in their sale of alcoholic drinks, excluding beer. Violence arising from alcohol consumption is predominantly directed to other members of the black community, so in that sense provides little threat to established interests. However, there is no doubt that drinking can also provide a form of companionship and solidarity. Gordon observes that drinking together is one of the most important rituals of friendship in a Namibian mine. Friendly relations and mutual trust are engendered by drinking together from a common pot in a context where tales of poisoned beer abound. 'Everyone, young and old, sits within conversational range around the beer bins which emphasizes the egalitarian basis of compound society' (Gordon, 1977: 116).

(i) Millenarian or other-worldly beliefs

A common form of psychological resistance to work is the adoption of religion or other-worldly beliefs, particularly those that stress relief from suffering in the next world. Often this might not be a coherent set of religious doctrines as in the case of the Mumbo cult mentioned earlier, but simply a belief in chance, fate, a lucky break or the evil machinations of such other person whose actions are wholly beyond control. These forms of withdrawal are all recorded by Lloyd in his study of Yoruba society [Nigeria] (Lloyd, 1974: 199, 200). Yet, while undoubtedly an opiate for most workers, religious belief and practice might also provide some elements in the construction of a workers' ideology (asceticism, solidarity, retribution) and some practical experience of organization. Because many African workers followed Islam or African Christian sects, employers were often suspicious of 'nativism' or 'Ethiopianism' being fanned by religious practices. This was undoubtedly the reason why at first all the independent churches were outlawed in the Rhodesian mine compounds (van Onselen, 1976: 184–5). That the colonial authorities and employers did not misapprehend the danger from independent religious movements is confirmed by Hodgkin's remarks in his classical study of *Nationalism in Colonial Africa*. According to Hodgkin, the main achievement of the independent churches was 'to diffuse certain new and fruitful ideas, in however confused a form, among the African mass, the peasants in the countryside and the semi-proletarianized peasants in the towns for the most part: the idea of the historical importance of Africans; of an alternative to total submission to the European power ...' (Hodgkin, 1956: 113).

When discussing forms of psychological resistance to the labour process, it is difficult to disentangle motive and intention from unconscious or dimly apprehended action and reaction. But the question of volition is less important than the capacity of workers to create some private domains and psychological 'space' free of the insistent pressures of the capitalist labour process.

(j) Theft

The last of the categories of 'hidden responses' considered here is that of theft. Many large industrial concerns calculate on a given proportion of raw materials, tools and product losses and simply pass on the increased prices to the customer. Worker theft can be usefully considered as a wage-supplement, which varies in volume with the rise or fall in real wages. To take one example from the Rhodesian mines, it appears that 'the volume of illegal gold trade increased as the wages of black miners fell' (van Onselen, 1976: 241). Besides the gold amalgam that was caught on large canvas strips under the mill, or by running a finger-nail across the copper plate over which the crushed gold passed, workers were engaged in many other 'crimes':

> Daily, hundreds of petty crimes were committed on the mining properties with the specific objectives of rectifying the balance between employees and their employers. African workers constantly pilfered small items of mine stores – such as candles – or helped themselves to substantial quantities of detonators and dynamite which they used for fishing. Wage rates were altered on documents and hundreds of work and 'skoff' tickets were forged by miners who sought to gain compensation for what they had been denied through the system.
>
> (van Onselen, 1976: 240)

In the much larger and more valuable diamond mining areas of South Africa and Namibia it is deemed necessary to have daily screenings of employees including anal searches and X-rays in order to reduce the numerous occasions when diamonds have been secreted in strange places or swallowed. In white settler societies, any club room conversation will reveal the elaborate charades domestic workers play with their employers – watering down the gin, moving the mark on the bottle, putting flour into the sugar and rice, etc. Theft has here been interpreted not as a legal or moral offence, but as a form of labour protest which has the effect of reducing the rate of exploitation of the workers by an informal wage supplement. Seen in this view 'theft' becomes an act of recovering some 'surplus value', which would otherwise be appropriated by the employer.

Hidden and overt forms of class consciousness

A quick glance at Table 1 will reveal that the sequential discussion of worker responses has stopped abruptly before category (k), the subsequent categories being those that are both better argued and documented in the existing literature and represent more obvious forms of class consciousness and action. By way of conclusion it is now necessary to relate the hidden to the overt forms of consciousness. Three theoretical positions can be briefly considered:

First, that hidden forms of resistance are both more pervasive and more important, they [express ...] a 'bedrock', 'grass-roots', 'genuine' sort of consciousness. Van Onselen seems to be inclined to this view, though by limiting his theoretical elaboration to a 'labour coercive economy' (for a discussion of this concept, see Trapido, 1971), that of a mining compound, it is easy to reply that in that context only the hidden forms of protest were possible. Yet the stress on the spontaneous actions of workers has deep roots among some left-wing theorists, including, for example, Trotsky, Rosa Luxemburg and C. L. R. James, some of whom see trade unionism and trade union leaders as the principal agencies by which workers are co-opted to the capitalist system. The danger of such a perspective is that it tends to romanticize the proletariat and seek explanations for its frequent failure to live up to its ascribed status as 'the truly revolutionary class' not by looking at its own organizational weakness and ideological limitations, but by finding other agencies which systematically are pulling the wool over the proletariat's eyes. This view can also easily overestimate the political significance of everyday protests that, by their very nature, cannot but be disconnected, individualistic and conducive only to a short-term effect. Certainly, in the forms of protest documented above, there is little sense in which we can see workers combining for a sustained long-term programme. They do not permanently seize the instruments of production, they only dimly see the possibility of governing themselves, they cannot establish themselves as what Marx called 'the general representatives' of their society. Only if such a development occurred could the proletariat establish its 'dictatorship' or legitimacy.

A second theoretical position could see the hidden forms of protest as indeed operating on a lower level of consciousness, but forming part of an incremental, escalating, chain of consciousness leading towards 'higher', more politicized forms of consciousness. This seems a somewhat more plausible position, though one should not be too dogmatic about whether the proletariat's consciousness is always on an upward spiral. In the absence of leadership, organization and a galvanizing issue (and in the presence of a repressive state or employer), there is little reason to assume that the process cannot be sidetracked or aborted. If protest can be kept on a sporadic and informal basis, it can ultimately be seen as a form of adaptation to the conditions of capitalist production. Nonetheless, those informal acts that do involve collective solidarity (e.g. drinking together or covering for a co-worker who is feigning illness) can lay the basis for an organization and leadership, if not a consistent ideology.

The idea of a step-by-step consciousness is now sometimes challenged by a third group of theorists who, following Lukàcs, have pressed for a theory of 'dual consciousness' (*New Left Review*, 52, 1968). What does this mean? The seeds of a dual theory are found in Marx and Engels's contrast in their essay, *The Holy Family*, between what any one proletarian or even the whole proletariat *imagines* to be their aim, and, on the other hand, what the proletariat *is* and what it consequently is compelled to do (see Mann, 1973: 45). This is a far-reaching proposition and one that challenges the arguments of those who, using various versions of subjectivist sociology (where reality is solely apprehended by the actor), seek to refute the notion of class consciousness by reporting worker opinions on the day a survey was carried out. On the other hand, while Marx and Engels hint at a dual consciousness theory, it remains open to a number of interpretations. For present purposes, I would distinguish overt from hidden forms of consciousness in this way. The former kind represents an extant, readily observed, open and self-aware form of consciousness (which may be conservative or revolutionary or any degree between the two). This is what the proletariat thinks, believes – imagines – to be its aim. The latter form of consciousness is represented (or mediated if you like) through the everyday forms of resistance described in this paper. It is a latent, unexplicit, subterranean form of consciousness. For the most part, workers are imprisoned within this second kind of consciousness, but they can transcend the prosaic limits of everyday actions and reactions in given circumstances, and with a leadership that is able to amplify and galvanize forms of dissent that have not previously gained a conventional expression.

In this paper I have not sought to show empirically how, and in what circumstances, the transition from a latent to an immediate and explicit consciousness is accomplished. Instead, by focusing on the hidden protests of African workers, I have tried to illustrate the variety and pervasiveness of their responses and their tenacity of purpose in resisting the capitalist labour process. Thus far African trade unions and revolutionary parties have only marginally been able to channel such dissent for progressive or revolutionary ends.

Especially adapted by the author from his article in *Review of African Political Economy*, no. 19, 1980, pp. 8–22.

REFERENCES

Beynon, H. (1973) *Working for Ford* Harmondsworth: Penguin.
Cohen, R. (1974) *Labour and Politics in Nigeria* London: Heinemann.
—— (1976) 'From Peasants to Workers in Africa' in Gutkind, P. C. W. & Wallerstein, I. (eds.) *The Political Economy of Contemporary Africa* Beverly Hills & London: Sage Publications.
Echenberg, M. J. (1975) 'Paying the Blood Tax: Military Conscription in French West Africa, 1914–1929', *Canadian Journal of African Studies*, 9: 171–192.
Gordon, R. J. (1977) *Mines, Masters and Migrants: Life in a Namibian Compound* Johannesburg: Raven Press.
Grillo, R. D. (1973) *African Railwaymen: Solidarity and Opposition in an East African Labour Force* Cambridge: Cambridge University Press.
Gutkind, P. C. W., Cohen, R. & Copans, J. (eds.) (1978) *African Labor History* Beverly Hills & London: Sage Publications.
Hodgkin, T. (1956) *Nationalism in Colonial Africa* London: Frederick Muller.
Isichei, E. (1976) *A History of the Igbo People* London: Macmillan.
Kapferer, B. (1972) *Strategy and Transaction in an African Factory* Manchester: Manchester University Press.
Lloyd, P. (1974) *Power and Independence* London: Routledge & Kegan Paul.
Lubeck, P. 'Unions, Workers and Consciousness in Kano, Nigeria' in Sandbrook, R. & Cohen, R. *q.v.*
Mann, M. (1973) *Consciousness and Action Among the Western Working Class* London: Macmillan.
Mason, M. (1978) 'Forced Labor and the Railway: Northern Nigeria, 1907–1912' in Gutkind, P. C. W., Cohen, R. & Copans, J. *q.v.*
Mason, T. (1981) 'The Workers' Opposition in Nazi Germany' *History Workshop*, 11, Spring 1981: 120–137.
Mihyo, P. (1975) 'The Struggle for Workers' Control in Tanzania', *Review of African Political Economy*, no. 4: 62–84.
Ranger, T. (1975) *Dance and Society in Eastern Africa* London: Heinemann.
Sandbrook, R. & Cohen, R. (eds.) (1975) *The Development of an African Working Class* London: Longman.
Sennett, R. & Cobb, J. (1973) *The Hidden Injuries of Class* New York: Vintage Books.
Stichter, S. (1975) 'The Formation of a Working Class in Kenya' in Sandbrook, R. & Cohen, R. *q.v.*
Trapido, S. (1971) 'South Africa in a Comparative Study of Industrialisation', *Journal of Development Studies*, 7 (3): 302–320.
van der Post, L. (1958) *The Lost World of the Kalahari* Harmondsworth: Penguin.
van Onselen, C. (1976) *Chibaro: African Mine Labour in Southern Rhodesia, 1900–1933* London: Pluto Press.
Wilson, F. (1972a) *Labour in the South African Gold Mines, 1911–1969* Cambridge: Cambridge University Press.
—— (1972b) *Migrant Labour in South Africa* Johannesburg: South African Council of Churches & Spro-Cas.
Wrench, K. (1974) *Speed Accidents* Discussion Paper, Series E. No. 17, Faculty of Commerce & Social Science, University of Birmingham.

Conclusion: Types of Struggle

Our selection of readings for this collection has focused largely on the social relations of class and gender. To understand how these relations are constituted, and how they are reproduced and challenged, requires consideration of forms of property and production, the nature and exercise of political power, and the workings of culture and ideology. We shall look at each of these in turn to distinguish different conditions of struggle as a basis for discussing types of struggle, their content and organization.

Property and production relations

The economies of Third World countries are characterized by different combinations of capitalist production and forms of household production. Capitalism presupposes the concentration of property in means of production on one hand, and, on the other, the existence of workers lacking sufficient or any means of production with which to earn their livelihood and who have to sell their labour power (or ability to work) for wages. Household production presupposes access to means of production which are worked with family labour to satisfy the needs of the household.

A number of the readings provide glimpses of the historical formation of a working class, a process in which people are dispossessed of alternative ways of securing their livelihood (9, 16, 30). The readings also illustrate different degrees and forms of this process of *proletarianization*. Examples of working classes which are fully proletarianized in the sense of maintaining and reproducing themselves through wage labour include the metalworkers of São Paulo (18), the miners of La Lota in Chile and Siglo XX in Bolivia (11, 29), the women *beedi* workers of Nizamabad (16), the sugar estate workers of El Valle and the agricultural day labourers of Bori Arab (9, 22). Two of our accounts also describe groups of militant and organized wage workers in public sector employment (17, 28).

This relationship constituted by the capitalist ownership of means of production and the formation of a proletariat implies several areas of struggle. The ways in which capitalism has developed in Third World countries, and these countries' mode of integration with the world economy, have dispossessed more people of means of production to work with than there are jobs available to them, with the consequence of widespread unemployment and underemployment. The latter was seen in the case of the day labourers of Bori Arab: 'If they don't get work, they often just lie around and try to sleep because there is no food and they have no strength to do more' (p. 180). There is thus a large 'reserve army of labour' of people seeking work, which enables capitalists to enforce low wages and harsh conditions.

Wages which are insufficient for family reproduction (the maintenance of all family members, not just wage earners) mean that the wives or companions of male workers have to engage in cash-earning activities to supplement household incomes

(9, 27, 29(i)). In addition to struggles to obtain and retain wage employment and to survive and raise families on very low wages, there are struggles arising within capitalist enterprises over conditions of work and pay (11, 16, 18, 20(ii)).

One of the striking features of Third World economies, by comparison with those of industrialized capitalist countries, is the importance of household production side by side with capitalist enterprises and sectors. Households attempt to satisfy their needs by producing subsistence goods, for instance peasants cultivate foodstuffs for their own consumption, or produce goods and services for sale to others (petty commodity production), or combine these two activities in some way.

The places described in the readings that approximate most to an apparently non-commercialized, peasant subsistence agriculture are also those which are major sources of labour migration: southern Mozambique, the Senegal river valley, and the Mapuche reservations of southern Chile (4, 12, 20; 10; 7). Migratory labour systems assume that a substantial part of the costs of family reproduction are met through subsistence agriculture by the migrant's family, and that migrants 'retire' to their rural areas of origin when they are no longer needed by capitalist employers. In this situation, the social category of the 'reserve army of labour' corresponds to the population of particular geographical areas. Also, according to the definition used above, this combination of (periodic) labour migration with peasant household production signifies only partial proletarianization.

In other cases, subsistence production by peasants is combined with production for the market. The struggles which confront such peasants involve both their conditions of production and the realization and distribution of what they produce. Production organized on a household basis implies intrinsic limitations on the amount of labour that can be mobilized, the scale of production, and the cost and sophistication of the means of production utilized – all of which are exacerbated by difficult environmental and climatic conditions of cultivation.

When peasants have to gain access to land through sharecropping or some other form of rent, then part of their labour is owed as a payment to landowners, whether in the form of a share of the crop, a sum-of-money rent, or an obligation to perform unpaid labour (1, 3, 5, 6). Even when peasants own the land they farm they are typically subjected to domination by other groups through the mechanisms that link them to markets, and the wider economy more generally. In performing migrant labour, in marketing their produce, in seeking to obtain credit or access to improved means of production and expertise, peasants confront powerful groups and agencies: labour recruiters and employers, merchants, moneylenders, capitalist farmers, banks, or public and state agencies, as the conflict between the peasants' association of Jamaane and the SAED demonstrates (10). In different ways these 'external' forces cut into the control that peasants exert over the uses of their labour in production, or the amount of real income (and hence levels of consumption) they derive from their labour, or both.

The struggles of peasants thus focus around access to land (and other means of production), the demands of cultivation in often harsh or unpredictable ecological conditions, and the division of the product of their labour in face of the claims made on it by others through rents, taxes, interest payments, prices and other aspects of marketing arrangements.

Capitalist and household production exist in both agriculture and industry, countryside and town. The readings give a picture of the diversity of activities in urban petty commodity production, and of the diverse ways in which they are organized through households and highly individualized ventures. The 'informal sector' of urban petty commodity production comprises the provision of personal and other services, as well as goods, encompassing small-scale trading and hawking, domestic labour for others, the preparation of food for sale in the home or on the street, prostitution, the 'scavenging' of garbage for recycling and resale, and so on (11, 14, 24, 26, 27).

The 'informal sector' is thus highly differentiated with respect to its activities, the resources that households and individuals can mobilize to pursue them, and the incomes they derive from them. Despite this differentiation, the large numbers of people struggling to gain their living through urban petty commodity production has the effect of intensifying competition between them, subjecting them to control by a hierarchy of 'middlemen' (such as larger scale traders and suppliers). This increases the precariousness of the ventures they engage in, and depresses their incomes and standards of living.

We have suggested that different relations of property and production establish different social conditions of struggle, which affect whether struggles take a more collective or a more individual form. Before discussing this, we will look at some political, cultural and ideological aspects of class and gender relations.

Political relations

Political relations are those of effective power, of domination and subordination between different social groups, whose interests, ideologies and capacities for collective action are expressed in the forms of political organization they develop. In considering political relations the state (and the type of state) is of basic importance: in terms of which interests it represents, the ideologies it employs to legitimate the promotion of those interests, and the material means it uses to do so (the workings of the legal system, taxation and economic policy, education, the organization and uses of police and military, and so on). Equally important is the relative degree of coherence and effectiveness of state policies and practices, which in turn reflect the course and outcomes of social and political struggles.

Contemporary states exert (or attempt to exert) considerable control over those who live within their territory, for example, by regulating the movement of people, especially (but not only) across international boundaries (12, 19, 29(ii)). Residence and work permits and a host of other official documents can be seen as internal 'passports', used as a means of social control over subordinated classes, particularly when many people have to move around in search of work. In this respect official papers are both, as Adrian Adams put it, 'instruments of survival and signs of bondage' (p. 88; see also references to 'papers' in readings 9, 14, 19).

A critically important function of the state is to define legitimate political activity, and to suppress what is considered illegitimate. This means that struggles by peasants over land, say, or workers' conflicts with capitalists, often become simultaneously struggles over democratic rights of expression and organization. This occurs because such rights are constitutionally weak or non-existent (as in many Central and South American countries), or are denied by the practices of those who wield effective power. The latter was noted with respect to land rights established in law (5, 8), and what actually happens to land reform policies (6). Similarly, the strike of *beedi* workers to gain legally decreed conditions of work and pay confronted a local 'power bloc', including their employers, which was able to mobilize the material support of the police and the ideological support of the

press (16). As Lula put it, 'The fundamental question is the lack of liberty. And it
has to be won, it can't come through law.' (p. 145)

Cultural and ideological relations

Cultural relations provide collective identities based on common ethnicity, or
language, or religion, or nationality, ascribing distinctive 'ways of life' and values
to these shared characteristics. In this way, cultural relations can be articulated
without reference to (and indeed may appear to transcend) relations of class and
gender. On the other hand, cultural relations are not necessarily egalitarian either
'internally' (e.g. with respect to gender categories which prescribe the 'proper'
place and behaviour of men and women, or with respect to hierarchies like that of
caste), or 'externally' regarding other cultures (seen as superior or inferior).

Cultural differences can be a means of justifying the subordination of particular
groups and peoples by their 'inferiority'. The most important manifestation of this
in the contemporary world is the legacy of racism that accompanied European
colonialism, justifying it as a 'mission to civilize primitive and backward peoples'.
Examples of culturally subordinated groups in this collection include the
indigenous Indian peoples of Latin America (2, 7), and the 'untouchables' and
tribal people of India (22, 28). Cultural relations, therefore, can become a sphere
of struggle when those denigrated in this way assert their dignity as human beings.
The Mapuche resistance to encroachment on their reservation was a
demonstration of self-assertion by a culturally subordinated minority as well as the
action of a peasant community to defend its land (8). Other instances are the Dalit
movement in India (22), and the mass conversions to Buddhism of those
subordinated as 'untouchables' in the Hindu caste system. 'The Buddhist
movement gave us self-respect, the union helps us fill our stomachs.' (p. 228)

In pointing out how cultural relations can be a medium of domination and
subordination, and consequently an area of struggle, the distinction between
culture and ideology becomes blurred if we consider ideologies as the 'world views'
of social groups with different conditions of life and interests. The accounts in this
collection provide numerous examples of the complex ways in which different
cultural and ideological frameworks are drawn upon and combined to produce a
variety of forms of consciousness. The people encountered in these pages certainly
do not speak with a single voice! Rather than repeat the detail of the readings and
unravel its complexities concerning consciousness, we want to emphasize three
points about cultural and ideological relations.

First, the significance of class and gender is not exhausted by property and production relations, and those of political power, but also includes forms of domination
exercised through culture and ideology. Mao Tse-tung described four systems of
authority in traditional China – political, clan, religious and masculine – as 'the
four thick ropes binding the Chinese people, particularly the peasants' (p. 22).

Second, the meanings and identities provided by culture and ideology are 'lived'
through social relationships, and reinforce, modify or challenge the practices that
characterize those relationships. Consider, for example, the effect of ideological
relations which define the criteria for participation in public life. Aída Hernández
notes of the other female members of her cooperative that 'the women themselves,
actually believe that we, the compañeras [sisters] are inferior beings' (p. 186). This also
suggests that dominant ideologies are successful to the extent that those they

dominate accept the place assigned to them, whether justified by the authority of religion or myth, 'laws of nature', the superior wisdom of the state, or simply because 'that is the way things are'.

Ideological relations typically work in more complicated ways, however. The Popoloca Indians (2) and the women agricultural workers of Bori Arab (22) express an articulate and cynical consciousness about 'official' ideologies and the promises they hold out. Together with this ideological resistance at one level, they appear resigned to their circumstances because they feel they lack the capacity to change them. An important aspect of such capacity is formal education, defined as a necessary qualification for political activity by the dominant ideology which, at another level then, they have 'internalized'. 'If I had been educated I would have been a leader. But, as it is, I am only a bull for a festival.' (p. 183)

Our third point is that the construction of consciousness out of beliefs and values from different 'world views' (and the experience of different social worlds, for example, through labour migration) may be more or less consistent or contradictory, coherent or ambivalent. Rosendo Huenumán learned to speak the language of class struggle through his experiences as a miner, while retaining his identity as a Mapuche (11). Male trade unionists in Bombay regarded the Annapurna women (many of them workers' wives) who sold them meals as 'exploiters' (27). The working-class consciousness of the railwaymen of Sekondi–Takoradi was combined with elements of Fante regionalism (17).

Differences and unity

The Introduction states that our selection concentrated 'on the lives of those who are poor and who are subordinated socially, culturally, and politically'. The evidence of the readings and our discussion so far show that those who share these characteristics differ a great deal according to the conditions in which they struggle to gain a living, the social and cultural 'worlds' they occupy, their forms of consciousness, and their engagement in struggles of different kinds. Among these differences, two in particular stand out.

The first, and the most ubiquitous, kind of differentiation is undoubtedly that arising from gender relations, manifested in sexual divisions of labour, the norms of participation in 'public life', and the cultural and ideological relations that inform marriage and the practices of family existence. These can, and typically do, cross-cut the boundaries of social class in certain respects: the responsibility of *all* women for the tasks of domestic labour necessary to family reproduction, the 'duty' to provide their husbands with sons, and the deference due to husbands and their families, which can also be sources of conflict between women, for example, in the roles of mother-in-law and daughter-in-law (28).

However, the fulfilment of these demands, and possible resistance to them, assumes particular features in the lives of working-class and peasant women who also have to contribute to household income in the struggle for daily existence, thus experiencing the burdens of 'double work' (16, 20, 22, 27, 28, 29: the domestic responsibility of a middle-class woman is likely to involve supervising the work of servants, who in turn are likely to be the daughters or wives of workers, peasants, or 'marginals'). One answer to this slippery dialectic of class and gender is provided by Domitila Barrios de Chungara's reactions to the views of certain Western and middle-class feminists whom she encountered in Mexico (29(ii)). Other responses include the rejection of marriage (24, 25, 28), and the aspiration of Aída Hernández that her daughter will enjoy a marriage informed by political principles of equality between spouses (26).

The second major dimension of differentiation is between those who gain their livelihood through wage labour and those engaged in household or individualized production. The concentration of large numbers of propertyless workers in capitalist enterprises, and other large-scale employment, provides a distinctive basis of collective class organization and action. Household and individualized forms of production tend to separate producers from each other with respect to their access to means of production (limited and precarious though this may be) and their organization of production, and to individualize their relationships with members of other social classes and groups such as landlords, merchants, moneylenders and government officials.

Within this basic distinction, of course, a number of additional factors are important in determining what kinds of unity are more likely to develop between those occupying the same positions in systems of class and gender relations.

The pressures on workers of a large 'reserve army of labour' looking for jobs, and the power this gives capitalists, were expressed by a day labourer in Bori Arab in response to a call for unionization – 'Unity? How can we have unity? If I don't go to work, someone else will go, and I will lose. There is no unity among us. The [capitalist] farmers, though, they have unity.' (p. 181) Similarly, there appeared to be no effective trade union organization among the workers of El Valle, one of whom was dismissed 'for non-fulfilment of the quasi-military regulations' of the sugar estate he worked for, and was subsequently 'blacklisted' – another demonstration of the unity of capitalists (p. 67). On the other hand, agricultural workers in a number of Third World countries, particularly those employed in large plantations and estates, have histories of struggle that have produced strong organizations and a militant consciousness (see also 20(ii)).

In the industrial and urban capitalist sectors, workers in large enterprises tend to organize themselves more readily, though rarely without struggle. The readings show examples of union organization and strikes by workers in both sophisticated modern plants owned by multinational corporations (18) and in primitive, semi-industrial 'factories' (16). Where workers are also concentrated in particular types of communities, for example the 'company' towns and villages characteristic of mining in many countries (not only those of the Third World), this often gives an additional element of solidarity to their consciousness and actions (11, 29; see also 17).

The engineering workshops of Howrah reflect a situation intermediate between capitalist and petty commodity production (15). They are small-scale capitalist enterprises employing a few workers, but the owner is also typically a skilled craftsman who works alongside the others, perhaps consulting as well as supervising them. In these 'face to face' conditions, as M. P. Ghosh notes, 'an appearance of close social and family ties is maintained' between employers and workers, in contrast to the ways in which capital and labour confront each other in large capitalist enterprises.

Different types of household and individualized production were indicated in the section on property and production relations. They have distinctive social characteristics with important effects for different types of struggles. While based in the property and production relations of landowners and sharecroppers as social classes, Indra Lohar's relationship to his former landlord Bibhuti evidently took a very personal form, including 'loyalty' (5), analogous in this sense to the relationship between small workshop owners and their employees.

The fact that peasants are not directly employed and supervised by others, as wage workers are, is associated with values of 'freedom' and 'independence' (see p. 84), that often represent aspirations rather than the realities of their existence – an ideological resistance to the fate of dispossession. The description of the conditions of sharecropping in north-east Brazil in the commentary to Reading 1 provides a stark contrast with the poem's declaration that the peasants driven to town by drought and famine had been 'kings' in their fields.

However, the particular forms of class relations and traditions of community that characterize some peasantries do provide a basis for more unified struggles (3, 8, 10, 20(i)), and through the linkages with a wider political context can lead to the formation of regional and national peasant organizations (3, 6, 23).

In the case of the urban 'informal sector' the readings illustrate various forms of differentiation and cooperation. Relations within and between the workshops of Howrah are expressed in familial and quasi-kinship terms, presenting one image of the 'urban village' (15). These small capitalist engineering businesses stand at the top of the hierarchy of 'informal sector' activity, while the autobiography of Miguel Duran provides a vivid picture of life at the bottom and an image of the 'urban jungle' – 'a war of all against all' fuelled by desperation (14).

Other types of urban petty commodity production fall between these two poles. The pressures of competition between those in the 'informal sector', the fragmented nature of the production of the goods and services they seek to sell, and the often personalized relationships of producers with suppliers, merchants and customers, make it extremely difficult to establish any effective wider organization. The notable exception to this among our readings is the organization of the Annapurna women of Bombay, but it is significant, first, that many of them are the wives of workers, and, second, that the initial impulse for their organization came from a woman trade union activist (27).

Survival, resistance and transformation

These three headings provide a means of drawing together, and further shaping, what we have suggested so far about conditions and types of struggle with particular reference to their content and organization.

We have already noted instances of everyday struggles for survival including the drudgery of long and arduous hours of labour for little return; the struggles to obtain and retain wage employment, or land, or other resources with which to earn a living in towns; the burden of double work for women peasants and workers, together with the restrictions imposed by male authority; coping with indignities and harassment at the hands of bureaucracy, courts and police; struggles for personal dignity in the face of political, cultural and ideological subordination.

At the level of struggles for individual survival we have seen how the precariousness of marital relationships, due to poverty and the search for work, imposes strains on women left to earn a living and raise children on their own. An effect of 'desertion' by husbands who are migrants might be sexual deprivation, as expressed in the metaphor of the poignant lament by a Moroccan woman (21). A more widely noted effect is the breakdown of marriages – 'Maghalangu [the labour recruiter] is taking the man away who, upon his return from Joni, may find that his wife has gone with another man!' (12).

The relative instability of the 'nuclear' family can be 'compensated' by the operation of extended family ties. Children are often brought up by grandparents and other relatives (7; this was also the experience of Ivan Martin – 13). Relatives are also called upon for help in finding jobs and housing (11, 14, 17, 28), in pooling resources and placing orders in 'informal sector' businesses (14, 15), in acquiring an education (11), and generally performing a 'social welfare function' (p. 138).

The readings also illustrate various expressions of resistance, and the analysis by Robin Cohen alerts us to forms of both collective and individual resistance that tend to remain 'hidden' (30). As he makes clear, however, many of these 'subterranean' expressions of resistance simultaneously represent accommodation to conditions of exploitation and oppression, in that they do not provide either ideological or material means for challenging them directly.

The same is true, for example, of ideological resistance combined with fatalism about the possibilities of change that we noted above. The woman street cleaner who we quoted enjoys both self-respect due to the Buddhist movement and a full stomach, helped by a strong trade union (22); her proletarian sister in Bori Arab often has an empty stomach and not much regard for the leaders of her local Buddhist community (28).

A different example of resistance is provided by those women who reject the demands of marriage and male authority to earn their living through prostitution. The poem in Reading 25 celebrates the prostitute's life by comparison with that of a peasant's wife in a way that suggests the possibility of transformation at an individual level. Janet Bujra's account, however, analyses the social contradictions of prostitution as a 'way out' (24). She argues that prostitution is ultimately a defensive measure rather than an offensive one which challenges the conditions that give rise to and reproduce the oppression of women, and she quotes Kate Millett: 'To be a rebel is not to be a revolutionary. It is more often but a way of spinning one's wheels deeper in the sand.' (p. 209)

This is a useful distinction which can also be applied to the story of Rhygin – 'the mythical urban hero: reggae star, stud, *ganja* trader and a gunman.' (p. 106) His story reflects, rather than points beyond, the contradictions of the society that produced him: marijuana smoking may express 'hidden' resistance (30) but its effect is to pacify, while the accolade of 'stud' signifies prowess in the sexual exploitation of women. Rhygin's saga of personal defiance no doubt has a potent symbolic appeal to the urban dispossessed and 'marginals', particularly those who are male and young, but the message of his song is that of the individual rebel – 'I'm gonna get my share now, what's mine' rather than 'We're gonna get our share now, what's ours' (13(iii)).

A similar distinction, albeit in a very different setting, informs D. P. Bandyopadhyay's account of Indra Lohar (5). While determined and courageous, Indra Lohar's struggle against eviction from the land he had farmed for many years was a solitary one, helpless against the force and brutality of the locally powerful and the remote bureaucracy of the High Court of Calcutta.

Turning now to collective struggles by workers and peasants, the boundaries between survival, resistance and transformation tend to become blurred. These struggles can combine elements of *defence* against further · exploitation and oppression, such as harsher discipline and higher workloads in factories and capitalist farms, declining real wages, victimization of union activists and strike breaking by police, loss of land, the raising of rents and taxes, and so on; of *resistance* to the power of capitalists and landowners, and the legal, political and ideological forces that support them; and of *transformation* when such struggles develop ideologies and forms of organization and solidarity that challenge existing structures of exploitation and oppression and point the way beyond them to alternative forms of society.

The most dramatic example of the latter in our readings is presented by the peasant movement in Hunan in the 1920s, when a specific combination of historical factors made possible a frontal assault on existing relations of property, production and power (3). It is important to note that the peasant movement of Hunan represented only one episode in a protracted process of transformation in China that has experienced many vicissitudes and conflicts over its direction to the present day.

Other collective struggles described in the readings may be less significant as events in contemporary history, but no less dramatic to those participating in them. At the level of a particular community the resistance by the Mapuche to the heavily armed police detachment sent to enforce their eviction expresses a dynamic of struggle not so different from that unleashed in China on a much greater scale. Moreover, the success of their resistance paved the way for the Mapuche to establish collective farming, timber working and construction, and to build and run a school – the beginnings of a process of transformation in relations of production and distribution, and of enhancing the educational and technical capacities of the community (8). Likewise, in organizing cooperative agriculture the peasants' association of Jamaane sought to transcend the social and technical limitations of peasant household cultivation, to overcome the legacy of 'backwardness' associated with the area's remoteness and history as a reserve of migrant labour, and at the same time to maintain control over their organization of production against the threat of incorporation into a large-scale state 'development' programme (10).

Some of the workers' struggles described here reveal considerable initiative and energy 'from below', together with the sophistication of leaders who have to be able to articulate their ideas and to assess their strategy and tactics in relation to the balance of forces at the level of national politics (17, 18, 19). It was noted above that struggles for ostensibly limited demands, such as higher wages and better conditions of work, can have a much wider political impact, according to the circumstances in which they occur. Such struggles can also be seen as the 'school' in which workers acquire new forms of consciousness and political and organizational skills that are of longer term significance. This was the result of Rosendo Huenumán's experiences as a miner (11, 8), and is also conveyed in Mao Tse-tung's and Domitila Barrios de Chungara's ideas of struggle as a process of education (3, 29). And in the words of a Peruvian woman – 'I didn't understand. But then, each day, I saw more and more, and I began to realize what it all meant to fight together against those who were exploiting us.' (p. 186).

People change as a result of participation in struggles, and acquire a new self-confidence in their collective ability to organize and control the conditions of their lives. As well as the evidence from workers' and peasants' struggles, an interesting example is that of the Annapurna women who have begun to learn organizational skills, who show a new interest in education, and who are standing up to their husbands more. Mira Savara shows that the organization of the Annapurna has by no means transformed their social existence, but that some of the elements necessary to transformation have been introduced into their lives for the first time.

Our main point in conclusion is that the experience of collective struggles for even immediate and limited ends can disclose both the need and potential for more fundamental and longer term transformation. The different kinds of organizations that have been described in the readings – trade unions, peasant associations, producers' cooperatives, women's organizations – provide an accumulated experience of struggles, of contradictions and defeats as well as successes, that any wider movement for social transformation will be able to draw on and learn from. The examples of energy, courage, capacity for solidarity, for organization and leadership, provided by many of the working people whose lives have featured in these accounts, indicate the most important resource that any wider movement for social transformation would have to mobilize.

Index

A

alcohol 26, 112, 186, 188, 199, 229, 254–5

B

birth control 11, 187–8, 204, 205, 221, 223–4, 239
bureaucracy 19, 40–1, 46, 53–4, 56, 57, 81, 87, 155

C

caste 128, 174, 175, 177, 178, 181, 182, 183, 184, 219, 226, 228
chiefs 32, 34, 51, 52, 53, 54, 58, 137, 141n, 165, 166, 249
childhood: autobiographical accounts 45–50, 111–14
children 33, 115, 116, 119, 129, 170, 179, 184, 187, 188, 202, 203, 204–6, 214, 227, 234–5
class: specific references to 16, 19, 87, 102, 127, 143–52, 175, 176, 177, 178, 180, 214, 219, 232, 245–8, 256–7
colonialism 32–5, 70–4, 135–7, 183, 197, 248–51, 255
co-operatives 27, 29, 61–2, 185–6, 189–90; and state supervision of 74–6
corruption 120, 130, 133, 134, 136, 138–40, 155
courts 37–40, 53, 54, 57, 61, 231
crime 27–8, 112–17, 255–6

D

demonstrations 17, 167–8
dispossession (of land) 10, 40, 64, 175; resistance to 19, 50, 51–61
divorce 178, 181, 192–5, 200–4, 206–7, 211n, 228–31
domestic labour 174, 182, 189, 214, 234–5; as paid occupation 66, 96–7, 98, 215, 217–25

dress 33, 43, 106, 109, 118, 136, 167, 180, 183, 195, 206, 227, 231, 241
drought 6–10, 77
drugs 25, 106, 116, 245, 254

E

education 12, 112, 129, 139, 155, 156, 182, 184; lack of 52, 55, 122, 124, 128, 219, 222; aspirations to 28–9, 55–6, 66, 96–7, 223
elections 131, 152, 186, 189, 233

F

factories 97, 98, 129–30, 142, 146–9, 176, 179, 183, 214, 225–6, 251, 252; industrial workshops 126–7
food 17, 26, 33, 66, 77, 86, 102, 112, 176, 180, 219
food aid 9, 76, 82, 181–2
forced cultivation 34–5, 164, 165–6
forced labour 32–3, 73, 249–50

H

housewives 177, 224, 233–6, 241
housing 57, 61–2, 66–7, 101, 108–9, 119, 122, 133, 167, 171, 179, 194, 202, 208, 219, 229, 241
hunger 6–10, 13, 107, 120, 123, 180, 183, 241, 250

I

illegitimacy 205
illness 33, 49, 64, 122, 130, 165, 207, 253–4
indebtedness: rural 19, 63–4, 83–4, 85; urban 123, 184, 220
indigenous peoples 45–6, 46–63, 175, 213, 214
inheritance 37, 200, 231–2
insecurity of employment/income: specific references to 66, 99, 122–3, 125, 146, 149, 164, 175, 180

L

labour contractors/recruiters 65, 104, 154, 156, 184, 213, 214–15, 249

labour migration 10, 12, 13, 65, 71, 77–8, 81, 103–5, 128, 138, 153–8, 164, 170, 173–4, 175, 184, 192–8, 218–19, 244–5, 248–9

landlords/landowners 33, 35–42, 103, 175, 177; actions against 17–20, 50, 53–4, 56–7, 59

land reform 36, 40–1, 43–4, 46, 175, 185, 190

land tenure 13, 44, 73–4, 177, 192, 200–1; see also 'official papers'

language 9, 11, 13, 52, 57, 68, 80, 88, 237, 244–5, 252–3

leadership 44, 78–9, 135–6, 144, 146, 147, 149, 176, 183, 185, 189, 190, 226, 237, 257

loans 62, 218, 221–4; interest on 218, 220

M

magistrates 20–1, 37–40, 54, 57, 61

male authority 23–4, 115, 181, 186–7, 188–9, 191, 192, 203, 206–7, 230

marriage 169–70, 173, 175–6, 178, 188, 193, 195, 201–4, 206–9, 211n; 'common law' marriages 65–6, 116–24, 181

merchants 27, 29, 114

mining 98, 99–102, 104–5, 164, 170, 233–5, 239, 245, 252

N

newspapers 56, 58, 61, 85–6, 99, 130, 144, 145

O

official papers: personal documents 32, 58, 65, 88, 97, 99, 122, 155, 156, 157, 165, 236–7, 256; property titles 36–7, 48, 51, 53, 54, 59, 200

P

peasants: specific references to 10, 11, 14–15, 43, 44, 47, 62, 63–4, 68, 84, 102, 177; and cultivation 78–9, 171, 191, 192, 197, 199–200, 215; peasant organizations 15–30, 44, 67–9, 78–90, 185, 186

plantations (large-scale agriculture) 32–3, 64, 164, 166–8, 197, 214, 247–8

police 21, 24, 34, 38–40, 50, 54, 57, 58–61, 106, 113, 114, 130, 157, 248; militia 20, 233

political parties 14, 23, 24–5, 31n, 57, 58, 62, 103, 107, 110n, 131–6, 140, 142, 150, 151–2, 179, 226

pregnancy 178, 204, 205, 215–16, 239; and childbirth 49, 195

prices of food 18, 27, 89, 132, 155, 234; of other commodities 118, 123, 194, 195, 199, 206, 211n

prisons 32, 113, 114, 115, 178

prostitution 112, 115–16, 178, 191–6, 198–211, 212, 238

R

religion 9, 12, 22–4, 26, 44, 69, 80, 175, 177, 183, 244, 255

rent: for land 18, 43, 44, 213; for housing 99, 101, 124, 133, 140n, 155

S

sexual harrassment 119, 172, 178, 199, 220, 223, 227, 229, 231

sharecropping 10, 36–42, 76, 85

slavery/slaves 178, 191, 196–8, 200, 208, 210n, 211n

state, the: specific references to 14, 19, 22, 74, 183, 232, 235

strikes 130, 132–40, 142–7, 179, 185, 221, 228, 232, 245

T

taxes 18, 28, 71, 77, 133, 165, 251

trade 70, 191, 196; petty trade 48, 66, 114, 117–24, 138, 192, 193, 217–24, 234, 236

trade unions 51, 61, 62, 102, 107, 128, 130, 132–40, 142–50, 157, 158, 176, 179, 181, 213, 214, 216, 217, 233, 220–1, 226–32

U
unemployment: rural 6-8, 15, 19,
    175; urban 99, 106-10, 137, 138,
    154, 155, 157, 235

W
wages 47, 96, 97, 98, 101, 102, 127,
    129, 132, 138, 144-6, 151, 152n,

167, 177, 179, 180, 182, 190,
200, 201, 214, 215, 216, 219,
234, 250-1, 255
water: for cultivation 30, 35, 70-6,
    78-9, 82, 86, 89; for consump-
    tion 33, 182-3, 208, 219, 231
women's organizations 23, 128, 164,
    166, 179, 181, 217-25, 233-42